TWO DOORS TO

ETERNITY

Making The Most Important
Decision of Your Life

by

Christopher H. K. Persaud

Dedication

Dedicated to my father, Hiram (1924 -2004), my mother, Ruth (1924 – 1985), and my brother John(1949 – 2013). I miss them dearly and look forward to the day when we will all meet again in Christ's glorious and eternal kingdom.

TABLE OF CONTENTS

INTRODUCTION...1

PART ONE ANSWERING SOME CRUCIAL QUESTIONS................................5

1 IS THERE A GOD? 6

2 JESUS CHRIST – WHO IS HE? 33

3 THE DEVIL OR SATAN – IS HE REAL? 52

4 IS THERE A HEAVEN?..71

5 IS THERE A HELL?.. 97

6 WHAT IS ETERNITY? 127

PART TWO WORLD RELIGIONS & PHILOSOPHIES - THE STANDARD FOR COMPARISON...139

7 BIBLICAL CHRISTIANITY... 140

PART THREE FALLING SHORT OF THE STANDARD................................173

8 JUDAISM...174

9 ROMAN CATHOLICISM... 192

10 EASTERN ORTHODOXY... 227

PART FOUR_CHRISTIANITY COMPARED WITH MAJOR RELIGIONS & PHILOSOPHIES 247

11 CHRISTIANITY COMPARED WITH MAJOR RELIGIONS & PHILOSOPHIES – ATHEISM 248

12 CHRISTIANITY COMPARED WITH MAJOR RELIGIONS & PHILOSOPHIES - BUDDHISM 271

13 CHRISTIANITY COMPARED WITH MAJOR RELIGIONS & PHILOSOPHIES – HINDUISM, YOGA & REINCARNATION 289

14 CHRISTIANITY COMPARED WITH MAJOR RELIGIONS & PHILOSOPHIES – ISLAM 321

PART FIVE_CHRISTIANITY COMPARED WITH NEW RELIGIONS, PHILOSOPHIES & CULTS 344

15 CHRISTIANITY COMPARED WITH NEW RELIGIONS, PHILOSOPHIES & CULTS - JEHOVAH'S WITNESSES: THE WATCHTOWER BIBLE & TRACT SOCIETY 345

16 CHRISTIANITY COMPARED WITH NEW RELIGIONS, PHILOSOPHIES & CULTS – MORMONISM: THE CHURCH OF JESUS CHRIST OF LATTER-DAY SAINTS 365

17 CHRISTIANITY COMPARED WITH NEW RELIGIONS, PHILOSOPHIES & CULTS – SEVENTH DAY ADVENTISM 388

18 CHRISTIANITY COMPARED WITH NEW RELIGIONS, PHILOSOPHIES & CULTS – THE NEW AGE MOVEMENT 416

19 CHRISTIANITY COMPARED WITH NEW RELIGIONS, PHILOSOPHIES & CULTS -EVOLUTIONISM 440

20 CHRISTIANITY COMPARED WITH NEW RELIGIONS, PHILOSOPHIES & CULTS – SATANISM & THE OCCULT 465

21 CHRISTIANITY COMPARED WITH NEW RELIGIONS, PHILOSOPHIES & CULTS - OTHER NON-CHRISTIAN/ANTI-CHRISTIAN RELIGIONS & PHILOSOPHIES...486

PART SIXTWO DOORS TO ETERNITY 551

22 TWO DOORS TO ETERNITY - MAKING THE MOST IMPORTANT DECISION OF YOUR LIFE...552

NOTES...579

INTRODUCTION

Christian scholarship teaches in unmistakable terms that Almighty God devised a plan of salvation for sinful humankind ever since the *Fall* in the Garden of Eden, a paradisial location wherein God placed the first man and woman. God's first children, a man named Adam and his wife Eve, chose to disobey the directives of their Creator, who subsequently banished them from his holy presence. An omniscient, omnipotent, and omnipresent God, however, in his unparalleled mercy and concern for humankind, formulated a strategy to redeem his wayward creation unto himself so its members could exercise their free will to obtain the gift of everlasting life and not be alienated from him for all eternity.

The term "eternity," used from a perspective of theological rumination, conveys the following overwhelming inferences.

(a) Time without beginning or end; infinite time

(b) The state or quality of being eternal

(c) The timeless state following death

(d) The afterlife; immortality.

The Holy Bible unequivocally says everyone, from the time of God's creation of the first human beings in his image to the end of time, will be ushered into eternal existence. People who, up to such a time, will have accepted God's begotten Son Jesus Christ's atoning sacrifice for people's sins on the Cross via his crucifixion and resurrection will live forever with

1

God in unprecedented joy and peace in a place called *Heaven*. People who will have rejected Christ's offer of eternal life will face an eternity of permanent estrangement from God in a dreaded location called *Hell*.

Heaven and hell are real places – One paradisial and sublime, the other terrifying and agonizing.

While theologians and Biblical scholars agree on the nature of heaven and envisage it as an environment of wondrous, unending peace and happiness, there exist two basic schools of thought about what constitutes hell. Both versions ring of unspeakable and unparalleled anguish and horror.

One school of thought teaches that at the final judgment of humankind, before the ushering in of eternity, people who would have rejected Jesus Christ as Savior will be permanently annihilated and completely destroyed and consequently separated forever from Almighty God. The end will be excruciating, conclusive, and irrevocable! Hell would not be a nice place to be, even for a nanosecond. The implications concomitant with the condemnation to such a place are mind-boggling.

The second premise about the nature of hell revolves around a presupposition even more petrifying than the forgoing one. It tells of a location of everlasting torment and terror. The situation, as with the previous version of the nature of hell, is irreversible.

It is disquieting that many Christian leaders and other disseminators of Christ's Gospel trivialize the message of salvation from sin and the inheritance of eternal life. Heaven and hell are unpopular and discomfiting subjects that so-called ministers of the Gospel are reluctant to discuss or present to their congregations. Congruently, many believers prefer not to have to listen to sermons about accountability and divine judgment, even though the latter two considerations essentially encapsulate the Christian Gospel's message of redemption and the promised habitation in God's eternal kingdom.

At the forefront of the unwillingness of people to address and contemplate the ramifications of jettisoning Biblical teachings about salvation, heaven, and hell is the devil, or Satan, history's greatest deceiver.

The Bible says God created an angelic being named Lucifer. He was perfect and righteous and was the most powerful of God's creations. However, pride led Lucifer to crave worship due to God alone. He initiated a rebellion in heaven and persuaded a third of the angels to revolt against God. Michael, one of God's archangels, led God's angels in a battle against Lucifer and his angels and defeated them. God then cast Lucifer (Satan) and his angels (demons) out of heaven.

Satan continues his rebellion today since he hates God and his plans. He also leads people to defy God and all that is good. He opposes Jesus Christ, God the Son who took on the form of a human being to redeem humankind from its sins and restore the previously unflawed relationship between God and his creation.

Satan utilizes diverse forms of deceit and trickery to steer people away from God. He concocts false religions and doctrines, including so-called alternatives to a created universe and life; he masquerades as an "angel of light" (2 Corinthians 11-14) and leads people to think he is a righteous spirit being who has nothing but their interests at heart. He persuades people to

3

believe that a relationship with Jesus Christ is unnecessary to gain entrance into heaven and that just being good and moral is sufficient.

Satan's greatest deception, however, might be to prompt people to believe he does not exist, or if he does, he is not Satan – an unspeakably evil entity bent on facilitating their condemnation to hell and estranging them from God forevermore.

Nothing is more important in a person's life than accepting Christ's atoning sacrifice made on the cross more than two thousand years ago in order to save his or her soul, and enlisting the help of God's Holy Spirit in warding off the devil's unceasing attempts to entrap him or her into rejecting or abandoning God's offer of salvation.

PART ONE

ANSWERING SOME
CRUCIAL QUESTIONS

CHAPTER ONE

IS THERE A GOD?

In December 2004, long-time British professor and philosopher Anthony Flew, regarded by many as "the world's most acclaimed atheist," renounced his atheism in favor of theism.

Dr. Hugh Ross, an astrophysicist and one of the world's leading cosmologists, likened Professor Flew's dramatic conversion to having the same impact on the academic world as an announcement that Billy Graham had renounced Christianity would have on the Christian Church!

Dr. Andrew Corbett, National President of ICI Theological College Australia, made the following comment about Professor Flew's surprising conversion to a belief in God and creationism.

One of the reasons cited by Prof. Flew was "the evidence." He admitted that for a long time, the growing problem of Evolution's inability to explain how life began, or for that matter, how anything began (see Chapter Eighteen – Christianity Compared with New Religions, Philosophies & Cults: Evolutionism)*, led him to the inevitable conclusion that it was an inadequate answer in the face of the evidence. Then, when the DNA Genome code was unraveled, the evidence for Design became "undeniable." These two pieces of evidence (1) the existence of life demanding a Life-Source and (2) the* *scientific evidence of an extremely complex code in the make-up of that life - DNA) were enough for Professor Flew to renounce atheism.* [1]

A Young Boy's Search For God

The following narrative appears in the first person.

I have always been terrified of the prospect of drowning. Growing up, I would try to envision how terrible the suffering must be for someone who would die by drowning. It was a kind of morbid fixation, and the mania related not only to drowning per se but to any scenario in which a person could not breathe, and suffocation resulted. I later realized my trepidation stemmed from a most unfortunate and troubling experience I had in the nineteen-sixties when I was about twelve or thirteen years old. At the time, our family lived in Leonora, a quaint village in rural Guyana (then British Guyana) at the top of the South American continent. My father worked as a bookkeeper at one of the country's sugar estates. The latter were a number of strategically sited sugar-producing locales, which functioned under an umbrella organization headquartered in the nation's capital city of Georgetown. By virtue of my father's occupation, we lived in a reasonably spacious house equipped with many of the comforts that eluded the majority of other residents in the area.

Numerous canals or trenches (waterways) channeled raw sugar cane (in floating vessels called "punts") from nearby cane fields to the factory for processing into sugar. One such canal ran along the side of a roadway situated a few yards behind our house. The canal held a strange fascination for the people who lived in the neighborhood. It was an allure tinged with a discernible measure of fear. For as long as I could remember, at least one person, invariably a child, would drown in the canal each year. In a rustic Guyanese village in the 1960s where the immediate community comprised of an easily measurable number of residents who also formed a closely knit, extended family, the demise of one of its members was a prominently distressing event. There was a keen sense of awareness of just about everything that transpired in the community.

Gradually, a frightening legend grew around the sad occurrences of young children losing their lives in the dark, mysterious waters of the canal. Word went around that an 'evil spirit" in the form of an oversized alligator roamed the waters in search of victims each year. The alligator would lure children, especially, into the canal to their deaths. Rural Guyana in the 1960s was not without its own 'urban legends," and people who seldom ventured beyond the boundaries of a confined communal life were susceptible to the pull of superstition and panic.

I admit I fell victim, at least in part, to the fearsome tale of the "spirit" alligator, notwithstanding the strong Christian influence exuded by my mother and the generally stable religious atmosphere that pervaded our home. I have always considered myself a committed Christian believer, even as a young boy. The earnestness of my relationship with Jesus Christ, however, hardly went beyond the precincts of a Christian's traditional walk with God. I constantly wished for a closer, more meaningful bond with the miracle-working Galilean but understood little exactly what it meant or entailed. Chapter Two: *Jesus Christ – Who Is He?* explicates the life and teachings of Jesus Christ and presents a strong case for his Godhood and the wherewithal through which sinful humankind may obtain eternal life in a place called heaven.

In the mid nineteen-sixties, a new family moved into our neighborhood, about five houses from where we lived. We, my siblings and I quickly became friends with the two boys and their sister, who, with their parents, were a shining example of an engaging and principled family. The brothers were about my age, while their sister was a few years younger. She was a lovely and endearing child, about nine or ten years old if my memory serves me correctly. No one was prepared for the heartbreaking and traumatic event that would unfold a number of months later.

One day, it was around noon. I was at home when I heard a commotion outside and decided to investigate. I had stayed home from school for a reason I do not recall. I saw a group of people on the roadway, and it was obvious their attention was focused on some sort of activity taking place in the canal. I remember seeing my new friends' mother sitting by the roadside frantically motioning to some men who were in the water. It looked as though they were searching for something...or someone! I ran and joined the group of people, and to my utter dismay, realized our new friend, Jenny, was missing. It had become a force of habit in the neighborhood for searches for missing children to begin within the locality of the dreaded waterway.

A number of men were combing the area in the hope of finding the child, should she be under the water, before it was too late. The tension and anxiety mounted to a fever pitch as the child's mother became disoriented and wailed uncontrollably. She, and most of the others present at the scene, feared for the worst. I then witnessed a scene that tugged at my very insides. It remains with me to this day!

The girl emerged from the water as though she floated to the surface. Actually, she was being raised and pushed upwards by the man who found her lying at the bottom of the canal. Her eyes were closed, and the green dress she wore clung to her body. The men girl brought the girl out of the water and laid her at the side of the road. Her mother, by then, had fainted. The child was not dead. There were noticeable movements of her arms and legs. My father, who was on his lunch break - his office was within a short walk from our home and the home of the girl - appeared on the scene. He administered mouth-to-mouth resuscitation but to no avail. Though still alive at the time, the little girl had swallowed too much water and had all but suffocated, having been underwater for what had to be a long period of time. Jenny died shortly afterward, and the entire community plunged into mourning.

The sight of a dying, or for all I knew at the time, a dead person, known closely to me, being brought out of the water was too much for me to bear. I became totally unsettled. All around me suddenly grew dark, and I felt dizzy. It had never happened to me before, but I realized I was about to pass out. With great effort, I managed to reach a nearby shed and grabbed on to one of its supporting columns. It was some minutes before I returned to my normal self.

I knew some of the children who drowned in the canal in the years before Jenny died! There were others I knew also, who lost their lives in the dark, treacherous waters of the canal after our dear friend died. She was the only one whose demise I actually witnessed, however, and the tragedy seemed to affect me more than all the others! We lived in our home along the roadway and canal for several more years, and I could never really shake the insidious, foreboding atmosphere of dread and apprehension surrounding the legend of the evil "water spirit." I daresay many others who rallied in the neighborhood shared a similar unease. Legend or not, the tale caused much worry and agitation of mind for the residents of the rural district of Leonora for many years.

While I later thought the terrifying tale about the "evil alligator" was born of superstition and ignorance, I also realized it could have been a ruse by the devil (Satan) to trigger confusion in the minds of people. I feel certain the Lord watched over the other members of my family and me during those times of uncertainty and trepidation. Chapter Three, *The Devil, or Satan – Is He Real?* explores who Satan is and analyzes his agenda of deception and hate as he and his demonic followers ceaselessly try to lead people away from God and his promise of eternal life.

Over the years after Jenny's death, I gradually came to understand the gravity of establishing a personal relationship with Jesus Christ. My Christian upbringing had laid the foundation for living a Christ-centered existence, and I slowly but surely learned about eternity and the afterlife. Such issues assumed paramount importance, and God's Holy Word, the Bible, expounded the consequences of making a decision for or against Christ and his unprecedented sacrifice on the cross for the atonement of the sins of humankind. He died and rose from the dead so repentant sinners could spend eternity with him.

My friend Jenny was no more with us, but I knew she was in Jesus' keeping, awaiting the glorious day when all of God's children, including my own loved ones and I, would be reunited and enjoy God's and each other's company forever. [2]

Does God Exist?

Does God exist? - It is probably history's most asked question and one of life's most fundamental inquiries. The overwhelming answer to this question is "Yes," although there are myriad rationalizations and beliefs about God's identity, nature, sovereignty, and agenda.

The Holy Bible says there is a God and that nature demonstrates a Creator.

The heavens declare the glory of God; the skies proclaim the work of his hands. (Psalm 19:1, NIV)

The Book of Romans says God reveals enough of himself in the world for people to know of him.

For since the creation of the world God's invisible qualities—his eternal power and divine nature—have been clearly seen, being understood from what has been made, so that people are without excuse. (Romans 1:20, NIV)

The early Christian church originated and developed from eyewitness accounts, evidence, and solid reasoning. The following biblical passages attest to such an assertion.

Many have undertaken to draw up an account of the things that have been fulfilled among us, just as they were handed down to us by those who from the first were eyewitnesses and servants of the word. (Luke 1:1,2, NIV)

For we did not follow cleverly devised stories when we told you about the coming of our Lord Jesus Christ in power, but we were eyewitnesses of his majesty. (2 Peter 1:16, NIV)

Now, the Berean Jews were of more noble character than those in Thessalonica, for they received the message with great eagerness and examined the Scriptures every day to see if what Paul said was true. (Acts 17:11m, NIV)

Even Jesus himself pointed to corroboratory evidence when defending his claims. (John 5:31-47).

Outside of and beyond the Bible, there is confirmatory evidence of the presence of God in the fields of archaeology, science, history, literature, and human experience. As expected, some dissenters distort information gleaned from the forgoing areas of research and investigation to attack the idea of God's existence. Yet, the balance of human experience, science, and philosophy, for the most part, seems to indicate there is a God. Much of what human beings assume as part of daily life, including the capacity to reason and engage in moral behavior, would be unexplainable facets of human existence if God, as a designer and creator of the universe and of life, did not exist.

Many geniuses throughout history have been believers, and many have been atheists as well. Notable scientists who acknowledged the existence of

13

God and were practicing Christians included Isaac Newton, Johannes Kepler, Louis Pasteur, Francis Bacon, Galileo Galilei, and Michael Faraday. A salient question about God is not whether he exists but whether one is open to evidence that supports his existence.

The question "Is there a God?" harbors more than purely intellectual connotations. Indeed, how a person purposes answer the question may strongly reflect an ingrained bias towards an objective or impartial response. In other words, there are reasonable and unreasonable approaches, and open-minded and closed-minded ways to look at the same information. If, for instance, an individual commits himself or herself to rejecting God, most forms of evidence and reason espousing God's existence will be considered meaningless. By the same token, the individual who harbors a steadfast predisposition to subscribe to the belief that God exists will not depart from his or her conviction regardless of most arguments to the contrary.

Historical, scientific, and personal evidence for the existence of God are pointless to the individual who nurtures a deliberate resolve to disbelieve. Still, people generally do not want to seem unreasonable, so many who refuse to believe God exists often raise other objections. Sometimes, the demurrals translate into patently ridiculous requests or mandates for proof, i.e., a demand for the provision of a particular miracle or a natural phenomenon of some sort. However, if people are not ready to accept commonplace or mundane yet credible evidence of God's existence, they are just as liable to reject miraculous confirmation.

Arguments For The Existence Of God

Arguments for the existence of God derive from a number of different perspectives. Three well-known viewpoints are the cosmological argument, the scientific argument, and the philosophical argument.

The Cosmological or First Cause Argument

The *Cosmological Argument*, in natural theology and natural philosophy (not cosmology), is an argument for the existence of God that derives from alleged facts concerning causation, explanation, change, motion, contingency, dependency, or finiteness with respect to the universe or some totality of objects. [3]

The *Cosmological Argument,* also called the *First Cause Argument*, bears upon three pivotal dictums, i.e., (a) everything has a cause, (b) there must have been a first cause, and (c) the first cause was itself uncaused.

Origin of the Cosmological Argument

Plato (428/427 or 424/423 – 348/347 BC), the Athenian philosopher, and Aristotle (384 – 322 BC), the Greek philosopher, developed "first cause" or cosmological arguments in the 4th and 3rd centuries BC. The arguments maintain everything that exists or occurs must have had a cause. So, if one could go back in time far enough, one would discover a *first* cause. Aristotle, a deist, posited this first cause was the creator of the universe. Thomas Aquinas (1225 – 1274), an Italian Christian philosopher, expanded on Aristotle's ideas in the 13th century AD and molded the first cause concept into a framework in which the cause of the universe itself is uncaused, i.e., the *First Cause* is God.

The Mechanics of the First Cause Argument

The first cause argument avers the existence of the universe was dependent on the presence and involvement of an original being or entity. Such a notion proceeds from the presumption that the universe had a beginning. There must, the first cause argument contends, be something that caused the beginning, i.e., a first cause of the universe.

The history of the universe consists of a series of events stretched across a seemingly endless span of time. Each one of these events caused a succeeding one and was the result of a preceding event. The present world came from a past world, which in turn came from a previous world.

If one traces the series of events back in time, then what does he or she find? There would seem, from an initial evaluation, to be two possibilities. There is the possibility of eventually reaching back to the first event in the series, i.e., the cause at the beginning of the universe that set everything in motion, or the possibility of finding no first event, i.e., the past stretches back into infinity.

The cosmological or first cause argument suggests the second course of events could not have been possible. In other words, the past could not have stretched back into infinity but rather must have had a beginning. The argument then progresses by inferring if the universe had a beginning then something from the outside brought it into existence. This being or entity outside the universe, this Creator, the first cause argument says, is God.

The Impossibility of Traversing an Infinite Series

If someone said he or she had just counted down from infinity to zero, starting with "infinity minus zero" and carrying on until he or she reached "infinite minus infinity, i.e., zero," then anyone would know this claim was false. Just as it is impossible to count up from zero to infinity, so it is impossible to count down from infinity to zero. If someone started counting down from infinity and kept going, then he or she would still be counting to this day, i.e., he or she could not finish such an exercise. This is because it is impossible to traverse an infinite series.

The Past Cannot be Infinite.

The concept of the universe having an infinite past is as problematic as the idea about someone counting down from infinity. If the universe had an infinite past, then counting down from infinity to time zero or to the present would be totally unachievable. The fact the present has been reached shows the past is not infinite but finite.

Since the past cannot go back forever, then the universe must have had a beginning. A pertinent question is whether something caused this beginning or whether the universe just burst into existence out of nothing. Nothing exists without a cause, i.e., nothing comes from nothing. For something to come about, there must be something already existent in order to bring it into existence. It follows if the universe had a beginning then something brought it into existence. In other words, the universe had a Creator.

The First Cause Must be Uncreated, Eternal

If the Creator of the universe were an entity or being like the universe i.e., something that exists in time and came into existence, then it too would have had to be created. Nothing comes from nothing, not even God. The ultimate or first cause of the universe, therefore, never came into existence; the ultimate Creator must be a being that exists outside of time, an eternal being with neither beginning nor end.

The First Cause or Cosmological argument, then, points to the existence of a Creator who transcends time. Combined with the Ontological argument (see later in this chapter), this would render strong credibility to the idea there is a perfect, necessary, and eternal Creator.

The Cosmological Argument - What Does The Bible Say?

In its very first verse, the Bible declares God created the universe. "In the beginning God created the heavens and the earth." (Genesis1:1, NIV) Also, the Scriptures say, "The LORD made the heavens." (1 Chronicles 16:26, NIV). God himself is not a physical part of the universe, as confirmed by 2 Chronicles, which states, "But who is able to build a temple for him, since the heavens, even the highest heavens, cannot contain him?" (2 Chronicles 2:6, NIV) One also knows "the LORD, the everlasting God," is eternal and infinite (Genesis 21:33, NIV), and he "rules forever by his power." (Psalm 66:7, NIV). The Bible clearly refers to God as the uncaused First Cause who created the universe by willing it into existence.

18

The Scientific Argument

DNA (deoxyribonucleic acid) – The Genetic Wonder

In 1990, the Human Genome Project set out to determine the sequence of the chemical base pairs that comprise human DNA (deoxyribonucleic acid). The Human Genome Project (HGP) was an international scientific research project with the goal of determining the sequence of nucleotide base pairs making up human DNA and identifying and mapping all the genes of the human genome from both a physical and a functional standpoint.[4] It remains the world's largest collaborative biological project ever undertaken.[5] It took 13 years to complete the decoding of the DNA molecule, and the results were stupefying.

Amazing Facts about DNA

During the DNA decoding process, scientists discovered something extraordinary - an exquisite 'language' composed of some 3 billion genetic letters. Scientists also determined the amount of information in human DNA is roughly equivalent to 12 sets of The Encyclopedia Britannica - an incredible 384 volumes' worth of detailed information enough to fill 48 feet of library shelves.

According to molecular biologist Michael Denton (b. 1943), a British-Australian proponent of intelligent design and a Senior Fellow at the Discovery Institute's Center for Science and Culture, a teaspoon of DNA molecules, each of which is actually only two-millionths of a millimeter thick, could contain all the information needed to build the proteins for all the species of organisms that ever lived on the earth, and "there would still be enough room left for all the information in every book ever written" [6]

Dr. Stephen Meyer (b. 1958), an American scientist, college professor, and an advocate of the pseudoscientific principle of intelligent design, remarked, "One of the most extraordinary discoveries of the twentieth century was that DNA actually stores information—the detailed instructions for assembling proteins—in the form of a four-character digital code." [7] Meyer is director of the Center for Science and Culture at the Discovery Institute in Seattle, Washington, USA. Who or what could miniaturize such information and place this enormous number of 'letters' in their proper sequence as a genetic instruction manual? God perhaps?

DNA Comprises a Full-Fledged Language

The key elements of an authentic language are (a) an alphabet or coding system, (b) correct spelling & grammar, including the proper arrangement of the words, (c) meaning or semantics, and (d) an intended message or purpose. The genetic code, or DNA, satisfies all these requirements and is, therefore, a full-fledged language.

"The coding regions of DNA," explains Stephen Meyer, "have exactly the same relevant properties as a computer code or language." [8] The only other codes found to be true languages are all of human origin. Although we do find that dogs bark when they perceive danger, bees dance to point other bees to a source, and whales emit sounds, to name a few examples of communication by other species, none of these is a bona fide language. They represent only low-level communication signals.

The only types of communication considered high-level are human languages, artificial languages such as computer and Morse codes, and the genetic code (DNA). No other communication system contains the basic characteristics of a language. Bill Gates, the founder of Microsoft, commented that "DNA is like a software program, only much more complex than anything we've ever devised." [9]

DNA – The Product of Intelligent Design

Most scientific scholars, including some prominent atheists, increasingly believe the type of high-level information found in DNA could not have evolved, even though they remain reluctant to acknowledge the involvement of a supernatural entity in the production of the remarkable molecule. Some seem to express muted acceptance of a kind of extraordinarily intelligent force at work, but this is as far as they will go. However, they must know if one claims the genetic code gradually evolved, especially in line with the Darwinist presumption, he or she contradicts all the known rules of how matter, energy, and the laws of nature work. In fact, no example of one information system inside a living cell gradually evolving into another functional information program has ever been identified in nature.

Lee Strobel, the acclaimed American Christian author and former investigative journalist, says, "The data at the core of life is not disorganized; it's not simply orderly like salt crystals, but it's complex and specific information that can accomplish a bewildering task—the building of biological machines that far outstrip human technological capabilities" [10]

Michael Behe, a prominent American biochemist and advocate of the pseudoscientific principle of intelligent design (ID), and professor at Pennsylvania's Lehigh University, says information in the genetic code is primarily an immensely complex instruction manual that was majestically designed by a more intelligent architect than human beings.

Even Francis Crick, one of the discoverers of the genetic code and an agnostic, after decades of work on deciphering it, admitted, "an honest man, armed with all the knowledge available to us now, could only state that in some sense, the origin of life appears at the moment to be almost a miracle, so many are the conditions which would have had to have been satisfied to get it going." [11]

Yet another remarkable feature of the genetic code and DNA information is the ideal number of genetic letters in the DNA code necessary for storage and translation. Moreover, the copying mechanism of DNA, to meet maximum effectiveness, requires the number of letters in each word to be an even number. Of all the possible mathematical combinations, scientists calculated the ideal number for storage and transcription is four letters - and this is exactly what exists in the genes of every living thing on earth - a four-letter digital code. Werner Gitt (b.1937), the well-known young earth creationist and German engineer, states: "The coding system used for living beings is optimal from an engineering standpoint. This fact strengthens the argument that it was a case of purposeful design rather than a (lucky) chance." [12]

Evolutionary Theory Cannot Provide an Answer

Secular educators around the world persist in promoting Darwinian evolution as though it were fact. Increasingly, however, scientists are questioning the overall logic and scientific veracity of the controversial hypothesis. Former atheist Patrick Glynn says, "As recently as twenty-five years ago, a reasonable person weighing the purely scientific evidence on the issue would likely have come down on the side of skepticism (regarding a Creator). That is no longer the case...Today, the concrete data points strongly in the direction of the God hypothesis. It is the simplest and most obvious solution ..." [13]

Evolutionism teaches living things evolve through chance mutations and natural selection. Yet to evolve means to change certain aspects of a living organism gradually until it becomes another type of creature, and this can only be achieved by changing the genetic information. Genetic information, however, is basically the same in a bacteria or a plant as in a human being. A bacterium has a shorter genetic code, but qualitatively, it gives instructions as precisely and exquisitely as it does in humans. One finds the same prerequisites of a language—alphabet, grammar, and semantics - in simple bacteria and algae as in humans.

Molecular biologist Michael Denton says each cell with genetic information, from bacteria to man, consists of "artificial languages and their decoding systems, memory banks for information storage and retrieval, elegant control systems regulating the automated assembly of parts and components, error fail-safe and proof-reading devices utilized for quality control, assembly processes involving the principle of prefabrication and modular construction ... and a capacity not equaled in any of our most advanced machines i.e., a capability of replicating its entire structure within a matter of a few hours." [14]

Consequently, it is well-nigh impossible for the genetic information of bacteria to evolve gradually into information for another type of organism when only one or a few minor mistakes in the millions of letters in that bacterium's DNA can kill it. Evolutionists are at a loss to explain how genetic information can transform itself, unaided and unguided, into something different and eventually occasion the formation of a new species. As a matter of fact, horizontal evolution, or evolution from one species into another species, has never been observed in nature or in a science laboratory. As Lee Strobel writes: "The six feet of DNA coiled inside every one of our body's one hundred trillion cells contains a four-letter chemical alphabet that spells out precise assembly instructions for all the proteins from which our bodies are made ... No hypothesis has come close to explaining how information got into biological matter by naturalistic means." [15]

The German engineer Werner Gitt puts it succinctly: "The basic flaw of all evolutionary views is the origin of the information in living beings. It has never been shown that a coding system and semantic information could originate by itself (through matter) ... The information theorems predict that this will never be possible. A purely material origin of life is thus ruled out." [16]

24

The Holy Bible records a declaration made by Israel's King David thousands of years ago about the marvelous human body. He was addressing the supernatural, intelligent designer and creator of the universe and of all life. King David's words of praise to Almighty God remain relevant and incontrovertibly true today. He said: "For you formed my inward parts; you knitted me together in my mother's womb. I praise you, for I am fearfully and wonderfully made. Wonderful are your works; my soul knows it very well. My frame was not hidden from you when I was being made in secret, intricately woven..." (Psalm 139:13-15, ESV).

The Facts Point to the Existence of God

A growing number of scientific scholars today are refuting evolutionary theories about the origin of life that have pervaded scientific scholarship for very many decades. Discoveries in the realm of molecular genetics, especially as they pertain to DNA (deoxyribonucleic acid), leave agnostic scientists at a loss to explain adequately, the origins of biological systems at the molecular level. Consequently, many level-headed professionals are gravitating to a case for a supernatural designer and creator of life and of the universe and are abandoning blind reliance on impotent, woefully unscientific evolutionary theories.

Dr. Stephen Meyer considers recent discoveries about DNA as the "Achilles heel" of evolutionary theory. He observes: "Evolutionists are still trying to apply Darwin's nineteenth-century thinking to a twenty-first-century reality, and it's not working ... I think the information revolution taking place in biology is sounding the death knell for Darwinism and chemical evolutionary theories." [17]

25

Dr. Meyer's conclusion? "I believe the testimony of science supports theism. While there will always be points of tension or unresolved conflict, the major developments in science in the past five decades have been running in a strongly theistic direction." [18]

Dean Kenyon (b.1939), Professor Emeritus of Biology at San Francisco State University and a young Earth creationist, who repudiated his earlier book on Darwinian evolution - mostly due to the discoveries of the information found in DNA - states: "This new realm of molecular genetics (is) where we see the most compelling evidence of design on the Earth." [19]

Just recently, one of the world's most famous atheists, Professor Antony Flew (see beginning of this chapter), admitted he couldn't explain how DNA originated and developed through evolution. He now accepts the need for an intelligent source to have been involved in the making of the DNA code. Professor Flew said, "What I think the DNA material has done is show that intelligence must have been involved in getting these extraordinarily diverse elements together. " [20]

The author directs the reader to Chapter Nineteen, *Christianity Compared with New Religions, Philosophies & Cults – Evolutionism,* for more on what many learned scholars increasingly consider one of the greatest hoaxes perpetrated in the name of science – Darwinian evolution or evolutionary theory!

The Philosophical or Ontological Argument

A Brief Outline of the Ontological Argument

A *philosophical argument* for God's existence, also called an *ontological argument*, is a case presented for God's existence based entirely on reason or logic. According to this argument, there is no need to go looking for physical evidence of God's existence; one can determine he exists just by analyzing the possibility. Philosophers and other scholars call such arguments *a priori* arguments.

The ontological argument dates back to Saint Anselm (1033 -1109), a Benedictine monk, abbot, philosopher, and theologian of the Catholic Church, who held the office of Archbishop of Canterbury from 1093 to 1109. Anselm's argument was the first of its kind in the Western Christian tradition. [21] Anselm proposed his idea about God's existence in his 1078 work *Proslogion* and defined God as "a being than which no greater can be conceived." [22] He argued that a concept of this being must exist in the mind, even in the mind of the person who denies the existence of God.

French philosopher René Descartes (1596 -1650) also used the ontological argument, which states once an individual mentally grasps the concept of God, he or she realizes God's non-existence is impossible. Such a theory, if successfully imparted, demonstrates the existence of a perfect being or entity, which, from all commonsensical perspectives, cannot fail to exist.

There are certain assumptions one can tell are false without even having to conduct any type of inquiry. The theory that the earth is square and the hypothesis that heavy metal objects cannot travel through the air are both obviously false claims. It is common knowledge today that the earth is round and airplanes can fly. One does not need to fear falling off the earth if he or she ventures too far from home. Also, if someone lives within close proximity to an international airport, as this writer does, he or she will see and hear huge "metal objects" (passenger jet planes) roar overhead incessantly.

The ontological argument contends that the idea God doesn't exist is just as absurd as the notion the earth is flat. According to the ontological argument, one knows the claim God doesn't exist is false without having to analyze or research it in any detail. Just as knowing the phrase "the earth is round" points to the unlikelihood of a flat earth, the ontological argument says knowing what "God" means makes it obvious God's non-existence is impossible. The submission God does not exist is, therefore, an exercise in self-contradiction.

God by Definition is Perfect in Every Way

There are many things an entity would have to be in order to be properly called "God." For instance, it would have to be omnipotent or all-powerful, omniscient or all-knowing, and omnipresent or ever - present. Merriam - Webster describes "God" as the entity or "being perfect in power, wisdom, and goodness who is worshiped as creator and ruler of the universe." Something cannot properly be referred to as "God" unless it is perfect. This is the central characteristic of the ontological argument. It is a gross misrepresentation to attempt to identify as God, someone, or something that isn't perfect in every way.

St. Anselm - God is "That Than Which Nothing Greater Can Be Conceived"

If something is perfect, then it couldn't possibly be better than it is, i.e., there can't be anything better than perfection. In other words, if a thing is perfect, then it is impossible to imagine it being better than it is in its present state.

Saint Anselm, the originator of the ontological argument, taught that God is "that than which no greater can be conceived." He describes the concept in the *Proslogion* as follows:

(Even a) fool, when he hears of ... a being than which nothing greater can be conceived ... understands what he hears, and what he understands is in his understanding.... And assuredly that, than which nothing greater can be conceived, cannot exist in the understanding alone. For suppose it exists in the understanding alone: then it can be conceived to exist in reality, which is greater.... Therefore, if that than which nothing greater can be conceived, exists in the understanding alone, the very being, than which nothing greater can be conceived, is one, than which a greater can be conceived. But obviously, this is impossible. Hence, there is no doubt that there exists a being than which nothing greater can be conceived, and it exists both in the understanding and in reality. [23]

The forgoing perplexing extract from the *Proslogion* may be summarized as follows:

29

- It is a conceptual truth (or, so to speak, true by definition) that God is a being than which none greater can be imagined, i.e., the greatest possible being imaginable.

- God exists as an idea in the mind.

- A being that exists as an idea in the mind and, in reality, other things being equal, is greater than a being that exists only as an idea in the mind.

- Thus, if God exists only as an idea in the mind, then one can imagine something that is greater than God, i.e., a greater imaginary god.

- However, one cannot imagine something greater than God (for it is a contradiction to suppose one can imagine a being greater than the greatest possible being imaginable).

- Therefore, God exists.

  Consequently, it is impossible to envisage there being anything greater than God or to imagine God being better than he already is.

Other Arguments for God's Existence

Shown below is a lengthy list of arguments for God's existence, all in accordance to some extent with Christian scholarship. An additional argument for God's existence, the *Scientific Argument*, which is technically an upshot of the *Design Argument*, appears earlier in the chapter.

1. The Argument from Change

2. The Argument from Efficient Causality

3. The Argument from Time and Contingency

4. The Argument from Degrees of Perfection

5. The Design Argument

6. The Kalam Argument (the First Cause Argument)

7. The Argument from Contingency

8. The Argument from the World as an Interacting Whole

9. The Argument from Miracles

10. The Argument from Consciousness

11. The Argument from Truth

12. The Argument from the Origin of the Idea of God

13. The Moral Argument

14. The Ontological Argument

15. The Argument from Conscience

16. The Argument from Desire

17. The Argument from Aesthetic Experience

18. The Argument from Religious Experience

19. The Common Consent Argument

20. Pascal's Wager[24]

Note:

The discussions in this chapter serve to support a case for God's existence, explain what he is like, and help confirm he created the universe. They do not, however, say why he created the universe or what he expects of humankind. Such deliberations are addressed elsewhere in this book.

In Part Four and Part Five of this book, the author compares Christianity with various world religions, philosophies, and cults. While most of the belief systems acknowledge the existence of God, their deities are fundamentally dissimilar to the God of the Bible or the God of biblical Christianity. Admittedly, there may be allusions to God, Jesus Christ, and the Holy Spirit in some of the worldviews, even presumed connections, but such associations are basically misrepresentations of the Christian Gospel.

CHAPTER TWO

JESUS CHRIST – WHO IS HE?

JESUS CHRIST IN WORLD RELIGIONS & PHILOSOPHIES

Jesus Christ, more than anyone else in history, is the religious leader most frequently mentioned by religious scholars and philosophers, whether they happen to be Christian or otherwise. Every major religious movement regards Jesus as an outstanding, important spiritual figure; some see him as God Himself. In addition to his status as history's preeminent religious leader, Christ is easily the most influential individual to have lived on earth. He is unique to the degree he defies comparison with anyone else. Just about every religious faith or belief system considers it an obligation to research and analyze the Galilean's life and teachings.

The author presents, in encapsulated form, the following perspectives about Jesus Christ derived from the philosophies of a number of the world's more prominent religions and worldviews.

Judaism – The main teachings about Christ include the following. [1]

- Jesus was the Virgin Mary's son. Orthodox Jews, however, deny Christ's virgin birth.

33

- Jesus was a rabbi and popular teacher. Orthodox Jews do not accept him as the Messiah.

- Jesus had many disciples and followers.

- Jesus was a popular teacher, revered by his followers and respected by his opponents.

- Christ was a miracle worker.

- Christ claimed to be the Messiah. While ancient Jews denied Jesus was the Messiah, they acknowledged he made such a claim publicly.

- Ancient Jewish texts (Talmud and Toledot Yeshu) affirm Jesus' crucifixion. However, they do not contain reports about his resurrection.

- Jesus' followers reported he rose from the dead.

Islam – Main teachings about Christ include the following. [2]

- Jesus Christ was born of a virgin. The Quran describes Mary as a virgin prior to Jesus' birth and records a conversation between Mary and Allah during which Allah tells Mary she will conceive without sexual interaction.

- Jesus is to be revered and held in high regard.

- Jesus was one of God's most important prophets.

- Jesus was a wise teacher. Muslims acknowledge Jesus as divinely inspired.

- Jesus was a miracle worker.

- Jesus ascended to Heaven.

- Jesus will come again.

Ahmadiyya (Muslim revivalist religion) – The main teachings about Christ include the following. [3]

- Ahmadiyya Muslims uphold the Christian claim that Jesus (called "Yus Asaf") was born of a virgin.

- Jesus was a great prophet.

- Jesus was a divinely wise teacher.

- Jesus was a miracle worker.

- Jesus suffered crucifixion on the Cross but did not die. He traveled to India and preached and healed the sick.

Baha'i – Main teachings about Christ include the following. [4]

- Jesus was a manifestation of God. The Baha'i faith, however, places Jesus alongside other messengers from major religious movements, including Abraham, Muhammad, the Buddha, Krishna, and Zoroaster.

- Jesus was born of a virgin.

- Jesus spoke for God while He was on earth. In fact, Baha'is consider the words of Jesus to be the words of God.

- Jesus was a wise teacher.

- Christ had both a divine and human nature.

- Christ was a miracle worker.

- Jesus died on the cross as an atonement for humanity's sins. The Bahá'í faith acknowledges Jesus died, and his death and (spiritual) resurrection serve to redeem fallen humankind.

Hinduism – The main teachings about Christ include the following. [5]

- Jesus was a holy man. Most Hindus evaluate "spirituality" on the basis of behavior and practice. Virtues such as tolerance, love, non-violence, self-sacrifice, and humility are held in high esteem and considered to be characteristics of "holy men" known as Sadhus. Based on the above requirements and Jesus' teachings, he qualifies as a "Hindu Saint."

- Jesus was a wise teacher. Most Hindus respect the teachings of Jesus, and some have even committed themselves to such teachings. Mahatma Gandhi saw Jesus as a symbol of superior ethics and venerated his teachings.

- Jesus is a 'God.' Some Hindus are more than willing to acknowledge Jesus as divine, if not 'uniquely' divine. Jesus, however, is supposedly only one of many "ishtas" (forms of the divine) in the history of humankind; others being Rama, Krishna and Buddha.

Buddhism – The main teachings about Jesus include the following. [6]

36

- Jesus was an enlightened man. Most Buddhists acknowledge and respect the fact Jesus lived a self-sacrificial life and had compassion for those who were in spiritual need.

- Jesus was a wise teacher. Most Buddhists respect the teachings of Jesus to a high degree, especially Jesus' teachings related to loving one's neighbor and the need to demonstrate kindness and forgiveness.

- Some Buddhists, including the 14th Dalai Lama (Tenzin Gyatso), have even recognized Jesus as a " bodhisattva" (one who dedicates his life sacrificially to the service and betterment of others). While they see Jesus as a wise teacher, they do not regard him as divine.

- Jesus was a holy man. The current Dalai Lama often describes Jesus as a "holy man" and includes Jesus on his list of holy people. In fact, the Dalai Lama does not typically elevate Buddha to a greater status than Jesus when discussing the two individuals.

The New Age Movement – The main teachings about Jesus include the following. [7]

- Nothing could be more diverse than the New Age Movement when related to the identity of Jesus. Perhaps most striking however, is the pluralism and relativism existing within the movement. Any attempt to identify Jesus as the singular God of the universe is surely rejected. Many New Age believers are willing to acclaim the teachings of Jesus, however, and often describe the "Christhood" of Jesus as something all of us could attain. In this sense, Jesus is seen as a man who completed a process of "spiritual evolution" over successive generations of reincarnation and became an enlightened master.

- Probably the only area of agreement among most New Age believers is Jesus was a wise and moral teacher. Many New Age spiritual movements describe Jesus as some sort of sage, teacher, or philosopher. They typically highlight those areas of his teachings aligning with the principles of Eastern mysticism, and they often distort the words of Jesus to accomplish this objective. They also typically ignore Jesus' teaching about his own identity. Many revere Jesus' moral teachings and some argue the ethics of Jesus are not those of the Christians who follow him. These New Age believers particularly respect what they believe Jesus taught about peace and love for one's enemies, the hypocrisy of the rich and religious leaders, and the rights of women and children.

The author directs the reader to the following chapters of "Two Doors to Eternity" for detailed comparisons between biblical Christianity and the belief systems mentioned above (except Ahmadiyya): *Judaism* (Chapter Eight), *Buddhism* (Chapter Twelve), *Hinduism* (Chapter Thirteen), *Islam* (Chapter Fourteen), *The New Age Movement* (Chapter Eighteen), and *The Baha'i Faith* (Chapter Twenty - One: Other Non-Christian/Anti-Christian Religions & Philosophies).

"Two Doors to Eternity" also compares biblical Christianity with the following worldviews, i.e., *Roman Catholicism* (Chapter Nine), *Eastern*

Orthodoxy (Chapter Ten), *Atheism* (Chapter Eleven), *Jehovah's Witnesses* (Chapter Fifteen), *Mormonism* (Chapter Sixteen), *Evolutionism* (Chapter Nineteen), *Satanism & the Occult* (Chapter Twenty), and *Christian Science, Transcendental Meditation, Freemasonry, Hare Krishna, Secular Humanism, The International Churches of Christ* (formerly Boston Church of Christ), *Postmodernism, Unification Church* (The Moonies), and *Unitarian Universalism* (Chapter Twenty - One: *Other Non-Christian/Anti-Christian Religions & Philosophies*). Unavoidably, Jesus Christ, history's foremost religious figure and spiritual leader, and God to over 2.2 billion people, is part of just about every discussion presented.

Biblical Minimalism

The study of biblical history and archaeology (Biblical minimalism) generally is not, as the appellation might imply, an undertaking to uphold biblical claims to authenticity of any sort. Rather, the exercise is often an unobtrusive attempt by minimalists to accomplish just the opposite, i.e., discredit biblical assertions and concomitantly strip the Bible of its supernatural nuances and invalidate the Scriptures' eschatological inferences.

Essentially, minimalists confer little credence on the biblical record and trivialize the importance of the Bible to the historical record, placing more trust in evidence from other sources. They persist in disputing the Bible's claims until an archeologist digs up confirmatory proof or until other manuscript evidence comes to light to substantiate the Scriptures. Modern critical scholarship, accustomed to controverting myriad affirmations of historicity in various spheres of inquiry stares in awe at the Holy Bible, which continues to be a source of embarrassment to what ostensibly may be termed the "scientific" study of the past.

A principal objective of minimalists aimed at discrediting the Scriptures is to subject their record of the life and teachings of its main Character, Jesus Christ, to widespread and often debatable or controversial methods of research and analysis.

The Jesus Seminar was a group of about 50 Biblical scholars and 100 laymen founded in 1985 by Robert W. Funk, a religionist and pioneer in modern biblical scholarship, and that originated under the auspices of the Westar Institute. [8] The seminar was very active through the 1980s and 1990s, and into the early 21st century. Members of the Seminar used votes with colored beads to decide their collective view of the historicity of the deeds and sayings of Jesus of Nazareth.[9] They produced new translations of the New Testament and Apocrypha to use as textual sources and published their results in four reports: The Five Gospels (1993), [10] The Acts of Jesus (1998), The Acts of Jesus: The Search for the Authentic Deeds of Jesus (1998), [11] and The Gospel of Jesus (1999).[12]

The Jesus Seminar came under criticism from a wide array of scholars and laymen regarding its method, assumptions, and conclusions. [13, 14] Various aspects of the Jesus Seminar fell under stern condemnation, including:

- The composition of the Seminar & the qualifications of its members.

- The use of a flawed voting system.

- Creating a Jesus based on the presuppositions of the Seminar's members.

- Inappropriate emphasis on flawed criteria.

- Bias against canonical sources and partiality in favor of non-canonical sources.

In addition to the many scholarly critiques, there was a huge conservative backlash against the Jesus Seminar and its questionable modus operandi. Although never formally disbanded, the seminar effectively ceased functioning as "The Jesus Seminar" in 2006, shortly after the death of Robert Funk in 2005.

If people were to render any measure of plausibility to the garblings of Jesus Seminar members and other nonconformists, one would ask why would someone like Jesus Christ, supposedly a common man with no extraordinary capabilities, have had such a huge impact on world history – to the extent 2.2 billion people today venerate him and follow his teachings? [15]

Jesus Christ In History

No capable historian would claim Jesus Christ is not a historical figure. There is an overabundance of evidence from the early Christian era to show he did exist. As biblical theologian and historian F.F. Bruce wrote, "The historicity of Christ is as axiomatic for an unbiased historian as the historicity of Julius Caesar." [16] Ancient documents produced by respected historians and writers like Tacitus, Flavius Josephus, Suetonius, and Pliny the Younger, among others, contain unmistakable references to the existence of Jesus of Nazareth.

The Roman historian Tacitus (AD 56 – 120), writing about the great fire of Rome in AD 64 during the reign of Nero (AD 54-68), told of how the emperor blamed the Christians living in the city for starting the conflagration. Tacitus noted in his writings, *The Annals*, one of the earliest secular historical records that mentions Christ. The historian said:

> *Christus, from whom the name had its origin, suffered the extreme penalty during the reign of Tiberius at the hands of one of our procurators, Pontius Pilatus, and a most mischievous superstition, thus checked for the moment, again broke out not only in Judaea, the first source of the evil but even in Rome. . . .*[17]

Flavius Josephus (AD 37–100), a Jewish military general and historian, published a lengthy history of the Jews. While discussing the period during which the Roman procurator Pontius Pilate governed the Jews of Judaea, Josephus included the following account about Jesus Christ.

> *"Now there was about this time Jesus, a wise man, if it be lawful to call him a man; for he was a doer of wonderful works, a teacher of such men as receive the truth with pleasure. He drew over to him both many of the Jews and many of the Gentiles. He was [the] Christ. And when Pilate, at the suggestion of the principal men amongst us, had condemned him to the cross, those that loved him at the first did not forsake him; for he appeared to them alive again the third day; as the divine prophets had foretold these and ten thousand other wonderful*

42

things concerning him. And the tribe of Christians, so named from him, are not extinct at this day. [18]

Suetonius (AD 69 – 122), a chronicler of the Imperial dynasty and a court official during the reign of the emperor Hadrian (AD 117-138) wrote, "As the Jews were making constant disturbances at the instigation of Chrestus (an alternate spelling of Christus), he expelled them from Rome." [19] The decree expelling Christians from Rome probably dates back to AD 49 during the reign of the emperor Claudius. In another work, Suetonius observed, "Punishment by Nero was inflicted on the Christians, a class of men given to a new and mischievous superstition." [20] The inference here undoubtedly relates to the nascent Christian faith.

Plinius Secundus (AD 61 -113), a lawyer and author, more commonly known as Pliny the Younger, governor of Bithynia in Asia Minor, corresponded with the emperor Trajan in AD 112 about how to treat Christians who refused to pay homage to the emperor. Secundus said:

Having never been present at any trials concerning those who profess Christianity, I am unacquainted not only with the nature of their crimes or the measure of their punishment, but how far it is proper to enter into an examination concerning them." Plinius mentions Christianity, Christians, and the name of Christ ten times in the short letter, even remarking that Christians "addressed a form of prayer to Christ, as to a divinity. [21]

The Emperor's reply commended Pliny for his actions:

You have adopted the right course, my dearest Secundus, in investigating the charges against the Christians who were brought before you. . . . If indeed they should be brought before you, and the crime is proved, they must be punished; with the restriction, however, that where the party denies, he is a Christian. . . .[22]

There are many other ancient secular attestations to the historicity of Jesus Christ, but the forgoing four instances help confirm Christ and his revolutionary teachings, which later became the doctrines of the Christian faith, were familiar to Roman officials at the highest levels as early as the reign of Claudius (AD 41-54). Certainly, the Roman governor Pontius Pilate knew Jesus Christ and chronicled his trial and execution. Unfortunately, such records apparently did not endure over the centuries.

The early accounts, notwithstanding dissenting opinions by some, provide unbiased support for many of the biblical claims about Jesus, including his teachings, his miracles, his crucifixion, his resurrection, and even his divinity! The truth of the matter is many critical scholars do not want to believe these things, even from the pens of historians whom they hold in high regard. This is because they realize if they acknowledge the work of these chroniclers, it perhaps would require or challenge them to follow Christ's teachings - and they will do anything to avoid making such a commitment!

Jesus Christ – Who Really Is He?

Few people would question whether Jesus Christ existed. Historically, most people acknowledge the Galilean rabbi walked the earth in the land of Israel about 2000 years ago. Much debate, however, swirls around the subject of Jesus' identity, i.e., who really was he? Did he perform miracles? What did he teach? Did he rise from the dead? Is he God? Is he coming back to judge the world?

As intimated earlier, almost every major religion presents Jesus as a prophet, a good teacher, or a godly man. The Holy Bible, however, declares Jesus was infinitely more than any or all of these embodiments.

Clive. S. Lewis (1898 – 1963), the well-known British writer and lay theologian, made the following incisive statement about Christ in his book *Mere Christianity*.

I am trying here to prevent anyone from saying the really foolish thing that people often say about Him (Jesus Christ): 'I'm ready to accept Jesus as a great moral teacher, but I don't accept his claim to be God.' That is the one thing we must not say. A man who was merely a man and said the sort of things Jesus said would not be a great moral teacher. He would either be a lunatic—on a level with a man who says he is a poached egg—or else he would be the Devil of hell. You must make your choice. Either this man was, and is, the Son of God, or else a madman or something worse. You can shut him up for a fool, you can spit at him and kill him as a demon, or you can fall at his feet and call him Lord and God. But let us not come up with any patronizing nonsense about his being a great human teacher. He has not left that option open to us. He did not intend to. [23]

Considering Jesus Christ merely on the basis of his exemplary life and his superior moral teachings will not remove the stumbling blocks to Christianity raised by an unbelieving world. The real test of what one thinks of him must revolve around who he claimed to be and what he accomplished during his brief sojourn on earth. The ultimate conclusion must be that there is no Christianity without Christ; everything about the faith centers on him.

The predominant theme of the Scriptures is the Person and the work of Jesus Christ. The Holy Scriptures say He is God. He became a human being, died by crucifixion, and was buried. He rose from the dead. He is the only, all-sufficient Savior of the world and He will come again to this earth. The removal of these all-important tenets from God's Holy Word negates the cardinal message of Christ's Gospel and ruptures the consistency of the unified story and revelation of the Old Testament and the New Testament.

The Holy Bible is the incontrovertibly truthful Word of God. The following biblical extracts clearly identify who Jesus Christ is and explain why he came to earth as God incarnate.

Jesus Christ is God

- *He was pre-existent with the Father* - "The same was in the beginning with God. All things were made by him; and without him was not anything made that was made" (John 1:2,3, KJV)

- *He is the Son of God* - His enemies admitted: "He...said also that God was his Father, making himself equal with God" (John 5:18,

KJV). Peter confessed: "And we believe and are sure that thou art the Christ, the Son of the living God" (John 6:69, KJV). Jesus affirmed: "I and my Father are one." (John 10:30, KJV)

- *He was sinless, as only God can be* - Jesus challenged his enemies: "Which of you convinceth me of sin?" (John 8:46, KJV) Peter testified: "...Christ also suffered for us, leaving us an example that ye should follow his steps: who did no sin, neither was guile found in his mouth" (1 Peter 2:21,22, KJV). Paul stated: "For he hath made him to be sin for us, who knew no sin; that we might be made the righteousness of God in him." (2 Corinthians 5:21, (KJV)

- *He forgives sin, as only God can* - The Scribes said: "Who can forgive sins but God only?" (Mark 2:7, KJV) Jesus said: "But that ye may know that the Son of man hath power on earth to forgive sins..." (Matthew 9:6 (KJV) Also, see John 8:1). Peter wrote: "Who his own self bare our sins in his own body on the tree, that we, being dead to sins, should live unto righteousness: by whose stripes ye were healed" (1 Peter 2:24, (KJV)

- *He performed miraculous works* - He healed the sick: Matthew (8:9-13; Luke 4:31-44; 5:12-15; John 4:43-5:16). He fed the hungry (John 6; Mark 8). He raised the dead (Luke 7:11-18; John 11:1-46).

Jesus Christ Became Man

- *Jesus Christ became man* - "And the Word was made flesh and dwelt among us...full of grace and truth." (John 1:14, (KJV). Also, see Philippians 2:7-8.

- *The Holy Scriptures prophesied Christ's miraculous birth 800 years before his coming* - "Behold a virgin shall conceive, and bear a son, and shall call his name Emmanuel." (Isaiah 7:14, (KJV)

- *The prophecy was fulfilled to the letter* - "Fear not, Mary: for thou hast found favor with God. And, behold, thou shalt conceive in thy womb, and bring forth a son, and shalt call his name Jesus." (Luke 1:30, 31, KJV)

- *Jesus demonstrated human characteristics* - He became tired (John 4:6), He thirsted (John 19:28), He ate food (Luke 24:40-43), He showed feelings (Mark 6:34), He wept (John 11:35), He knew temptation (Hebrews 4:15), and he died (John 19:30).

Jesus Christ Fulfilled His Father's Plan

- *Jesus died on the Cross* - This is the fundamental theme of the Gospel.

  The fact of Christ's death - One-fourth of the Gospels addresses Christ's Passion and Resurrection. (a) For this purpose, he came into the world (John 12:27). (b) The Scriptures prophesied Christ's death hundreds of years before he died (Isaiah 53:3-8).

48

The meaning of Christ's death - (a) It was a ransom for sin (Matthew 20:28; Romans 3:24; 1 Peter 1:18). (b) It was to pay the penalty for sin (Romans 3:24; 1 John 2:2; 4:10). Man was the object of God's wrath because of rebellion and sin, but God took the initiative in satisfying his wrath by sending his own Son to Calvary.

Jesus' death is a reconciliation - The enmity between humankind and God ended with Christ's death (Romans 5:10), which restored humankind to God (2 Corinthians 5:18, 19).

Jesus' death is a substitution - He died in sinful humankind's place (1 Peter 3:18; 2 Corinthians 5:21). (e) In summary, Christ's death dealt completely with the matter of sin (1 Peter 2:24; Hebrews 9:26; Hebrews 10:12).

- *Christ rose from the dead* - This is unique and elemental to Christianity.

The reality of the Resurrection - (John 20:1-10; 1 Corinthians 15:4).

The credibility of the Resurrection - Jesus predicted it (Matthew 13:39-41; Luke 24:1-7).

The tomb was empty - (John 20:11-13).

Many witnesses saw him alive after his resurrection - The women (Luke 23:55, 56), Mary Magdalene (John 20:1, 2, 11-18), and Peter and the other disciples (John 20:3-9, 19, 20, 24-31; 21:1-14).

The Results of Christ's Work

- *Christ ascended to His Father* (Luke 24:49-53; Acts 1:6-11).

- *Christ is humankind's eternal Mediator* (1 Timothy 2:5; Hebrews 8:6; 1 John 2:1.

- *Christ is humankind's Savior* - "Thou shalt call his name Jesus: for he shall save his people from their sins." (Luke 1:30, 31, KJV). "Him hath God exalted with his right hand to be a Prince and a Savior, for to give repentance to Israel, and forgiveness of sins."(Acts 5:31, KJV)

- *Christ is the only Savior* - "Salvation is found in no one else, for there is no other name under heaven given to men by which we must be saved."(Acts 4:12, NIV)

- *Christ is a complete Savior* - "Wherefore he is able also to save them to the uttermost that come unto God by him, seeing he ever liveth to make intercession for them." (Hebrews 7:25, (KJV)

- *Christ is a personal Savior* - "That if thou shalt confess with thy mouth the Lord Jesus, and shalt believe in thine heart that God hath raised him from the dead, thou shalt be saved. For with the heart, man believeth unto righteousness; and with the mouth confession is made unto salvation." (Romans 10:9,10, KJV)

The Consummation of Christ's Accomplishments

- *Christ shall return again to this earth* - (Acts 1:11; Hebrews 10:37; John 14:3).

- *Believers in Christ shall receive resurrected bodies to begin a new, undying life* - (1 Thessalonians 4:17-18; 1 Corinthians 15:51-58).

- *He will reign as King of kings and Lord of lords over His new creation* - (2 Peter 3:10-13; Revelation 22:3-5).

Jesus' True Identity

Why is the question about Jesus' true identity so important? Why does it matter whether Jesus is God? Jesus has to be God because if he is not God, his death would not be sufficient to pay the penalty for the sins of the whole world (1 John 2:2). Only God could pay such an infinite penalty (Romans 5:8; 2 Corinthians 5:21). Jesus has to be God so that he could pay humankind's debt. Jesus had to be a man so he could die in order to atone for humankind's sins. Salvation is available only through faith in Jesus Christ. Jesus' deity is why he is the only means of salvation. His deity is why he proclaimed, "I am the way and the truth and the life. No one comes to the Father except through me." (John 14:6, NIV)

CHAPTER THREE

THE DEVIL OR SATAN – IS HE REAL?

The celebrated American evangelist William (Billy) F. Graham (1918 – 2018), considered by many "one of the most influential Christian leaders of the 20th century," [1]offered the following response to a man who wanted to know what the devil's (Satan's) most successful trick was. Dr. Graham's answer to the man's question condenses the message of the Christian faith, i.e., that of trusting Jesus Christ as one's Savior in order to fend off Satan's constant attacks and so secure a place in God's kingdom for all eternity[1].

> *I'm thankful you want to be on guard against the devil's schemes—because the devil is real, and he will do everything he can to deceive us and turn us away from God. The Bible urges us to be alert to the devil's schemes, "in order that Satan might not outwit us." (2 Corinthians 2:11, NIV)*

> *The devil has many tricks up his sleeve (so to speak)—but surely one of his most successful is to make us believe he doesn't even exist. We may admit that evil is real—but then deny that behind it are demonic spiritual forces bent on our destruction and death. Or we may deny the devil's true nature by turning him into a harmless cartoon character with a red suit and pitchfork. But Jesus said, "He was a murderer from the beginning, not holding to the truth, for there is no truth in him."* John 8:44, NIV)

Someone has said that the devil doesn't need to think up any new tricks—because the old ones still work! It's true; lust, pride, power, discouragement, doubt, money, escapism, pleasure, hate, anger, jealousy, selfishness—the ways he attacks us are almost endless. If one temptation doesn't work, he'll try another—and he'll keep on trying.

But listen: The most important fact about Satan is that he is a defeated foe! By His death and resurrection, Jesus Christ conquered death and Hell and Satan—and someday, His victory will be complete. In the meantime, make sure of your commitment to Christ, and turn to Him every day for the strength you need. [2]

Does The Devil Really Exist?

The Bible states in no uncertain terms that Satan or the devil exists. The Scriptures describe Satan as the enemy of man (Genesis 3:15), the father of lies (John 8:44b), and the accuser (Revelation 12:10), among other things. Isaiah 14:12–17 say Satan was originally an angelic being, but he craved the honor and worship due only to God. Subsequently, God cast him out of heaven (see Ezekiel 28:11–17).

Ever since God cast Satan out of heaven along with the angels (now demons) who chose to rebel with him, the devil has made it his purpose to oppose God and lead people into rebellion as well. How powerful is Satan? He is not God's counterpart because God has no equal. He is not God's opposite because God has always existed, and he created all that exist now, including angels, human beings, and other living things. Although the devil's power is laughable compared to the capabilities of God, he is a real threat to humans and has the capacity to ruin a person's life to the point of eternal damnation. He possesses a considerable measure of authority in this world. He is called "the god of this age" (2 Corinthians 4:4, NIV) and "the prince of the power of the air." (Ephesians 2:2, KJV) That's why people are to "be alert and of sober mind (because) the devil prowls around like a roaring lion looking for someone to devour." (1 Peter 5:8, NIV)

The devil spreads his malevolence via attitudes of self-centeredness, lust, greed, vanity, jealousy, envy, resentment, competition, strife, bitterness, and hate. Essentially, the deplorable traits classified as "human nature" are actually Satan's nature. He broadcasts his sinisterness directly and indirectly, often utilizing film, television, the Internet, and other forms of media, and entraps unsuspecting people the world over. Satan influences and manipulates people from an early age, and though they don't necessarily exhibit abominable characteristics at birth, they soon absorb the fiendish miens broadcast by the devil. When one looks at the world and its untold evils, one observes the tragic, reprehensible deeds and omissions of men and women deceived by Satan's diabolical agenda.

The Holy Bible says Satan is a created being, and Almighty God created him and all the angels, including those whom he cast out from his presence after they rebelled against him. This begs the question - How could a loving God create something as evil as the devil?

Satan's History

The Bible reveals God created angels and they inhabited the Earth long before he created Adam and Eve. Job 38:4-7 records the angels shouting for joy when the Creator made the Earth. The angels bore the capacity to reason and choose between good and bad.

The Book of Ezekiel in the Old Testament states God created an archangel of awesome, majestic beauty, dazzling brightness, and supreme knowledge and put him in charge over the Earth and the angels on Earth:

Thou sealest up the sum, full of wisdom, and perfect in beauty. (Ezekiel 28:12, KJV)

Thou hast been in Eden the garden of God; every precious stone was thy covering, the sardius, topaz, and the diamond, the beryl, the onyx, and the jasper, the sapphire, the emerald, and the carbuncle, and gold: the workmanship of thy tabrets and of thy pipes was prepared in thee in the day that thou wast created. (Ezekiel 28:13, KJV)

Thou art the anointed cherub that covereth; and I have set thee so: thou wast upon the holy mountain of God; thou hast walked up and down in the midst of the stones of fire. (Ezekiel 28:14, KJV).

The prophet Isaiah called the archangel angel "Heylel," meaning 'Light-Bringer' in Hebrew and "Lucifer" in Latin. (Isaiah 14:12)

The Book of Exodus in the Old Testament explains the meaning of "the anointed cherub that covers" spoken of in Ezekiel 28. Exodus 25 relays God's instructions to Moses on how to pattern the Ark of the Covenant. The top of the chest would be a mercy seat, depicting the very throne of God in heaven, and two cherubs would be stationed at the mercy seat, one on each side with their wings covering the likeness of God's throne. The symbolism was that these superior angels were involved in the administration of the government of God over all creation. Lucifer was stationed at that throne of God, trained to rule, and then placed by God in charge of the angels on Earth.

Lucifer and the angels under his governance then underwent an appalling change.

The Bible says the angels who God placed on Earth sinned (2 Peter 2:4). Sin is the transgression of God's law (1 John 3:4), the latter that facilitates peace, harmony and love. Isaiah 14 and Ezekiel 28 of the Old Testament shed light on what happened to Lucifer and the angels who fell under his jurisdiction.

Lucifer was perfect until he allowed thoughts contrary to God's law into his mind. His mind became filled with vanity, jealousy, envy, lust, competition and greed. The Bible says, "Thou wast perfect in thy ways from the day that thou wast created, till iniquity was found in thee." (Ezekiel 28:15, KJV)

Lucifer was no longer satisfied with ruling just Earth—he wanted to rule the entire universe like God. He said, "I will ascend into heaven, I will exalt my throne above the stars of God." (Isaiah 14:13, KJV). He was the first rebel and he also encouraged the angels under his authority to betray God by injecting feelings of resentment and bitterness into their minds.

Lucifer then led the angels under his watch into outright rebellion and attempted to overthrow God from his throne. The archangel, who once was God's most trusted friend, became God's principal adversary. God then banned Lucifer, who became Satan, and his followers, who became demons, from his kingdom and restricted them from roaming the Earth. The prophet

Isaiah lamented, "How art thou fallen from heaven, O Lucifer, son of the morning! How art thou cut down to the ground!" (Isaiah 14:12, KJV). Jesus Himself told His disciples, "I beheld Satan as lightning fall from heaven." (Luke 10:18, KJV).

Satan today still rules the Earth over which God gave him authority a long, long time ago. However, the evil one's days are numbered.

God did not create a devil but a resplendent, perfect super-angel. Yet Lucifer allowed his beauty and perfection to fill him with vanity and a craving for self-glory. Envious of God's power, he resented God's authority over him and rebelled. He became Satan, God's chiefest adversary and humankind's greatest threat to obtaining everlasting life!

Satan's Agenda Of Deception

The Lie In The Garden Of Eden

Satan's primary objective is to deceive people, and he is an ingenious liar. God created Adam and Eve with free will to choose and make decisions, just like people today. The Garden of Eden, in which God placed the first members of his human creation, apparently contained many types of fruit-bearing trees, the fruits of which they were free to consume. The only instruction God gave to Adam and Eve was not to eat from a particular tree. It was a simple, straightforward instruction. He warned them that if they disobeyed him, they would surely die.

Satan saw an opportunity to tempt Eve. He lied to the woman and said, "You will not certainly die...For God knows that when you eat from it your eyes will be opened, and you will be like God, knowing good and evil." (Genesis 3:4,5, (NIV)

Satan deceived Eve, persuading her to believe God was withholding something wonderful from Adam and her, i.e., they could be like God. Only it was not true! Adam and Eve believed Satan's lie rather than respecting God's wishes. Satan is very adept at distorting the truth and exposing people to harm. The consequences of Adam and Eve's insubordination were devastating.

Satan Accuses God of Being Unloving & Unjust

The devil is an expert at playing on people's consciences and emotions. His greatest desire is to alienate people from God or prevent them from approaching God's Throne of Grace. He will seek either to cause one to deny God's existence or to slander God and lie about the latter's character. Satan tries to impress upon people that God doesn't love them. He points to the myriad ills of the world and people's trials and tribulations and tells them if God were loving and just, he would prevent pain and suffering.

God, however, is incomparably loving and merciful and repeatedly affirms his love for humankind. He says, "I have loved you with an everlasting love; I have drawn you with unfailing kindness." (Jeremiah 31:3, NIV). The Gospel of John reminds the Christian that "This is love: not that we loved God, but that he loved us and sent his Son as an atoning sacrifice for our sins." (1 John 4:10, NIV). The Scriptures echo one of the most endearing expressions of God's love for people everywhere.

For God so loved the world that he gave his one and only Son, that whoever believes in him shall not perish but have eternal life. (John 3:16, NIV).

In a world riddled with sin and evil, a world under Satan's governance, all kinds of problems are inevitable. Satan and his demons lead people to sin. They are the ones who are unloving and unjust, not God! Satan is the originator of wickedness and deception, even though humans, being moral agents endowed with the capacity to choose between good and evil, make the ultimate decision whether to commit sin.

However, if someone has a relationship with God and places him at the helm of his or her life, the Creator is ready to help the believer overcome any problem. One does not have to shoulder or solve his or her problems by himself or herself. God is able to give his children wisdom and real strength in the midst of their trials. He offers them resolution and comfort like no one else.

Peace I leave with you; my peace I give you. I do not give to you as the world gives. Do not let your hearts be troubled and do not be afraid. (John 14:27, NIV).

Satan Accuses People of Being Unfit for God's Kingdom

The Old Testament relates the story of Satan appearing before God and accusing a just and holy man named Job of being imperfect. Satan said if Job suffered enough, he would curse God. Job, even though he experienced unbelievable tragedy and hardship, did not curse God. A merciful God eventually blessed Job and restored everything he had lost.

Satan undermines people and condemns them before God. He tells them God will reject them because they are not good or holy enough to deserve their Creator's blessings. He pinpoints their failures and their shortcomings in the process. God, however, makes it unambiguously clear in his Holy Word that if an individual repents of his or her sins, trusts Jesus Christ as his or her Redeemer, and purposes to change for the better, he will accept such an individual as his own through the dispensation of his infinite grace. No one needs to be perfect or sinless to obtain salvation and an eventual place in God's kingdom.

Jesus Himself said of Satan when he rebuked the Jewish leaders who sought to incriminate him, "You belong to your father, the devil, and you want to carry out your father's desires. He was a murderer from the beginning, not holding to the truth, for there is no truth in him. When he lies, he speaks his native language, for he is a liar and the father of lies." (John 8:44, NIV). Jesus describes the stunning contrast between the devil and God when he says, "The thief comes only to steal and kill and destroy; I have come that they may have life, and have it to the full." (John 10:10, NIV).

Three Stories Of The Supernatural

While the devil, more often than not, strikes at people indirectly through deceit, temptation, the spread of false teachings, and other forms of inveiglement, he and his demons sometimes attack potential victims directly. Such confrontations can be terrifying and overwhelming, and save for the intervention by an omnipotent and compassionate God, people would have no recourse against such dark and sinister assaults.

The author recalls three incidents in which evil supernatural forces or entities confronted him and/or members of his family. The events took place many years ago in Guyana, South America. The narratives appear in a first-person format. The stories first appeared in *God in Our Midst: Making the Most Important Decision of Your Life*, the author's first full-length book, published in 2003 by Xlibris Corporation, USA.

Story One - The Georgetown (Guyana, South America) Hospital Incident

I experienced a frightening encounter with what I felt certain was a paranormal entity one night in April 1978, shortly after being admitted into a hospital in Georgetown, Guyana's capital city, following a serious motor vehicle accident.

As a result of the accident, I suffered a dislocated left hip, fractured left knee and right elbow, and, worst of all, an almost completely severed right hand, which hung on to my arm by only ruptured skin. There were also minor cuts and bruises on my body. The once sturdy British-made car in which I was a passenger became a total write-off.

A couple of days after admittance into the hospital, I relocated from the emergency department to an area called "Seamen's Ward." It was a section of the building in which, they said, ailing seamen of bygone days stayed. I shared a large, partitioned room with a kindly older gentleman.

One night, not long after my stay in the hospital began, I experienced a most terrifying ordeal. It was very early in the morning, around two or three o'clock, when, in a dazed state, I realized a woman dressed in a nightgown was trying to push me off the bed on which I lay. I must mention at this point that my injured leg and foot were in a kind of "traction" apparatus. In other words, I had to lie on my back all the time with a kind of pulley, having a weight at its end attached to my left leg and foot. This was done so the head of the dislocated femur or thighbone would be kept in the hip socket and help initiate healing. Any sudden, forceful movement could cause another dislocation.

The woman, it was more of an apparition, climbed on top of me, moved to my side and sat on my feet in its violent attempts to move me from the position in which I lay. Whatever it was that attacked me, it made no sound. There was a menacing look on its face as it relentlessly tried to harm me. I yelled and panted as I tried to fight it off. I called out to God in my attempt to ward off the assault. The whole incident lasted about five minutes. By the time it ended, I was fully awake and gasping for breath. My roommate had heard the commotion and wanted to know what had happened. A thick, drawn curtain separated our areas in the room and he could not have seen anything. He was, of course, taken aback at my story, and I sensed he too was scared.

I prayed for the light of day. I seized the earliest opportunity to summon the matron or head nurse. I was quite panicky and nervous. All that took place seemed so real! I demanded to be relocated to another room or ward. No other room was available, however. What disconcerted me further, though, was the look of fear on the matron's face as I related the story to her. Had something of this nature occurred before in the ward? The matron excused herself and hurriedly left the room.

The next day when my wife Pamela came to see me, I requested she bring a pocket Bible on her next visit. I slept with the little book on top of my chest from then on. It was easy to do this, actually, with my leg being in "traction' and my having to lie in one position all the time. I constantly repeated prayers of protection as I read from the Scriptures. Needless to say, from then on, I slept peacefully, and there were no other fear-provoking occurrences during the rest of my stay at the hospital.

Someone, or something evil and quite likely of a preternatural nature, tried to cause me harm. Whatever it was, it had to contend with a third party to the fiasco, and I do not mean the gentleman on the other bed in the room. The Lord Jesus was there, and my assailant knew it had no recourse but to leave the scene a defeated foe. [3]

Story Two - The Possessed Child

My mother was a deeply religious woman. Her father (my grandfather), the latter whom I never had the privilege of knowing, was also a godly individual. As a matter of fact, both my maternal and paternal grandfathers were lay preachers, also known as "catechists." They were not ashamed of Christ's Gospel and boldly espoused its teachings. When we were children, my mother told my other siblings and me about her father and his encounters with the unknown. He met and overcame, through God's providence, entities termed "evil spirits." We would later learn the "evil spirits" were really Satan's demons engrossed in their campaign to antagonize and lead astray, people who would fall prey to their cunning and subterfuge. They continue to do so today.

At various stages in her life, my mother apparently had a few preternatural encounters of her own. One such meeting took place in the middle nineteen-seventies in Leonora, a small rural district in Guyana, South America (mentioned earlier in this chapter). My mother was a teacher at the Leonora Government School at the time of the incident. She related to us the following story.

There was a student, about seven or eight years old, who one day fell into a kind of trance. Her countenance changed from a bubbly, animated one to a wild-eyed, serious expression. The child started to sway forward and then backward. She did so to the extent that she was almost parallel to the floor in either direction without losing her balance and while still on her feet! She spoke perfect English, something beyond her capability when she was her usual self. Her hair became loose as she swayed to and fro. The episode lasted for a few minutes. The other children who were nearby became terrified and ran away. The child, after the rocking ceased, became normal again but suffered a severe headache. This frightening transformation apparently had taken place before and was a continuing occurrence…until my mother intervened!

I had never had any reason to question the honesty and integrity of my mother, especially in issues associated with her life as a practicing Christian and her relationship with the Lord Jesus Christ. I was not going to start then.

My mother told us she confronted the child on one occasion after the latter began to behave strangely. She proceeded to question the child, or whoever or whatever was resident in her at the time. Astonishingly, the girl replied in the voice of a full-grown man! My mother, being the child of God she was, had suspected earlier and now was sure the student was demon-possessed. After finding out when and where the spirit had taken possession of the girl, my mother asked it to leave the child. The spirit bluntly refused and said it would not go away. This made my Mom mad. Now, this fellow, this being within the child, didn't know it, but it was never advisable to make my mother mad, especially when the matter at hand had to do with the Lord's work! She immediately commanded the demon to leave the child's body. This time, she used special authority with which she was vested. She used the "name that is above every other name, the owner to which every knee will bow, in heaven and on earth and under the earth." (Philippians 2:9-10, NIV). Yes, she uttered the name "Jesus!" The spirit fled, and the child returned to normal.

During the course of the incident, before the evil spirit bolted, my mother gave the child a copy of the New Testament to grasp. The demon refused to hold the holy book. It flattened out the child's hand so as to make the book drop to the floor. My mother, upon seeing this, forcibly closed the child's hand over the New Testament. The entity resident in the child knew what the message on the pages of the Scriptures represented, and it did not like it a bit! In the end, it had no choice but to acknowledge the superiority of the power of God and His Holy Word. [4]

As incredible as the forgoing story appears, it is nevertheless true. My brother-in-law, who now resides in Florida, USA, and who was a teacher at the Leonora Government School at the time, was witness to one of the earlier incidents involving the child's unusual behavior. He assured us the occurrences really did take place. During the episode in which he was a bystander, the entity within the child terrorized schoolchildren and teachers who were nearby. A teacher, who was a committed Christian, managed to free the girl of her tormentor, who reluctantly left her.

Story Three - The New Amsterdam (Guyana, South America) Incident

I recall an unusual and frightening experience that took place in Guyana, South America, during the early nineteen-seventies. I was a senior public accountant at the time and was in charge of a team of accountants. Together, we traveled to various locations in the country and audited the books and records of clients conducting business in a hodgepodge of manufacturing, production, service, and financial industries. On one occasion, we visited a client in New Amsterdam in the County of Berbice. Berbice is one of three counties that comprise the geographical makeup of Guyana. Generally considered Guyana's second largest city, New Amsterdam is a quaint town with a number of older, well-kept buildings and is situated some twenty miles or so from the country's capital city of Georgetown in the County of Demerara. The Berbice River separates the two counties and one would use a passenger ferry to get from one county to another.

Our client was a bank, and atop its offices was a guesthouse where we stayed, two persons to a room. The bank manager and his family lived in a part of the house.

We began our assignment on schedule and made good progress during the first day or two. It was late during what must have been the second or third night of our stay when a macabre event unfolded.

We had settled down, anticipating a good night's rest after a day's tiring work. It was well into the night when we heard the loudest of noises. The noise jolted us out of our sleep, actually. The home was a huge one with numerous rooms, and the unoccupied spaces seemed to help intensify the deafening sound. We thought a section of the building had collapsed. My primary concern was for the safety of the bank manager's family. He, the manager, had gone out earlier and apparently had not yet returned. My roommate was hesitant to venture out of our room, as was yours truly. The place became eerily silent. We realized after a while that no one was willing to leave his or her room to investigate what we thought was a very strange occurrence.

I finally decided to look into the matter myself and headed towards the kitchen area, which was the logical direction to take given the layout of the house. I was going past a nearby washroom and saw that the door was wide open. I looked in and reeled in shock. I had found the answer to our dilemma. I was also bewildered and unsettled.

On the floor, in front of the commode, lay pieces of what used to be the toilet seat and cover. Both parts were completely separated from the toilet bowl. It seemed as though someone…or something ripped off the toilet seat and cover and, in one sweeping motion, raised them high in the air and then smashed them against the floor. I had never before seen anything like it.

There were no tools or heavy objects nearby with which anyone could have possibly dislodged the toilet seat and cover. For someone to tear or yank the toilet seat and cover from the commode with his or her bare hands, such an individual had to have the strength of a superhuman. For the sturdy material of which the parts were made to be broken the way they were, the force with which they were sent to the floor had to be unbelievably powerful. Probably the most startling fact was that no one was around. Two accountants were in the kitchen and were too terrified to leave. All of the doors allowing entry into the house were locked.

Someone or something was angry we were in the house that night!

Not without some measure of trepidation, I ventured into the washroom and looked around nervously. It was empty, and a strange silence enveloped the immediate vicinity. I was unable to determine what had transpired. I managed to pull myself together, surveyed the area where the scattered pieces of the toilet seat and cover lay, and purposed to be as practical as possible, in as much as logic and practicality seemed inept considerations at the time.

I proceeded to pick up the pieces of material from off the floor and put them in a corner. I shook my head in disgust and muttered a question under my breath as to who would do such a foolish thing. Somehow, I was no longer afraid.

The other accountants, including my roommate, were understandably spooked after I informed them about the peculiar nature of my discovery in the washroom. Everyone thereafter hurriedly retired to his or her room.

I went back into my room, took out a copy of the "New Testament" I normally carried with me when I traveled, and read a few Psalms of protection and guidance. A wave of calmness and assurance overtook me and I slept well during the rest of the night.

Needless to say, the rest of our stay at the house was without incident. [5]

RESPONDING TO SATAN

Satan will tempt the prospective Christian into committing wrongs, and he will utilize even more devious ways than usual to do so. This is because the evil one realizes his chances to lead the believer away from God will gradually disappear. God's Holy Word assures Christians he is ever at their side to lead and protect them, i.e., "You have never been tempted to sin in any different way than other people. God is faithful. He will not allow you to be tempted more than you can take. But when you are tempted, He will make a way for you to keep from falling into sin." (1 Corinthians 10:13, NLV).

God desires a relationship with every one of his children and wants everyone to share in his love. He did not create people to live in darkness and confusion but to know and experience the truth. Jesus says in the Gospel of John, "I am the Light of the world. Anyone who follows Me will not walk in darkness, but will have the Light of Life." (John 8:13, NLV).

At creation, God gave mankind authority over the earth (Genesis 1:28). When Adam and Eve willingly disobeyed God, they gave up some of their authority and subjugated themselves to the devil. Yet, at the cross, Jesus stripped Satan of his authority, as the following scriptures declare.

"Now is the time for judgment on this world; now the prince of this world will be driven out" (John 12:31, NIV).

"The reason the Son of God appeared was to destroy the devil's work." (1 John 3:8, NIV).

Satan has no authority over those who are in Christ except when they give it to him by believing his lies. The Christian need not be apprehensive or fearful, and in times of adversity of any kind, he or she should cling to the assurance of God's providence and protection. The psalmist beautifully reminds us of this provision when he faithfully proclaims, "The Lord is my light and my Salvation, whom shall I fear? The Lord is the stronghold of my life, of whom shall I be afraid?" (Psalm 27:1 NIV).

The Holy Bible plainly says Satan does exist, and it reveals his sinister plan to lead people astray. However, those who give their lives to Christ need not be intimidated by Satan, as his power is infinitely inferior to God's. The key is to submit to God and resist the devil (James 4:7), knowing that Christ defeated him for good at the cross and his (Satan's) end, i.e., eternal judgment - is inevitable (Revelation 19:20).

CHAPTER FOUR

IS THERE A HEAVEN?

AN OVERVIEW OF HEAVEN

Relatively few people object to the existence of *Heaven* from a moral or ethical perspective. The idea of a rewarding afterlife appeals to most people, particularly since they believe they will go to such a place if it indeed exists. Among people who deny the possibility of heaven are those who believe in some form of reincarnation or simply in oblivion after death. The Holy Bible, however, describes a real, eternal, and conscious eternity after death for all people. Those who trust in Christ will experience this in a temporal state in the presence of God, without sickness or death. The Book of Revelation, the final book of the Holy Bible, articulates God's glorious promise to his obedient children.

Then I saw a new heaven and a new earth, for the first heaven and the first earth had passed away, and the sea was no more. And I saw the holy city, New Jerusalem, coming down out of heaven from God, prepared as a bride adorned for her husband. And I heard a loud voice from the throne saying,

> *"Behold, the dwelling place of God is with man. He will dwell with them, and they will be his people, and God himself will be with them as their God. He will wipe away every tear from their eyes, and death*

shall be no more, neither shall there be mourning, nor crying, nor pain anymore, for the former things have passed away." [1]

Part Four (*Chapters 11-14*) and Part Five (*15-21*) of this book critique the issues of heaven and hell as imparted by major non-Christian religions and other philosophies and belief systems and compare and contrast such beliefs with mainstream Biblical doctrine.

A common objection to heaven's existence stems from popular culture and has little to do with spiritual contemplation. Many people reject the idea of heaven because of its sometimes idealistic or simplistic portrayal as a realm of fluffy clouds, harps, white robes, and aimless repose. Others dislike the idea of an unceasing worship service. Neither of these views of heaven is a biblically supported concept.

The Bible affirms that heaven, defined as "the place where God dwells," does indeed exist. The apostle Paul speaks about being "caught up to the third heaven," but he was prohibited from revealing what he experienced there (2 Corinthians 12:1-9). If a third heaven exists, there must be two other heavens.

The first heaven, frequently referred to in the Old Testament, is the "sky" or the "firmament." It refers to the earth's atmosphere or the immediate sky. It is where birds navigate, and clouds drift. Biblical references to the first heaven appear in (Deuteronomy 11:17; 28:12; Judges 5:4; Acts 14:17). [2]

The second heaven is interstellar or outer space, which is the abode of the stars, planets, and other celestial bodies (Genesis 1:14-18).

The Scriptures refer further to the second heaven in (Deuteronomy 17:3; Psalms 19:4, 6; Jeremiah 8:2; Isaiah 13:10). [3]

The third heaven, the actual location of which is unknown, is the dwelling place of God. Jesus promised to prepare a place for true Christians in heaven (John 14:2). The third heaven is also referred to as the heaven of heavens and houses the Throne of God. Additional Scriptural references to the third heaven appear in (1 Kings 8:27, 30; Psalms 2:4; Matthew 5:16; Deuteronomy 10:14; 2 Chronicles 2:6; 2 Corinthians 12:2, 4). [4]

Heaven is also the destination of Old Testament saints who died trusting in God's promise of the Redeemer (Ephesians 4:8). Whoever believes in Christ shall never perish but have eternal life (John 3:16).

The Bible says after the return of Christ, believers will live with God in a New Jerusalem on a reformed Earth. The "heaven" promised to Christians is a restored Garden of Eden. The apostle John had the privilege of seeing and reporting on the heavenly city (Revelation 21:10-27). The Apostle John testified that heaven (the new earth) possesses the "glory of God" (Revelation 21:11), i.e., the very presence of God. Heaven has no night since the Lord Himself is the light. The sun and moon are no longer necessary (Revelation 22:5).

God's city glistens with the brilliance of costly stones and crystal-clear jasper. Heaven has twelve gates (Revelation 21:12) and twelve foundations (Revelation 21:14). The river of the water of life flows freely through the Garden of Eden, and the tree of life is available once again, yielding fruit monthly, with leaves that "heal the nations" (Revelation 22:1-2).

Notwithstanding John's eloquence in describing heaven, the magnitude of heaven's splendor is beyond the ability of finite human beings to comprehend (1 Corinthians 2:9).

In heaven, there will be no more tears, no more pain, and no more sorrow (Revelation 21:4). There will be no more separation because death will have been conquered (Revelation 20:6). The most wonderful aspect about heaven will be the presence of the Lord and Savior Jesus Christ (1 John 3:2). God's children will revel in the presence of the Lamb of God whose love for humankind is so great he sacrificed himself so everyone who accepts his offer of salvation can enjoy his presence in paradise forever.

Jesus Christ Is The Only Way To Heaven

The Christian faith's most unequivocal exhortation revolves around one's accepting Jesus Christ as his or her Savior, the latter who, through his atoning sacrifice on the cross, provides the only means of salvation from one's sins and a place in God's kingdom. The Bible specifically says there is only one God, one faith, and one way to God the Father – and that way is through his Son, Jesus Christ, and his sacrificial death on the cross.

The Bible makes numerous pronouncements about Christ's role as the Redeemer of lost humankind, a few of which appear below.

Jesus answered, "I am the way and the truth and the life. No one comes to the Father except through me. (John 14:6, NIV).

For God so loved the world that he gave his one and only Son, that whoever believes in him shall not perish but have eternal life. For God did not send his Son into the world to condemn the world but to save the world through him. Whoever believes in him is not condemned, but whoever does not believe stands condemned already because they have not believed in the name of God's one and only Son. (John 3:16-18, NIV).

The Father loves the Son and has placed everything in his hands. Whoever believes in the Son has eternal life, but whoever rejects the Son will not see life, for God's wrath remains on them. John 3:35-36, NIV).

For the wages of sin is death, but the gift of God is eternal life in Christ Jesus our Lord. (Romans 6:23, NIV).

Salvation is found in no one else, for there is no other name under heaven given to mankind by which we must be saved. (Acts 4:12, NIV).

Satan and his demonic servants, as mentioned elsewhere in this book, are specialists at deceiving people, and they employ various means to achieve their objectives. Some of the devil's more devious schemes, and there are many, include propagating the following lies as he deems them expedient.

- People will go to heaven if they are good enough. It is not necessary to accept Jesus Christ as Savior.

- Jesus Christ was simply a wise man who lived a long time ago.

- People can earn their way to heaven, i.e., via works, and do not need the dispensation of God's grace through Christ's atoning sacrifice on the Cross.

- All religions and belief systems are basically the same, and they all lead to one God.

- Since the devil is not real, God is not real either.

- There is no accountability to God because he does not exist.

- God will judge no one because he loves everyone.

- Essentially, no form of behavior should be condemned since sin is relative.

- The devil does not exist.

- There is no hell.

God's Holy Spirit, which indwells the hearts of Christian believers, is only too willing to guide and protect them against the wiles and perniciousness of Satan and his demons. Chapter Three – *The Devil, or Satan: Is He Real?* and Chapter Five – *Is There a Hell? look* into more detail about Satan and his agenda of evil and misdirection.

Testimonies About Heaven's Existence

The following six testimonies by people who experienced the reality of heaven and returned to share their amazing stories with the world at large provide undeniable proof of a paradisial location in which those who love and serve God will live for eternity. Very many other testimonies are available in a variety of media, including on the worldwide Internet, but the lack of space in this book delimits their inclusion.

Ian McCormack

Sourced in the main from Christian Broadcasting Network (CBN) [5]

In 1982, the actor Ian McCormack was an adventurous 26-year-old. He was diving for lobsters off the island of Mauritius (in the southwest Indian Ocean) one evening when five box jellyfish, one of the most venomous creatures in the world, stung him. The box jellyfish's poison can kill an individual in four minutes. By the time an ambulance arrived, Ian's body was completely paralyzed, and necrosis had started to set into his bone marrow.

On the way to the hospital, McCormack began to see his life flash before him. He knew he was near death. He was an atheist and didn't know whether or not there was an afterlife. As he lay dying, he saw a vision of his mother, who was the only Christian in his family, praying for him. She encouraged McCormack to cry out to God from his heart, and God would hear him and forgive him. He didn't know what to pray, so he cried out that if God were real, God would help him pray. Instantly, God showed McCormack the Lord's Prayer.

A Dark & Deathly Place

The doctors at the hospital tried to save MacCormack's life by injecting anti-toxins and dextrose into his body but to no avail. Ian's body then lay lifeless for about 15 minutes. Ian prayed from his heart and gave his life to the Lord. "I didn't understand it at the time, but that was my prayer for salvation," he says. He claims an incredible peace came over his heart, and fear left him.

Ian then died. He says, "I knew my spirit had left, I had gone somewhere, and yet I didn't know I was dead." He found himself in a very dark place and did not know where he was. He reached out and found he couldn't touch anything. He tried to touch his face, but his hand would go right through it. McCormack sensed the darkness that enveloped him wasn't just a physical darkness but a spiritual darkness. He had an eerie feeling that something or someone else was present in the vicinity, and he or she was observing what was going on.

Within the darkness, Ian heard voices screaming at him, telling him to "shut up" and that he "deserved to be there," and he was in hell. Then he began wondering why he'd gone there because he'd prayed just before he died and asked God to forgive him of his sins.

A Heavenly Light

Then, a luminous beam of light radiated through the darkness and started to lift him upward. He found himself being translated into it. McCormack then entered an opening and found himself inside a long, narrow tunnel. At the far end of the tunnel, he could see the source of the light. Then he watched as a wave of the light broke off the source and moved up the tunnel towards him. This light passed through McCormack, and he could feel a wave of warmth and comfort flood his soul.

Coming out of the end of the tunnel, he found himself standing in the presence of overwhelming light and power. He wondered if this were just an energy source or if perhaps there could be someone standing in the midst of this light. Ian felt pure love flow over him. He found himself weeping uncontrollably. As he stepped closer to the light, he could feel a presence healing his broken heart. Suddenly, the light opened up, and Ian could see Jesus standing in front of him. His garments were shimmering white in color, and his hands were outstretched as if to welcome him.

The scene opened out into a brand new world - green pastures, a crystal clear stream, and rolling green hills. Ian could see the awesome light radiating throughout the entire creation – a perfect world totally untouched by man. Ian knew he belonged here and that God had created him to live here.

A Choice to Return

God asked Ian, "Now that you have seen - do you wish to step in, or do you wish to return?" Ian thought, "I don't want to return. I wish to step in. I have no one to go back to, and no one has ever loved me...I wish to step in." As Ian was about to say goodbye to his life on earth, he He had a vision of his mother standing before the tunnel. When he saw her he knew that she was the one person in his life that had shown him love and prayed for him every day. He knew it would break his mother's heart if he died because she would have no way of knowing God had heard his prayer in the ambulance and had forgiven him of his sins.

Ian decided to return, but God told him he must be prepared to see things in a new light - God's Heavenly perspective, not his temporary earthly standpoint. God also showed Ian a vision of his family and thousands and thousands of other people who would not get a chance to hear about him if Ian did not return to earth.

Ian returned to his physical body. The doctor trying to save Ian's life had a scalpel and was prodding the base of his foot. Ian started to move, which terrified the doctors, nurses, and orderlies. God healed Ian completely, and he walked out of the hospital the next day. Over the next six weeks Ian read the entire Bible and was never the same again. Ever since Ian's near-death experience, he has shared the Gospel and told people what God did for him in over 60 nations around the world.

Ian MacCormack's story about his visit to heaven and back appears in the book *A Glimpse of Eternity: One Man's Story of Life Beyond Death.* [6]

Don Piper

Sourced from *Guideposts.com* [7] (A first-person story by Don Piper)

Most people who know me know I died on January 18, 1989, went to heaven, and was prayed back to earth about ninety minutes later. However, many don't know the rest of the story—a part I didn't know myself until more than a year afterward. One powerful revelation came out when I ate at a Chinese restaurant with Dick and Anita Onarecker.

More than a year before, on a cold, rain-slicked rural road a few miles from the gates of a retreat center, a tractor-trailer truck crossed the center stripe of the two-lane highway on a bridge over Lake Livingston in the East Texas Piney Woods area (USA) and hit my vehicle head-on. I was killed instantly. The report stated, "Dead on the scene," and the medics summoned the coroner. Although the accident involved three cars, there were no serious injuries to the other people.

Because of the accident, traffic backed up in both directions. Dick and Anita were heading home from a church conference. They had stopped for take-out coffee and were about half a mile from the scene of the accident. With so many cars backed up, they left their car and walked to the scene of the accident to see if they could be of assistance. Anita gave her hot coffee to an elderly man in one of the accident vehicles. Dick sought out the emergency medical technicians. After Dick identified himself, one EMT said, "The man in the red car is dead; several people are badly shaken up but not seriously hurt." Dick told me, "The Lord spoke to me in a clear voice: 'Pray for the man in the red car.' "

When Dick asked permission to get under the tarp placed over my red Escort, an EMT refused. "The demolished car is too gruesome," he said. Dick persisted, and the man relented. Despite the misty rain, Dick pulled back the tarp and crawled inside my Escort. He found my horribly mangled body slumped in the front seat. He prayed desperately for me, not knowing at that time for whom he was praying.

Even my intimate friends would not have recognized me. I suffered two crushed legs. One was severed, as was my left arm. The steering wheel impaled my chest. In addition to obvious wounds, I was bleeding from the ears and eyes. My best recollection of what I heard was that Dick took hold of my only intact limb, my right hand, and prayed fervently and urgently. He prayed that I would live and be delivered from internal injuries. He paused a few times and sang hymns.

At one point, he began singing, "What a Friend We Have in Jesus." I started to sing with Dick. At the shock of hearing my singing with him, he scurried from under the tarp and yelled, "The man is alive!" Once again, he crawled under the tarp and continued to pray— with even more intensity. We continued to sing while firefighters, now on the scene, tried to extricate me. I was unaware of the activity, so I can only report what Dick and others told me.

In my next moment of consciousness I was in the darkness, singing hymns along with a voice I didn't recognize. The powerful hand that gripped mine infused me with strength, encouragement, and the will to survive. For the next year, after my ordeal, I was in a hospital bed most of the time and underwent sixteen surgeries (more would follow). Excruciating pain filled my body constantly. I slowly recovered through God's grace.

Sometime later, even though I wore heavy leg braces and was still in agony, I was alive and able to stand at the pulpit of the man who had prayed me back to life. I told Dick's congregation about their pastor's fervent prayers, our hymn singing in the wrecked car, and his strong hand that supported me and infused me with the courage to hold on. Many people cried that day—and tears came to my own eyes as I relived that experience.

While we ate lunch at the Chinese restaurant after the worship service, Anita smiled and leaned toward me. "I need to correct something you said in the pulpit this morning." I returned her smile, but I thought that's exactly what every preacher doesn't want to hear - he or she made a mistake during a sermon.

Anita continued, "I enjoyed hearing your testimony this morning. I know it wasn't easy for you." I said, "No, it wasn't." "There's just one thing. The part where you talked about Dick holding your hand and praying for you - that didn't happen." I responded and said, "I have many gaps in my memory, Anita, and some of my facts come from those who were there. But of one thing, I am absolutely positive. I vividly remember holding his hand. That's what inspired me to hold on." She peered intently at me. "You were holding a hand as Dick prayed. But it wasn't Dick's hand." I don't know if I protested or stared silently. "But how," I said. Anita continued, "No one could have reached your hand while you were trapped inside your car. You were twisted so far to the right that your right hand was actually on the floor of the passenger's side. Dick reached through the back window of your car and placed his right arm between the front seats and your right shoulder— your unbroken arm." I agreed. Anita then said, "Your right hand was beyond Dick's reach."

I stared at her uncomprehendingly. "But I remember the hand—it was so powerful. I know a hand grasped mine. I drew enormous strength and help from that hand. It gave me the power to hang on." "There was a hand, all right." Anita interrupted, then added, "But it wasn't Dick's."

"If it wasn't Dick's hand, whose hand was it?" I asked. Anita responded, "I believe you know." Just then, I understood. God sent one of His ministering spirits—an angel—not only to hold my hand but also to infuse me with a will to live. There had been three of us inside that demolished car. It had been a heavenly trio.

The book *Ninety Minutes in Heaven: A True Story of Death & Life* describes Don Piper's story about his death in a car accident and his ninety-minute experience in heaven. [8]

Colton Burpo

Sourced from HeavenVisit.com and Art-Souls Works.com [9, 10]

Looking at Colton Burpo today, you would never know that he almost died as a four-year-old in 2003. His father, Todd, wrote about the near-death experience in the book *Heaven is for Real*.

"He started throwing up in the toilet," remembers Todd. "At first, we thought he had the stomach flu because the doctor said it was going around." Colton's condition only got worse as the days passed. His doctor discovered his appendix had burst, and infection was spreading in his body. Time was running out.

"We knew we were in bad shape when the nurse said, 'You need to come out to the hallway.'" recalls Todd. "They separated us from everyone else, and someone came and started talking to us. 'We need to have surgery on your son.' " Colton's mom Sonja remembers, "It was tough, seeing your boy lifeless, when he was a very vibrant child."

"It was at that moment we were looking at each other, and I remember my wife holding Colton in that hallway. It was just us, and Colton wasn't even moving," says Todd. "We went to the surgery preparation area. I remember them taking him away and him just yelling at me, 'Daddy, don't let them take me. Daddy, don't let them take me.'"

"Then I went back to the pre-op room, and I was finally alone," remembers Todd. "And I just broke down. I was mad at God. I was just frustrated and fed up. And I remember telling him, 'God, after all I've done for you, and now you're gonna take my kid? Is this how you treat your pastors?'" "I was calling our prayer chain," remembers Sonja. "I was calling anyone on the other line to get Colton on the prayer chain because it was bad."

"We were in the waiting room maybe an hour and a half total," says Todd. "And then I remember the nurse coming out, 'Is Colton's daddy out here?' I said, 'Yes.' And the nurse said, 'Well, Colton is in recovery, and he is screaming for you.'"

"And I'm sitting there with him," says Todd. "And I remember my son in that room looking up at me, and he says, 'Dad, do you know I almost died?' And my first thought was that maybe he overheard the nurse say so. Or maybe they thought he was under anesthesia, and he wasn't. It wasn't until four months after we got out of the hospital that we finally listened to our son."

"And that's where I got to see heaven," said Colton. "Jesus and some angels came and flew me up to heaven."

Todd asked Colton, "What did Jesus look like?

Colton remembered, "I knew that the first person I saw was Jesus. He was wearing white robes with a purple sash, and He just came down nicely and gracefully."

Colton continued to talk about Jesus having "markers," so eventually, Todd had to ask what he meant by "markers?"

"He drops his toys down, stands up, and just points," says Todd. "'Dad, they are right here.' And he takes his fingers and points to the palms then he bends down and touches the tops of his feet, and looks up at me. 'That's where Jesus's markers were, Dad.'"

"I was in the throne room of God to start with," says Colton. "So I got to see what that looked like. I was upset because I didn't know what was happening. What God did was He used people or things that I liked to calm me down. From then on, I felt better."

"One day, we were traveling," remembers Todd. "And Colton looked up at me and said, 'Dad, you used to have a grandpa named "Pops," didn't you? And I said, 'yeah.' Colton said, 'He's really nice.' So I said, 'Really?' 'Yeah, you used to play with him as a kid and fix… work with him on the farm and shoot stuff with him.' And I said, 'Well, yes, how do you know that?' 'Well, he told me.'"

Colton told his parents the angels sang to him so he would not be afraid. He told them he sat on Jesus' lap, surrounded by winged angels. Colton could describe everyone he saw in Heaven and shared details about Jesus, the Archangel Michael with his special sword, Mary, John the Baptist, and even his unborn sister, who had died in his mommy's tummy.

Colton's revelations about his experience did not end there. Colton was able to describe Jesus in both detailed character and appearance. Colton said Jesus then sent him back to earth to answer Todd's prayers.

As Colton shared more and more of his experiences with his parents, they didn't know what to think. Of course, they wanted to believe their son, but they could not understand his experience. Colton had been very sick, but he hadn't actually died on the operating table, like others who died and then claimed to return to life.

Skeptics have tried to explain away Colton's experience based on his knowledge of Bible stories. Colton's parents were skeptical too - then Colton unexpectedly began to share even more astonishing revelations that further confirmed his heavenly visitation was true.

Meeting His Older Sister in Heaven

Colton asked his parents why they were sitting in separate rooms during his surgery. He said he saw them from Heaven. His parents knew there was no way Colton could know this. The boy also explained that he met his great-grandfather, a man who died three decades before Colton was born. Colton pointed him out to his parents in a photo – a photo Colton had never seen, one of when his great-grandfather was about 30 years old. Colton even knew his nickname, 'Pops.'

Colton, who has an older sister and a younger brother, started talking about missing his 'other' sister. While Colton had never been told he had another sister, he told his parents he met her in Heaven. Unbeknownst to Colton at the time of this revelation, his mom had miscarried a baby a few years earlier - before Colton was even born.

While Colton's vivid accounts of Heaven surprises some in the Christian community, many realize God sometimes works in mysterious ways. Although some people remain uncertain about Heavenly encounters, Colton's childish innocence, his unwavering conviction, and remarkable accounts of heaven and God's love lend much credibility to his story. So much so that a few years after Colton shared his experiences with his family, his father, Todd decided to write a book. It took some time, but once written, the *Heaven is For Real* book immediately became a best seller. Soon, the book was adapted into a movie. The film became an instant success. Knowing the truth about heaven changes everything for believers and seekers alike.

Today, Colton, a healthy twenty-four-year-old, shares the story about his heavenly journey with boldness. He says, "I learned that heaven is for real, and you're going to like it."

Colton Burpo's experience in heaven is the subject of the book *Heaven Is For Real* and the motion picture of the same name. [11]

Mahesh Chavda

Mahesh Chavda's search for truth began with the Hindu faith. This is not surprising since he was born (in 1946) to devout Hindus. His father and mother, Keshavlal and Laxmiben Chavda, were members of the princely Rajput caste. His father was a well-known and loved figure in Mombasa, Kenya, where he was a civil servant in the British colonial government. After his father died, when Mahesh was only five, his mother continued training him for a life of Hindu devotion.

The young Hindu, however, became disillusioned with his religion as he grew older. One day, when he was about sixteen, his seven-year-old niece introduced him to a missionary named Sid Pierce. Pierce discussed the Christian faith with Mahesh. She handed him a book and told him, "If you are seeking truth, you will find it in this book."

Mahesh started to read the Bible the missionary gave him and soon became enthralled by the New Testament stories of Jesus Christ. The Galilean's life seemed so different from the lives of the priests of the Hindu religion. The Gospel of John was especially captivating as he read about the many times Jesus claimed to be God and identified himself with the truth. Mahesh felt drawn to Jesus and thought seriously about accepting him as his Savior. However, he was indecisive about embracing Christ. He revisited everything that had taken place in his life – his proud Rajput ancestry, the years spent studying the Hindu scriptures and living by its tenets. It was difficult to abandon the many aspects of an existence enveloped in Hinduism.

Mahesh continued to struggle with indecision and uncertainty. His fascination with Jesus, however, never left him but only grew. As he was reading his Bible late one night at his desk, he closed the book and said to himself, "Enough is enough. I am never going to think about Jesus Christ again. I am never going to read this book again. My mind is made up."

Chavda recalls he immediately found himself in a strange and wonderful place. His body was still there at the desk, but in spirit, he was somewhere different, somewhere wonderful, somewhere he had never been before. He thought, very simply and clearly, "I am in heaven!" Mahesh claims he saw streets of transparent gold, grass as thick as a blanket, colors more vivid than any he had ever seen and heard music that he experienced more than felt.

Mahesh says, "I felt I was home. This was where I wanted to be, where I was supposed to be. This was why I had been created." He then became aware of a brilliant white light coming toward him. Within that light was a man. He sensed immediately this was Jesus – even though he had never seen any pictures of him. Jesus, even though he looked like an ordinary man and

89

walked like an ordinary man, was so resplendent Mahesh could hardly bear to look at him.

Chavda remembers, "As he came closer to me, I could see that he was smiling. It was the same kind of smile you see on the face of a mother or father when he or she picks up their little baby, a smile of utter love and delight. I stood there gazing into his eyes. He stretched out his hand and, placed it on my shoulder and said to me simply, 'My little brother.' "

Suddenly, in the same way it began, the experience ended. Mahesh was once again in his house with his head resting on his Bible – but he noticed something strange. At the outset of his remarkable experience, after his head fell forward onto the desk, his Bible was closed. He had just made a decision never to open it again. However, after he found himself back in his room, the Bible was open. Chavda reports, "I looked down and saw that it was opened to chapter eighteen of Luke's Gospel, the story of the rich young ruler…I knew how the story ended. The young man had turned away from Jesus with inexpressible sadness in his heart because he could not bring himself to pay the price of becoming Jesus' disciple." An inner voice then asked him, "Are you going to turn away from me the same way he did?" He replied, "No sir!"

Chavda recalls, "Then I did something that to my knowledge, no ancestor of mine had ever done or no one in all the eight hundred years of our family history could even have imagined doing. I got down on my knees and said, 'Jesus, I'm sorry. Please forgive me for all the wrong things I've done. I want you. I want to give my life to you. Please come and live in my heart.' "

Mahesh Chavda honored his commitment to follow Jesus. Today, he and his wife Bonnie pastor the All Nations Church in Charlotte, North Carolina, USA. As a result of their international ministry, over 750,000 people have come to Jesus.

Mahesh Chadva and his wife Bonnie are the authors of several inspirational books, including Mahesh's popular *The Hidden Power of Healing Prayer.* [12]

Curtis "Earthquake" Kelley

Sourced from Christian Broadcasting Corporation (CBN).com [13]

Bishop Curtis "Earthquake" Kelley was born in Stamford, Connecticut, USA. He is the seventh of eleven children born to Robert and Erma Jean Kelley. Curtis' father was violently abusive, an alcoholic, and dabbled in voodoo and obeah (a form of witchcraft). His mother is a devout Pentecostal Christian.

Curtis' father abused him when he was a child. His older brothers were drug dealers, so drugs were always accessible to him, even at the age of four. When he was five, Curtis witnessed his voodoo-practicing grandmother cast a spell on a man, and he fell over. He wanted to have the same power.

Curtis repeated the words he heard his grandmother say and immediately felt a dark presence envelop him. He started practicing voodoo. Curtis' father and a voodoo witch planned to take him to Haiti, where he would learn voodoo. The then-serving Haitian president, Francois "Papa

Doc" Duvalier, was an active occultist. Curtis wanted to go because he expected to gain money, power, and control.

As Curtis's dad and the voodoo witch were sneaking him out of the apartment one morning, Curtis' mother intercepted them. The women each grabbed one of Curtis' arms and started tugging at him. Somehow, Curtis' mother lost her grasp on him, and he, his father, and the witch started to run for the back door. However, before they made it to the doorway, Curtis' father and the witch ran away. Curtis believes they saw something that frightened them, probably an angel who interceded as a result of his mother's prayers.

To Hell and Back

Curtis' mother would constantly pray for the salvation of her family and planned a getaway. One day, while his father was away, they rented a U-Haul, emptied the entire apartment, and fled to Milwaukee.

Curtis was free from his father's abuse but still in bondage to drugs. In 1971, at age fifteen, he overdosed on large quantities of cocaine, pills, and marijuana. His brothers then took him to a bar, where he says sixty hooded creatures attacked him.

Curtis exclaimed to his brothers, "Take me home!" He wanted to go home because he knew his mother could pray away the things that were tormenting him. Curtis saw the ground open up around him as countless spirits announced, "We've come to take you away." His brothers took him to a car to go home. On the way home, Curtis died.

Curtis felt the spirits grab him by the mouth, yank him out of his body, and pull him down into a dark, reddish pit. He heard screams. There were snakes, demons, and every foul thing imaginable. It had a terrible smell. It was very lonely and isolated.

Curtis was swarmed by thousands of spirits. Then, the whole place was illuminated with a Great Light. Curtis saw two hands come down, grab him by his shoulders, and pull him up out of the pit. The evil spirits were still trying to hold on to him and were saying, "No! He belongs to us!" The hands gently pulled him out and put him back into his body. Then he heard a voice say, "Because of your mother's prayers and because you were chosen to work for us, you were saved."

Curtis believes the voice was God's voice. He came back. He couldn't see or walk, and as his brothers dragged him to the stairs, he blacked out. Curtis woke up in a mental hospital. He had lost his memory, along with certain body functions. His sister, who had become a Christian, constantly invited him to participate in revival services at church. One evening, the pastor singled Curtis out and asked him to come forward.

As Curtis walked to the front on his own, he heard a voice say, "I love you." "It was like a tank fell off my shoulders," he says. He saw a vision of himself helping people instead of dragging them down into the evil world of drugs and the occult. At that point, he accepted Jesus Christ and the Holy Spirit into his life.

Now Curtis ministers worldwide - China, London, Pakistan, Haiti, and resides with his wife, Selena Kelley, in Little Rock, near Mojave, California, in the USA. He also distributes food and clothing to people within the community, develops relationships with at-risk young people, and offers his message of hope to troubled youth.

Bound to Lose, Destined to Win is Curtis Kelley's autobiography that tells of his visits to heaven and hell. [14]

Alec Rex

Sourced from *Christ is Coming, Prepare to Meet the Lord* (Testimonies of Heaven and Hell, End Times, Jesus Christ) [15]

Alec Rex was driving down a busy street in Adelaide, Australia, on February 15, 2016, when he suffered a massive heart attack. He slumped forward on the steering wheel. Traffic stopped around him, and a woman came rushing over to his car.

The young woman started to perform CPR on Alec, but she felt certain he was dead. Providentially, an ambulance was among the vehicles caught in the traffic jam. Alec recalls, "A couple doctors raced over and started working on me. In the police report, it says they resuscitated me five times. That means I died five times. They put me in the ambulance and took me to the hospital. I was dead."

Alec then shocked the doctors. He says, "They didn't know what to do with me. I was thrashing about, punching them. I came back to life. They were stunned. According to the MRI, my heart was badly damaged because of a blockage in one of the main arteries. They put a stent inside. They said to my wife there was a possibility I would have a 10 percent chance of living. If I survived, I would be a vegetable."

Doctors also discovered pneumonia in Alec's lungs, so they placed him in an induced coma following his surgery. There seemed to be no hope for Alec. God, however, was about to demonstrate his power in a way that would surprise the doctors and everyone else.

While Alec was hovering between life and death, he was transported to a nether region beyond this world. He recounts, "In front of me was like a veil, the gates of Hell. I was at the gates of hell, but not in hell."

He heard a voice say, "Jesus, I know, but you I don't." Then another voice said: I am the Lord God. I am going to heal you and make you new." Alec realized the second voice belonged to Jesus, and the Lord could read his thoughts.

Jesus' presence provided the light for Alec to see. Others there couldn't see the Lord or hear him. Jesus assured Alec he would heal him and show him the power of the Holy Spirit. Alec then observed an astonishing scene. "Around me was a sea full of people," he recounts. "I couldn't see their faces. They were joined together in chains." The Lord told him they were people who called themselves Christians, but they couldn't forgive their brothers and sisters.

During his near-death experience at the gates of hell, Alec says Jesus also told him a worldwide revival was coming. There will not be anything like it.

Alec was in a coma for three weeks. During that time, doctors and family debated about whether to turn off his life support. Then, God breathed new life into his body. "They were going to switch off the machine," he recounts. "God brought me back to life. It is a medical fact I was dead for 20 minutes in the hospital. My brain is now 100%. Praise God! Everything changed. I am one miracle after another."

After Alec came out of the coma, the head ICU nurse told his wife, Beth, "Your husband's vital signs are 100%." The next morning, Dr. Matthew Worthley, a cardiologist and professor at the Royal Adelaide Hospital, came into his room, looked at his file, and said, "You were dead, but you're alive. You're a miracle." A vascular heart surgeon, Dr. Raja, shook his head in amazement and said, "I was there when you came back to life. I was there when they took the MRI of your heart. It was so badly damaged. I can't understand it. There is no sign of a heart attack, no sign of any scarring. Your heart is 100%."

As Alex left the hospital, he got a standing ovation from the nurses. He remembers, "I thanked all the nurses and doctors. There were doctors there with tears."

While Alec is grateful to be alive, he is even more ecstatic about what God is doing. "I believe the bridegroom is coming soon — two years, five years, 10 years — I don't know when, but it's exciting."

Heaven exists, as does hell. One's soul just does not cease to exist after death. An individual will either go to heaven to live forever with Almighty God and His Redeemer Son Jesus Christ, or experience indescribable, everlasting torment in hell, the latter which is the subject of the next chapter.

CHAPTER FIVE

IS THERE A HELL?

AN OVERVIEW OF HELL

The devil, or Satan, labors to persuade people he does not exist. It's one of his chiefest ploys. It follows if Satan does not exist, hell or a place of eternal damnation may not exist either. Maybe God Himself does not exist. So, does hell exist?

Trendy but inaccurate assumptions about hell lend to misconceptions in the minds of a great many people. Frequently imagined as a burning wasteland, a dungeon full of cauldrons, or a netherworld filled with ghosts and goblins, hell increasingly conjures up visualizations that border on the nonsensical instead of the earnestly profound. Other popular depictions of hell often involve a flaming torture chamber or a location where evil creatures reside—and where heroes and heroines enter to battle evil. Such versions of hell are figments of the imagination.

The Holy Bible speaks of the reality of hell in the same terms as it does about the reality of heaven (Revelation 20:14–15; 21:1–2). In fact, Jesus spent more time warning people about the dangers of hell than he did in comforting them with the hope of heaven. The concept of a real, conscious, unending existence in hell is just as biblical as the premise of a real, everlasting presence in heaven. It is impossible to separate the two doctrines.

Notwithstanding the Bible's unambiguous teaching about the existence of both heaven and hell, it is not unusual for people to acknowledge the certainty of heaven while rejecting the likelihood of hell. It seems much simpler to entertain the idea of a pleasant afterlife than it is to ponder the implications of an existence rife with terror and anguish. Such a strategy is not dissimilar to the one undertaken by some people when it comes to dangerous kinds of behavior like illegal drug use and substance abuse. The assumption they will get what they want in spite of the possibility things might go wrong does not deter them from choosing unwisely or recklessly. Christian preachers do a great disservice to the Christian Gospel by refusing to contemplate fundamental subjects like hell and eternal damnation, which they conveniently omit from their teachings and sermons so as not to unsettle their audiences.

All have sinned against God (Romans 3:23). The just punishment for that sin is death (Romans 6:23) since sin is ultimately against God (Psalm 51:4). Since God is infinite and eternal, the punishment for sin if it remains unpardoned through the refusal to accept Jesus Christ as Savior and Redeemer, must also be infinite and eternal. Hell is this infinite and eternal sentence people will inherit because of unforgiven sin.

The Scriptures repeatedly describe the punishment of those who will occupy hell. The picture painted is terrifying, to say the least. Hell consists of "eternal fire" (Matthew 25:4, NIV) and "unquenchable fire" (Matthew 3:12, NIV), a place of "shame and everlasting contempt" (Daniel 12::2, NIV), a location where "the fire is not quenched" (Mark 9:48, NIV), a place of "torment" and "fire" (Luke 16:23,24, NIV), and "everlasting destruction"

(2 Thessalonians1:9, NIV), a place where "the smoke of their torment will rise forever and ever" (Revelation 14:10, NIV), and a "lake of burning sulfur" where the wicked are "tormented day and night forever and ever." (Revelation 20:10, NIV).

The suffering of the wicked in hell will be as never-ending as the bliss of the righteous in heaven. Jesus himself indicates punishment in hell will be just as everlasting as life in heaven (Matthew 25:46). The wicked will forever be subject to the fury and the wrath of God. Those in hell will acknowledge the perfect justice of God (Psalm 76:10). Those who go to hell will know their condemnation is just and they alone are to blame (Deuteronomy 32:3-5). The Bible makes it clear hell is to be avoided at all costs (Matthew 5:29–30).

Jesus Christ The Only Way To Avoid Hell

In Chapter Four – *Is There a Heaven?*, the author cites biblical protocol that requires an individual to embrace Jesus Christ in order to gain entry into heaven or paradise. This subsection adds a further dimension to Christ's involvement in the lives of people and asserts, in addition to providing the only means through which one may enter heaven, he represents the only means whereby one may avoid hell, because there is no neutral ground.

In essence, when one accepts Jesus Christ as his or her Savior, he or she secures eternal salvation and simultaneously evades eternal damnation. It's a two-fold blessing – unlike any other! By the same token, when one rejects Jesus' offer of salvation, he or she remains unsaved and consequently endangers his or her soul for eternity. It's a two-fold curse – unlike any other! One cannot become a child of God without faith in Jesus. The

99

Scriptures say, "Yet to all who did receive him, to those who believed in his name, he gave the right to become children of God." (John 1:12, NIV) and "For you are all sons of God through faith in Christ Jesus." (Galatians 3:26, NASB).

Salvation through Jesus Christ is a gift from God according to the selfless dispensation of his grace. Nobody earns a gift. A gift is made available freely by the giver. God's Holy Word says, "For it is by grace you have been saved, through faith—and this is not from yourselves, it is the gift of God - not by works, so that no one can boast." (Ephesians 2:8-9 NIV) God's unmatchable promise of love and compassion for humankind reverberates in the following phenomenal biblical pronouncement, which reads:

> *For God so loved the world that he gave his one and only Son, that whoever believes in him shall not perish but have eternal life.* (John 3:16, NIV)

Testimonies About The Existence Of Hell

The testimonies of six individuals who visited or experienced heaven appeared in the previous chapter. A few of those narratives contained references to hell. The focus of the following six testimonies lends toward expanding on the subject of hell.

Of course, there will be those who, for one reason or another, would dispute the veracity of the stories about heaven and hell presented in the preceding chapter and this one. The inclination to doubt or query the stories may stem from (a) an affiliation with alternative or non-Christian religions,

(b) an atheistic or agnostic disposition, (c) ostensible scientific disputation, (d) irrationality from a nonspiritual perspective, and (e) misconstrued symbolism.

Some professed Christians even, especially those who traverse a path that jettisons supernatural concomitance with religious doctrine, may be reluctant to accord the stories a significant measure of plausibility. Yet other Christians may disagree with "revelations" about heaven and hell that may contradict preconceived notions of such locations.

While some of the details might perturb and/or startle some readers, there is no intention to aggrandize the stories. The goal is to communicate, in as truthful a manner as possible, the remarkable experiences of six people - there exist very many others - who feel deeply obligated to testify to others about the existence of heaven and/or hell.

Mickey Robinson

Sourced from HeavenVisit.net [1] Beautiful Heaven & Horrible Hell (A first-person story)

Flying conditions on the night of the parachute jump were poor due to a combination of intense heat and high humidity. However, I was a professional skydiver and had demonstrated my skill before crowds of thousands. I was obsessed with the sport. I had jumped with some of the world's best skydivers. I was 100% committed to skydiving, and I felt in complete control of my life.

That night, with a full load of six, the plane cleared the runway, going well over 100 miles per hour. Suddenly, without any warning, the engines totally failed. The pilot turned to me and said, "We're going down!" The plane plunged towards the earth and impacted where the wing joined the fuselage. It then spun, cart-wheeled, and slammed into the ground. I was flung forward and hit my face against the hard interior wall. Injured and in shock, three skydivers escaped the wreckage and ran. A fourth also exited. He saw the pilot and me moving around and assumed we would also get out. As he left, the plane burst into flames. The fuel tank had ruptured, and gasoline had splashed everywhere. Terrified, the man bolted, screaming, and suddenly realized that we were still inside the plane. Running back into the flaming wreckage, he saw that I was aflame from head to toe, trying to free my leg, which was trapped in a hole where the wing had been torn apart. He yelled for the pilot to unbuckle himself and attempted to pull me loose. Alas, I was stuck!

I became desperate! I was in flames, trapped in the wreckage, and unable to wrench myself free! My rescuer's second attempt succeeded, as with what seemed to be super human strength, he pulled me loose from the parachute harness. Dragging me from the plane, he threw me on the ground and rolled me around to put the fire out. It took several attempts as the fire kept re-igniting. He finally doused the flames and turned to help the pilot, but it was too late. The poor man had been burnt to death.

I lay on the ground, severely injured. The skin on my arm and hand was falling off. There was also a serious cut on my face. I asked how badly I was burned and was told it was hard to say because of the smoke. Actually, they were convinced I would never make it off the field alive. When the medics cut off what remained of my clothing, they saw that I had sustained very serious third-degree burns over a third of my body. The prognosis was not good at all.

In the days and weeks that followed, I became deathly ill. My entire body became infected, and I lost much weight. I suffered from internal bleeding and was in tremendous pain. I also had a head injury and a contusion on my brain. My body was fighting as hard as it could against death, but it was a losing battle. I was blind in my right eye. As time went on, my body became rigid, and the nerves in both my legs died. My muscles became flaccid, and my feet curled up like withered claws over the end of the bed. Even with help from outside medical experts, the expectation was I was going to die.

During my stay at the hospital, I had a life-changing experience. I suddenly left my physical body and was no longer in the hospital room - I had entered a kind of spiritual realm. Immediately, I became aware of two things i.e., the spiritual world was real, and there was no perception of time as I knew it. It was awesome! I found myself traveling or going somewhere and had no control over what was happening.

I saw what appeared to be a closing doorway. A great, sweeping darkness began to surround me as if trying to envelop me. Coming through the still open space in the doorway was a beam of the purest, whitest light I had ever seen. The doorway began closing faster and faster. The implication of what was taking place then dawned on me. If the door closed completely, I would be cut off from this light for all eternity.

I felt a sense of deep hopelessness and horror. I want people to know there is such a thing as eternal separation. I was permitted not only to see but to experience what it would be like to be in a state of eternal separation from God. Eternal separation is torment beyond belief. I began to cry out to God, and a repentance process began. I cried out. "God. I'm sorry! Please give me another chance!" I stood at the very edge of eternity with this door closing and the darkness beginning to encase me. I knew that in an instant, I could be separated for eternity from the source of all Life!

The grace and mercy of God are beyond man's comprehension!

I was instantaneously caught up in Heaven. What a contrast! Eternal hopelessness compared to eternal love and comfort. I knew now I would never die. I had a deep awareness of eternal life - and the blessed assurance I would always be comforted and cared for. The Bible says, "...in your presence there is fullness of joy; at your right hand are pleasures forevermore." [2] The glory and power of God were everywhere; over me, under me, around me, vibrating through me.

The Lord told me that I was coming back to earth. I traveled back to the life I had come from and settled into my physical body. I could actually feel my spirit pressing through my flesh. Suddenly, I could see again out of my physical eyes and hear out of my physical ears. As I began to return to normal consciousness, I realized that I was speaking in a beautiful language and wondered what was happening. I realized that I was alive; the temperature of 106 degrees fell, and I fell into a natural sleep for the first time since the injury. I woke up several hours later, and for the first time in my life, I knew what true peace was.

I have experienced many marvelous healings since my accident. Around five years after the accident, I regained sight in my blind eye. Also, today I can walk again. Doctors felt sure such healings were impossible, given the terrible injuries I suffered.

Even though at first I did not understand what had happened to me spiritually, I knew I was saved, born-again, and filled with the Holy Spirit. Today, I enjoy life! I play with my children, run, snow ski, and ride horses. I would not wish for anyone to go through what I did. Yet, the experience taught me the utter importance of living by God's strength. People everywhere need to make the conscious decision to stop relying on their own power and abilities and to live by the strength and guidance of God.

Mickey Robinson's story of his experience about heaven, hell, and miracles appears in the book *Falling into Heaven: A Skydiver's Gripping Account of Heaven, Healings and Miracles* by Broadstreet Publishing Group, LLC (2014). [3]

Tamara Leroux

Sourced from Evidence for Christianity & Christian Broadcasting Network, CBN.com [4]

A lot of people seem to think that all of the evidence for Christianity consists of paraphernalia from ancient sources. But that is not the case at all. The truth is God has provided for us thousands upon thousands of eyewitnesses who are alive today who have seen heaven or hell. For example, have you ever heard the amazing story of how Tamara Laroux was delivered from hell? It is an amazing near-death experience that you will never forget, and as you can see from the posted video (shown on the source website – see Chapter Five, Note 4 at the back of this book for the website's

URL), this is a woman that is very, very credible. Atheists have a really hard time explaining the very real experiences multitudes of people around the world are having. The truth is God has not left us without a witness. He has not left us without evidence. The evidence for Christianity is all around us if we are willing to just stop and look at it.

When Tamara Laroux was a young woman, she got to a point in her life where she felt like life was simply not worth living anymore. She was in an extraordinary amount of emotional pain, and one day, she finally decided she was going to commit suicide. On that fateful day, she initially pointed the gun at her head, but a voice told her to point it at her heart instead. At that moment, Tamara was given a vision of what she would look like in the future if she shot herself in the head, and it scared her. So she decided she would kill herself by shooting herself in the chest instead, which is what she did. She committed suicide by shooting herself in the chest. But it was not the end for Tamara Laroux. In fact, Tamara Laroux discovered that life after death is very, very real.

Very shortly after committing suicide, Tamara Laroux found herself in hell. It was horrifying beyond description. The burning and the pain were unbearable.

The following is how a CBN article described what Laroux saw in hell...

Tamara says she entered ultimate darkness – a darkness so black that there was absolutely no light. Her cry for forgiveness turned to a violent scream. "I realized my soul had been transformed into a being of sin and death," she says. "I became everything the Father is not." Loneliness

106

surrounded her as she looked across the fiery pit and saw hundreds of souls just like her – screaming in agony. "Each one was a formless being begging for another chance," says Tamara.

Though they were right next to each other, they were not allowed to communicate with one another. "We were together, yet we were in total isolation from one another," she says. Behind her was an indescribable creature with dragon-like heads upon his body. "He stood fiercer than anything that the earth has ever seen," she says. "I was only allowed to see a glimpse of him, and for thatI am grateful."

But fortunately, she did not stay there. Just before shooting herself, Tamara said the following words: "God, please forgive me!" Perhaps that one act is what saved her. Tamara Laroux was delivered. A great hand lifted her out of hell and brought her to a place where she was able to see heaven. What she saw there was beautiful beyond description.

The following is how Laroux describes what she saw:

I saw the hand of God literally come down. I knew that He was coming for me. He hand-picked me up, and instantaneously, I was no longer a being of tormented sin. I was now being cleansed. God took me over the Heavens.

It was beyond peaceful, gorgeous, and magnificent. However, I was not allowed to stay, and I was certainly not allowed to see anything specific. But I was able to feel His presence in its entirety, perfect serenity, and joy for the first time; complete, whole joy.

After that, she was brought back into her body and made a miraculous recovery. Now, she is sharing her story with the world. The testimony of Tamara Laroux should be a huge wake-up call for all of us.

Tamara Leroux's story about her visits to heaven and hell and returning to life is the subject of the 2018 book, *A Second Chance at Heaven – My Surprising Journey Through Hell, Heaven and Back to Life.* [5] Tamara and her husband Rodney are the founders of *Life Change International*, an organization committed to sharing the uncompromised truth of the Gospel. Together, they have shared the truth of the Gospel in over 40 countries. Their ministry reaches millions in the United States and abroad with the power of God's love.

Bill Wiese

Sourced from Christian Broadcasting Network, CBN.com [6]

In his book "23 Minutes in Hell," Bill Wiese describes his personal experience of November 22, 1998. Wiese says that he was lying in bed at 3:00 am when he was plunged into hell – not in a dream, but in actuality – not because he had died and was being punished, but because God wanted him to experience hell and warn others. Wiese believes that after 23 minutes of torment, Jesus came to rescue him from hell and returned him to earth, where he landed, shaking, on his living room floor.

Although Bill had been a Christian for 28 years, he had never thought much about hell. After his extraordinary experience, Bill spent six years searching the scriptures to find out what the Bible says about hell. He cites more than 150 scripture references to hell, all of which he discovered lined up exactly with what he experienced. Bill pleads to those who read his story and says, "Even if you don't believe my story, I hope you will believe the scriptures and avoid hell just the same."

After being catapulted out of his bed into the very pit of hell, Wiese arrived in a cell measuring approximately 15 feet by 10 feet by 15 feet. It had walls of rough stone and rigid bars on the door. As he lay on the floor, Bill felt extremely weak, and as he looked around, he realized he was not alone in the cell. Two enormous beasts, approximately 10-13 feet tall and very menacing, were also there.

Bill recognized the beasts were entirely evil and were looking at him with pure hatred. He became paralyzed with fear. He says the creatures resembled giant reptiles but took on human form. The first one had bumps and scales all over its body, a protruding jaw, gigantic teeth, and sunken eyes. This ferocious beast paced around the cell like a caged bull. The second beast had very long arms and razor-sharp fins all over its body and claws about a foot long. Bill could hear the creatures talking and although he could not identify their language, somehow he could understand their words. They were spewing forth blasphemous words expressing extreme hatred for God. They then turned their attention toward Bill, and he felt the malevolence and loathing being directed at him.

Two more creatures entered the cell, and Bill knew these four beings had been "assigned" to torment him. Suddenly, the light vanished, and it became pitch black. One of the creatures picked up Bill and somehow, he perceived the creature possessed the strength of more than a thousand men. The beast threw him against the wall, and he crumbled to the floor, feeling as if every bone in his body had been broken. The second beast grabbed Bill from behind in a bear hug and pressed its sharp fins into his back. It then reached around and plunged its claws into Bill's chest and ripped it outwards. Bill's flesh hung from his body like ribbons as he fell to the floor.

Bill pleaded for mercy, but the creatures showed him none. He says the mental anguish was indescribable. He was extremely nauseous due to the terrible, foul stench coming from the creatures. He says if one takes every rotten thing he or she can imagine – an open sewer, rotten meat, spoiled eggs, sour milk, dead rotting animal flesh, and sulfur, and magnifies them a thousand times, the smell might come close to the stink he experienced. Bill somehow dragged himself out of the cell, and with tremendous effort, he got to his feet. He was horrified as he heard the screams of untold multitudes crying out in torment. It was deafening, and the screams seemed to go right through Bill, penetrating his very being. The fear was so intense he couldn't bear it, but even worse, he couldn't die. Hell was so terrifying, so intense, and so hostile he could not exaggerate the horror. The heat was unbearable, as was the thirst.

Eventually, Bill returned, screaming, to his living room, where he explained the experience to his wife, Annette. She noticed it was 3:23 am when she woke in their bedroom to Bill's screams, which came from their living room. Although Bill and Annette had been Christians for many years, he believes God allowed him to experience hell in order to draw people's attention to His Word and point them to what the Holy Bible has to say about hell.

In Bill's book, *23 Questions about Hell: Everything You Want & Need to Know,* he answers some of the most common questions about hell and eternity. The book draws its answers from the Bible as well as Wiese's personal experience. Bill says although he had a miraculous vision of hell that he shares freely, he doesn't want people to take him at his word. He says, "Many people fail to read the Bible and thereby remain uninformed. We hope to change that by inspiring people to search God's Word for themselves."

After Bill's vision, he and Annette traveled around the USA for seven years, sharing his experience with people. In 2000, they began Soul Choice Ministries and, soon after, began traveling and spreading Christ's Gospel full-time. According to Bill, "Each year we provide books to inmates, sow ministry trips as God directs us, and we are honored to give a significant amount of our proceeds to missions and other ministries. Our desire is to see at least one billion souls come to Christ and witness a healthy, reverential fear of the Lord restored to the Church."

Bill Wiese recounts the story about his visit to hell in the book *23 Minutes in Hell: One Man's Story about What He Saw, Heard & Felt in that Place of Torment.* [7]

Athet Pyan Shinthaw Paul

Sourced from HeavenVisit.com [8]

The immediate testimony is somewhat lengthy. The author apologizes for any inconvenience occasioned by reading it.

My Early Years

My name is Athet Pyan Shinthaw Paulu. I am from the country of Myanmar. I was born in 1958 in the town of Bogale, in the Irrawaddy Delta area of southern Myanmar (formerly Burma). My parents were devout Buddhists, like most people in Myanmar. Our lives were very simple. At the age of 13, I left school and started working on a fishing boat. At the age of 16, I became the leader of the boat.

One day, when I was 17, we caught a large number of fish in our nets. The fish attracted a large crocodile, which followed our boat and tried to attack us. We were terrified, so we frantically rowed our boats toward the riverbank as fast as we could. The crocodile followed us and smashed our boat with its tail. No one died, but the attack greatly affected me. I no longer wanted to fish.

Not long after, my father's employers transferred him to Yangon City (formerly Rangoon). I entered a Buddhist monastery at age 18 to be an apprentice monk. Most parents in Myanmar try to enroll their sons in a Buddhist monastery, at least for a time. It is considered a great honor for a son to serve in this way. We have been observing this custom for many hundreds of years.

A Zealous Disciple of Buddha

I became a full-fledged monk at age 19 in 1977. The senior monk at my monastery gave me a new Buddhist name, U Nata Pannita Ashinthuriya. The senior monk's name was called U Zadila Kyar Ni Kan Sayadaw. He was the most famous Buddhist monk in all of Myanmar at the time. Everyone knew who he was. He was widely honored by the people and respected as a great teacher. He died in 1983 in a car accident. His death shocked everyone. At the time he died, I had been a monk for six years.

I tried hard to be the best monk I could and to follow all the precepts of Buddhism. Some monks move deep into the forests, where they live a life of self-denial and poverty. I sought to deny my selfish thoughts and desires, escape from sickness and suffering, and break free from the material cycles of this world. I even relocated to a cemetery once.

I studied the holy Buddhist teachings just like all my forefathers had done before me. My life continued as a monk until I got very, very sick. I was in Mandalay at the time and had to be admitted to the hospital. The doctors carried out various tests and told me I suffered from both yellow fever and malaria. My condition worsened, and after a month in the hospital, the doctors told me I would not recover. They discharged me and sent me home to die.

A Vision that Changed My Life Forever

I went back to the monastery where other monks cared for me. I grew weaker and weaker and was lapsing into unconsciousness. I learned later that I actually died for three days.

While I was dead or comatose, I had an unforgettable spiritual experience. I seemed to be caught in a very, very powerful storm. A tremendous wind flattened the whole landscape until there were no trees or anything else standing, just a flat plain. I walked very fast along this plain for some time. No one else was there. I was all alone. After a while, I crossed a river. On the other side of the river I saw a terrible, terrible lake of fire. In Buddhism, there is no concept of a place like this. I was confused at first and didn't know it was hell until I saw *Yama*, the king of hell. Yama is the name ascribed to the king of hell in numerous cultures throughout Asia. His face and his body were like a lion's, but his legs were like a naga's or serpent spirit's. He had a number of horns on his head, and his face was very fierce. I became extremely afraid. Trembling, I asked him his name. He replied, "I am the king of hell, the Destroyer."

The Terrible, Terrible Lake of Fire

The king of hell told me to look into the lake of fire. I looked, and I saw the saffron-colored robes that Buddhist monks wear in Myanmar. I looked closer and saw the shaven head of a man. When I looked at the man's face, I saw it was U Zadila Kyar Ni Kan Sayadaw, the famous monk who had died in a car accident in 1983. I asked the king of hell why my former leader was in this lake of torment. I said, "Why is he in this lake of fire? He was a very good teacher. He helped thousands of people understand that their worth as humans is far greater than the animals." The king of hell replied, "Yes, he was a good teacher, but he did not believe in Jesus Christ. That's why he is in hell."

I was told to look at another person who was in the fire. I saw a man with very long hair wrapped on the left side of his head. He was also wearing a robe. I asked the king of hell, "Who is this man?" He replied, "This is the one you worship: Gautama (Buddha)." I was very disturbed to see Gautama in hell. I protested, "Gautama had good ethics and good moral character. Why is he suffering in this lake of fire?" The king of hell answered me, "It

114

doesn't matter how good he was. He is in this place because he did not believe in the Eternal God."

I then saw another man who looked like he was wearing a soldier's uniform. He had a large wound on his chest. I asked, "Who is this man?" The king of hell said, "This is Aung San, the revolutionary leader of Myanmar. Aung San is here because he persecuted and killed Christians, but especially because he didn't believe in Jesus Christ."

I looked and saw another man in the lake of fire. He was a very tall man and he was dressed in military armor. He held a sword and a shield. The man had a wound on his forehead. He was taller than any person I had ever seen. The king of hell said, "This man's name is Goliath. He is in hell because he blasphemed the Eternal God and His servant David." I was confused because I didn't know who either Goliath or David was. The king of hell said, "Goliath is recorded in the Christian Bible. You don't know him now, but when you become a Christian, you will know who he is."

I also saw a creature whose job is to stoke the flames beneath the lake of fire to keep it hot. This being asked me, "Are you going into the lake of fire too?" I replied, "No! I am only here to observe!" The appearance of this creature stoking the fire was very terrifying. He had ten horns on his head and a spear in his hand. The spear had seven sharp blades. The creature told me, "You are right. You came here just to observe. I cannot find your name here." He said, "You must now go back the way you came." He pointed me toward the desolate plain that I had first walked along before I came to the lake of fire.

The Road of Decision

I walked a long time until I bled. It was hot, and I was in great pain. Finally, after walking for about three hours I came to a wide road. I walked along this road for some time until I came to a fork. One road, going off to the left, was wide. A smaller road went off to the right. There was a signpost at the fork saying the road to the left was for those who do not believe in the Lord Jesus Christ. The smaller road to the right was for believers in Jesus.

I was interested to see where the wider road led so I started to walk along it. There were two men about 300 yards ahead of me. I tried to catch up with them so I could walk with them, but no matter how hard I tried, I couldn't catch up with them, so I turned around and went back to the fork in the road. I watched the two men as they walked down the road away from me. When they reached the end of the road, they were suddenly attacked. The two men cried out in great pain! I also cried out when I saw what happened to them! I realized the wider road ended in great danger for those who traveled along it.

Looking into Heaven

I started walking down the believers' road instead. After traveling for about one hour, the surface of the road turned to pure gold. It was so pure that when I looked down at it, I could see my own reflection perfectly. I then saw a man standing in front of me. He was wearing a white robe. I also heard beautiful singing. Oh, it was so beautiful and pure! The man in the white robe asked me to walk with him. I asked him, "What is your name?" but he did not answer. I asked him his name six times, and eventually, the man answered, "I am the one who holds the key to heaven. Heaven is a very, very beautiful place. You cannot go there now, but if you follow Jesus Christ, you can go there after your life has finished on the earth." The man's name was Peter.

Sent Back with a New Name

Then Peter said, "Now get up and go back to where you came from. Speak to the people who worship Buddha and who worship idols. Tell them they will go to hell if they don't change. Those who build temples and idols will also have to go to hell. Those who give offerings to the monks to earn merit for themselves with go to hell. All those who pray to the monks will go to hell. Those who chant to idols will go to hell. All those who don't believe in Jesus Christ will go to hell." Peter told me to go back to the earth and testify about the things I had seen. He also said, "You must speak in your new name. From now on, you are to be called Athet Pyan Shinthaw Paulu, i.e., "Paul who came back to life."

I walked back along the gold road. I heard beautiful singing again, the kind of which I had never heard before or since. Peter walked with me until I was ready to return to the earth. He showed me a ladder that reached down from heaven to the sky. The ladder didn't reach the earth but stopped in mid-air. I saw many angels on the ladder, some going up to heaven and others going down the ladder. They were very busy. I asked Peter, "Who are they?" Peter answered, "They are messengers of God. They are reporting to heaven the names of all those who believe in Jesus Christ and the names of those who don't believe." Peter then told me it was time to go back.

117

It is a Ghost!

The next thing I became aware of was the sound of weeping. I heard my own mother cry out, "My son, why did you leave us now?" I also heard many other people weeping. I realized I was lying in a box (coffin). I started to move. My mother and father started shouting, "He is alive! He is alive!" Other people who were farther away did not believe my parents. I then placed my hands on the sides of the box and sat upright. Many people were struck with terror. They cried out, "It is a ghost!" and ran away as fast as their legs could carry them. Those who remained were speechless and trembling.

I learned later I was just moments away from being cremated in the flames. In Myanmar, people are placed in a coffin, the lid is then nailed shut, and the whole coffin is burned. When I came back to life, my mother and father were looking at my body for the very last time. Soon after, the lid of my coffin would have been nailed shut, and I would have been burnt to ashes!

I immediately started to explain the things I had seen and heard. People were astonished. I told them about the men I had seen in the Lake of Fire and told them Christianity is the one true religion. Buddhists and others have been deceived for thousands of years! The people were astonished because they knew how zealous a monk I had been.

Epilogue

Athet Pyan Shinthaw Paulu today remains a faithful witness to the Lord Jesus Christ. Burmese pastors claim he led hundreds of other monks to faith in Christ. The uncompromising nature of Athet Paulu's message offended many people who refused to accept the biblical teaching that Jesus Christ is the only way to heaven. Following his "resurrection" experience, Paulu began to proclaim the Gospel of Christ and exhorted other monks to forsake false gods and follow Jesus Christ with all their hearts.

Athet Paulu's conversion to Christianity and his zeal to spread the Christian Gospel cost him tremendously. In a bid to get his message out to as many people as possible, this modern-day Lazarus began distributing audio and video cassette tapes to tell people about his vision. The police and Buddhist authorities in Myanmar did their utmost to gather these tapes and destroy them. Anyone in Myanmar who possessed any of these tapes ran the risk of persecution and imprisonment.

Paulu's fearless testimony landed him in prison at least once, but the authorities failed in their bid to silence him. Upon his release from jail, he continued to testify of the things he saw and heard during his vision about heaven and hell. His current whereabouts are unknown.

Howard Storm

Sourced from TopTenz.com

Howard Storm, before becoming a minister of the United Church of Christ, was an ardent atheist and a Professor of Art at Northern Kentucky University, USA. Anything relating to religion repulsed him. He didn't believe in the afterlife or anything science couldn't explain. However, his perspective on life changed dramatically after he allegedly died and went to hell in 1985. Howard was in a hospital bed at the time, dying from a punctured stomach.

Howard vividly describes his brief stay in hell and how Jesus Christ rescued him. Right after he died, some "unknown beings" invited Howard to follow them. At first, the entities were friendly and warm. Howard describes them as "more like silhouettes, or shapes." He couldn't clearly identify them because they were in a fog or haze. The closer Howard got to them, the deeper they went into the haze.

The strange beings started to become aggressive towards Howard after a while. Eventually, they attacked him viciously. More specifically, according to Howard, the creatures "began to tear off pieces of my flesh." The beings beat Howard to death. An "inner voice" urged Howard to pray. Reluctantly, he uttered phrases that he thought were religious since, at the time, he didn't know how to pray. Miraculously, the strange beings stopped attacking him, and they disappeared.

The inner voice then urged Howard to ask Jesus to save him. Deep within himself, he screamed, "Jesus, please save me!" And true enough, Jesus did save him, and gave him an opportunity to turn his life around. Howard subsequently underwent a dramatic transformation. Today, he is a devoted follower of Jesus Christ.

Howard Storm's extraordinary experience, whereby he saw what hell is like, is featured in the 2005 book *My Descent into Death: A Second Chance at Life.*[9]

Aline Baxley

Sourced from Heaven, Hell, Rapture, and End Times! HeavenVisit.com [10] – *A first-person account.*

The Accident

I received the Lord in my life when I was eleven years old. I married at the age of seventeen, left the church, and headed into a world of sin. By the age of forty, I was in my second marriage, a complete alcoholic, and hooked on drugs and cigarettes. I was running from the call of God on my life. My mother knew I didn't care if I lived or died. I had made several attempts to take my life. I was so possessed by alcohol and drugs that I couldn't believe God could or would set me free again. I had turned my back on God so many times that I didn't even have the right to ask Him to forgive me again.

A week before I was involved in a terrible motor vehicle accident, I told my mother, "Mama, if there is Heaven and if there is a Hell, my Hell would be to be separated from my God I have loved so much all my life." Mama got on her knees like she always did. She prayed, "God, you heard her words. She's not afraid of death or Hell. Somehow, show her a portion of Hell and turn her back around and put the fear of you back in her heart."

The Accident That Sent Me To Hell

One week later, I fell asleep at the wheel of my car. I went over an embankment and was thrown out. I had my neck broken, four major breaks to my spine, nine broken ribs, a crushed left lung, and crushed kidneys. My mother was called to the hospital, and two doctors met her at the door and told her my only hope was God. I would have to have a miracle from God Almighty.

In the meantime, I found myself walking in the Valley of the Shadow of Death. The valley was so deep, dark, and wide that I was afraid to even move an inch. I started crying out for God to let me stay on my feet and not let me move. I was in a place of thick, gross darkness. I couldn't see my hands before me. I had always loved the 23rd Psalm. I started quoting it: "Yea, though I walk through the Valley of the Shadow of Death..." but I couldn't go on. I couldn't say, "His rod and staff would comfort me." I stood there with sin in my life – undone, to meet that Almighty God up there. The only thing alive within me was the Word, and the Word turned into Jesus Christ. He started interceding on my behalf as my high-priest unto God the Father to protect my soul in that Valley of Death.

In the right-hand corner appeared the mighty Death Angel. I started crying. "What is the Death Angel here for?" He had arrived so that on the command of the Father, he would have to separate me and my Lord. The Death Angel carried me out to that outer, outer darkness. I found myself in Hell, screaming, hollering, gnashing my teeth, begging the Death Angel not to leave me in Hell. Souls were around me by the hundreds and thousands, screaming and gnashing their teeth, just trying to die.

I saw a great gulf and all these souls trying to climb up to God the Father, but the only way through the deep gulf was through the precious Blood of Jesus Christ, the Blood I had taken so lightly. Then God showed me the Lake of Fire, where the third of the angels were in chains of darkness.

There were red-hot-piercing flames going through all of Heaven and earth. Yet they gave no light. The Lake of Fire was in total darkness. Hell was enlarging itself and the mighty, earth-quaking voice of God began to speak. He began to penetrate the atmosphere as He spoke to me. He said, "You were right not to fear the devil, though I let him kill you with the first death. You fear Me. I am the One that can destroy both your body and your soul."

God Spoke To Me In Hell.

During the days that I lay in a coma, I waited in that dark valley. It seemed an eternity, but it was just a few days in earth-time. During this time my sister was in great intercession for my life. At last, after what seemed ages, a bright light began to shine. It was so holy, so righteous, I wasn't fit to even look up to this Almighty light. I covered my eyes and fell flat on my face in that dark, deep valley. Here, for the second time, that Almighty voice of God began to speak to me. All God would say to me was Romans 11:29, "For the gifts and calling of God are without repentance." I screamed, "God forgive me!" I thought I was dying at this point, as my crushed lung began swelling and my right lung deflated, and for four minutes, I didn't breathe. They were trying to force a copious volume of oxygen into my lungs, but there was no improvement. They tested me after four minutes. There was no life at all – another minute, and they would have pronounced me dead and would have taken me off all life-sustaining machines. I didn't know what they were doing to try to save my life, but I knew I was dying. There appeared in the Heavens a beautiful scroll. A hand appeared and began rolling it out. There, in a matter of seconds, I saw my entire life before me – everything I had ever done.

There Is A Heaven, And There Is A Hell!

I truly found out there is a Heaven, I saw the lights of paradise. But there also is a Hell. I've walked into Hell. God answered my mother's prayer that He would let me experience Hell. My Hell would be separation from my God, whom I loved so much and whom I had accepted as my Savior at the age of eleven. When the soul sees it's going to be separated from its God for all eternity, it plunges into such a terrible spiritual fire as can never be kindled on earth. It is the spiritual torture of a soul that has once known God and now is cast into that outer, outer darkness, separated from God, its Creator, forever and ever.

We just begin to live when we die the first death. "It is appointed unto men once to die, but after this the judgment." (Hebrews 9:27). You have an appointment with God, and you are going to keep that appointment. The Bible describes Hell (and I found this to be true) as a place of future punishment for sinners and unbelievers. Hell is a Lake of Fire, a place of torment, a place where lost souls never die, and the fire is not quenched, a place of weeping, wailing, and gnashing of teeth, a place where sinners drink of the wine of the wrath of God, a place where the smoke of their torment ascends up forever and ever. The fire of Hell consumes the flesh, but it cannot consume the soul. I am a living witness that Hell is real.

There will be no unbelievers in Hell, but it will be too late! Every soul in Hell will give anything in this world to be me or you, back in this life, with one more chance to cry out, "God forgive me!" If we come to that dark Valley of Death with unrepented sin in our lives, there will be no second chance. God is a God of love as well as a God of wrath, and woe be unto those upon whom His wrath falls.

Where Will You Spend Eternity?

Where will you spend eternity? It will be in one of two places, Heaven or Hell, with its lake of fire and brimstone. Unless you repent of your sins and believe in the Lord Jesus Christ as your Lord and Savior, it will be Hell. God did not create Hell for you, my beloved; He created Heaven for the soul of man, and He created Hell for the devil and his angels. If we go there, it will be our fault.

Jesus made a way for you and me by the shedding of His precious Blood. You can be free from all your sins and make Heaven your eternal home forever. Accept Jesus into your life. He will heal your broken heart and set you free from drugs, alcohol, disease, and all sins. If the Lord could set me free, He can also set you free. Beloved, I am living witness: There is a Hell. I have walked there. I have been there screaming, hollering, weeping, wailing, gnashing my teeth, begging God not to command the Death Angel to leave me in Hell. Wide is the road that leads to Hell and destruction, but NARROW is the path that leads to everlasting life (Matt 7:13). Choose life with Christ, and receive Him into your heart today. Tomorrow may be too late.

In Summary

The undergirding implication in the forgoing testimonies and those in the preceding chapter regarding the existence of heaven and hell is one of paramount importance, i.e., one must embrace Jesus Christ as Lord and

Savior in order to get to heaven. Marginal or peripheral inconsistencies with perceived biblical concepts about heaven and hell should not function to engender skepticism in the minds of people who might otherwise accept the Christian message of salvation for their souls and everlasting life in a place called paradise.

Jesus Christ represents the only means through which one may avoid hell's eternal torment. Christian believers must be prepared to attest to this incontrovertible truth and persuade people who do not yet know Christ to understand their souls remain jeopardized with every passing second they neglect to allow him into their lives.

CHAPTER SIX

WHAT IS ETERNITY?

Eternity, in common parlance, refers to an infinitely long period of time. As indicated in the introduction of this book, the term commonly harbors the following connotations, (a) time without beginning or end, i.e., infinite time (b) the state or quality of being eternal (c) the timeless state following death, and (d) immortality, i.e., the afterlife. When the Greeks coined the word "eternity" (*Aeon*), the intended meaning was "the fullness of time." The term, therefore, may scholastically refer to the past, present and future all being experienced in continuity.

The forgoing definitions notwithstanding, many people consider eternity a deep mystery. Eternity is an important concept in many religions, where a god or gods are said to endure eternally. The next sub-section deals with the subject of God and eternity from the standpoint of Christian erudition.

God And Eternity

Eternity, as "the fullness of time," wherein the past, present, and future all converge in unbroken sequence or reality, must be an ideal environment for God, the eternal designer and creator of life and the cosmos. God does not have to wait for things to happen, nor does he have to reminisce about the past. Everything is before him in the present. For him, all things *just are*, not *were,* or *will be.*

God lives in eternity. Humans live their lives in serial time. God lives in the fullness of time. God is not waiting and wondering who will get to heaven. He is not watching history unfold like a movie. As God sees it, 10,000 years ago is just as present as 10,000 years from now. Eternity as the fullness of time, from God's perspective, includes all past and future events as part of the present.

The Bible confirms God's eternality and eternity as the fullness of time on numerous occasions.

But do not forget this one thing, dear friends: With the Lord a day is like a thousand years, and a thousand years are like a day. (2 Peter 3:8, NIV)

Your eyes foresaw my actions; in your book all are written down; my days were shaped, before one came to be. (Psalm 139;15, NAB)

A thousand years in your sight are like a day that has just gone by, or like a watch in the night. (Psalm 90:4, NIV)

Then there is simply God's name: "I AM." In this name, there is no past, no future, just an eternal now, i.e., a continuous, all-enveloping present.

Jesus answered, "I tell you the truth, before Abraham was even born, I Am! (John 8:58, NLT).

"Fullness of time" as it relates to God and eternity gives rise to a few thought-provoking issues.

- *Is God waiting for events to unfold?* - God is not waiting on anything. He did not wait for anyone to be born; he is not waiting

128

for anyone to die. He is not waiting to judge anyone. He is not waiting for anyone to enter heaven (or hell). He is not waiting for the end of the world. Everything is accomplished. Everything is done, and yet everything is also underway. The day of one's birth is present to God. The day of one's death is present to him. The full sweep of history is before God in one glance, one comprehensive current scene. God lives in eternity, as mentioned above, and humans live in serial time and do not see as God sees, yet everything is there.

- *What about people's freedom?* - The fact that everything is predetermined does not mean people's freedom is meaningless. Although God already knows and has always known every decision everyone makes, it does not mean one does not freely decide what to do or what not to do. God's sovereignty and knowledge do not negate one's freedom. People are moral agents and retain the prerogative to exercise their freedom to act in order to try to control the direction of their lives.

The term "election" is sometimes associated with the term "predestination" and often gives rise to the misconception that because God specifically chose certain people for the carrying out of his divine plan of redemption for humankind, he also selected others for eternal damnation. Herbert M. Wolf (1938-2002), the noted American biblical scholar and professor of Old Testament studies, made the following insightful comment.

- *In each case, foreknowledge precedes election and is intricately linked with God's will and purpose. Yet, we should not think of this as some kind of fatalism or determinism. God does not force anyone to become a believer but works in a person's heart so that the individual freely chooses to receive Christ as Savior.* [1]

The terms *predestination* and *election*, when used in connection with God's foreknowledge, invariably relate to positive and/or good news.

- *Are humans capable of understanding eternity and the fullness of time?* - Humans are created beings, and for as long as they exist, they will occupy a plateau of knowledge, awareness, and character remotely similar to God's. Even after donning their glorified bodies and moving to the eternal center with God at time's end, it seems likely God's children will never understand time and events as comprehensively as he does. Yet because humans will move to eternity, to the fullness of time, it may mean once they are in heaven the whole course of their lives somehow will mysteriously be available for their review and assessment. How and in what manner or mode they will experience such revelation is not clear. How and to what degree people would want to go back and "visit" the past is difficult to determine. Hypothesizing what eternity i.e., the fullness of time, might be is one thing; describing how one might experience it is something altogether different and understandably is beyond the realm of people's current understanding.

130

- *What about prayer?* - A seemingly pertinent question is if everything about everyone is predetermined by God, what is the purpose of prayer? A likely answer may be that as far as human beings are concerned, time and decisions must unfold. Although God always knows what people will or will not do, humans cannot predict the future and, therefore, must pray. God's omniscience is irrelevant in such a situation. People ought to pray and acknowledge God is omnipotent and omniscient and he knows whether they would pray. God also knows the answers to such prayers and has already acted accordingly.

- *Are the Souls in heaven waiting for anything?* – If eternity is the fullness of time and if past and future are contained in a perfect *now*, it would seem the souls in heaven are not waiting for anything. People who have died are not likely to wait for their families to join them since the future is already present to them. They are not waiting for their bodies to rise, for such events are already a part of eternity. From a temporal or serial time perspective, these things have yet to occur and must unfold, but in eternity, it would seem they are elements of an ever-present picture.

Eternity & The Afterlife

Many people consider the term *afterlife* synonymous with the term *eternity*, though not substitutional when it relates to the fullness of time, as discussed above. Indeed, many biblical scholars view the concept of the afterlife in conjunction with eternity as the fullness of time.

People invariably harbor a penchant for the possibility of an afterlife. Consequently, people over the centuries developed numerous theories about the belief. Many people nurture an inborn resistance against the idea life ends with the grave. Funerals and memorial services customarily feature talks about the afterlife, complete with euphemisms to describe what happens after life on earth is over. The dead supposedly relocate to other realms of existence where souls continue to live and/or embark on some kind of progressive path toward an optimal state. The destinations to which eulogists and other sympathizers allude are invariably happy, paradisial locations, even though such portrayals are often nebulous and without cogent assurance. Essentially, people like to think something pleasant and enduring awaits them after they die.

The afterlife characterizes a definitive mystery. William Shakespeare, the renowned British playwright, mused in his masterpiece *Hamlet*, "...The undiscovered country, from whose bourn no traveler returns, puzzles the will..." [2]

There is a book, however, compiled over a period of 1400 to 1800 years by over 40 different authors that contradicts William Shakespeare and multitudinous others who labor to determine whether there is an afterlife. The book is the Holy Bible, and it tells the story of a man named Jesus Christ.

A Word About Near Death Experiences (NDE's)

The fond expectation of an afterlife in which a deceased individual supposedly lives indefinitely, often in spirit form, is buoyed by reports of so-called near-death experiences (NDEs). An NDE is a personal experience associated with death or impending death. When positive, such experiences may encompass a variety of sensations, including detachment from the body, feelings of levitation, total serenity, security, warmth, the experience of absolute dissolution, and invariably the presence of a light. When negative, such experiences may include sensations of anguish and distress.[3] NDEs are a recognized element of the beliefs of myriad religions that teach about an afterlife. [4, 5]

Chapter Four - *Is There a Heaven?* and Chapter Five - *Is There a Hell?*, document a number of near-death experiences from the standpoint of Christian familiarity whereby people describe visits to or visions of heaven (a place of everlasting joy) and hell (a place of eternal torment) and subsequently share their experiences with others.

The perceived authenticity of many NDEs notwithstanding, the author believes there are instances where some such experiences do not reflect God's involvement. There is interaction instead with evil supernatural forces that seek to mislead the individual experiencing the NDE into thinking there is no hell and that all people will go to a paradisial place after death. Consequently, there is no need to accept Jesus Christ as Savior. Such NDEs proceed from the devil and serve to dissuade people from seeking salvation from their sins and eventual residence in heaven. One must remember Satan and his demons are master deceivers, and they seize every opportunity to misinform and lead prospective believers of Christ's Gospel astray. Surely, the devil would cunningly utilize so-called NDE's in attempts to accomplish his sinister agenda.

133

Additionally, some people experience NDEs in which God supposedly communicates with them and warns them about a multitude of so-called sins or incidental deeds or omissions that would condemn people to hell. Such NDEs lead people to believe if each and every minor misdeed committed relegates even the Christian believer to an eternity of torment, then why should he or she even bother to embrace Christ since it already seems like a lost battle. Such NDEs also proceed from the devil, and their messages do not conform to biblical doctrine. Further, some NDEs, although incorporating certain aspects of biblical doctrine, may harbor cunning distortions of the identities of God, Jesus Christ, and the Holy Spirit. It behooves people, including those involved in NDEs, to test and analyze experiences against the revelations of God's Word, the Holy Bible.

NDEs that are not revelations from God may steer people toward developing a morbid fear of Satan and his demons to the exclusion of venerating God fully and trusting in his omnipotence, omniscience, omnipresence, and predisposition to love his children unconditionally. God's most earnest yearning is to have as many people as possible approach his Throne of Grace in seeking residence in his everlasting kingdom. His love for his children transcends all other forms of amity and compassion.

Jesus Christ, The Ultimate Authority & Witness To Eternity & The Afterlife

One traveler did return from the "undiscovered country" (see William Shakespeare's reflection above), i.e., one who went over to the other side and came back to tell all people what to expect after they die. He alone possesses the authority and knowledge to speak truthfully about the afterlife.

More importantly, this individual holds the key to unlock the door to the afterlife sought by humankind. He is Jesus Christ, who died and returned to life. The New Testament Book of 1 Corinthians records the story of hundreds of reliable witnesses who saw and interacted with the risen or resurrected Christ.

> *For what I received I passed on to you as of first importance: that Christ died for our sins according to the Scriptures, that he was buried, that he was raised on the third day according to the Scriptures, and that he appeared to Cephas, and then to the Twelve. After that, he appeared to more than five hundred of the brothers and sisters at the same time, most of whom are still living, though some have fallen asleep. Then he appeared to James, then to all the apostles, and last of all he appeared to me also* (1 Corinthians 15:38, NIV).

Jesus Christ, the one person who can speak with real authority and experience concerning the afterlife or eternity, presents three basic truths about the subject of life after death.

- There is an afterlife.

- After an individual dies, he or she is headed for one of two possible destinations – heaven or hell.

- There is only one way through which an individual can guarantee himself or herself a blissful, unending experience after death – by trusting Jesus Christ as his or her Savior and Redeemer.

There Is An Afterlife

First, Christ teaches there is an afterlife in a number of biblical passages, including one that describes an encounter with the Sadducees, who do not subscribe to the teaching of one's resurrection. He reminds them of their own Scriptures, which affirm God is not the God of the dead, but of the living (Mark 12:24-27). Jesus clearly tells them those who died centuries before are very much alive with God, although they do not marry, becoming instead like angels. Jesus later comforts his disciples with the hope of being with him in Heaven:

> *Do not let your hearts be troubled. You believe in God; believe also in me. My Father's house has many rooms; if that were not so, would I have told you that I am going there to prepare a place for you? And if I go and prepare a place for you, I will come back and take you to be with me that you also may be where I am. You know the way to the place where I am going.* (John 14:1-4, NIV).

Two Destinations

Having established the existence of eternity and an afterlife, Jesus also speaks authoritatively about the two places of eternal habitation that await people who die: one in which God is present and one in which he is absent. In the story of the rich man and Lazarus, Jesus describes these two destinations, "The time came when the beggar died, and the angels carried him to Abraham's side. The rich man also died and was buried. In Hades, where he was in torment, he looked up and saw Abraham far away, with Lazarus by his side." (Luke 16:22-23, NIV). An important aspect of the story is there is no indeterminate state for those who die; their eternal destiny will already have been determined. The New Testament Book of Hebrews says, "...it is appointed for man to die once, and after that comes judgment." (Hebrews 9:27, KJV)

Jesus makes it clear when he says, "These (unbelievers) will go away into everlasting punishment, but the righteous into life eternal." (Matthew 25:46, KJV) The foregoing Scriptural passage confirms there are two destinations awaiting people after they die. One is in the Father's house with Christ. The other is a place of torment, a place of "outer darkness" where there is "weeping and gnashing of teeth." (Matthew 8:12, 22:13, 25:30, KJV)

Gaining Admission into Heaven

The inevitability of going to heaven or hell after one dies prompts the question - What determines one's eternal destination? Christ's answer is unequivocal! One's eternal destination depends on whether he or she has faith in God and what he or she decides with respect to Christ. The Lord himself had much to say on this subject, with perhaps the most profound declaration of its kind found in the Gospel of John.

For God so loved the world that he gave his one and only Son, that whoever believes in him shall not perish but have eternal life. For God did not send his Son into the world to condemn the world but to save the world through him. Whoever believes in him is not condemned, but whoever does not believe stands condemned already because they have not believed in the name of God's one and only Son.(John 3:16-18, NIV)

Those who repent of their sins and put their faith in Christ as their Savior and Lord will enjoy an afterlife or eternity in God's company. Those who reject Christ, and he is the only means of salvation (John 14:6), face an eternity of estrangement from God. There is no neutral ground. There is no second chance should death visit while one remains undecided or has refused to embrace Jesus.

As life on this earth ends, life in one place or the other essentially begins since a decision for or against Christ would have already been made. The apostle Paul rejoiced in the fact that for the Christian believer, death holds no threat. He said,

> *When the perishable puts on the imperishable, and the mortal puts on immortality, then shall come to pass the saying that is written: 'Death is swallowed up in victory.' 'O death, where is your victory? O death, where is your sting?'* (1 Corinthians 15:54-55, ESV)

For those who will spend eternity in heaven, death merely facilitates the entrance into an everlasting period of bliss in the presence of God and his Son, Jesus Christ, the *One* who opened heaven's door for humankind through his own death and resurrection.

PART TWO

WORLD RELIGIONS & PHILOSOPHIES - THE STANDARD FOR COMPARISON

CHAPTER SEVEN
BIBLICAL CHRISTIANITY

A STANDARD FOR COMPARISON

It is invariably a practical approach, in most undertakings where philosophical and/or religious doctrines and dogmas are contrasted, to select a lone worldview to serve as a standard for comparison among the different belief systems. The author selects *Biblical Christianity* as the standard against which he measures other religions and worldviews for the following reasons.

Firstly, the Christian faith, as it proceeds from the teachings of the Old Testament and embodies a renewed covenant between God and humankind, which is undergirded by Christ's Gospel in the New Testament, represents one of the oldest religions in history.

Secondly, adherents of the Christian faith number an unbelievable one-third of the world's population or 2.6 billion people. Such a statistic places the worldview on a unique plateau. In the last 100 years, the number of Christians in the world quadrupled from about 600 million in 1910 to more than two and a half billion. Today, Christianity is the world's largest religious group. [1]

Thirdly, Christians are geographically widespread, unlike followers of any other religious or philosophical worldview – so far-flung that no single continent or region can indisputably claim to be the center of global Christianity. Today, only about a quarter of all Christians live in Europe (26%). A plurality (more than a third) are in the Americas (37%). One in every four Christians lives in sub-Saharan Africa (24%), and about one in eight in Asia and the Pacific (13%). [2] Such far-reaching dispersion attests to a kind of globalism no other religion in the world can match.

Fourthly, and this fact is concomitant with the second and third observations above, the Bible, or the holy book of Christianity, is the bestselling publication of all time, with approximately 78.5 million Bibles being distributed globally per year. There are approximately 6 million books about Christianity in print today.[3] Also, the Bible appears in more languages than any other book in history.

Fifthly, the author of *Two Doors to Eternity* is a born-again Christian, firmly persuaded through the auspices of the Holy Spirit that the Christian Gospel is God's unerring Word and there is no other means through which one can attain salvation and enter into God's everlasting kingdom except through the Redeemer Jesus Christ. The author subscribes firmly to the biblical assertion that all who reject Christ's offer of eternal life and die unsaved will suffer in hell for all eternity.

Lastly, and most importantly, it is entirely commonsensical to expect an omnipotent, omniscient, and omnipresent God to measure or judge humankind by his standards, his Word, and nothing else. This is where God's Holy Word, with its originality and truthfulness, upon which true biblical Christianity stands, comes into play. The use of the Bible, or biblical

Christianity, as a standard for comparison among other religions and philosophies, therefore, leaves no room for false or misguided contemplation, religious or secular.

There are, of course, other considerations that impact the author's decision to use Christianity as a criterion for evaluation in relation to other belief systems. Among such factors are (a) the strong measures of authentication of the Holy Bible as an original record of Christian history, (b) archaeological discoveries that substantiate Old Testament and New Testament history, and (c) compelling arguments for the exceptionality and truthfulness of biblical prophecy.

The forgoing deliberations notwithstanding, the reasons outlined above may well be subjective in the eyes of some impartial observers. While to the Christian believer, they suffice as persuasive representation in making a case for Christianity, the non-Christian understandably would require additional or alternative submissions.

The author, in presenting *Two Doors to Eternity*, aims to provide such information in no small measure.

WHAT IS BIBLICAL CHRISTIANITY?

The term *Biblical Christianity*, as used in this book, refers to an approach towards biblical scholarship that employs resilient effort in searching carefully for the real meaning of God's Holy Word without modifying anything to conform to changing norms and attitudes, especially from secular moral and philosophical standpoints. A biblical Christian undertakes the task of researching and examining the Bible with reverence and respect, under the guidance of the Holy Spirit, mainly because he or she believes it is true and authoritative and represents God's immutable revelations to humankind.

The Dangers Of Heresy

As early as late in the first century, leaders of the then-nascent religion of Christianity realized the importance of demarcating between true Christian dogmas and emerging heterodox teachings and keeping them separate. Among Christianity's most dangerous foes are heretics within the belief system itself who entertain and advance views and theories contrary to the time-honored, commonly received truths undergirding the faith, i.e., the doctrines contained in the Old Testament and New Testament or God's inspired, conclusive Word about his plan of redemption for sinful humankind.

Biblical Christians have had to guard against unorthodox, misguided decriers of Christ's Gospel for centuries – from the Gnostics of the first and second centuries to today's liberal and often irreverent moralizers. Conversely, mainstream Christians simultaneously have to be cautious against being unfairly judgmental of other well-meaning believers who harbor certain viewpoints dissimilar to their own.

Biblical Christianity refers to a universal assemblage of believers from a multitude of churches and denominations. It is inevitable there will be certain beliefs and areas of scholarship that particular groups would prefer to emphasize instead of others. Such a stance is generally acceptable as long as it does not detract from the fundamentals of the Gospel message. The central, indispensable teaching that galvanizes biblical Christians everywhere reads, "...Christ died for our sins according to the Scriptures...he was buried...he was raised on the third day according to the Scriptures." (1 Corinthians 15:3,4, NIV)

Of course, Christianity encompasses many doctrines and truths germane to God's glorious plan of redemption for lost humankind, all of which appear in God's Holy Word. However, the foregoing scriptural declaration provides a definitive standard for comparing biblical Christianity with all other religions and philosophies.

Biblical Christianity As A Standard For Comparison Among Religions – Four Salient Considerations

The rest of this chapter revolves around four prominent aspects of the Christian faith that thrust the worldview to the fore as a standard for comparison among other religions, faiths, and philosophies.

1. Jesus Christ – His sacrifice & resurrection on behalf of sinful humankind.

2. The irrefutable Biblical record of Christ's Resurrection.

3. Humankind's fall from grace and its need of a Savior.

4. The truth and reliability of the Holy Bible.

Jesus Christ – His Sacrifice & Resurrection On Behalf Of Sinful Humankind

The resurrection of Jesus Christ istestament to the immense power of God. To believe in Christ's resurrection is to believe in God. If God exists, and if he created the universe and exercises dominion over it, then he must possess the power to raise the dead. If he does not have such power, he is not worthy of people's faith and worship. Only God who created life can resurrect it after death, only he can reverse the hideousness that is death itself, and only he can remove the sting of death and gain victory over the grave (1 Corinthians 15:54–55). In resurrecting Jesus from the grave, God reminds us of his absolute sovereignty over life and death.

The resurrection of Jesus Christ is also extremely important because it validates who Jesus claimed to be, namely, the Son of God and Messiah. According to Jesus, his resurrection was the "sign from heaven" that authenticated his ministry. (Matthew 16:1-4 NIV). The resurrection of Jesus Christ, attested to by hundreds of eyewitnesses (1 Corinthians 15:3–8), provides irrefutable proof he is the Redeemer and Savior of the world.

The death and resurrection of Jesus Christ also verify his sinless character and divine nature. The Scriptures say God's "Holy One" would never see corruption (Psalm 16:10, NASB), and Jesus never saw corruption, even after he died (see Acts 13:32–37). The resurrection of Christ provided the basis for Paul's resolute pronouncement, i.e., "Through Jesus the forgiveness of sins is proclaimed to you. Through him everyone who believes is set free from every sin." (Acts 13:38-39, NIV)

The crucifixion and subsequent resurrection of Jesus Christ is not only the supreme confirmation of his deity; it is also undeniable validation of the Old Testament prophecies that foretold Jesus' suffering and resurrection (see Acts 17:2–3). Christ's resurrection also substantiated his own claims he would rise on the third day after his crucifixion (Mark 8:31; 9:31; 10:34). If

Jesus Christ did not rise from the dead, then humankind had no hope its members would be resurrected either. In fact, if Christ did not rise from the dead, humankind would have no Savior, no salvation, and no hope of eternal life. As Paul said, "People's faith would be "useless," "and if Christ has not been raised, your faith is futile; you are still in your sins. Then those also who have fallen asleep in Christ are lost." (1 Corinthians 15:14-19, NIV)

Christ's death and resurrection serve as authentication of the eventual resurrection of human beings, which is a basic tenet of the Christian faith. Unlike other religions, Christianity boasts a founder who transcends death and promises his followers they will do the same. Founders of every other religion ended up in the grave. As Christians, believers know God became man, died for their sins, and rose from the dead on the third day. The grave could not hold him. He lives, and he sits today at the right hand of the Father in heaven (Hebrews 10:12).

Christians, because they know they will eventually be resurrected to new life, can endure persecution and danger for Christ's sake, just as the Lord did during His sojourn on earth. Jesus' sacrifice and resurrection have inspired thousands of Christian martyrs throughout history to willingly trade their earthly lives for the promise of everlasting life in heaven.

Christ's resurrection is a triumphant and glorious victory for every believer. He is coming again! The Holy Bible assures all who embrace Jesus Christ as Lord and Redeemer that they will spend eternity with him in paradise.

Brothers and sisters, we do not want you to be uninformed about those who sleep in death, so that you do not grieve like the rest of mankind,

146

who have no hope. For we believe that Jesus died and rose again, and so we believe that God will bring with Jesus those who have fallen asleep in him. According to the Lord's word, we tell you that we who are still alive, who are left until the coming of the Lord, will certainly not precede those who have fallen asleep. For the Lord himself will come down from heaven, with a loud command, with the voice of the archangel and with the trumpet call of God, and the dead in Christ will rise first. After that, we who are still alive and are left will be caught up together with them in the clouds to meet the Lord in the air. And so we will be with the Lord forever. Therefore encourage one another with these words. (1 Thessalonians 4:13-18, NIV)

The Biblical Record Of Christ's Resurrection – Difficult To Refute

The following arguments for the authenticity of the Biblical record of Christ's resurrection are difficult to repudiate, even by those staunchly opposed to the Christian Gospel and its unique message of redemption for lost humankind.

Christ's Burial By Two Prominent Jewish Followers

The New Testament says Joseph of Arimathea, a prominent member of the Jewish community and a sympathizer of Christ's ministry, sought and received permission from the Roman Governor Pontius Pilate to take possession of and bury the young rabbi's body. Nicodemus, a Jewish follower of Jesus, made available a mixture of about a hundred pounds of myrrh, aloes, and other spices to be used in preparation for the burial.

The statement in the Gospel about Jesus being laid to rest by Joseph of Arimathea in the latter's newly hewn tomb helps validate the New Testament account of the young rabbi's death and resurrection. The passage reads, "Joseph took the body, wrapped it in a clean linen cloth, and placed it in his own new tomb that he had cut out of the rock. He rolled a big stone in front of the entrance to the tomb and went away. Mary Magdalene and the other Mary were sitting there opposite the tomb." (Matthew 27:59-61, NIV). The fact that two prominent Jewish men took charge of Christ's body, and used a rich man's tomb in which to inter him helps strengthen the Gospel story. As James P. Moreland (b. 1948), the well-known American philosopher, theologian, and Christian apologist, opines, "The mention of prominent men indicates that this account is not fictitious. If the disciples had created this story it would have been counterproductive to make up (include) a person that was supposed to be in a prominent position. This could easily have been refuted were it not true." [4]

Joseph of Arimathea, Nicodemus, and the women who looked on as the Romans interred Jesus' body noted the location of the Nazarene's tomb. In addition, the Jewish and Roman authorities ensured the tomb was specifically identifiable by marking it in a special way. The availability of so much information in the Gospels about Christ's burial place only enhances the accuracy of such an account, as dissenters could easily challenge and disprove the details if they were false.

Archaeological findings confirm the description of the tomb in which the Romans supposedly laid Christ's body as one belonging to a rich individual. Such burial places were relatively rare in Jesus' time. There is a strong indication the location of Christ's tomb, as indicated in the Gospels, is the same as the location of other similar tombs, some of which archaeologists excavated within a particular area near the Garden Gate at the north Wall of Jerusalem.

The Broken Roman Seal

The Roman authorities, working in conjunction with the Jewish leaders who wanted Christ's tomb secured and guarded, had an official seal made of wax and rope placed over the tomb. Such a procedure, in placation of the fears of the Jewish authorities, helped to make sure Christ's followers would not steal his body and then claim the empty tomb confirmed he rose from the dead as he said he would do.

During the time of the Roman Empire, the Roman seal in any form was an expression of power and authority. The unlawful breaking or destruction of this seal was an offense punishable by death. In fact, an individual found guilty of breaking a Roman seal faced death by crucifixion in an upside-down position. [5]

Jesus' disciples, like other Roman subjects, feared the cruel Roman overseers and most likely did not entertain the idea of breaking the Roman seal placed over his tomb. One must remember after the Romans and Jewish authorities arrested Christ, subjected him to a mockery of a trial, and abused him horrendously, his disciples distanced themselves from him. Peter, who was the *de facto* leader of the band of Jesus' followers after his arrest, denied his master three times after their persecutors confronted him. Most of the other disciples, if not all, hid from public view and attention.

It is extremely unlikely any of Jesus' disciples or his followers ventured to break the Roman seal set upon his tomb, yet visitors to the tomb found it broken on the morning of the third day after his burial.

The Large Stone Removed from the Tomb Opening

Historians presume the stone placed in front of Jesus' tomb to help prevent anyone from stealing his body weighed about one and a half to two tons. The people who visited the tomb on Sunday morning and found the huge rock missing were quite likely dumbfounded. Biblical scholars and secular historians as well, agree the heavy stone placed to block the entrance into, and ironically the exit from Christ's tomb, stood on an incline some distance away from the sepulcher itself. Two questions immediately come to mind if one were to mull over the hypothesis that Jesus' followers removed the stone and stole his body.

1. How could have one, two, three or even more individuals have moved the massive stone and left it at a distance away from the tomb? One needs to remember Christ's disciples ran away and hid after his crucifixion. Why would they suddenly congregate and attempt the daring and assumedly hopeless task of opening a very secure tomb and removing the Galilean's body?

2. How could an exercise such as the one mentioned above be performed without arousing the attention of the Roman guard on duty? In addition, it is worth noting the term "a Roman guard" could easily refer to a number of soldiers and not a single individual. Did all of the guards miss the carrying out of a

painstaking, protracted undertaking such as dislocating the huge stone and relocating it some distance away from the sepulcher?

The consensus held by Biblical and secular scholars alike about the aforementioned circumstances surrounding Christ's burial, the sealing of his tomb, and its subsequent unexplainable opening accords a considerable measure of believability to the New Testament record of Christ's resurrection. Clark H. Pinnock (b. 1937), the widely read Christian apologist, theologian, author, and Professor Emeritus of Systematic Theology at McMaster Divinity College in Hamilton, Ontario, Canada, makes the following assertive remark. "There exists no document from the ancient world (the New Testament record), witnessed by so excellent a set of textual and historical testimonies…Skepticism regarding the historical credentials of Christianity is based upon an irrational basis." [6]

The Empty Tomb

Three days after Jesus' death and burial, his followers and others came upon an empty tomb. All of the Gospels contain reports about the empty tomb, and if the story of the *Resurrection* were true, the bare tomb, of necessity, must be one of the earliest indications of such a miracle. It is safe to assume not even any of Christ's disciples, or his own mother as a matter of fact, anticipated the miracle of a resurrected Christ, this notwithstanding his own prediction that he would rise from the dead. The Gospel of Luke says, "On the first day of the week, very early in the morning, the women took the spices they had prepared and went to the tomb. They found the stone rolled away from the tomb, but when they entered, they did not find the body of the Lord Jesus."

Jewish and Roman historical sources alike report finding an empty tomb three days after the Romans laid Nazarene's body in it. These sources encompass writings from the time of the Jewish historian Flavius Josephus to the time of the compilation of the *Toledot Yeshu*, also called *Toledoth Jeshu* or the *Biography of Jesus*, a fifth-century work from a decidedly anti-Christian perspective. Paul L. Maier (b. 1930), the noted historical novelist and the Russell H. Siebert Professor of Ancient History at Western Michigan University in the USA, says notwithstanding the invectives contained in the Toledot Yeshu, there is the admission of Christ's tomb being empty on the third day after his burial. He refers to such an acknowledgment as "...positive evidence from a hostile source, which is the strongest kind of historical evidence. In essence, this means if a source admits a fact decidedly not in its favor, then the fact is genuine." [7]

The disciples of Jesus, after they realized his tomb was empty, as he said it would be on the third day after his burial, returned to Jerusalem with the astonishing news. They did not travel to any of the principal cities such as Athens or Rome, but back to Jerusalem where, if the tomb were not empty, people would have subjected them to much chastisement and derision. Jesus' tomb, indeed, had to be empty. Paul Maier makes a further incisive observation when he says, "...if all the evidence is weighed carefully and fairly, it is indeed justifiable, according to the canons of historical research, to conclude that the sepulcher of Joseph of Arimathea, in which Jesus was buried, was actually empty on the morning of the first Easter. And no shred of evidence has yet been discovered in literary sources, epigraphy, or archaeology that would disprove this statement." [8]

Jesus Christ died on the cross and rose from the dead as a promise to humankind that those who accept his sacrifice on the cross as atonement for their trespasses will live forever with him in Paradise.

The Missing Roman Guard

Roman military discipline in Christ's era, as it was before and after then, was stringent and inflexible. Soldiers and other military personnel who violated military regulations faced harsh castigation. The fear of their superiors' fury and the real possibility of execution for their infractions drove Roman soldiers, such as those assigned to guard Christ's tomb, to carry out their duties with utmost competence and dedication.

For the guards to be absent from the vicinity of Christ's open tomb on the first Easter morning meant some extraordinary event had taken place, something so astounding and remarkable as to render them incapable of fathoming its magnificence and/or to strike indescribable terror in their hearts and lead them to desert their station. Maybe it was an awe-inspiring, overpowering event whereby an angelic entity rolled away a two-ton stone as the guards stood transfixed, and even more astonishing, a dead man rising from his place of rest and exiting a cold stone tomb!

Whatever it was, the Roman guards risked their very lives by fleeing from their positions. They could not have fallen asleep, not all of them at the same time, and allowed a few scared, grief-stricken, and more or less feeble followers of the dead man to accomplish the physically improbable task of removing a huge stone from the doorway of their buried master's sepulcher and then, without being detected, escape with his body. Rather, a momentous, unprecedented incident transpired - a resurrection took place! All that was there for onlookers to see was an open and empty tomb!

The Case of the Linen Wrappings

Contrary to the generally accepted consensus among experts on the study of comparative religion that Jesus' tomb was empty on the morning of the third day after his death and burial, pointed research indicates this might not be an entirely accurate assumption.

One of Jesus' disciples – maybe John or Peter, probably witnessed a phenomenon of sorts after he entered his master's sepulcher. Christ's grave clothes lay on the surface where the body rested in the form of a kind of cocoon. It looked as though a solid cadaver literally left undisturbed the linen that held it, so the clothes retained an outer shell in the form of a human body. Additionally, the facecloth, which those who interred him used to wrap Christ's head, lay folded in a separate location in the sepulcher. Those who observed the spectacle were not likely to forget it in a hurry.

If Jesus' disciples did steal his body, as detractors from the Gospel accounts infer, why would they bother to fold his headcloth neatly and set it aside before spiriting the body away? More perturbing, what secular explanation is there for the cocoon-shaped, empty grave clothes left behind?

Eyewitness Accounts of a Resurrected Christ

The apostle Paul, in one of his letters to the Corinthians, spoke about the risen Christ appearing to over 500 people at the same time (1 Corinthians 15:3-8). The Gospel of Matthew (28:16-19) records a resurrected Jesus ministering to his followers before his ascension into Heaven.

Paul reminded his audience that a good number of the people who saw the resurrected Christ were still alive, and non-believers could question them about the experience. There is no record in the Holy Scriptures, or in any other reliable ancient document, about anyone interrogating the purported witnesses to the risen Jesus or, more significantly, about anyone disputing Paul's claim.

This is an extraordinarily persuasive argument for the truthfulness of the Gospel accounts of a crucified and risen Christ. Also, one needs to remember Paul wrote his epistles to the people at Corinth no more than a few decades after Christ's death and resurrection. Dr. Edwin M. Yamauchi (1937 -), Professor of History at Miami University, Ohio, USA, makes the following observation. "What gives a special authority to the list (of witnesses) as historical evidence is the reference to most of the five hundred brethren being still alive. St. Paul says, in effect, 'If you do not believe me, you can ask them.' Such a statement in an admittedly genuine letter written within thirty years of the event is as strong evidence as one could hope to get for something that happened nearly two thousand years ago." [9]

Critics of the resurrection story are wont to claim only Jesus' acquaintances and followers saw him after his death and burial. Such circumstances, they intimate, do not augur well for a believable story, and the Biblical account of the resurrection, therefore, may be untrue. A claim like the forgoing, firstly, is speculative, and secondly, even if it were true, Christ appeared only to his followers between the time of his resurrection and ascension to Heaven. There was likely a justifiable reason for such an approach. Maybe his showing himself to a select few was a tactic derived from a uniquely evangelistic perspective or from a special post-resurrection need for exclusivity among believers whom he would entrust to spearhead the religious movement later known as Christianity. Who knows? The likelihood that the Gospel account indicates Jesus chose to appear only to friends and followers after his resurrection should not perfunctorily provide grounds for the dismissal of such a report.

In the New Testament Book of the Acts of the Apostles (Acts 9:1-18; 22:1-16), one reads about Saul's (Saul of Tarsus) miraculous conversion from an impious persecutor of Christ's followers to a zealous, dedicated disciple of the Galilean miracle-worker. Saul, who afterward assumed the name Paul, underwent a life-changing experience as he traveled on a lonely road to the City of Damascus, initially bent on chastising the Christians who lived there. According to the Scriptures, Jesus confronted Saul and actually spoke to him. This was a post-resurrection event. Here, Christ showed himself not to a follower or friend but to one of his most ardent and hateful enemies. Paul subsequently became one of Christianity's foremost advocates for the truth of the resurrection.

The Witness of the Apostles

It is evident Jesus' apostles and close followers truthfully believed in his message of the salvation of one's soul and the importance of the acceptance of his sacrifice on the cross for the redemption of one's sins. These men and women would not have subjected themselves to the harassment and persecution meted out to them for preaching Christ's Gospel if they did not sincerely believe in his messianic identity and his godhood. The disciples were ordinary, worldly men who were content to live according to the dictates of an unobtrusive, materialistic society before they became disciples of the mesmerizing Nazarene. After their conversion, the disciples experienced a transformation into Spirit-filled advocates of Christ's sacrifice on the cross and his resurrection.

It is highly improbable that people totally committed to a worthy purpose would be a party to a hoax, would entertain a significant measure of doubt or trepidation, or persist with advancing a false doctrine, especially if such actions could lead to relentless persecution, the loss of their possessions and ultimately the loss of their lives. Jesus' disciples preached and defended his Gospel of humankind's redemption in the face of all of the forgoing challenges and threats.

Simon Greenleaf (1783-1853), American lawyer and jurist, one of the founders of Harvard Law School and a foremost legal mind in the annals of American history, made a stirring statement about the death and resurrection of Jesus Christ after he undertook a study of the four canonical Gospels of the New Testament in order to evaluate their worth as objective testimonial evidence. Greenleaf said: "It was impossible that the apostles could have persisted in affirming the truths they had narrated, had not Jesus Christ actually risen from the dead, and had they not known this fact as certainly as they did any other fact." [10]

Thomas Arnold (1795-1842), British educator and, historian and Professor of History at Rugby and Oxford, England, made the following remark about the validity of the Biblical account of Christ's resurrection. "I have been used for many years to study histories of other times and to examine and weigh the evidence of those who have written about them, and

I know of no better and fuller evidence of every sort to the understanding of the fair enquirer than the great sign which God hath given us that Christ died and rose again from the dead." [11]

Humankind's Fall From Grace and its Need of a Savior

Humankind's fall from grace, i.e., Adam and Eve's insubordination in the Garden of Eden, whereby they disobeyed their Creator, who placed them in a perfect location to live, plunged the entire human race and themselves into a state of sin. The effects of the *fall* were numerous and far-reaching. Sin affects every aspect of people's lives and bears upon their very existence on earth and upon their eternal destiny.

One of the immediate effects of the *fall* was humankind's separation from God. In the Garden, Adam and Eve had perfect communion and fellowship with God. When they rebelled against him, they adulterated that relationship. They became aware of their sin and felt ashamed in God's presence. They hid from him (Genesis 3:8-10), and people have been alienating themselves from God ever since. In order to reconcile themselves to their Creator, wayward human beings need an Intercessor or a Mediator and a Savior. Jesus Christ is such a mediator! Jesus Christ is such a Savior! Only Christ can restore humankind's fellowship with God and present its members as righteous and sinless in God's eyes, as Adam and Eve were before they sinned. "God made him who had no sin to be sin for us, so that in him we might become the righteousness of God." (2 Corinthians 5:21, NIV)

Because of the fall, physical death became a reality for all of creation. All men die, all animals die, all plant life dies. The "whole creation has been groaning," (Romans 8:22, NIV), waiting for the time when Christ will return to liberate it from the effects of death. Because of sin, death is an inescapable reality, and no one is exempt, "For the wages of sin is death, but the gift of God is eternal life in Christ Jesus our Lord." (Romans 6:23, NIV). Worse still, people not only die, but if they die without Christ, they will face an eternity of unmitigated anguish.

Another effect of the fall is people no longer acknowledge the purpose for which God created them. Man's highest purpose in life is to glorify God and enjoy him forever (Romans 11:36; 1 Corinthians 6:20; 1 Corinthians 10:31; Psalm 86:9). Love of God is the core of all morality and goodness. The opposite of loving God is loving oneself. Selfishness is the essence of what led to the *fall* in the Garden of Eden. Essentially, people seek to place themselves exclusively at the helm of their lives and usurp God's role.

When Adam and Eve chose to rebel against their Creator, they lost their innocence, incurred the penalty of physical and spiritual death, and had their minds darkened by sin. They also caused the minds of their descendants to become polluted. The apostle Paul said of pagans, "Just as they did not think it worthwhile to retain the knowledge of God, so God gave them over to a depraved mind."(Romans 1:28, NIV). Furthermore, he told the Corinthians that "the god of this age has blinded the minds of unbelievers so that they cannot see the light of the Gospel of the glory of Christ, who is the image of God." (2 Corinthians 4:4, NIV).

Jesus Christ the Savior provides the means through which humans may re-establish their blessed connection with God. He said, "I have come into the world as a light so that no one who believes in me should stay in darkness."(John 12:46, NIV). Paul reminded the Ephesians, "For you were once darkness, but now you are light in the Lord. Live as children of light."(Ephesians 5:8, NIV). The purpose of salvation, says Jesus, is "to open their (people's) eyes and turn them from darkness to light, and from the power of Satan to God, so that they may receive forgiveness of sins and a place among those who are sanctified by faith in me.' " (Acts 26:18, NIV).

The fall produced a state of depravity in humans. Paul spoke of those "whose consciences have been seared" (1 Timothy 4:2, NIV) and those whose minds are spiritually darkened as a result of rejecting the truth (Romans 1:21). In this state, man is utterly incapable of doing or choosing what is acceptable to God. According to the Book of Romans, "The mind governed by the flesh (the sinful mind) is hostile to God; it does not submit to God's law, nor can it do so." (Romans 8:7, NIV).

Without supernatural regeneration by the Holy Spirit, all people would remain in their fallen state. God, in his grace, mercy, and loving-kindness, however, sent his Son Jesus to die on the cross and suffer the penalty for humankind's sins, reconciling people to himself and availing to them the gift of eternal life. Christ's atoning death on the Cross reclaims what was lost because of the *fall* in the Garden of Eden.

The Truth and Reliability of the Holy Bible

The Holy Bible is God's unerring word produced over the course of many centuries by religious sages inspired by the Holy Spirit. God's Word consists of the Old Testament and the New Testament. As the Book of Proverbs states, "Every word of God is flawless; he is a shield to those who take refuge in him. Do not add to his words, or he will rebuke you and prove you a liar." (Proverbs 30:5-6 NIV) See also Psalm 119:160; Matthew 5:17, 18; Luke 16:17; John 10:35b; 1 Thessalonians 2:13; 2 Timothy 3:13-17; 2 Peter 1:20, 21; Revelation 22:18, 19)

In the strictest sense of the term, the original documents of the 66 books of the Bible, sometimes referred to as "autographs, are not in the possession of any individual or organization. In order to gain an understanding of how the original Bible came into being and how it compares to what it is today, it is necessary to look at the process relative to the book's original compilation and activities subsequent to its production.

Background of the Holy Bible

The assembling of the Holy Bible spanned a long period of time. Written by 40 authors over a period of nearly 1,500 years, the Scriptures comprises 66 books—39 in the Old Testament and 27 in the New Testament. The Old Testament contains three sections: (1) *The Pentateuch*, which is sometimes referred to as "The Law" and includes the first five books of the Bible; (2) *The Prophets*, which includes all the major and minor prophetic writings, and (3) *The Writings*, which includes Psalms, Proverbs, and a number of other books.

The New Testament also covers three segments: (1) *The Gospels*; (2) *Church History*, which basically includes just the book of Acts; and (3) *The Apostolic Writings*, which includes everything else.

Compilation of the Old Testament

The compilation or assemblage of the original Bible is traceable through reference to the Scriptures in a fairly accurate manner. The Old Testament prophet Moses, after he wrote the Pentateuch or the first five books of the Bible (Exodus 17:14; 24:4, 7; 34:27; Numbers 33:2; Joshua 1:8; Matthew 19:8; John 5:46–47; Romans 10:5), placed the texts in the *Ark of the Covenant* (Deuteronomy 31:24). The Ark of the Covenant, also known as the Ark of the Testimony, and sometimes as the Ark of God, (1 Chronicles 16:18, NLT), (1 Samuel 3:3, NIV), is a gold-covered wooden chest described in the Book of Exodus as containing the two stone tablets of the Ten Commandments. According to various texts within the Hebrew Bible, it also contained Aaron's rod and a pot of manna. [12]

Over time, rulers added other inspired texts to the first five books of the Bible. During the time of David and Solomon, religious designees put completed books in the temple treasury (1 Kings 8:6) to be cared for by the priests who served in the temple (2 Kings 22:8). Religious leaders added more books during the reign of King Hezekiah, i.e., David's hymns, Solomon's proverbs, and prophetic books such as Isaiah, Hosea, and Micah (Proverbs 25:1). In general, as the prophets of God spoke, religious sages recorded their words and included such writings in what later became the Old Testament.

Jewish religious leaders preserved the books during the exile of the Jews in the sixth century. The Jews returned from Babylonian captivity around 538 BC, and Ezra, the priest, afterwards added other inspired works to the compilation. Scholars placed a copy of the Torah in the Most Holy

162

Place of the second temple, the previous location of the Ark of the Covenant. Religious sages, adhering to a meticulous process, produced other copies of the Torah in order to protect and preserve the inspired writings. This collection of Old Testament books, written in the Hebrew language, is what Judaism calls the "Hebrew Bible."

In the third century BC, a team of 70 Jewish scholars translated the Old Testament books into Greek and called the finished work "the LXX" (which means "70"), or the "Septuagint," a Latin word derived from the phrase "the translation of the seventy interpreters." The Septuagint (LXX) is the earliest extant Greek translation of the Hebrew Scriptures from the original Hebrew. Paul and the other apostles later used and quoted from the Septuagint in their writings. The oldest manuscripts of the Septuagint include some first and second century BC fragments.

The Dead Sea Scrolls, also called The Qumran Caves Scrolls, are ancient Jewish religious manuscripts found in the Qumran Caves in the Judean Desert, near Ein Feshkha on the northern shore of the Dead Sea in 1947.[13] Various scrolls date anywhere from the 5th century BC to the 1st century AD. Historians believe Jewish scribes maintained the site to preserve God's Word and to protect the writings during the destruction of Jerusalem in AD 70. The Dead Sea Scrolls represent nearly every book of the Old Testament, and comparisons with more recent manuscripts show them to be virtually identical - the main deviations are the spellings of the names of some individuals and certain numbers quoted in Scripture.

The Dead Sea Scrolls are a testimony to the flawless preservation and accuracy of the Old Testament and help confirm that the Old Testament people use today is the same Old Testament Christ himself used. In fact, the Gospel of Luke records a statement made by Jesus regarding the assemblage of the Old Testament:

> *Because of this, God in his wisdom said, 'I will send them prophets and apostles, some of whom they will kill and others they will persecute.' Therefore this generation will be held responsible for the blood of all the prophets that has been shed since the beginning of the world, from the blood of Abel to the blood of Zechariah, who was killed between the altar and the sanctuary. Yes, I tell you, this generation will be held responsible for it all.* (Luke 11:49-51, NIV).

Jesus confirmed the authenticity of the 39 books of the Old Testament in these verses. An account of Abel's death appears in the Book of Genesis and Zechariah's in the Book of 2 Chronicles—the first and last books of the Hebrew Bible.

Compilation of the New Testament

The Council of Carthage, a synod held in the city of Carthage, Africa, in AD 397, officially settled the composition of the New Testament. The Synod of 397 issued a canon of the Bible on August 28, 397. The primary source of information about the third Council of Carthage comes from the *Codex Canonum Ecclesiæ Africanæ*. Among the various canonical writings sanctioned at the Synod of 397 were the following New Testament books: four books of the Gospels, one book of the Acts of the Apostles, thirteen Epistles of the Apostle Paul, one epistle of Paul to the Hebrews, two Epistles of the Apostle Peter, three of John, one of James, one of Jude, and one book of the Apocalypse of John. [14]

Notwithstanding the foregoing observations, religious leaders and theologians accepted the majority of the New Testament texts as authoritative much earlier. Marcion of Sinope, an early Christian theologian, proposed the first collection of New Testament books in AD 140. Although Marcion objected to certain doctrines about divinity and immortality in the Hebrew Scriptures and, affirmed the Father of Christ as the one true God and published his own list of New Testament books, [15] his pseudo-heretical actions effectively spurred early Church leaders to respond to his claims and eventually develop the New Testament canon.

The next proposed collection of New Testament books on record was the Muratorian Canon, also called the Muratorian Fragment. The Muratorian Canon is an ancient list of New Testament books - the oldest known list. The original document, probably written in Greek, dates to about AD 180 and lists 22 of the 27 books that later became the New Testament of the Christian Bible. The Canon included all four Gospels, Acts of the Apostles, thirteen of Paul's letters, and the books of 1, 2, 3 John, Jude, and Revelation. The church father Athanasius first identified the final New Testament canon in AD 367, and the Council of Carthage ratified it in AD 397.

Quotations from the early church fathers allow the reconstruction of almost the entire New Testament as it is known today. For example, Clement (c. AD 95) quotes from eleven New Testament books, Ignatius (c.

AD 107) quotes from nearly every New Testament book, and Polycarp (a disciple of John, c. AD 110) quotes from seventeen New Testament books. The entire New Testament can be compiled using the early church fathers' quotes, with the exception of 20 to 27 verses, most of them from 3 John. Such evidence points to the fact that early Christian leaders and theologians recognized the New Testament far earlier than the Council of Carthage in AD 397, and the New Testament in use today mirrors what it was 2,000 years ago.

New Testament Autographs, Manuscript Count & Integrity – Overwhelming Evidence of Accuracy and Truthfulness

Biblical scholars generally acknowledge scribes produced the New Testament autographs (original documents) between 45 A.D. and 95 A.D. There are about 5,600 known New Testament manuscripts in Greek alone. Some of these records originated as early as A.D. 125. The oldest, completely New Testament dates back to 367 A.D.

According to religious historians, eight thousand to ten thousand (8,000 to 10,000) Latin Vulgate New Testament manuscripts are in existence today. In addition, 8,000 manuscripts exist in the following languages:

- Ethiopic (an ancient South Semitic language that originated in southern Arabia)

- Coptic (a northern Afro-Asiatic language spoken in Egypt until at least the 17th century)

166

- Slavic (a group of closely related languages of the Slavic peoples and a subgroup of Indo-European languages)

- Syriac (a dialect of Middle Aramaic that was once spoken across much of the Fertile Crescent)

- Armenian (an Indo-European language widely spoken by Armenian communities in the Armenian diaspora).

Scholars contend there are some 86,000 quotations about the New Testament by the early church fathers and several thousand Lectionaries, or books used in church services, which contain Scripture quotations from the early centuries of Christianity. In fact, as mentioned above, experts feel that even if there were no manuscript copies of the Bible, the abundance of quotations from the early church fathers would suffice to enable scholars to reconstruct all but approximately 20-27 verses of the entire New Testament. The author refers to material dating back within 150 to 200 years from the time of Jesus Christ. Yet, some imprudent scholars rush to claim that the Christian Bible evolved through countless translations, additions, and revisions, insisting there was never a definitive version of the book.

Where there exist a large number of transcriptions of an original text, among which there are only a few trivial inconsistencies, the assumption is the copied or transcribed documents are representative of the contents of the original writing or autograph. This is especially true if writers generate the transcriptions at different times. An ancient manuscript, of course, would be in handwritten form as opposed to printed form.

In researching ancient literature, experts develop historiography, a tested approach to evaluating historical documents. There are three elementary tests appertaining to the study of ancient manuscripts or writings i.e., the bibliographic test, the internal evidence test, and the external evidence test. The bibliographic test, which encompasses research and analysis of actual manuscripts, falls into focus here for the purposes of the discussion at hand. According to this method, the more manuscripts there are, the less difficult it would be to attempt to reconstruct the original writing or the autograph. In addition, such an approach enables ample scrutiny for errors or discrepancies.

When experts apply the bibliographic test to Homer's Greek epic, *The Iliad*, considered by scholars to have the second-best manuscript tradition (a quantitative measure of manuscript copies) in history, the result is a manuscript count of about 650, by far the most for any other ancient manuscript - except one! Homer wrote The Iliad around 800 BC, but the whereabouts of the original manuscript are unknown. The versions of *The Iliad* people read today emerged from manuscript copies produced many centuries after Homer's lifetime. Scholars opine the oldest Iliad manuscript dates back to 200-300 AD - approximately 1,000 years removed from Homer's era. Yet, most experts take the presumed reliability of this manuscript and its many revisions for granted and consider the documents to be representative of Homer's original work.

The New Testament boasts, by leaps and bounds, a more solid manuscript tradition than Homer's *The Iliad*, or any other ancient work for that matter. The number of ancient manuscript copies of the New Testament books is overwhelming. There are in excess of 5,500 manuscripts, in Greek alone, of New Testament works today. Many of these texts or copies date back to times very close to when scribes created the original documents. As stated earlier, divinely inspired scribes prepared the New Testament books within the first century after the life of Jesus Christ. These "religious secretaries" produced some manuscript copies within a few decades after the Nazarene's death. The foregoing considerations notwithstanding, some historians and scholars of comparative religion rush to deny the historicity and authenticity of the Holy Bible, including the New Testament, while they presume other texts of much lesser claim to validity, including Homer's *The Iliad*, are trustworthy representations of original works.

Josh McDowell, the well-known Christian apologist, evangelist, and writer, in his widely read essay, *A Skeptic's Quest*, makes the following statement about the authenticity of the New Testament.

> *Let me tell you what I found in relation to the New Testament. When I wrote the book "Evidence That Demands a Verdict" in 1974, I was able to document 14,000 manuscripts of just the New Testament (that's not counting the Old Testament). In the revised edition I've been able to document 24,633 manuscripts of just the New Testament. The Number Two book in manuscript authority in all history is The Iliad by Homer, which has 643 manuscripts.* [16]

Sir Frederick Kenyon (1863 - 1952), a premier New Testament textual critic of the first half of the twentieth century, was optimistic about the general result of all of the hard work done by many scholars in their endeavors to establish the accuracy of the New Testament.

It is reassuring at the end to find that the general result of all these discoveries and all this study is to strengthen the proof of the authenticity of the Scriptures and our conviction that we have in our hands, in substantial integrity, the veritable Word of God. [17]

Scholars discovered other manuscripts after Kenyon's lifetime, but nothing emerged that challenged in a substantive way the meaning and content of the New Testament. Paul D. Wegner, Distinguished Professor of Old Testament Studies (Phoenix Seminary, USA), acknowledges:

Still, there are relatively few significant variants in the Bible, and among these variants, there is very little difference in meaning and content. [18]

While no one today possesses the original autographs of the New Testament, many extant copies do exist. Also, the work of biblical historians via the science of textual criticism provides proof of today's Bible as an accurate reflection of the work of the original writers.

Is Biblical Christianity Right?

Christians, by embracing a worldview based on Scriptural truth, may seem to non-Christians to be know-it-alls with no margin for error. Such a perception, however, is imprecise as Christians do not claim to be in possession of all truth because only God, who is omniscient, knows truth in its entirety.

Christians do not promote the idea there is absolutely no truth in non-Christian religions and other worldviews. Indeed, Christianity shares a number of common truths and upright morals with other belief systems. This is not to say that Christians, like adherents of other religions and philosophies, are sometimes not prone to venture tactlessly into areas of cultural and ideological contemplation. Foolishness and insensitivity are sometimes inescapable indiscretions, even among dedicated Christians.

While there are many other Christian doctrines, the teaching referenced below represents the cornerstone tenet of the faith, and it is for such a reason it features prominently in the author's decision to utilize Biblical Christianity as a standard against which to compare the rest of the world's major religions and philosophies, and lesser ones as well.

For what I received I passed on to you as of first importance: that Christ died for our sins according to the Scriptures, that he was buried, that he was raised on the third day according to the Scriptures. (1 Corinthians 15:3-4, NIV)

Biblical Christians believe that Jesus Christ is God, and he died for people's sins. Biblical Christians believe they are sinners through the blemish of inherent sin, a transgression committed by the first man and woman created by God (Adam and Eve), and by nature are spiritually dead. Their only hope for salvation from sin and, consequently, a place in God's kingdom for eternity is faith in Christ and acceptance of his death and resurrection. Biblical Christians are persuaded beyond any shadow of a doubt that God's Word, the Holy Bible, is the lone infallible rule of religious precept and practice.

Christians, in order to undertake practical and intelligent comparisons with other religions and philosophies, must be aware of what their own faith teaches and practice the edicts of such a faith without reservation. Biblical doctrines are not to be revised, adulterated, or stripped of their divine or supernatural corollaries. God provides confidence to the believer who opens himself or herself to what he (God) says. The apostle Paul reiterates the significance of God's involvement and the importance of the infusion of faith in the life of the Christian believer in the following scriptural passage.

> *Therefore I want you to know that no one who is speaking by the Spirit of God says, "Jesus be cursed," and no one can say, "Jesus is Lord," except by the Holy Spirit.* (1 Corinthians 12:3, NIV).

Christianity is not just a religion, philosophy, or way of life. It is a belief system with a message, or more particularly, an invitation to all who would approach Almighty God's Throne of Grace to contemplate seriously not only what they should do while here on earth but where they should choose to spend eternity, which never ends.

PART THREE

FALLING SHORT OF THE STANDARD

CHAPTER EIGHT

JUDAISM

JUDAISM - A BRIEF OVERVIEW

Jewish people are descendants of the ancient Hebrews. The term "Hebrew" is a derivative of the word "Eber," which was the name of one of the Old Testament patriarchs, Noah's grandsons (Genesis 10:21). Eber's ancestor was Shem, a son of Noah. The name "Shem" lends to the word "Semitic," which refers to a group of people that includes both Jews and Arabs. [1]

The history of the Jewish nation appears in the Old Testament, the only set of Scriptures recognized by Jews. The Old Testament includes the *Torah*, or Jewish Written Law, and consists of the five books of the Hebrew Bible that God gave to Moses on Mount Sinai. The Torah, also known as the *Chumash*, *Pentateuch,* or *Five Books of Moses*, contains all of the biblical laws of Judaism. [2]

Jews place great importance on the writings of the prophets contained in the Old Testament. The inspired sages who wrote the Old Testament underscored the enormous significance of justice, love, and humility, hoisting such virtues far above (a) the hollow ritualism of maintaining the external regulations of the Law and (b) neglecting to recognize its real intent. It is no wonder Jews around the world lead and support many charitable organizations.

The Romans destroyed Jerusalem and the Jewish Temple in A.D. 70 and left the Jews without a place to offer sacrifices for their sins, according to the Law of Moses (Deuteronomy 12). The Jews, following the devastating loss of their Temple, persistent persecution, and waves of expulsions from their own lands throughout ensuing centuries, relocated to almost every nation in the world and established communities and places of worship (synagogues) where they kept their faith alive.

The Jews are easily history's most persecuted people. Scattered all over the world, they have suffered horrendously at the hands of anti-Semites, including Arabs and Muslims, who encroached on Jewish and Christian lands in the Middle East to the point where today, the area inhabited by the people of Israel comprises less than one percent of total Middle Eastern territory. As if such greed and covetousness by Arabs and Muslims were not enough, they are hell-bent on taking even more of the minuscule portion of land on which the Jews presently live. [3]

The Nazis of Germany and its allies slaughtered more than six million Jews in the Holocaust during the Second World War (1939-1945), the worst genocide in the annals of history. The State of Israel was born in 1948 and became a homeland for Jews who immigrated from all over the world from lands to which they had to flee and/or to which subjugators banished them many years prior. In 1967, the Israelis captured all of Jerusalem, the first time they held the territory as a free people since 586 B.C.

Judaism – Its Religious Sects

Similar to most major religions, Judaism falls under several different sects. However, the branches of Judaism active today are not the same as those recounted in the Bible, so the ancient and modern eras must be viewed discretely. One should also note the term "Jewish" can refer to a religious identity, an ethnic identity, or a racial identity. However, from a religious standpoint, different sects conform to distinctive theological panoramas.

Jewish Religious Sects in the Ancient Era

Josephus, an early Jewish historian of Judea, defined four major, original sects of Judaism: *Pharisees, Sadducees, Essenes*, and *Zealots*. From a literal or unembroidered standpoint, Christianity began as a "sect" of Judaism, as well. Adherents of this later sect accept Jesus as the Messiah and are known as *Messianic Jews* (see separate sub-section). There were other, smaller groups with unique beliefs. The four mentioned by Josephus, however, were the chief divisions.

The Pharisees in New Testament times committed themselves to deep moral behavior and a scholarly approach to the Scriptures. Their stance on morality included a rigid adherence to behavioral aspects of Mosaic Law. Pharisees believed in a literal afterlife and the bodily resurrection of the dead. Christ not only criticized the Pharisees for their hollow legalism (Matthew 23:2–7) but also for distorting the commandments of God by way of their traditions (Mark 7:8–9).

The Sadducees differed significantly from the Pharisees in their theology. Sadducees did not believe in a literal afterlife or a bodily resurrection. In fact, the Sadducees' primary interest was politics, which made them useful conduits for the exercise of Roman authority. They saw the Old Testament law in a less rigid light than the Pharisees, though they adhered, in their own way, to its core concepts. The Sadducees tended to be aristocrats and were in control of the high priesthood. Annas and Caiaphas, mentioned in the New Testament (Luke 3:2), were Sadducees.

The Essenes were a monastic group. Unlike the Pharisees, Sadducees, and Zealots, the Essenes felt called to separate themselves from society in preparation for the end of the world. The Essenes, in a general sense of the term, could be considered a "doomsday sect." They felt the end times were imminent, and it was their duty to await the apocalypse patiently and passively. The Essenes produced written materials found millennia later, known as the Dead Sea Scrolls. These critically important documents show how carefully and accurately scholars preserved the Old Testament Scriptures over the centuries.

On the other side of the apocalyptic coin were the Zealots, by far the smallest of the four groups. Like the Essenes, the Zealots were something of a doomsday sect of Judaism. However, the Zealots believed their actions would directly influence when and how this apocalypse occurred. Specifically, they felt entrusted with a commission to commit acts of violence against the Roman occupiers and incite others to revolution. Theologically, Zealots were all but identical to the Pharisees, except for their fanatical, anti-Roman militancy. This view not only brought them into conflict with the Roman-friendly Sadducees, but it also accelerated Roman aggression against Jews, culminating in the destruction of the temple.

Jewish Religious Sects During the Transition Era (A.D. 70 to Early 18ᵗʰ Century)

The destruction of the temple by the Romans in A.D. 70 ushered in an era of division between the sects of Judaism existing at the time. As mentioned earlier, there have been no temples, no priests, and no sacrifices on behalf of the nation of Israel ever since the temple's demolition. Modern Judaic practice, for such a reason, is not the same as ancient Judaism. Political and religious changes over the first few centuries A.D. resulted in one particular Judaic school of thought becoming dominant, known today as Rabbinic Judaism.

The Rabbinic sect was the result of a consolidation of power within the sects of Judaism following the destruction of the temple and the Bar Kokhba revolt about 60 years later. The Bar Kokhba revolt (Mered Bar Kokhba) was a rebellion of the Jews of the Roman province of Judea, led by Simon bar Kokhba, against the Roman Empire. Fought circa 132–136 CE, [4] it was the last of three major Jewish–Roman wars, and known as The Third Jewish–Roman War or The Third Jewish Revolt.

The Rabbinic school grew out of the sect of the Pharisees, and it retained a heavy emphasis on scholars and rabbis. It taught there was a written Torah as well as an "Oral Torah," which required a tradition-based teaching authority in order to facilitate proper interpretation. In this way, Rabbinic Judaism proposed something similar to the magisterium of the Roman Catholic Church (the enmeshing of Scripture and tradition - see Chapter Nine: *Roman Catholicism*). The Rabbinic sect produced enormous

178

quantities of literature and helped define the *Halakha*, or interpretations of the Law.

As Rabbinic Judaism grew, mainline Judaism viewed Christianity less as a sect and more as a heresy. Christianity and Judaism were already growing apart in their spiritual approach prior to the Bar Kokhba revolt, and when Christ-following Jews refused to proclaim Simon Bar Kokhba as Messiah, mainline Rabbinic Jews branded them complete heretics. Christianity and Judaism effectively became completely separate theologies from then onwards. The Rabbinic period lasted until around the end of the 17th century.

Jewish Religious Sects of the Modern Era

In the early part of the 18th century, Judaism began to splinter as there emerged changes in the inter-relationships between Scriptural thought and societal norms. The resulting sects of Judaism essentially divided modern Jews into three groups: Orthodox, Conservative, and Reformed. The world's core Jewish population stood at 15.7 in September 2023., up from 15.6 million in 2022. [5]

As always with major religions, there developed numerous smaller, less influential sects of Judaism, such as Torah Judaism and Reconstructionist Judaism. The overwhelming majority of Jews in the world today are Orthodox, though Conservative and Reformed Jews are more common in the United States and certain parts of Europe.

Orthodox Jews adhere to the approach of Rabbinic Judaism, emphasizing traditional rituals, interpretations, and practices. Their core contention is that the Torah, handed down directly to Moses by God, is applicable in all ways and at all times. Most practicing Jews in the world today, except for those in the U.S. and parts of Europe, would be considered Orthodox.

The tensions between liberal-minded Reformed Jews and deeply conservative Orthodox Jews resulted in the growth of the third major sect of Judaism, referred to as *Conservative Judaism*. The practice of Conservative Judaism is significantly more common in the United States than in other parts of the world.

Messianic Judaism

Messianic Judaism is the term given to the belief system subscribed to by Jews who accept Yeshua (the Hebrew name for Jesus) of Nazareth as the promised Messiah of the Hebrew Scriptures. Messianic Jews do not stop being Jewish. They continue to remain faithful to their Jewish identity, lifestyle, and culture while following Yeshua, as revealed in the *B'rit Chadashah.*

B'rit Chadashah is the Hebrew name for the New Testament and means "New Covenant.' Like the Tanakh, the B'rit Chadashah may be divided into three main parts: Gospels/Acts (corresponding to Torah), Letters (corresponding to Ketuvim), and Revelation (corresponding to Nevi'im). [6]

Many Messianic Jews refer to themselves as "completed Jews" since they believe their faith in the God of Israel is "complete" or fulfilled in Yeshua (Jesus). In reality, Messianic Judaism began 2,000 years ago.

180

Yeshua himself was an observant Jew, most of the apostles and writers of the New Covenant were Jewish, and the vast majority of the early believers in Yeshua were also Jewish (Acts of the Apostles, chapter 2).

Traditional Rabbinical Jews do not believe Yeshua (Jesus) is the Jewish Messiah. Observant or "Torah mindful," Jews still wait faithfully for the appearance of the Messiah in accordance with the Rambam's (Rabbi Moses Maimonides, 1134-1204) teaching. *"I believe with perfect faith in the coming of the Messiah. However long it takes, I will await His coming every day."* [7] Most secular Jews do not believe in the physical coming of a personal Messiah, but some still look forward to a general Messianic milieu or Messianic Age.

Estimates today suggest there are over 2.5 million Messianic Jews in the world, and the number continues to grow. Messianic synagogues are also very popular, and recent approximations yield a tally of more than 780 congregations worldwide, including those in Israel. [8]

Messianic Jews celebrate the Jewish festivals and feast days as prescribed in the Hebrew Scriptures (i.e., Feast of Weeks, Feast of Tabernacles, etc.), but their observances are meant to demonstrate how Yeshua fulfills these Holy Days. Most Messianic Jews, if they celebrate Easter, remove the pagan influences and celebrate only what the Bible teaches, i.e., the Passover. Messianic Jews understand the declarations in the Old Testament (Old Covenant) were predictions of God's plans for humankind's future, such plans being revealed in the New Testament (New Covenant).

Jewish Customs And Laws

Orthodox Judaism

Orthodox Jews observe the teachings of three major books in relation to every facet of their lives.

1. The Torah (the Old Testament, the Jewish Written Law, the Chumash, the Pentateuch) is Judaism's most important text and consists of the first five books of the Tanakh, or the Hebrew Bible. These five books—which include the 613 commandments (mitzvot) and the Ten Commandments - also comprise the first five books of the Christian Bible. The word "Torah" means "to teach." In traditional teaching, the Torah exemplifies the revelation of God, given to Moses and written down by him. The Torah contains all of the rules by which the Jewish people structure their spiritual lives. 9

2. The *Mishnah* is about 1,000 pages in length and consists mainly of instructions for daily living known as *Halakah*, or "the way to walk." The *Mishnah* is the oral law in Judaism, as opposed to the written *Torah* or the Mosaic Law. Collected and committed to writing about AD 200, the Mishnah forms part of the *Talmud*. A midrash is a particular teaching within the Mishnah. [10]

3. The *Talmud* (compiled around AD 500) contains about 36 volumes. The Talmud proceeds from the Mishnah, with the addition of much material, including certain famous stories called the *Haggadah*. The *Talmud* is a central text of mainstream Judaism and consists

primarily of discussions and commentary on Jewish history, law (especially its practical application to life), and customs and culture. The Talmud also includes the *Gemara* or rabbinical analysis of and commentary on the Mishnah.[11] Some Orthodox Jewish laws and customs include the following.

Dietary laws. The Law of Moses forbids eating pork or shellfish (Leviticus 11:7, 10). The Law also forbids cooking a young goat in its mother's milk (Exodus 23:19). As a result, Orthodox Jews will not eat meat and dairy products together, going so far as to use separate dishes for meat and dairy foods. The Law of Moses forbids the consumption of fat or blood (Leviticus 3:17). Consequently, animals must be slaughtered in such a way so little blood stays in the flesh.

Sabbath laws. The Law of Moses calls for one to rest from work on the seventh day – the Sabbath or day of worship (Exodus 20:8-11). Orthodox Jews will not work, travel, use the phone, write, touch money, or pose for pictures on the Sabbath.

Conservative Judaism

Conservative Judaism promotes the laws of the Torah and Talmud but with certain concessions made for modern cultural preferences. Conservative Jews adopt a relatively lenient approach toward interpreting the Torah. The key interest in Conservative Judaism is the centrality of religion and the Jewish religious identity, including the preservation of the

Hebrew language. Conservative Jews maintain kosher dietary laws and the regular Sabbath but use both local and Hebrew language for liturgy. There is no gender separation during worship.

Reformed Judaism

Reformed Judaism, which emerged in Germany in the early 1800s, is by far the most theologically liberal sect. Reformed Judaism is primarily an "ethical monotheism" based on the interpretation of traditional practices rather than strict adherence to them. The belief system maintains that the principles of Judaism are more important than the practices.

Reformed Jews view concepts such as prayers in Hebrew, kosher dietary laws, and the separation of genders during worship as irrelevant or even archaic. The Scriptures, according to Reformed Judaism, are human developments subject to human interpretation and frailty. Reformed Jews, like Conservative Jews, do not regard the Scriptures as inspired or inerrant.

Common Customs and Observances

Orthodox, Conservative, and Reformed Jews all acknowledge the importance of a number of significant Jewish traditions, i.e., the observance and/or celebration of the Sabbath, the High Holy Days of Judaism (Rosh hah-SHAH-nah and Yom Kippur), and the Passover.

The Sabbath – The Jewish Sabbath begins at sundown on Friday and lasts until sundown on Saturday. As the sun sets on Friday, the woman of the house, with her family in attendance, lights the traditional candles and recites the age-old blessing: "Blessed art Thou, O Lord our God, King of the Universe, Who has sanctified us by Thy laws and commanded us to

184

kindle the Sabbath light." The man of the house then blesses the wine, everyone has a sip, and he slices the Sabbath loaf of challah bread.

Conservative and Reformed Jewish families attend a service at the synagogue after the Sabbath dinner. The main Orthodox service takes place on Saturday morning. Orthodox and Conservative Jews also attend a service on Saturday in the afternoon.

High Holy Days - Jews celebrate Rosh Hashanah (*Rosh hah-SHAH-nah*), or the Jewish New Year, in September or October of every year. The Jewish Day of Atonement, or Yom Kippur (YOME kee POOR), is observed 10 days after Rosh Hashanah. Jews participate in repentance and soul-searching during this 10-day period.

The Passover – The Jewish Passover occurs around the time when mainstream Christians celebrate Easter, i.e., late March or early April. The Passover observance in a Jewish home begins with a question from the family's youngest child: "Why is this night different from all other nights?" An older family member answers, "We were slaves to Pharaoh in Egypt. If God had not delivered our ancestors 'with a mighty hand and outstretched arm,' we would still be slaves. That is why this night is different." [12] The Jewish Passover represents an ancient ritual and celebration and encompasses everything from prayers and special foods to activities for children.

Judaism's Similarities With Christianity

Christianity and Judaism have many things in common. Both faiths share the Old Testament and its teachings. Adherents of both worldviews

185

believe in the same God – a God of holiness, justice, purity, righteousness, and unity. Christianity and Judaism both boldly proclaim, "The LORD our God, the LORD is one. Love the LORD your God with all your heart and with all your soul and with all your strength." (Deuteronomy 6:4-5, NIV). The moral and ethical teachings of the Holy Bible represent a considerable part of Jewish and Christian heritage.

Other similarities between Judaism and Christianity include the need to worship God, the importance of the family as a representation of God's decree of societal functionality, and the obligation to love other people and help those in need.

Messianic Jews, as explained earlier, worship Jesus Christ and acknowledge him as the Messiah promised in the Old Testament. Orthodox, Conservative, and Reformed Jews generally accept Christ as a great prophet and glean a lot of good from his teachings. Lamentably, this is as far as they will go!

Jesus Christ – The Source Of A Great Schism

The question as to who Jesus Christ is lies at the source of the greatest dissidence or non-conformity between Judaism and Christianity. Such dissent actually took root while Christ himself walked the earth. The Jews of that time were awaiting a Messiah (Anointed One) who would redeem them from their sins (Hebrews 2:16, 17).

Judaism, by the time of Jesus, consisted of a number of disparate structures, as intimated earlier. The Pharisees became tradition-bound and lacked the right attitude required by the laws in place. The Essenes repaired to ascetic desert communities. The Sadducees attached minimal importance to the supernatural elements of Judaic philosophy, and their sect seemed more aligned with Greek philosophy. The Zealots anticipated the arrival of a warrior-like king or deliverer who would conquer the despised Romans and restore the nation of Israel to its original glory.

Then Jesus came along – a meek, humble, and unpretentious young rabbi – and claimed to be the long-awaited Messiah, the Son of God! It is understandable the Jews thought he was an impostor and even crazy, notwithstanding the fact he was remarkably well-versed in the Holy Scriptures and performed many miracles, including raising the dead to life (John 11:41-44; Luke 7:11-17; Luke 8:40-42, 49-56). Jesus just did not satisfy the expectations of a people who longed for a deliverer who would free them from the depredations of a cruel Roman inspectorate.

The New Testament, which records Christ's life and ministry, is replete with references to Jesus as the Messiah or Christ (John 4:7-26, 39-42; Matthew 16:16; 26:63-65; Luke 24:26; John 8:28). Additionally, Christian theologians point to many Old Testament messianic prophecies fulfilled during Christ's earthly life and that helped confirm he was the promised Messiah. For instance, the Old Testament Book of Micah (Chapter 5:1-3) stated the Messiah would be born in Bethlehem. The fulfillment of this prophecy appears in the New Testament Book of Matthew (chapter 2:3-6). Isaiah (7:14) spoke about a virgin bearing a son who would be called Immanuel. The New Testament Book of Matthew (1:23) confirmed such an event. The Old Testament Book of Zechariah (9:9) prophesied the King (Messiah) would enter Jerusalem riding on a donkey. The New Testament

Book of Matthew (21:4, 5) records the fulfillment of this prophecy in what some religious scholars refer to as the Palm Sunday scriptural passage.

The Suffering Servant (Isaiah 53) Prophecy about the Messiah

Perhaps no other Old Testament prophecy or reference to the promised Messiah is as perspicuous and emphatic as the message contained in the Book of Isaiah. In chapter 49, the prophet Isaiah speaks about God's "servant," the Messiah King, who will suffer to redeem his people from their sins and help turn them to the Lord (Isaiah 49:5-26).

Chapter 53:3 of the Book of Isaiah predicts God's servant will be despised, rejected, sorrowful, and full of grief. The Gospel of John in the New Testament describes Jesus as one who came to redeem the world but whom the world, especially his own people (the Jews), rejected (John 1:10-12).

Isaiah 53, like the New Testament Book of 1 Peter, describes the redemptive ministry of the Messiah. Isaiah (53:4-6) foretells the Messiah would suffer great punishment for humankind's sins. 1 Peter (2:24, 25) recounts how the Messiah died for people's sins and says his suffering enables their obtaining salvation.

The Prophet Isaiah prophesies how the Messiah would die and provides the following startling details.

He was oppressed and afflicted,

Yet he did not open his mouth;

188

He was led like a lamb to the slaughter,

And as a sheep before its shearers is silent,

So he did not open his mouth.

By oppression and judgment, he was taken away.

Yet, who of his generation protested?

For he was cut off from the land of the living;

For the transgression of my people, he was punished.

He was assigned a grave with the wicked,

And with the rich in his death,

Though he had done no violence,

Nor was any deceit in his mouth.

(Isaiah 53:7-9, NIV)

The New Testament Gospel of Matthew (Matthew 27:57-60) and Gospel of Luke (Luke 23:32, 33) record how Jesus fulfilled every detail of the prophecy enunciated in Isaiah 53.

Old Testament Prophecy about Christ's Resurrection

The Old Testament, in addition to imparting prophecies about Christ's appearance as the Messiah, his work, ministry, trial, and crucifixion, contains an extraordinary prediction about the Galilean's triumphant resurrection. In the Book of Psalms, it reads: "For You will not give me over

189

to the grave. And You will not allow Your Holy One to return to dust (decay)." (Psalm 16:10, NLV)

The apostle Peter, when he taught the first sermon of the Early Church on the Day of Pentecost, quoted the above prophecy (Acts of the Apostles 2:27-31). Many people, including Jesus' disciples, saw the risen Lord and realized the prophecy was fulfilled. They called to mind what Jesus himself told them after his resurrection:

This is what I told you while I was still with you: Everything must be fulfilled that is written about me in the Law of Moses, the Prophets, and the Psalms...This is what is written: The Messiah will suffer and rise from the dead on the third day, and repentance and forgiveness of sins will be preached in his name to all nations, beginning at Jerusalem. (Luke 24: 44, 46, 47, NIV)

Judaism Falls Short Of The Criteria For Christian Conviction

Judaism, although in many ways the forerunner religion of the Christian faith, which derives from Old Testament theology, falls short of the standards of Christianity from a number of major perspectives.

Teaching about God – Jews believe the Lord God is one (Deuteronomy 6:4). Christians believe there is one essence of the Godhead in which reside three persons: Father, Son, and Holy Spirit, coequally and coeternally God (Matthew 3:13-17; 28:19; 2 Corinthians 13:14).

Teaching about Jesus Christ – While there are Jews who consider Jesus Christ a knowledgeable teacher or even a prophet, they reject him as the

Messiah and/or the Son of God. Christians believe Jesus is God as well as man, and he gave his life on the Cross to redeem all people from sin (Mark 10:45; John 1:13, 14; 1 Peter 2:24).

Teaching about sin – Jews believe man is not born good or evil but born free to choose between the two conditions or mindsets. Christians subscribe to the belief everyone is born in sin and falls short of God's standards (Romans 3:10, 23; 5:12).

Teaching about salvation – Judaic philosophy promotes the idea that anyone, Jew or Gentile, may obtain salvation through a commitment to the one true God and through living a moral life. Christians believe an individual attains salvation through faith and acceptance of Christ's atoning death on the cross (Romans 3:24; Ephesians 2:8, 9).

It is meet to remember *Messianic Jews* are akin to biblical Christians in that they acknowledge and believe Jesus Christ is the promised Messiah, Redeemer, and Savior. As such, Messianic Judaism falls within the precincts of biblical or mainstream Christianity.

In the final analysis, Orthodox, Conservative, and Reformed Jews, and other Jews affiliated with incidental Judaic worldviews, and who do not accept Jesus Christ as Savior and the only means to everlasting life in a paradisial location called Heaven, remain unsaved. Jews and Gentiles who are unsaved face an eternity of unmitigated suffering and torment in a place called hell.

CHAPTER NINE

ROMAN CATHOLICISM

MARTIN LUTHER AND THE PROTESTANT REFORMATION

In 1517, in the town of Wittenberg in East Germany, a professor of theology, composer, priest, and monk [1] named Martin Luther initiated a schism in the Catholic Church that gave rise to what religious scholars refer to as the Protestant Reformation. Luther ordained a priest in 1507 and came to reject several teachings and practices of the Roman Catholic Church. In particular, he disputed the view on indulgences. Luther proposed an academic discussion of the practice and efficacy of indulgences in his *Ninety-five Theses*, a work he produced in 1517. His refusal to renounce all of his writings at the demand of Pope Leo X in 1520 and the Holy Roman Emperor Charles V at the *Diet of Worms* in 1521 resulted in his excommunication by the Pope and condemnation as an outlaw by the Holy Roman Emperor.

The Diet of Worms was an imperial diet (a formal deliberative assembly)of the Holy Roman Empire called by Emperor Charles V and conducted in the Imperial Free City of Worms. Martin Luther was summoned to the diet in order to renounce or reaffirm his views in response to a Papal bull of Pope Leo X.

192

Luther taught that salvation and, consequently, eternal life are not earned by good deeds but are received only as the free gift of God's grace through the believer's faith in Jesus Christ as Savior and Redeemer. His theology challenged the authority and office of the Pope by claiming the Bible is the only source of divinely revealed knowledge, [2] and opposed sacerdotalism by deeming all baptized Christians to be members of a holy priesthood. [3] *Sacerdotalism* considers priests as essential mediators between God and man. Catholic, Orthodox, and Anglican forms of worship are sacerdotal. Sacerdotalism teaches that the priesthood is a special class of churchmen and is a necessary part of worship. People cannot approach God on their own but must seek him through a priest, whether it is for confessing sin, taking communion, or receiving grace.

Luther's translation of the Bible into the German vernacular (instead of Latin) made it more accessible to the laity, an event that had a tremendous impact on both the church and German culture. It fostered the development of a standard version of the German language, added several principles to the art of translation, and influenced the writing of an English translation, the Tyndale Bible.[4] Luther's hymns influenced the development of singing in Protestant churches. [5] His marriage to Katharina von Bora, a former nun, set a model for the practice of clerical marriage, allowing Protestant clergy to marry.[6]

In two of his later works, Luther expressed antagonistic views towards Jews.[7] In 1523, Luther proclaimed Jesus Christ was born a Jew, which discouraged mistreatment of the Jews and advocated their conversion by proving the Old Testament could be shown to speak of Jesus Christ. However, as the Reformation grew, Luther began to lose hope in large-scale Jewish conversion to Christianity, and in later years, as his health deteriorated, he grew more acerbic toward the Jews, writing against them with the kind of venom he had previously unleashed on the Anabaptists, Zwingli, and the pope. He directed his hateful rhetoric not at Jews alone but also towards Roman Catholics, Anabaptists, and nontrinitarian Christians.[8] Luther died in 1546.

Martin Luther raised 95 points of disagreement with the doctrines of the Roman Catholic Church. His complaints resulted in the emergence of the Protestant Church or Protestantism. The Protestant churches that grew out of the Reformation remain as vibrant and committed to the Christian Gospel today as they did at the outset. Roman Catholicism, also, is as strong as ever.

Background Of The Roman Catholic Church

The Catholic Church is a "Communion of Churches, both Roman, and Eastern, or Oriental, which is in full communion with the Bishop of Rome (the pope)."[9] The Church is also known as the *People of God*, the *Body of Christ*, and the "*Temple of the Holy Spirit*," among other names.[10] According to Vatican II's *Gaudium et spes*, the "church has but one sole purpose - that the kingdom of God may come and the salvation of the human race may be accomplished."[11]

The Communion of Churches comprises the *Latin Church* (or the Roman or Western Church) as well as 23 *Eastern Catholic Churches*, canonically called *sui juris churches*, each led by either a Patriarch or a Major Archbishop in full communion with the *Holy See* (the government or jurisdiction of the Catholic Church in Rome). "The Holy See," also called the See of Rome, is the apostolic episcopal see of the bishop of Rome, known as the Pope, ex-cathedra, the universal ecclesiastical jurisdiction of the worldwide Catholic Church, and a sovereign entity of international law. Founded in the 1st century by Saints Peter and Paul, by virtue of Petrine and Papal primacy according to Catholic tradition, it is the focal point of full communion for Catholic bishops and Catholics around the world organized in polities of the Latin Church, the 23 Eastern Catholic Churches, and their dioceses and religious institutes.

The Roman Catholic Church reports a worldwide membership of about 1.39 billion adherents as of 2022. [12] There are about 75.1 million Catholics in the U.S.A., i.e., approximately 23 percent of the country's population.

The Roman Catholic Church has assumed a significant role in world affairs for centuries and today remains an important player on the international political, social, and religious platforms. Leaders of nations continue to dispatch ambassadors to the Vatican in Rome in relation to various national and global concerns, just as they do to prominent governmental administrations around the world.

The Vatican (effectively the Roman Catholic Church) exercised considerable political influence in Western Europe during the Middle Ages. The Church's universities and monasteries assumed the status of recognized and reputable institutions of learning. During the 16th and 17th centuries, Catholic missionaries traveled to Asia, Africa, and the New World - the majority of Earth's Western Hemisphere, specifically the Americas, including nearby islands such as those of the Caribbean, and Bermuda and Oceania) and spread Western culture extensively.

The Catholic Church also wielded noteworthy influence in the areas of art, painting, sculpture, and music. Among famous Catholic painters and artists were Caravaggio, Benvenuto Cellini, Michelangelo, Raphael, Peter Paul Rubens and Leonardo da Vinci. Catholic sculpture is evident in many of the great cathedrals that exist today, such as the Notre Dame Cathedral in Paris, France, the Saint Patrick's Cathedral in Manhattan, New York, USA, and the Cathedral Basilica of the Sacred Heart in New Jersey, USA. Additionally, the Catholic Church became actively involved in the operation of schools, colleges, hospitals, orphanages, and homes for the aged and infirm around the globe. There is much for which the world should commend the Catholic Church.

Why, then, do mainstream or biblical Christians find themselves at loggerheads with practitioners of the Catholic faith? Why does there exist so much disagreement between the philosophies when Catholicism and Protestantism represent the two main offshoots of Christendom?

It is meet to mention mainstream Christians do not disagree en masse with Catholic ideology and tradition. There exist fundamental, affirmed Catholic teachings that are in agreement with biblical doctrines, such as belief in the Trinity of the Father, Son, and Holy Spirit; the deity of Jesus

Christ; the Virgin Birth of Jesus; the sinlessness of Christ; Jesus' atoning sacrifice on the cross, and his resurrection.

The problem with Catholicism lies in the worldview's tradition of adding to the Holy Scriptures over the years, sometimes obfuscating biblical truth and even distorting the message of Christ's Gospel. The Catholic Church has heaped various doctrines, rituals, and traditions on top of God's Word over hundreds of years, so adherents of the faith are no longer capable of recognizing true biblical precepts and instruction.

Catholicism's Unbiblical Traditions

Some major Catholic traditions and teachings with which mainstream Christianity finds itself at odds are as follows.

1. The belief the Apostle Peter was the first Pope, around whom the Christian Church developed.

2. The doctrine of purgatory after death whereby one's sins may be purged.

3. The practice of praying to the Virgin Mary and deceased saints on one's behalf.

4. The practice of kneeling before and praying to images.

5. Confession of one's sins to a priest for the absolution of one's sins.

6. The belief the Mass and sacraments are requirements for salvation.

7. The doctrine that salvation is obtainable only through the Roman Catholic Church.

8. Transubstantiation & The Eucharist of the Mass – the teaching that the bread and wine literally become the body and blood of Christ when taken during Communion.

9. Penance and the selling of indulgences.

10. The veneration and worship of Mary.

11. The canonization of dead saints.

12. The celibacy of priests.

13. The practice of praying the Rosary

14. The use of "Holy" water.

The Catholic Church incorporated the forgoing traditions into its praxes over many years, ultimately transforming them into institutional dogma in the mid-16th century. At the Council of Trent, the 19th ecumenical council of the Catholic Church, which was held between 1545 and 1563 in Trent in northern Italy, [13] church leaders issued condemnations of what it defined to be heresies committed by proponents of Protestantism and also issued key statements and clarifications of the Church's doctrine and teachings, including scripture, the Biblical canon, sacred tradition, original sin, justification, salvation, the sacraments, the Mass, and the veneration of saints.[14] It was at the Council of Trent where the Roman Catholic Church announced its official position that tradition was equal in authority with God's Word, the Holy Bible.

The decision at the Council of Trent ecumenical meeting to equate tradition with God's Word in relation to divine authority granted the

Catholic Church leeway to include traditions in the organization's catalog of doctrines as it saw suitable. One of the most contentious Catholic teachings from the perspective of biblical Christians revolves around Mary, the earthly mother of Jesus. Catholic tradition promotes ideas such as (a) Mary's immaculate conception, (b) her being born without original sin, (c) her living a sinless life, and (d) her not dying but being lifted up to heaven. Roman Catholics believe Mary truly became the Mother of God and the Mother of the Church.

The Error Of Adding Tradition To God's Holy Word

The Catholic Church presumes its right to add traditions to scriptural teaching derives from papal authority or the presumed sovereignty and infallible character of the Pope, who they claim is God's representative on earth. Of a truth, Jesus Christ himself cautioned the religious leaders of his day about additions and modifications to his teachings. The changes the Catholic Church made to Biblical doctrine and the traditions it merged with biblical Christianity over the centuries reflect the kind of aberrations the founder of the faith denounced.

In the Gospel of Mark, Jesus imparted sound advice about placing tradition ahead of adherence to scriptural teaching and thereby trivializing true biblical instruction. The Pharisees and other Jews were slaves to man-made ceremonies and enjoyed making a show of rituals in order to garner praise from onlookers.

The Pharisees and some of the teachers of the law who had come from Jerusalem gathered around Jesus and saw some of his disciples eating food with hands that were defiled, that is, unwashed. (The Pharisees and all the Jews do not eat unless they give their hands a ceremonial washing, holding to the tradition of the elders. When they come from the marketplace they do not eat unless they wash. And they observe many other traditions, such as the washing of cups, pitchers, and kettles.)

So the Pharisees and teachers of the law asked Jesus, "Why don't your disciples live according to the tradition of the elders instead of eating their food with defiled hands?"

He replied, "Isaiah was right when he prophesied about you hypocrites, as it is written:

These people honor me with their lips,

but their hearts are far from me.

They worship me in vain;

their teachings are merely human rules.

You have let go of the commands of God and are holding on to human traditions."

And he continued, "You have a fine way of setting aside the commands of God in

order to observe your own traditions!"

...Thus you nullify the word of God by your tradition that you have handed down. And you do many things like that."

(Mark, 7:1-9, 13, NIV)

Jesus admonished the religious leaders of his day for their hypocrisy in trying to appear righteous through relatively meaningless traditions. He questioned their real intentions and accused them of invalidating God's Word by their actions, which, in effect, confounded people and hindered them from becoming acquainted with the truth of the scriptures.

There is nothing iniquitous about religious tradition that characterizes or mirrors biblical doctrine. However, traditions contradictory to God's Word run afoul of true religious expression and warrant stern denouncement. Mainstream or Protestant Christians acknowledge the Bible as the standard of their faith and consider the scriptures sufficient for all aspects of religious edification. Roman Catholics do not consider the Bible the sole source of education and enlightenment in relation to their faith but combine tradition with the scriptures to provide the worldview's overall teachings and doctrines. As a matter of fact, in many instances, Catholic traditions and dogmas supersede biblical scripture as the final authority for Roman Catholic believers.

Scripture Alone Vs Scripture Plus Tradition

One of Protestantism's major beliefs revolves around the unparalleled importance of the Bible or the Holy Scriptures as the sole authority upon which to determine Christian doctrine and base its practice. The *sola scriptura* or "Scripture alone" aphorism controverts the Roman Catholic practice of combining the scriptures or the teachings of the Bible with so-called "Sacred Catholic traditions" to determine what religious principles the Christian faith should follow. The Catholic Church, as mentioned earlier in this chapter, enacted legislation at its ecumenical meeting at the Council of Trent (1545 -1563) to retain the right and power to interpret the Holy Scriptures according to what it believed the Bible says.[15] Essentially, the Catholic Church claims doctrines and traditions developed by the church over the years are as spiritually authoritative as the canons contained in the Bible itself.

The term *Sola scriptura* refers to the acknowledgment that the Bible, and the Bible alone, satisfies all the requirements of spiritual authority. The Holy Scriptures, which proceed from inspiration by God, clearly and unequivocally contain everything the Christian believer needs to know, believe, and practice. The foregoing notwithstanding, the Holy Bible is not a catch-all for knowledge about everything. It is not meant to be. While unlike the texts of other religions and belief systems, the Bible is unique in its accurate references to history, science, medicine, and archaeological substantiation, it is essentially a book of divine pertinence. The primary, indispensable dispatch of the Holy Scriptures revolves around humankind's redemption from sin and the method of obtaining God's grace toward such an end.

A requirement to be privy to everything Jesus did, especially his actions and omissions that did not impact his ministry in a consequential manner is more or less extraneous, even though Roman Catholic apologists allude to

John 21:25 in an attempt to justify complementing the scriptures by adding to a closed biblical canon.

Jesus did many other things as well. If every one of them were written down, I suppose that the whole world would not have room for the books that would be written. (John 21:25, NIV)

The fact the Bible refers only in passing to the multitudinous activities of Christ certainly does not mean the scriptures are incomplete. The following statement declares an unequivocal, uncluttered truth.

If you declare with your mouth, "Jesus is Lord," and believe in your heart that God raised him from the dead, you will be saved. (Romans 10:9, NIV)

Knowledge of everything that Jesus did during his earthly ministry is not a requirement for obtaining salvation or redemption from one's sins.

Looking at the issue from another perspective, it behooves the enquiring student of comparative religion to recognize an element of possible exaggeration in the Apostle John's words about the number of books required to accommodate stories about Christ. John's statement is likely a well-meaning estimation rooted in overwhelming adoration for the mesmerizing founder of the Christian faith. Further, it should be noted there are possible semantical plays on the terms "whole world" and "room for the books that would be written." The world around the time of Christ was remotely similar in size to the modern world, and the number of written/published books at the time was infinitesimally small in comparison to what one would expect to be the tally today.

Contrary to the belief by some people, *sola scriptura* does not mean one can entertain idiosyncratic beliefs and interpret the Bible to conform to such ideas. The Christian Church is under commission to broadcast the truth but must, however, remain compliant with biblical veracity. The Protestant believer must trust his church only to the extent it remains sincere to the teachings of the Bible.

Additionally, adherence to the *sola scriptura* principle does not preclude acknowledgment of the fact early Christian sages communicated the Word of God by word of mouth. It is obvious disseminators of Christ's gospel circulated news orally during the initial 20 or 30 years of the Church's existence. This period of verbal transmission preceded the production of the Apostle Paul's letters to the various churches and before the actual authoring of any of the Gospels.

Roman Catholics argue the Holy Bible is primarily an "institutional book" because the Church produced or at least decided what should comprise the New Testament. Evangelical Protestants counter such a superficial classification with the rejoinder that the Church ascertained what texts should make up the New Testament as the Holy Spirit revealed which writings were inspired and trustworthy.

Also, the nascent Christian Church always had the advantage of being able to reference the Old Testament, which foreran the New Testament and pointed to God's new covenant with humankind. New Testament writers often quoted from the Old Testament as they worked under the guidance of the Holy Spirit, [16] as attested to by the following biblical extract.

Above all, you must understand that no prophecy of Scripture came about by the prophet's own interpretation of things. For prophecy never had its origin in the human will, but prophets, though human, spoke from God as they were carried along by the Holy Spirit. (2 Peter 1:20,21, NIV)

Interpreting The Holy Scriptures

The Catholic *Dei Verbum* document contains the following statement about the interpretation of Scripture, "All that has been said about the manner of interpreting Scripture is ultimately subject to the judgment of the Church which exercises the divinely conferred commission and ministry of watching over and interpreting the Word of God." [17] While the Catholic Church encourages believers to read the Bible, it dissuades them from trying to interpret it for themselves, as the extract from the *Dei Verbum* decree stipulates.

Evangelical Protestants, however, place heavy importance on the work of the Holy Spirit as it guides them in discerning what God tells them through the Scriptures. Believers should search the Bible themselves for edification and direction. The Gospel of John confirms the expediency of the forgoing convention.

But when he, the Spirit of truth, comes, he will guide you into all the truth. He will not speak on his own; he will speak only what he hears, and he will tell you what is yet to come. (John 16:13, NIV)

The Roman Catholic Church is adamant about its position as the only accurate and authoritative source of the Holy Scriptures. Such doggedness proceeds from Christ's statement in Matthew 16:18, 19 (NIV), which follows the Apostle Peter's answer to his master's inquiry, "Who do you say I am?" Peter tells Jesus that he (Jesus) is the Christ, the son of the Living God. Jesus responds to Peter and says only God could have revealed such truth to him and then utters the following declaration.

> *And I tell you that you are Peter, and on this rock I will build my church, and the gates of Hades will not overcome it. I will give you the keys of the kingdom of heaven; whatever you bind on earth will be bound in heaven, and whatever you loose on earth will be loosed in heaven.* (Matthew 16:18-19, NIV)

Peter – The Church's Foundation?

The *Catechism of the Catholic Church* contends Jesus made Peter the "rock" of his Church, handed him the keys, and appointed him shepherd of the entire flock of believers. Specifically, the creed reads, *"This pastoral office of Peter and the other apostles belongs to the Church's very foundation and is continued by the bishops under the primacy of the Pope, who, as Vicar of Christ and as pastor of the entire Church has full, supreme and universal power over the whole Church, a power which he can always exercise unhindered."* [18]

Evangelical Christians disagree with the Catholic Church's interpretation of Matthew 16:18, 19 and point out Jesus did not actually say he would build his Church upon Peter, but upon "this rock." The Greek (original) text unambiguously refers to Peter as *Petros*, which means "a small stone," and to "this rock" as *petra*, which translates into "a very large

Gibraltar-size rock." Many of the early Church fathers were of the opinion the rock to which Christ alluded in Matthew 16:18, 19 referred to Peter's *confession of faith* and not the apostle himself. [19]

Catholics are amiss in postulating Jesus intended to make Peter the foundation on which the Christian Church would be built. The Scriptures unambiguously identify Christ, and no one else, as the Church's foundation and provide the following declarations to such an effect.

For no one can lay any foundation other than the one already laid, which is Jesus Christ. (1 Corinthians 3:11, NIV)

Consequently, you are no longer foreigners and strangers but fellow citizens with God's people and also members of his household (the Church), built on the foundation of the apostles and prophets, with Christ Jesus himself as the chief cornerstone. (Ephesians 2: 19-20, NIV)

Peter, although the notional leader of the group of apostles who undertook to spread Christ's Gospel, never considered himself remotely close to an authoritative figure such as a pope or church leader. He was more like an elder who exhorted his fellow elders to *"be shepherds of God's flock"*(1 Peter 5:2, NIV).

There certainly exists no conclusive evidence of the Roman Catholic Church's claims about Peter's ascendancy to a foundational status relative to Christ's church on earth. Catholic leaders, in their zeal to have Scripture conform to their assessment of religious tenets, combined subjective traditions with biblical teachings to produce what they wished were true.

Catholics view couched religious doctrines such as the Immaculate Conception, the bodily assumption of Mary, and papal infallibility as Scriptural truth even though they are not. The fact that such doctrines may be markedly conjectural does not prevent or dissuade Catholic theologians from incorporating them into their worldview's ideology.

Apostolic Succession

The doctrine of apostolic succession is the belief Christ's twelve apostles passed on their authority, wisdom, and powers to successors, the latter who then passed on such influence and qualities to their successors, such repetition continuing through the centuries up to the present time. The Roman Catholic Church combined the idea of Peter as the leader of the apostles with the concept he later became the first bishop of Rome, to construct the peripheral doctrine that Roman bishops who followed Peter were *ipso facto* the delegated leaders of the Church. Additionally, apostolic succession, combined with Peter's implicit seniority among the apostles, resulted in the Roman bishop being the supreme authority of the Catholic Church, i.e., the Pope.

Nowhere in the Scriptures does it say Jesus, the apostles, or any other New Testament writer proposed the idea of "apostolic succession." Further, Peter never assumed the role of absolute supremacy over the other apostles. The apostle Paul, in fact, rebuked Peter for leading others astray and said:

> *When Cephas came to Antioch, I opposed him to his face because he stood condemned. For before certain men came from James, he used to eat with the Gentiles. But when they arrived, he began to draw back and separate himself from the Gentiles because he was afraid of those*

208

who belonged to the circumcision group. The other Jews joined him in his hypocrisy so that by their hypocrisy, even Barnabas was led astray.

When I saw that they were not acting in line with the truth of the gospel, I said to Cephas in front of them all, "You are a Jew, yet you live like a Gentile and not like a Jew. How is it, then, that you force Gentiles to follow Jewish customs? (Galatians2:11-14, NIV).

Peter no doubt had a prominent role in the lives of the apostles. Perhaps he was the putative leader of the apostles, although the book of Acts records the apostle Paul and Jesus' brother James as also having prominent leadership roles. Peter was not the commander-in-chief or supreme authority over the other apostles. Even if the tradition of apostolic succession could be demonstrated from Scripture, which it cannot, the apostolic succession would not necessarily result in Peter's successors being superior to the successors of the other apostles.

Catholics point to Matthias being chosen to replace Judas as the twelfth apostle in Acts chapter 1 as an example of apostolic succession. While Matthias did indeed "succeed" Judas as an apostle, this is in no sense an argument for continuing apostolic succession. Matthias being chosen to replace Judas is only an argument for the church replacing ungodly and unfaithful leaders (such as Judas) with godly and faithful leaders (such as Matthias). Nowhere in the New Testament is any of the twelve apostles recorded as passing on his apostolic authority to a successor. Christ ordained the original apostles, not their so-called successors, to build the foundation of the church.

The foundation of the church originates from the New Testament – the record of the deeds and teachings of the apostles, the latter derived from the auspices of God's leading through the Holy Spirit. The church never needed apostolic successors who would occupy positions of authority and supplement the Scriptures with man-made traditions. Christianity's canon is closed. The church thrives on biblical doctrines accurately recorded and preserved, and God has already provided such enablement through his Holy Word.

The doctrine of apostolic succession is not biblical. The concept of apostolic succession cannot be found in Scripture. The genuine church follows what the Scriptures teach and compares all doctrines and practices to Scripture in order to determine what is true and right. The Roman Catholic Church alleges that a lack of ongoing apostolic authority results in doctrinal confusion and chaos. Such a charge is unfortunate and disingenuous. The apostles of yore warned about false teachers arising and taking it upon themselves to deceive the world. Sadly, Catholic leaders figure among those who would mislead others.

> But there were also false prophets among the people, just as there will be false teachers among you. They will secretly introduce destructive heresies, even denying the sovereign Lord who bought them—bringing swift destruction on themselves. (2 Peter 2:1, NIV)

Of a truth, the lack of definitive authority among non-Catholic churches results in many different interpretations of the Bible. However, the differences in construal are not the result of the Scripture being unclear or nebulous. Rather, they are the result of even non-Catholic Christians

210

persisting with the disreputable tradition of interpreting Scripture in accordance with their own misrepresentative leanings. If people prayerfully study the Bible in its entirety and in its proper context, they will easily determine the truth. Doctrinal differences and denominational conflicts are a result of some Christians refusing to agree with what Scripture says, not a consequence of there being no "supreme authority" to interpret Scripture.

Alignment and conformity with scriptural teaching, not apostolic succession, are the principal factors in determining the authenticity of a church. The Word of God is the guide the church should follow (Acts 20:32). The Scriptures are infallible and represent the measuring standard for religious teaching and practice (2 Timothy 3:16-17) and form the criteria with which to compare doctrines and traditions (Acts 17:10-12). Apostolic authority persisted through the writings of the apostles, not through apostolic succession and the musings of posterior, probably unrepresentative religious personnel.

Salvation Through Faith Or Faith & Works?

Protestants, in addition to considering *sola scriptura* (the Bible alone) as the means of final scriptural authority and truth, rely on *sola fide* (faith alone) as the sole means of salvation. Catholics, on the other hand, believe one must obtain salvation through faith plus "good works" and God's grace facilitated through the Seven Sacraments, which are as follows:

1. *Baptism* (Matthew 28:19) for infants and adults – Baptism imparts sanctifying grace and erases original sin. The Catholic believer

maintains sanctifying grace only through "spiritual battle" by following a program of "good works." [20]

2. *Confirmation* (John 14:26) is the completion of baptism, the giving of the Holy Spirit in a deeper outpouring. Baptized children are confirmed at age 12.

3. *The Holy Eucharist* (Matthew 26:26-28; John 6:35-38) is also called Holy Communion and is the most important sacrament of the Catholic Church. During Mass, it is claimed Christ is represented as an unbloody sacrifice for sin through the miracle of transubstantiation.

4. *Penance* (confession or reconciliation, John 20:19-23) is a means whereby a Catholic believer is forgiven by God – through the ministry of a priest – for the sins he or she commits after baptism.

5. *Anointing of the Sick* (James 5:14, 15) (formerly *Extreme Unction*). In performing this sacrament, the priest lays hands on the sick or dying believer, prays over him or her in the faith of the Church, and anoints the believer with oil, sometimes blessed by the bishop. [21]

6. *Holy Orders* (1 Timothy 3:1; 2 Timothy 1:6; Titus 2:15) refers to the ordaining of Catholic ministers at three levels, i.e., bishops, presbyters (priests), and deacons. Only bishops may confer the Sacrament of Holy Orders. [22]

7. *Matrimony* (Genesis 2:18, 21-25; Ephesians 5:22, 33) refers to the sacrament in which Christ joins a Christian man and woman in a grace-giving, lifelong union or relationship. Divorce and remarriage proscribe the Catholic adherent from partaking in Eucharistic communion but not from the Church.

The Holy Eucharist & Penance – Major Doctrinal Departures From Biblical Christianity

The sacraments of *The Holy Eucharist* and *Penance* represent two of the most significant doctrinal differences between Catholicism and Protestantism.

The Holy Eucharist - Roman Catholics believe when a priest consecrates the bread and wine during the Mass, such elements, through the miraculous process of *transubstantiation*, become the actual body and blood of Christ.[23]

According to the Catechism, the Eucharist is not only a memorial of Christ's Passover but also a sacrifice in which he gives participants the very body he relinquished for humankind on the cross and the very blood he poured out for the forgiveness of sins. The Catechism of the Catholic Church actually states... *"The Eucharist is thus a sacrifice because it re-presents (makes present) the sacrifice of the cross...in this divine sacrifice, which is celebrated in the mass, the same Christ Who offered Himself once in a bloody manner on the altar of the cross is contained and is offered in an unbloody manner.*[24] Use of the term "unbloody manner" supposedly denotes Christ does not actually suffer or die again, only that the sacrament re-presents his selfless act of sacrifice so the Catholic believer can be a part of the event.

Evangelical Protestants see no rationale or justification for repeatedly re-presenting Christ's sacrifice. There is no need for believers to become part of Jesus' atoning death on the cross, which was a one and only offering of himself to enable humankind to become righteous by choice through acceptance of his gift of eternal life. Representing Christ's sacrifice over and over again through the celebration of the Mass is, in actuality, a contradiction of the Christian Gospel. The following extracts from the New Testament Book of Hebrews help confirm the futility and meaninglessness of practices like the Holy Eucharist.

> *Just as people are destined to die once, and after that to face judgment, so Christ was sacrificed once to take away the sins of many; and he will appear a second time, not to bear sin, but to bring salvation to those who are waiting for him.* (Hebrews 9:27,28, NIV)

> *Then he said, "Here I am, I have come to do your will." He sets aside the first to establish the second. And by that will, we have been made holy through the sacrifice of the body of Jesus Christ once for all.* (Hebrews 10:9, NIV)

> *Day after day every priest stands and performs his religious duties; again and again he offers the same sacrifices, which can never take away sins. But when this priest had offered for all time one sacrifice for sins, he sat down at the right hand of God, and since that time he waits for his enemies to be made his footstool. For by one sacrifice he*

has made perfect forever those who are being made holy. (Hebrews 10:11-14, NIV)

Penance (confession or reconciliation) - Penance or confession is another key sacrament for Catholics as it revolves around acts of atonement or mollification the believer must perform in order to receive forgiveness for his or her sins.

Catholics differentiate between "mortal" and "venial" sin. A mortal sin is supposedly a grave offense committed with "full knowledge and deliberate consent" and leads to the loss of sanctifying grace.

Sanctifying grace, in Catholicism, is a permanent disposition that perfects the soul itself to enable it to live with God and to act by his love. Sanctifying grace is the grace of salvation and must be maintained. Those dying in sanctifying grace go either to purgatory or directly to heaven. Sanctifying grace is also known as justifying grace or habitual grace. [25]

Mortal sin must be confessed and forgiven (under ministerial jurisdiction), or the transgression "causes exclusion from Christ's kingdom and the eternal death of hell." [26] Mortal sins allegedly include adultery, fornication, lying, stealing, drunkenness, blasphemy, lustful or hateful thoughts, and neglecting the duty to family, job, country, and the underprivileged. [27]

A venial, or easily forgiven sin, is a much less serious transgression than a mortal sin, and although it can weaken a believer's faith and moral fortitude, it does result in the loss of sanctifying grace. [28] Among venial sins are white lies, overeating, immoderate consumption of alcohol, and driving too fast. Catholics must confess venial as well as mortal sins, including venial sins inclined to grow in number and be left unaddressed. The *Catechism* warns the believer about the cumulative effect of venial sin and says, "Deliberate and unrepented venial sin disposes us little by little to commit mortal sin." [29]

The contrite Catholic believer's sin may be absolved after he or she confesses to a priest. However, to remedy all the taint one's sin causes, he or she must undertake to make amends or "do penance." The priest or confessor assigns a penance commensurate with the gravity of the sin committed. [30] Acts of penance may take the form of repeating certain prayers, engaging in self-discipline such as fasting, and carrying out prescribed "works of love," which could be anything from a kind word to listening to someone patiently.

Protestants, while they agree the forgoing deeds and attitudes are commendable, do not believe they represent a means of securing salvation. Salvation is a gift of grace and cannot be earned, even though good works may help evidence a saved condition. Protestants also recognize the importance of Christian believers confessing their sins and faults to one another (James 5:16) and helping each other grow spiritually. However, the teaching that one believer (a priest) is capable of absolving another believer's sin is a stark contradiction of the biblical premise. An individual's relationship with God cannot be arbitrated by a priest or anyone else since, as the Bible declares, "...there is one God and one mediator between God and mankind, the man Christ Jesus." (1 Timothy 2:5, NIV)

216

Justification & Sanctification

Catholics, although they acknowledge Christ's blood "has become the instrument of atonement for the sins of all men,"[31] nevertheless maintain faith in what Christ did on the cross in and of itself is not enough.[32] Catholicism says faith in Christ is the beginning of salvation and lays the foundation for justification. The believer must endeavor to supplement his or her faith with good works because "man has to merit God's grace of justification and eternal salvation."[33] Catholics believe good works help infuse righteousness into them, facilitate the eradication of their sins, and enable their souls to merit heaven.[34]

Protestants define justification differently from Catholics. They articulate being justified does not mean one has to be made righteous and holy but is already declared righteous and holy through faith in Christ, even though a sinful nature still exists. Christ's atoning sacrifice on the cross imputes righteousness to Christians, i.e., those who accept him as Lord and Savior. *The Biblical Dictionary of Theology* states, "The righteous work of Christ manifested in his death on the Cross is reckoned to the account of the believer as a gift of righteousness apart from human merit or works."[35]

Protestants subscribe to the idea they enter the process of sanctification after being fully justified by faith, the latter which occurs upon their accepting Christ as Lord and Savior. Sanctification, therefore, begins the moment one becomes saved or washed by regeneration and renewed in the Holy Spirit (Titus 3:5). Sanctification, according to the majority of

Protestants, is a process that continues throughout a Christian's life [36] as he or she attends to living according to God's will.

> *Therefore, my dear friends, as you have always obeyed—not only in my presence, but now much more in my absence—continue to work out your salvation with fear and trembling, for it is God who works in you to will and to act in order to fulfill his good purpose.* (Philippians 2:12-13, NIV)

In summary, while "good works" are essential in the lives of Roman Catholics and Protestants alike, adherents of the two denominations view justification and sanctification differently. Protestants believe they are fully justified through faith in Christ immediately upon accepting him as their Redeemer, and their saved condition predisposes them toward the performance of good works as they grow in the Christian life according to God's plan (Ephesians 2:8-10). Catholics, on the other hand, do not believe faith alone provides justification, and they must work toward justification all their lives. In effect, Catholics combine justification and sanctification into one process.

The Catholic Doctrine Of Purgatory

The *Catechism of the Catholic Church*, paragraph 1030, contains the following statement about *purgatory*, a paradoxical state of joy and suffering in which the departed Catholic believer's soul undergoes preparation for final suitability for heaven. "All who die in God's grace and friendship, but still imperfectly purified, are indeed assured of their eternal salvation, but after death they undergo purification, so as to achieve the holiness necessary to enter the joy of heaven." [37] As the soul submits to the burning, purifying love of God, it sheds itself of immature self-love, and "real self then emerges, perfected, totally absorbed in God." [38]

Further, the Catholic Encyclopedia refers to purgatory as "a place or condition of temporal punishment for those who, departing this life in God's grace, are not entirely free from venial faults, or have not fully paid the satisfaction due to their transgressions." In other words, Catholic theology describes purgatory as a place where a Christian's soul goes after death to be cleansed of the sins for which full atonement was not made during life.

The doctrine of a purgatorial or an expiatory experience is totally at odds with biblical scholarship. Christ died to pay the penalty for all of humankind's sins. The Scriptures clearly say, "But God demonstrates his own love for us in this: While we were still sinners, Christ died for us" (Romans 5:8, NIV), and "He was pierced for our transgressions, He was crushed for our iniquities; the punishment that brought us peace was upon Him, and by His wounds we are healed." (Isaiah 53:5, NIV)

Jesus suffered on the cross for people's sins so they could be delivered from having to atone for their transgressions. While people who sin are to seek forgiveness and make amends as far as it is possible, i.e., physical restitution, change of attitude, and even possible incarceration, forgiveness and cleansing of sin are supernatural acts that only God can perform. To say people must suffer in a similar manner as Christ did for their sins is to say that Jesus' suffering was insufficient. To say people must atone for their sins by being cleansed in Purgatory is to deny the adequacy of the atoning sacrifice of Jesus (1 John 2:2). The very idea that people have the opportunity after death somehow to make amends for transgressions committed during their earthly lives is intemperately contradictory to what the Bible teaches about salvation.

Catholics point to the following biblical passage from 1 Corinthians as evidence of the state of purgatory.

If anyone builds on this foundation using gold, silver, costly stones, wood, hay or straw, their work will be shown for what it is, because the Day will bring it to light. It will be revealed with fire, and the fire will test the quality of each person's work. If what has been built survives, the builder will receive a reward. If it is burned up, the builder will suffer loss but yet will be saved—even though only as one escaping through the flames. (1 Corinthians 3:12-15, NIV)

The passage in 1 Corinthians 3 refers to an illustration of the works of a believer being judged. If his or her works are of good quality, i.e., "gold, silver, costly stones," he or she will pass through the fire unharmed and will be rewarded for such works. If a believer's works are of poor quality, "wood, hay, and straw," such works will be consumed by the fire, and he or she will receive no reward. The passage does not say a believer passes through the fire, but rather a believer's works pass through the fire, and refers to the believer "escaping through the flames," not "being cleansed by the flames." (1 Corinthians 3:15 NIV)

Purgatory, like many other Catholic dogmas, proceeds from a misunderstanding of the nature of Christ's sacrifice. Catholics view the Mass/Eucharist as a re-presentation of Christ's sacrifice because they fail to

220

understand Jesus' once-for-all sacrifice was absolutely and perfectly sufficient (Hebrews 7:27). The Catholic view of meritorious works being contributory to salvation is due to a failure to recognize Jesus' sacrificial payment has no need of additional "contribution" (Ephesians 2:8-9).

The very idea of Purgatory and its attendant practices, i.e., prayers for the dead, indulgences (see below), and praiseworthy works on behalf of the dead, among others, fail to recognize Jesus' death was enough to pay the penalty for ALL of the people's sins. Jesus, who was God incarnate (John 1:1, 14), paid an infinite price for humankind's transgressions. He died for people's sins (1 Corinthians 15:3), and is the atoning sacrifice for their sins (1 John 2:2). To limit Jesus' sacrifice to atoning for original sin or sins committed before salvation is an attack on the Person and Work of Jesus Christ. If an individual, in order to be saved, must pay for, atone for, or suffer because of his or her sins, then Jesus' death was not a perfect, complete, and appropriate sacrifice.

The Bible clearly states after death, believers will be "away from the body and at home with the Lord." (2 Corinthians 5:6-8, NIV) See also Philippians 1:23. It does not say believers will be "away from the body, in Purgatory with the cleansing fire." This is so because Jesus' flawless sacrifice enables God's children to be ushered in immediately into the Lord's presence after death - fully cleansed, free from sin, glorified, perfected, and ultimately sanctified.

Indulgences – Lessening The Time Spent In Purgatory

An *Indulgence*, according to the Catechism of the Catholic Church, is "the remission before God of the *temporal* punishment due to sin whose guilt has already been forgiven." A properly disposed Catholic, therefore, can obtain an indulgence under prescribed conditions through the help of the Church, which, as the minister of redemption, dispenses and applies with authority the treasury of the satisfactions of Christ and the saints. An indulgence is partial if it removes part of the temporal punishment due to sin or plenary if it removes all punishment. Only the Pope can grant a plenary indulgence. Bishops, archbishops, and cardinals may effect only partial indulgences.

Catholic believers already in purgatory, the Catechism teaches, cannot help themselves, but believers on Earth can do so on their behalf and help them obtain heaven faster by praying for them, offering Mass for them, and performing good works, which includes gaining indulgences. Believers who seek indulgences generally wish to shorten their own or someone else's time in purgatory. [39]

According to the *Catechism*, the Church utilizes the authority purportedly conferred on the apostle Peter to bind and lose sins (Matthew 16:19) and intervenes on behalf of individual Christians by opening a "treasury" of the merits of Christ and the saints (the spiritual treasury of the Church). In essence, indulgences relate to God's "indulging" or being compassionate to a believer by availing an inexhaustible supply of spiritual merits accumulated in the Church's treasury through the work of Christ and the prayers and good works of the Virgin Mary and the saints. [40] The merits or indulgences are then used to cover or remove the temporal punishment for venial or mortal sins for which the believer did not finish making amends before death.

Are Catholics Saved Or Assured Of Salvation?

The question, "Are Catholics saved or assured of salvation?" cannot be answered with a universal "yes" or "no." In the same way, neither can the questions "Are Baptists saved?" or "Are Presbyterians saved?" or "Are Methodists saved?" be answered from a unanimous standpoint. One is not saved by being Catholic, Baptist, Presbyterian, or Methodist. Salvation is by grace alone, through faith alone, in Christ alone. Jesus himself says, "I am the way and the truth and the life. No one comes to the Father except through me." (John 14:6, NIV). See also Ephesians 2:8-9. It is probably safe to assume there is no denomination or grouping of the Christian faith in which every member is a true or faultless adherent of the Christian Gospel.

Further, there are an estimated 1.4 billion Roman Catholics in the world. Among those 1.4 billion adherents, there is a significant amount of latitude in beliefs and practices. Roman Catholics in the United States do not have identical beliefs and practices as Roman Catholics in Italy. Catholics in Latin America are not perfectly analogous in precept and practice with Catholics in Africa. While the Roman Catholic hierarchy advances the notion all Roman Catholics hold to the same beliefs and observe the same practices, in reality, this is untrue. Such diversity within Catholicism is another reason why the question "Are Catholics saved?" cannot be answered unequivocally.

Should the question about Catholics and salvation assume a more clearly delineated form than a general inquiry if Catholics are saved, then the answer may be more definitive. For instance, were one to ask, "Are Catholics who adhere to official Roman Catholic beliefs and practices saved?" the answer would be "No!" The answer is "no" because the official teaching of Roman Catholicism is salvation is not by faith alone, or through grace alone, or in Christ alone. The Roman Catholic Church insists one must perform good works and observe the rituals of Roman Catholicism in order to be saved.

A summary of the official Roman Catholic position on the requirements for a believer to obtain salvation is as follows:

1. One must receive Christ as Savior by faith.

2. One must be baptized in the Trinitarian formula, i.e., in the name of the Father, Son, and Holy Spirit.

3. One must be infused with additional grace by observing the Catholic sacraments, especially the Eucharist (Mass).

4. One must die without any unconfessed mortal sins.

If one accomplishes the above, Catholic scholarship posits, he or she will be saved and granted entrance into heaven, likely after an extensive time of further cleansing in purgatory.

Notwithstanding the Roman Catholic Church's claim that its jurisdictional ascendancy derives directly from the apostle Peter's, and imputedly the apostle Paul's commission from Jesus Christ to head the universal Christian Church, Catholic doctrine towards the attainment of salvation, i.e., taking the forgoing four requirements as a whole, is significantly different from the apostle Paul's teaching on the all-important subject. Paul exhorted his audiences to "Believe in the Lord Jesus, and you will be saved" (Acts 16:31, NIV).

Furthermore, John 3:16 ascribes salvation to everyone who believes in Christ. The Book of Ephesians explicitly teaches that salvation is not by works.

For it is by grace you have been saved, through faith—and this is not from yourselves, it is the gift of God— not by works, so that no one can boast. (Ephesians 2:8-9, NIV)

Ephesians then clarifies the fact that good works do not result in salvation but result from salvation.

For we are God's handiwork, created in Christ Jesus to do good works, which God prepared in advance for us to do (Ephesians 2:10, NIV)

It is important to remember not all Catholics hold to the Roman Catholic understanding of salvation. There are Catholics who truly and fully believe salvation is by grace alone and through faith alone. There are Catholics who observe the sacraments as an aspect of spiritual growth and intimacy with God, not as an attempt to earn salvation. Many Catholics believe in the biblical doctrine of salvation and do not understand or recognize the marked dissimilarities between the teachings of the Roman Catholic Church and the authentic Christian Gospel.

Are Catholics saved? Do Catholics go to heaven? It depends. If the question is "Are there saved Catholics?" then the answer is "Yes." If the question is, "Will a person go to heaven if he or she holds fast to the official Roman Catholic doctrine of salvation?" then the answer is "No."

In the final analysis, the official Roman Catholic doctrine and comprehension about salvation unto eternal life fall short of or outside the precincts of biblical Christianity.

CHAPTER TEN

EASTERN ORTHODOXY

Eastern Orthodoxy or Orthodox Christianity, surprisingly is not much understood by Christian Protestants, including evangelical Christians. Many students of comparative religion consider Orthodox Christians similar to Roman Catholics but without the appurtenances of papal governance.

While Eastern Orthodoxy, or *Orthodoxy* (termed sans "Eastern" because the worldview today is prevalent in the West and also remains widespread in the East) does share a fair number of similarities with Roman Catholicism, there are some major differences. Also, contrary to popular thinking, Orthodoxy is not represented today by a single, main Orthodox Church. The Orthodox branch of Christianity detached itself from the church in Rome in 1054 following the *East-West Schism* triggered by disputes over doctrine and the authority of the Pope.

There are at least 13 autocephalous or independent, self-governing Orthodox Christian churches, including the four ancient patriarchates still existing in the Middle East – Constantinople, Alexandria, Antioch, and Jerusalem. Nine other autocephalous Orthodox churches can be found in Russia, Siberia, Romania, Georgia, Cyprus, Greece, Poland, and Albania. In addition, Orthodox churches exist throughout the world – particularly in Western Europe, North and South America, and Australia. Baptized

Orthodox believers around the world number approximately 200 – 260 million.[1] The mean estimate is around 190 million.

The Orthodox Church at Constantinople, while it enjoys a certain measure of honor deriving from historical relevance, exercises no power or influence in the internal affairs of the other Orthodox churches.[2]

Eastern Orthodox Christianity – The Visible, True Church?

The Orthodox Church rejects the Roman Catholic Church's claim to be the one true Church. The well-known contemporary Eastern Orthodox hierarch and theologian Kallistos Ware (born Timothy Richard Ware) writes, *"Orthodoxy, believing that the Church on Earth has remained and must remain visibly one, naturally also believes itself to be that one visible church."* [3] Ware contends the Orthodox Church guards and teaches the true belief about God, glorifying him with right worship as it preserves the original apostolic faith.

Orthodoxy alleges the Eastern Church preserved the faith, staying true to the decisions of the first seven General (Ecumenical) Councils of the Church, held between 325 and 787. The seven ecumenical councils include the following: the First Council of Nicaea in 325, the First Council of Constantinople in 381, the Council of Ephesus in 431, the Council of Chalcedon in 451, the Second Council of Constantinople in 553, the Third Council of Constantinople from 680–681 and finally, the Second Council of Nicaea in 787. The meetings represented an attempt by Church leaders to reach an orthodox consensus, restore peace, and develop a unified Christendom.

The Western Church (Rome), Orthodox Christians say, embraced heretical beliefs and practices via the development of the papacy and claims to unencumbered primacy or dominion over all other churches. A crucial issue of contention, Orthodoxy asserts, is the Western or Catholic Church's adoption of the *filioque* doctrine, which it included in the Nicene Creed without any input from the Church's General Council. [4]

The filioque is a Latin term that deals with the church controversy concerning the phrase "and from the Son," which was intended to indicate the *Holy Spirit* proceeds from both the Father and the Son (double procession) and not from the Father alone. The controversy contributed to the split between the Eastern and Western churches in A.D. 1054. The Eastern Church, or the Orthodox Church, rejected the filioque and maintained that the Holy Spirit proceeds from the Father alone, whereas the Western church, the Roman Catholic Church, accepts the filioque. [5]

Orthodoxy & Apostolic Succession

Orthodox Christians, like Roman Catholics, assign considerable meaning to the doctrine of apostolic succession. However, they view the role of bishops from a different perspective. While Catholicism claims bishops continue the work of the apostle Peter, or the first pope, and today's pope enjoys sovereignty as the leader of the Church, Orthodoxy does not place the pope in an office of unquestioned supremacy, even though it views the apostle Peter and the incumbent or serving pope as possessing a certain measure of preeminence. All bishops, nevertheless, along with the pope, "share equally in apostolic succession." [6]

Evangelical Protestants, as emphasized elsewhere in this book, do not subscribe to the Catholic or Orthodox doctrine of apostolic succession. They reject the suggestion such activity ever took place. While Protestants acknowledge the very foundation of the Church proceeds from "the apostles and the prophets, with Christ Jesus himself as the chief cornerstone" (Ephesians 2:20, NIV), they view the work of the apostles as unique and their powers and authority as untransferable. The New Testament, with Jesus as the architect of the Christian Gospel, resulted from the work of the biblical prophets and the Lord's apostles. The biblical canon closed thereafter without the necessity of any addition or deletion. The communication of God's message of salvation unto eternal life to humankind was complete.

Scholars and theologians would later be free, of course, to research and study God's Word, the Holy Bible, and present their objective or subjective opinions to the world at large, but not to continue the work of the apostles and prophets as inheritors of any kind of ascendant authority. Religious scholars and leaders are incapable of doing so anyway. The doctrine of apostolic succession is a null and void proposition and is in stark contradiction to proper Christian comportment.

The power and authority of Peter and the rest of Christ's apostles, born of divine conferment, never passed to anyone. Nowhere do the Scriptures intimate such a transition occurred. The "apostolic age" ended around the end of the first century with the death of John, the last apostle. Although it is true Christ's apostles appointed religious leaders to oversee local congregations as the nascent Church grew leaps and bounds after Christ's departure, they did not possess the wherewithal to transform such leaders into apostles or endow them with any kind of extraordinary ability. Only God could do such a thing, and no biblical evidence says he did. Pastors, bishops, and deacons only had authority inasmuch as they stayed true to the tenets of the Gospel as proclaimed by the original apostles. [7]

Orthodoxy & The Addition Of Tradition To Scripture

Orthodox Christians, unlike Protestants, consider the Church as wielding the ultimate authority in interpreting Scripture. Protestants believe only the Scriptures are authoritative, and all believers possess the right and responsibility to research and study God's Holy Word for themselves rather than rely on the Church to determine dogmatically what the Scriptures mean.

Protestants elevate God's Holy Word above all else, including the Church, as the ultimate authority in connection with the Christian faith. Orthodox believers regard the Church as superior to the Scriptures in establishing institutional doctrine and tradition, the latter oftentimes derived from the spiritual eccentricities of religious leaders. They contend Scripture is just a part of a larger convention representing a comprehensive whole, i.e., the "fullness of the Christian faith." Orthodoxy resembles Catholicism in this regard.

Unlike Protestants, whose criteria for religious and/or spiritual truth pivots on the Holy Scriptures (*sola scriptura*), and unlike Catholics, who deem the pope or papal authority the conclusive definition of sacred uprightness, Orthodox Christians point to an "internal norm" for determining spiritual authority, i.e., the Spirit of God living within the Church. [8] Orthodoxy sees the work of the Holy Spirit in the Church, or Christian Tradition, as being inclusive of accessing and using the following texts, i.e., the Holy Bible, the Nicene/Constantinopolitan Creed, the Decrees of the Seven Ecumenical Councils, the writings of the Fathers, the canons of the Church, the service (liturgical) books, and holy icons.

Timothy Ware makes the following controversial statement about Orthodoxy's view of the Holy Bible's authority - *"The Bible is not something set up over the Church; it is something that lives and is understood within the Church"* [9] A troubling explication of Ware's subjective interpretation is the Bible gets its authority from the Church, and not the other way around.

Orthodox scholars submit the Church existed and flourished prior to the production of any of the New Testament books. Also, because the Church initially decided which books would comprise the Holy Scriptures, only the Church may interpret them with authority. [10] The statement that the Church existed and thrived before the New Testament books were written is a presumption mired in partisanship. The Christian Church, from a perspective of inclusiveness, became complete and ratified only after Christ's crucifixion, resurrection and the conferring of the Holy Spirit at

232

Pentecost. The New Testament records details of this New Covenant, which promised God would forgive sin and have a close, unbroken relationship with his people. The promise was first made to Israel and then extended to everyone who comes to Jesus Christ in faith. (See Jeremiah 31:31-34; Matthew 26:28; and Hebrews 9:15). Previous biblical pacts between God and humankind, like the Adamic, Abrahamic, Palestinian, Mosaic, and Davidic covenants, formed only part of an as yet unfinished agreement.

Protestants differ sharply from Orthodox Christians and Roman Catholics as well in their view of the authority of the Holy Bible. To such an end, John Calvin, the French Protestant theologian, pastor, and reformer in Geneva during the Protestant Reformation, declared *the Word of God (the Holy Bible) gave birth to the Church.* [11] The following biblical extracts from the Book of 2 Timothy and the Book of 2 Peter lend ample credence to the Bible's superiority over the Church as the prevailing source of authority. Such influence proceeds from the inspired (God-breathed) writings of men who acted under the inspectorate of the Holy Spirit.

All Scripture is God-breathed and is useful for teaching, rebuking, correcting and training in righteousness... (2 Timothy 3:16, NIV)

> *Above all, you must understand that no prophecy of Scripture came about by the prophet's own interpretation of things. For prophecy never had its origin in the human will, but prophets, though human, spoke from God as they were carried along by the Holy Spirit.* (Peter 1;20, NIV)

John Calvin was a principal figure in the development of the system of Christian theology, later called Calvinism, aspects of which include the doctrines of the absolute sovereignty of God in the salvation of the human soul from death and eternal damnation.

It is rather simplistic, as Orthodox and Catholic scholars are wont to do, to suggest the Church "decided" which books would encompass the Holy Scriptures. The Church labored for about 200 years under spiritual direction to determine which writings possessed "divine authority" and belonged to the canon of Scripture that became today's Holy Bible.

No church created the canon, but the churches and councils gradually accepted the list of books recognized by believers everywhere as inspired. It was actually not until 367 AD when the church father Athanasius first provided the complete listing of the 66 books that belonged to the biblical canon. [12]

Orthodoxy Versus Reformation

Orthodox believers decry the Reformers' "mistake" of dividing and separating the "organic whole" of Scripture and tradition. Reformers (Protestants) say Scripture transcends the Church and does not require the Church's sanction or confirmation but speaks directly to a believer's heart and mind. Orthodox theologian Georgi Florovsky rejects such thinking and considers the Reformation mindset a sin because it encourages the subjective interpretation of Scripture. [13]

Orthodox and Roman Catholic theologians complain about perceived problems surrounding scriptural interpretation caused by a superfluity of

Protestant denominations that freely interpret the Bible under the supposed guidance of the Holy Spirit.

It is not incorrect to say that Protestant churches do differ on certain religious doctrines. However, the practice of interpreting the scriptures prayerfully for oneself is by no means a fatalistic undertaking. As Bible scholar Don Fairbairn ruminates, "Evangelicals have never affirmed that all interpretations of Scripture are equally valid." Fairbairn notes evangelical Protestants observe definite rules as to what constitutes a correct interpretation of the Bible and emphasizes:

> ...(Protestant) insistence on the responsibility of individual believers to seek truth in the Bible themselves serves as a check on potential misuses of the Scriptures by a person or a group of people. If a group proclaims a false interpretation, other Christians who have access to the Bible (which is an understatement - author's emphasis) can recognize the error and correct it. [14]

In retrospect, the so-called "weakness" of Protestantism, i.e., its diversity and multiple denominations, is actually a great strength - simply because no one church, pope, or council should wield total or unencumbered jurisdiction over the interpretation of Scripture.

Orthodoxy & The Seven Sacraments

Orthodox Christians observe the same seven sacraments commemorated by Roman Catholics, with certain deviations with respect to the interpretation of and emphasis on some of the practices. Orthodoxy considers *baptism* and *the Eucharist* the two most important sacraments.

Baptism marks the beginning of the Orthodox believer's life in the Church. The sacrament, administered to infants and adults, is supposedly a "bath of regeneration" that cleanses an individual of original and actual sins and enables him or her to be born again.

The *Eucharist* or *Divine Liturgy* is central to all Orthodox precepts and practices and deemed "the center of the life of the Church and the principal means of spiritual development, both for the individual Christian and the Church as a whole." [15] Orthodoxy believes the very body and blood of Christ are present in the bread and wine served during the Eucharist. However, they desist from using the term "transubstantiation" (as Catholics do) to refer to the changing of the elements into the body and blood of Christ and instead conclude the transformation, while, a fact, is beyond human elucidation.

The Orthodox see the Eucharist as a conciliatory sacrifice "offered on behalf of both the living and the dead." [16] Timothy Ware says the Eucharist is not a new sacrifice or a repetition of the sacrifice on Calvary because the Lamb (Christ) was sacrificed only once and for all time. Instead, during the Eucharist, the events of Christ's sacrifice – The Last Supper, Crucifixion, and Resurrection – are made present even though they are not repeated. [17] Such an intimation is distinctly problematic for many people and escapes inborn rationality, notwithstanding the possible inference of divine concomitance.

The Orthodox Church addresses the issue of sins committed after baptism through the sacrament of confession or repentance. Confession, however, does not take place in an enclosed area with a grill separating the confessor and the attending priest. It is done in the open, often in a room set apart for such activity. The parties do not face one another but stand or sit side by side in order to underscore the idea the priest is not the judge, but God himself is. The priest often offers advice to the penitent individual after listening to his or her confession and may occasionally assign a penance, but such a course of action is not imperative and is often forgone. [18]

Orthodoxy holds fast to the doctrine of *theosis,* i.e., going through the process of deification to attain salvation. Consequently, there is no emphasis on making amends for temporal punishments or chastisement, as in Roman Catholicism. Indulgences are also unnecessary and need not be invoked to compensate for sins on behalf of anyone living or dead.

Orthodox believers pray for the departed, but not because they think their souls are in purgatory. Orthodoxy teaches that the souls of people who have died are in a place of rest that is unlike a purgatorial state where there is ongoing punishment or cleansing. Souls in the restful location envisaged by Orthodox believers do not have to undergo any kind of purification in order to enter heaven but are being strengthened by the prayers offered by the faithful still on earth as they are being prepared for their appearance before Christ on Judgement Day.

Orthodox Practice Of Praying To Saints And Icons

Orthodox Christians pray to the saints, especially Mary because these individuals allegedly have achieved deification. Additionally, Orthodoxy insists the saints, including Mary, are not mediators but intercessors, and praying to them does not amount to worship but veneration.

The terminology utilized in the forgoing observations about Orthodox practices gives rise to some measure of semantic disquiet, even before one attempts to address attendant theological ramifications. The term *deification*, for instance, harbors three connotations, i.e., (a) the condition of being treated like a god, (b) an embodiment of the qualities of a god, and (c) the elevation of a person (as to the status of a god).[19] What this means is Orthodox Christians, contrary to their denial, revere saints and Mary as gods. Also, a *mediator* is one who acts as a link between parties, as is an *intercessor*.[20] There is actually no difference between the two functions. Consequently, the Orthodox claim that Mary and the saints are intercessors and not mediators, and praying to them does not constitute worship but veneration, is a perplexing submission, if not willful misdirection.

Orthodoxy considers Mary as the saint most completely deified. The Orthodox Church venerates her as *Theotokos* (mother of God) in keeping with a decision taken at the Third General Council at Ephesus in A.D. 431. The Orthodox Church, like the Roman Catholic Church, shares the doctrine about Mary's perpetual virginity but rejects the teaching about her immaculate conception.

Orthodox scholars believe there is evidence for an early and strong tradition concerning the *Assumption of Mary* into heaven (often shortened to *the Assumption*), but they do not think the subject is as important or on par with such doctrines as the Trinity and Christ's virgin birth. The

238

Assumption of Mary, according to the beliefs of the Catholic Church, and Eastern and Oriental Orthodoxy as well, [21] is the bodily taking up of the Virgin Mary into Heaven at the end of her earthly life.

Orthodox tradition includes the wide use of icons or colorful, stylized paintings of Jesus, the apostles, and Mary and other saints, which adorn the walls of many Orthodox churches. The iconostasis (plural - iconostases) is a wall of icons and religious paintings, separating the nave from the sanctuary in a church. The nave is the central part of a church, typically extending from the narthex to the chancel and flanked by aisles. Orthodox believers are known to prostrate themselves in front of the icons, kiss them, and burn candles before them. Protestants, of course, view the forgoing activities as constituting idol worship or idolatry, a practice expressly forbidden by God and articulated as such in the Scriptures in no uncertain manner. Orthodox believers voice their disagreement with the allegation of idolatry by proposing the befuddling and derisible contention that the veneration exhibited by the worshiper is not toward the icons or pictures but toward the individuals therein.

Another puzzling assertion by the Orthodox Church in relation to icons is they serve the purpose of religious edification. Those who might be ignorant of the teachings of the Orthodox Christian faith or those who cannot avail themselves of the time to study may visit a church and see on its walls all they need to know and understand the faith.[22] A confounding presumption allied to such a doctrine is Orthodox Christians consider icons a source of revelation equal to the Bible.

Revisiting the issue of praying to Mary and the saints, there is absolutely no scriptural basis to pray to anyone other than God alone. No one in heaven can mediate on people's behalf except Jesus Christ. Only God can hear and answer the prayers of believers. The temple veil was torn in two (Hebrews 10:19–20) after Jesus died on the cross. In a sense, the veil was symbolic of Christ himself as the only way to the Father (John 14:6). The splitting of the temple veil availed the believer on earth just as much access to God's throne of grace, in Jesus' name, as anyone in heaven (Hebrews 4:16).

The Bible nowhere instructs believers in Christ to pray to anyone other than God. The Bible nowhere encourages or even mentions believers asking individuals in heaven for their prayers. No saint can take Jesus' place. The Bible says, "For there is one God and one mediator between God and men, the man Christ Jesus." (1 Timothy 2:5, NIV). There is no one else who can mediate with God for Christians. Since Jesus is the only mediator, Mary and the saints cannot be mediators or intercessors. Further, the Bible says Jesus Christ himself intercedes for believers before the Father. The book of Hebrews states, "Therefore He is able to save completely those who come to God through Him because He always lives to intercede for them?" (Hebrews 7:25, NIV).

Romans 8:26–27 says the Holy Spirit also intercedes for believers. Why then, even if it were possible to do so, would anyone petition Mary and the saints to approach God's Throne of Grace on his or her behalf when the second and third Persons of the Trinity, i.e., the Redeemer Jesus Christ and the Holy Spirit, already perform such functions?

Orthodoxy Emphasizes Deification Above Justification

The Orthodox idea about sin and salvation differs from the Protestant and Catholic views to a great extent. Humankind, Orthodoxy says, while its members fell into sin through the *fall* in the Garden of Eden, does not wallow in a totally corrupt, sinful nature. Humans did not inherit guilt through Adam and Eve, but instead inherited death, mortality and corruption.[23] Further, Orthodox Christians do not share the view God created humankind in communion and fellowship with himself but instead assigns to his creation the task of achieving such a status. Adam and Eve's sin in Eden and the sinful nature and deeds of people after them represent a "departure from a path" and not a plummet from a state of blessedness. [24]

Orthodox adherents, unlike Protestants, do not consider Christ's crucifixion on the cross as his suffering God's wrath as a substitute for sinners but as only a victory over sin and death. Protestants believe acceptance of Jesus' atoning sacrifice at Calvary fully restores humankind's fellowship with God. Orthodox, on the other hand, see Jesus' death on the cross and God's grace as the means to enable humankind to "become god, to obtain *theosis* ('deification' or 'divination')." [25] Orthodox scholars point to 2 Peter as a source of the concept of *theosis*:

> *Through these he has given us his very great and precious promises,*
> *so that through them you may participate in the divine nature, having*

escaped the corruption in the world caused by evil desires. (2 Peter 1:4, NIV)

Orthodox theologians presume the concept of *theosis* also appears in other passages of Scripture such as Psalm 82:6, Ephesians 4:24; 5:1, 1 John 3:2). Even cursory, hurried analyses of these Scriptural references negate or put to naught, the Orthodox notion of *theosis* (deification) or man becoming god.

The Orthodox Church, in its defense, claims *theosis* is not similar to *pantheism*, i.e., the belief that God is everything and everyone, and everyone and everything is God. Christians might become "gods," but they still possess a human nature. To be deified is to become a partaker of the divine nature, but one does not become a divine being. [26] Yet, as mentioned previously, the Orthodox Church says believers pray to Mary and the saints because they have achieved *deification*, which, as the earlier foray into semantics revealed, relates to (a) the condition of being treated like a god (b) an embodiment of the qualities of a god and (c) the elevation of a person (as to the status of a god). In effect, then, Orthodoxy says Mary and the saints to whom people pray are divine beings or gods and not just "partakers of a divine nature." The truth is Mary, and the saints to whom believers pray are simply the souls of departed believers. They are incapable of responding to such petitions.

Protestants say the Orthodox doctrine of "deification towards salvation" ignores the doctrine of justification by faith. Theologian Donald Fairbairn says, "Most elements of the Orthodox understanding of salvation actually pertain to sanctification." [27] Further, Fairbairn inspects 2 Peter 1:4, the scriptural passage Orthodox scholars identify as a source of the *theosis* premise, and points out the words that occur in the middle of a passage about sanctification. He says 2 Peter 1:3 mentions beforehand God's divine power, which enables believers everywhere to live godly lives through their knowledge of Christ Himself. Christians, because of the precious promises of salvation they have already received, can 'participate in the divine nature' and escape the world's corruption.

Believers, after being justified by faith in Jesus Christ, add various qualities to their stature as Christians that help expedite the process of sanctification, which is a lifelong undertaking. The following scriptural passage lists the objectives in such a regard.

> *For this very reason, make every effort to add to your faith goodness; and to goodness, knowledge; and to knowledge, self-control; and to self-control, perseverance; and to perseverance, godliness; and to godliness, mutual affection; and to mutual affection, love.* (2 Peter1:5-7, NIV)

Christians become more effective and productive by acquiring these qualities, more so because they are already recipients of salvation through trusting Christ as their Savior.

Donald Fairbairn laments the fact Orthodox believers neglect to emphasize salvation is a free gift facilitated through God's grace. Such an omission results in a failure to "distinguish between justification as God's free acceptance of unworthy sinners *and* sanctification as the process of becoming righteous, a process that involves human activity and effort." [28]

Amidst Differences - Jesus Christ, The Central Figure

While there exist a number of significant differences between Eastern Orthodoxy and Protestantism, there are also some telling commonalities. For instance, evangelical Protestantism and Orthodoxy share a belligerent defense of the fundamental truths of Christianity. Both Churches rally together in the face of liberalism, secularism, and modernism in their many guises. Protestant scholar Daniel Clendenin lends credence to the forgoing observation when he says, "Fidelity and an unwavering loyalty to the apostolic faith characterize eastern Christianity." [29]

Admittedly, the Orthodox "sin of the Reformation" grievance against Protestantism - whereby the latter elevates Scripture over and above the Church and tradition - remains a real bone of contention between the two major factions of the worldview. However, this does not mean Orthodoxy robotically ostracizes Protestant believers and/or relegates them to a no-man's land where they might be unable to obtain salvation unto eternal life. Orthodox bishop and theologian Timothy Ware contends it is incorrect to assume those who are not Orthodox can't possibly belong to the Church. Ware says, "Many people may be members of the church who are not visibly so...Invisible bonds may exist despite an outward separation." [30] Clive Staples Lewis, the renowned British writer and lay theologian, ruminated, "At the center of differing Christian viewpoints...there is something or a Someone, who against all divergences of belief...speaks with the same voice." [31]

The three main branches of Christendom, i.e., Biblical Christianity (Protestantism), Roman Catholicism, and Eastern Orthodoxy, although they persist in embracing certain doctrines they consider non-negotiable, appear to hold fast to one indisputable, unchallengeable tenet of Christianity, i.e., Jesus Christ is at the center of the faith. He is the Lord of the universe, who died and rose again to life three days later, *according to the Scriptures.*

Christ's invitation is open to all who put their faith directly in him alone:

All those the Father gives me will come to me, and whoever comes to me, I will never drive away. (John 6:37, NIV)

Are Orthodox Believers Saved Or Assured Of Salvation?

Orthodox doctrine suggests humankind did not fall from perfect fellowship with God but departed from the path for attaining perfect fellowship and inherited mortality and corruption, but not Adam and Eve's guilt. [32] Protestants say humans degenerated from a perfect state with God and inherited Adam and Eve's guilt (Romans 5:12-21). The Orthodox Church claims believers attain salvation through the process of *theosis*, whereby believers become deified (like God). Protestants, on the other hand, say justification comes through faith in Jesus Christ (Romans 3:24; Ephesians 2:8, 9). The Christian then becomes sanctified by walking with Christ (Ephesians 2:10; 2 Peter 1:3-11).

As in the case of Roman Catholics, who insist one must perform good works and observe the rituals of Roman Catholicism in order to be saved, Eastern Orthodox devotees who believe salvation comes through the process of *theosis* are not saved. Salvation is by grace alone, through faith alone, in Christ alone. John 3:16 ascribes salvation to everyone who believes in Christ. Ephesians 2:8–9 (NIV) explicitly teaches that salvation is not by works so that no one can boast. Ephesians 2:10 (NIV) explains and clarifies the fact good works do not result in salvation, but result from salvation.

As it is with Roman Catholics, one needs to realize not all Orthodox Christians may hold fast to their Church's understanding of salvation. Surely, there are Orthodox believers who firmly believe salvation is by grace alone, through faith alone. Many Orthodox Christians follow the biblical doctrine of salvation and do not realize the official teaching of the Orthodox Church about the issue differs diametrically from what the Bible actually teaches.

The author repeats the questions fielded in the final sub-section of the chapter on Roman Catholicism and answers them accordingly: Are Eastern Orthodox Christians saved? Do Orthodox believers go to heaven? It depends on the attendant circumstances. If the question is "Are there saved Orthodox Christians?" then the answer is "Yes." If the question is, "Will a person go to heaven if he or she holds fast to the official Eastern Orthodox doctrine of salvation?" then the answer is "No."

In the final analysis, the official Orthodox doctrine and understanding of salvation, like the formal Roman Catholic creed relating to the subject, falls short of or outside the boundaries of biblical Christianity.

246

PART FOUR

CHRISTIANITY COMPARED
WITH MAJOR RELIGIONS & PHILOSOPHIES

CHAPTER ELEVEN

CHRISTIANITY COMPARED WITH MAJOR RELIGIONS & PHILOSOPHIES – ATHEISM

No two religions or philosophies are the same. It is true that sometimes there exist moral commonalities in various belief systems, but generally, there are certain considerations that differentiate worldviews from salient supernal and/or spiritual perspectives. Consequently, choosing to endorse or support one religion or philosophy, by default, culls or rejects other worldviews.

The forgoing observation notwithstanding, it is not sufficient to jettison alternate belief systems summarily because they differ from a particular worldview. One ought to be prepared to compare and contrast the multitudinous aspects or components of dissimilar belief systems and present a compelling case for his or her own choice of a religious worldview.

The presence of faith, while undoubtedly essential for living the Christian life, finds a valuable parallel in a tendency to advocate for the Gospel. The Book of Jude of the New Testament clarifies such an idea.

Beloved, while I was very diligent to write to you concerning our common salvation, I found it necessary to write to you exhorting you *to **contend earnestly for the faith** which was once for all delivered to the saints* (emphasis author's). (Jude 1:3, NKJV)

In the immediate and subsequent ten chapters, the author researches and analyzes a number of the world's more popular religions and philosophies and their teachings with a view toward evaluating same against the doctrines contained in the Holy Bible, or the Christian Gospels, the latter which he utilizes as a standard for comparison.

The author considers the issues of sin, salvation, and the afterlife unquestionably important, and he undertakes constructive critiques of non-Christian and anti-Christian belief systems with the objective of encouraging, not coercing, prospective believers to consider embracing the Christian faith. This is how Jesus taught his disciples to spread his Gospel of love, compassion, and eternal life.

Atheism

Atheism is actually an ancient belief or worldview and upholds the idea that God, or a supreme overseeing entity, does not exist. The Old Testament contains a Psalm (a sacred song or poem used in worship) written by David, King of Israel and Judah, around 1000 B.C., which mentions atheism:

The fool says in his heart, 'There is no God.' They are corrupt. They do abominable deeds; there is none who does good. (Psalm 14:1, ESV)

Atheism is sometimes confused with *Agnosticism*, which postulates the existence of God is impossible to be known or proven. The word "agnostic" essentially means "without knowledge." While atheism suggests God does not exist - an untenable position, agnosticism argues that God's existence cannot be proven or disproven, i.e., it is impossible to know whether God exists. Agnosticism is, therefore, a more intellectually honest form of atheism. God's existence cannot empirically be proven or controverted.

The number of people worldwide who embrace some sort of atheistic affiliation or another seems to be waning, as intimated by a January 22, 2024, LIFEWAY Research article.

While Christianity and other religions are growing around the world, the global atheist population is falling. The current growth trend for atheism is -0.12%, with their number falling from 147 million in 2020 to 146 million in 2024. Atheism peaked around 1970 with 165 million people.. [1]

The decline of atheists notwithstanding, there are 500 to 750 million atheists in the world today. [2]

Atheists, many of whom in European and Western societies are liberals, habitually deride religionists, including Christians, as lacking in intelligence and practicality. They consider people who believe in God and creationism out of touch with reality and subscribe instead to *evolutionary theory and the Big Bang theory* as answers to the origin of life and the universe - this notwithstanding their own palpably splintered understanding of scientifically deficient propositions, which falsehearted scientists have imposed on a largely ignorant and unsuspecting global audience for decades on end. The author directs the reader to Chapter Nineteen, *Christianity Compared with New Religions, Philosophies & Cults – Evolutionism,* for more on the patently absurd theory of evolution.

A Question Of Faith

Regrettably, atheism is not simply an issue about acknowledging or denying the existence of God. Further, acknowledging God's existence is not necessarily the same as honoring his desire to have people approach his Throne of Grace in repentance and in seeking forgiveness of their sins. It is God's desire for people to believe in him by faith and accept his gift of salvation, as the following scriptural passages attest.

The Lord is not slow in keeping his promise, as some understand slowness. Instead he is patient with you, not wanting anyone to perish, but everyone to come to repentance. (2 Peter 3:9, NIV)

For God so loved the world that he gave his one and only Son, that whoever believes in him shall not perish but have eternal life. (John 3:16, NIV)

The Old Testament records the following instances whereby God clearly demonstrated his presence and sovereignty.

The Book of Kings relates the story of the 450 false prophets of Baal and the 400 false prophets of Asherah, who failed in their attempts to call upon their god to set fire to the bull offering laid before them at Mount Carmel in Northern Israel of old. The prophet Elijah prayed, and fire fell and consumed the sacrifice. The Israelite witnesses subsequently proclaimed, "The LORD, He is God! The LORD, He is God!" Elijah then announced the end of a long drought; clouds gathered, the sky turned black, and it rained heavily. Ahab, the king of Israel at the time, had been asked to summon the people from all over Israel to Mount Carmel to witness the contest between Elijah and the representatives of Baal and Asherah. The incident confirmed that all who were present at Mount Carmel acknowledged God's presence. (1 Kings 18:17-46 (General)

The Book of Exodus mentions another occasion whereby people admitted to the existence of Almighty God and experienced his unmatched benevolence. The prophet Moses and the Israelites, fleeing from Egypt and its dictatorial Pharaoh, found themselves trapped at the edge of the Red Sea (a seawater inlet of the Indian Ocean, lying between Africa and Asia). Moses called upon God and stretched out his hand over the sea, and the Lord drove the sea back with a strong east wind and turned it into dry land. The waters divided, and the Israelites went through the sea on dry ground, with a wall of water on their right and on their left. Pharaoh's armies tried to follow Moses and the Israelites and drowned as the turbulent water rushed back to refill the supernaturally created chasm. (Exodus 13:17-22, 14 (General)

The Old Testament story about Noah and his family was yet another instance of people acknowledging God's existence and presence. Noah and his family were faithful believers who loved and respected God. They tried to live according to his laws and adhere to his directives. God instructed Noah and his sons to construct a huge ark in which to house and transport themselves and pairs of animals, birds, and other living things, as a deluge of unprecedented proportions was imminent. Noah and his family knew of God's existence and his capacity to accomplish the impossible. The rest of the world at the time also knew of God's existence, but men and women would not change their evil ways. They refused to follow God. They even mocked and laughed at Noah and his family. They lacked faith and trust in God. Then the great flood came! (Genesis 6:8-22, 7 (General).

Did the recognition of God's existence and/or presence elicit change in the attitude of the people who gathered at Mount Carmel, or in the minds of the false prophets? It does not seem so. Did the Israelites, even though God delivered them from the Egyptians, wholeheartedly follow God in the wilderness and in the Promised Land after they left Mount Sinai, where God gave them the Ten Commandments? No! They rebelled numerous times and even challenged him. (Numbers 11:1, 14:1-2; 16:1-3; 21:5)

Mere acknowledgment of or belief in the existence of someone or something does not necessarily signify allegiance or obeisance. An individual who admits God exists, especially the God of the Bible, but does not subscribe to his omniscience, omnipotence, and omnipresence and submit to a strategic plan of redemption and divine purpose might as well be an atheist or agnostic. He or she flounders outside the peripheries of a life assigned to an eternity of either unmitigated joy or unceasing torment. If someone is not prepared to accept God's existence by faith, then he or she is definitely not ready to accept Jesus Christ as Savior by faith (Ephesians 2:8-9). God's desire is for people to become practicing Christians, not just theists or those who simply believe he exists.

God's Existence Revealed In Various Ways

The importance of faith as a parallel consideration in acknowledging God's existence is significant; nonetheless, God reveals Himself to humankind in a number of different ways. Concomitantly, it is philosophically impossible for one to be an atheist since, to be an atheist, one must possess infinite knowledge before he or she can be absolutely certain God does not exist.

The following arguments for God's existence help put to naught many an atheist's perfunctory dismissal of the reality of a divine, overseeing entity who created the cosmos life and who set in motion the physical laws that govern the functioning of the universe.

The following discussions allow for a different perspective than the approach adopted in Chapter One – *Is There a God?,* whereby the author presented three complementary and widely acknowledged submissions about the truth of God's existence, i.e., (a) The Cosmological or First Cause Argument, (b) The Scientific Argument, and (c) The Philosophical or Ontological Argument.

God's Existence Revealed Through Creation

The first words of the Old Testament echo an unassailable truth, i.e., *"In the beginning God created the heavens and the earth."* (Genesis 1:1, NIV) Likewise, the first words of the New Testament announce the fascinating, incontrovertible statement, *"In the beginning was the Word, and the Word was with God, and the Word was God."* (John 1:1, NIV)

The foregoing scriptural passages, the very first statements of the two collective books comprising the Holy Bible, convey an irrefutable message, notwithstanding numerous efforts by atheists and agnostics throughout history to disprove them. They tell about the eternality of God and his wondrous handiwork in creating the universe and all life. The Psalmist declares, *"The heavens declare the glory of God; the skies proclaim the work of his hands."* (Psalm 19:1, NIV)

One looks at the night sky and beholds its celestial wonders. One looks at nature and observes its exceeding beauty and diversity. One looks at living creatures and marvels at their makeup and construction, from the single cell to more complex organisms with their multiple trillions of such cells, all operating in unbelievable synchrony and purpose to evidence the miracle of life. One looks at the human brain, the eye, and the heart and shudders at their astonishing composition and the precise, integrated functioning within themselves and with each other. Consequently, one begs the question – How can there not be a superlative planner, designer, and creator of the universe and of life?

The author contends the Big Bang and evolutionary theories are invalid, escapist suppositions devoid of even token substantiation, and in reality, are woefully wanting from the standpoint of true scientific precept and practice. In addition, the Big Bang and evolutionary theories transgress native logic and inborn common sense. See Chapter Nineteen: *Christianity Compared with New Religions, Philosophies & Cults – Evolutionism* for more details on evolutionary theory.

God's Existence Revealed Through a Desire to Know Him

Humankind, for the most part, has been on a search to find a supreme and/or divine creator or architect of the cosmos and life since the dawn of time. God himself instilled in the minds of the creatures created in his image a desire to identify a figure or personage whom they look up to and call "Father" or "God."

> *For since the creation of the world God's invisible qualities—his eternal power and divine nature—have been clearly seen, being understood from what has been made, so that people are without excuse.* (Romans 1:18, 20, NIV)

In other words, people possess the intrinsic realization there exists a supernatural entity who created everything and everyone, and who deserves humankind's adulation and obeisance. Sadly, very many members of God's creation neglect to acknowledge such an obligation and instead choose to follow false gods. Atheism is one such god.

The following scriptural passages allude to humankind's rejection of God's existence and its ingratitude to its Creator and warn of a righteous God's consequential wrath.

> *The wrath of God is being revealed from heaven against all the godlessness and wickedness of people, who suppress the truth by their wickedness, since what may be known about God is plain to them, because God has made it plain to them.* (Romans 1:18-19, NIV)

For although they knew God, they neither glorified him as God nor gave thanks to him, but their thinking became futile and their foolish hearts were darkened. Although they claimed to be wise, they became fools and exchanged the glory of the immortal God for images made to look like a mortal human being and birds and animals and reptiles. (Romans 1:21-23, NIV)

256

Therefore God gave them over in the sinful desires of their hearts to sexual impurity for the degrading of their bodies with one another. They exchanged the truth about God for a lie, and worshiped and served created things rather than the Creator—who is forever praised. Amen. (Romans 1:24-25, NIV)

God's Existence Revealed Through Human History

Proof of God's existence spans thousands of years, i.e., from the time of the beginning of the Old Testament era to the end of the New Testament era. The Old Testament spanned the period from creation (4000 BC) to the period of the Persian Empire when King Cyrus (600 or 576 BC – 530 BC) allowed the Jews to return from captivity and rebuild their temple. The Old Testament ended around 400 BC.[3] The New Testament era began in 500 B.C. and ended in A.D. 100. [4] Allusion to the presence of proof of God's existence being available for thousands of years, i.e., an era from the beginning of the Old Testament era to the end of the New Testament, does not suggest he was non-existent before then. God is eternal and has always existed.

The remarkable nature of Christendom's two religious texts enables invaluable insights into the history of the Christian faith proper, which encompasses the eras of the Old Testament and the New Testament. The first tells about the creation of the universe and all life, including the first man and woman, and the second chronicles the life of the Messiah Jesus Christ, from his entrance into the world as an infant to his ultimate sacrifice on the cross as atonement for humankind's sins, followed by the spread of his Gospel to people everywhere.

Furthermore, the continuing dissemination of the Christian Gospel from the time of Paul, i.e., around A.D. 100 and the other apostles to the present day to people from the far corners of the earth is testimony to the influence and uniqueness of the Christian faith, which in turn attest to God's presence and his continuous sovereignty over all. The growth of Christianity over the centuries and its persistence as the globe's premier religious worldview staggers the imagination. Despite unceasing attempts by those opposed to the Gospel's doctrines to suppress and destroy the faith, Christianity today numbers around 2.2 billion believers among its adherents. [5]

The Old Testament records a widespread deluge or floods around 2348 B.C., a year-long global catastrophe that destroyed the physical world, reshaped the continents, buried billions of creatures, and laid down the earth's rock layers. It was God's judgment of man's wickedness, and only eight righteous people and representatives of every kind of land animal escaped the catastrophe.[6] Following the great flood of 2348 B.C., the Old Testament prophet Noah and his extended family, whom God spared from the civilization-ending deluge, became the forerunners of a whole new world. God had not given up on his wondrous creation. He still wished to steer recalcitrant humankind toward reconciliation with himself. The post-flood world, however, like the pre-flood global civilization, alienated itself from its creator. People rejected God and his laws and followed the lure of reprobate morals and desires.

A loving and just God, pained by humankind's continuous rebellion and disregard for his holy and principled standards, decided to embark on a unique strategy to draw his wayward children unto himself. He loved his creation so much that he chose to become a man and live among men and women on earth. Just over two thousand years ago, history's most consequential interaction to date between a divine Creator and humankind took place when an infant was born in a lowly stable in Bethlehem, a southwestern village of Jerusalem in ancient Judea. The baby's name was Jesus, and he was a living representation of what Almighty God looked like. If one wants to see what God looks like, all he or she needs to do is look at Jesus Christ. The Bible says, "The Son is the image of the invisible God, the firstborn over all creation." (Colossians 1:15, NIV)

God, who is an invisible Spirit (John 4:24), showed his visible form in the person of Jesus Christ. The Creator of the universe and all life became a man so his children could see what he was like and, more importantly, get to know him personally. He did not leave his children wallowing in doubt and insecurity. He communicated his presence to the world at large so people, including those who doubted, could believe in him and his plan of salvation for all. The untiring spread of Christ's Gospel today is an extension of the affirmation of God's existence.

God's Existence Revealed through His Word, the Holy Bible

The most remarkable book ever written, the Holy Bible, corroborates God's existence. Translated into more than 1800 languages, the Bible is the bestselling book of all time. Hardly anyone who undertakes to scrutinize and examine the Bible honestly and constructively would deny it is the supernatural imprint of God. All scripture (the Bible) is God-breathed. The

259

apostle Peter says, *"Men spoke from God as they were carried along by the Holy Spirit."* (2 Peter 1:21, NIV)

The Bible is actually a compilation of 66 different books written by 40 different authors over a period of 1500 years. [7] The exclusiveness of such a literary accomplishment is unmatched, quite apart from any relevance to genre or claim to legitimacy. Nevertheless, the books of the Bible, from Genesis to Revelation, provide remarkable details about God's expectations for the redemption of lost humankind. In disclosing his strategy for delivering his disobedient children from sin and damnation, God reveals himself continuously as a God of love to a largely incredulous world.

Another astonishing, unparalleled feature of the Bible is the impeccable unity and concord of its message, which threads through the entire book, despite the unbelievable number of authors involved, the length of time spanning the production of the book, and the enormous length of the book's full text.

Historical and geographical accuracy and archaeological findings further confirm the Holy Bible's authenticity and, concomitantly, its revelation about God's existence and dominion. Wide documentation by theological and scientific scholars also helps to verify the truthfulness of the Bible.

An inimitable, mind-boggling feature of the Holy Bible, and a means by which it attests to God's presence and involvement in the affairs of humankind, is the fulfillment of hundreds of prophecies uttered by Biblical prophets inspired by the Holy Spirit. A prophecy is a pre-written history. Fulfilled prophecy is one of the most powerful indications the Bible is truly the Word of God. J. Barton Payne's *Encyclopedia of Biblical Prophecy* lists 1,239 prophecies in the Old Testament and 578 prophecies in the New Testament, for a total of 1,817. [8]

There were over 300 Old Testament prophecies about the Messiah fulfilled by the life of Jesus Christ. Josh McDowell, the popular Evangelical Christian apologist and evangelist, and author of over 150 books, separates the 300 prophecies into 61 different categories, and borrowing from the argument of noted Christian writer and co-founder of the American Scientific Affiliation, Peter Stoner (1888 – 1980), [9] he says if you just took 8 of these prophecies, the odds of a single individual coincidentally fulfilling all eight of these would be one in 10 to the 17th power. Since it is difficult to comprehend the size of such a number, McDowell offers the following illustration: "Suppose you took the state of Texas and spread silver dollars two feet deep across the whole state, then marked just one of them and buried it somewhere in the state. Then, if you chose one person, blindfolded him, and asked him to pick just one silver dollar, his chances of getting the marked one on his first try would be one in 10 to the 17th power!" [10]

Atheism is representative of a willful denial of the existence of the supernatural architect of the universe and the creator of all life and everything else he did on behalf of humankind. It is a morally and intellectually bankrupt philosophy, and its adherents place themselves in the perilous situation of entering eternity permanently estranged from Almighty God and his Redeemer Son Jesus Christ.

The New Atheism

A new, vituperative form of atheism emerged shortly after the September 11, 2001, terrorist attacks on the World Trade Center buildings in New York, USA. Islamic jihadists slaughtered over 3,000 innocent people in a pellucid demonstration of religious fanaticism. Countless observers in America and abroad immediately condemned the terrorists who carried out the despicable acts and unhesitatingly linked the perpetrations to mainstream Islamic beliefs.

Hardcore atheists joined in the fray and proceeded to lambaste religion in general, and as they are wont to do, singled out the Christian faith and Judaism for special condemnation. They neglected to acknowledge the fact that Christians and Jews themselves are constant, traditional targets and victims of Muslim extremists. Additionally, Christians and Jews, among the adherents of the world's other major religions and lesser-known worldviews as well, are the least inclined to engage in religious wars. This is true notwithstanding the misinformed claim by atheists, agnostics, and freethinkers that Christians maliciously engineered the violence and mayhem that accompanied the Crusades or religious wars that took place during the medieval period, specifically between 1095 and 1271. The Crusades, viewed from a proper perspective, were defensive wars whereby Christians sought to defend themselves, reclaim territories confiscated by Muslim antagonists over a period of four centuries after his death, and prevent further plundering and pillaging.

The New Atheist movement is buoyed by the histrionics of steadfast anti-religionists and God-haters like the irreverent evolutionary biologist

Richard Dawkins, the British polemicist and socio-political critic Christopher Hitchens, and the insufferable left-wing commentator and comedian Bill Maher.

Bill Maher volunteers the following incorrigible remark whereby he echoes the sentiments of many misguided atheists who seek to blame religion exclusively for the ills of the world.

Religion must die in order for mankind to live...The irony of religion is that because of its power to divert man to destructive courses, the world could actually come to an end.

Maher predicts the destruction of the human race will result from "religion-inspired nuclear terrorism." Maher's statement must bother anyone, religious or non-religious, with even a middling intellect or average powers of comprehension. He conveniently neglects the truth or probably lacks the wherewithal to realize that history's most crazed despots were people with hardly any religious affiliation and were the ones who perpetrated the worst genocides in recorded history. The author makes mention of eight instances of the unmitigated slaughter of innocent people. The events appear in order of descending mortality count.

1. *Nazi Holocaust (1933 to 1945) – 5 Million to 17 Million*

The Nazi Holocaust was the deadliest and most infamous genocide of the 20th Century. Over 6 million Jews were massacred between 1933 and 1945 by the Nazis and their allies under the leadership of the German madman Adolf Hitler. Nearly 78% of European Jews were killed in this genocide. Apart from 6 million Jews, it is estimated that around the same number of non-Jewish people were also killed over the course of the Holocaust.

2. *Holodomor (1932 to 1933) – 1.8 Million to 7.5 Million*

The number of people killed in the brutal manmade starvation in Ukraine, known as the Holodomor, is estimated at anywhere between 1.8 million individuals to 7.5 million. The majority of those who lost their lives were ethnic Ukrainians, a fact that has led to accusations that the government of the Soviet Union, which was at the time led by the dictator Joseph Stalin, intentionally orchestrated the genocide in order to reduce the risk of an uprising from Ukraine.

3. *Khmer Rouge Cambodian Genocide (1975 to 1979) – 1.3 Million to 3 Million*

In the Cambodian genocide between 1975 and 1979, between 1.5 and 3 million people were killed by the brutal policies of the Khmer Rouge regime. People were forced to relocate, forced into labor, and subjected to inhumane torture and other atrocities. Many people were killed by mass executions, while others died from disease, starvation, and malnutrition. This killing spree by the Khmer Rouge-led administration by the tyrant Pol Pot was undertaken with the objective of establishing a form of agrarian socialism in Cambodia.

4. *Kazakh Genocide (1931 to 1933) – 1.3 Million to 1.75 Million*

The Kazakh Genocide resulted in between 1.3 million to 1.75 ethnic Kazakhs losing their lives to famine and food shortage. Due to the involvement of the Soviet government in the carnage, scholars refer to the planned exterminations as genocide.

5. *Armenian Genocide (1915 to 1922) – 700,000 to 1.5 Million*

The Armenian genocide occurred between 1915 and 1922 in what was then known as the Ottoman Empire. During this time, as many as 1.5 million ethnic Armenians were brutally murdered by the actions of the Ottoman government, who were acting upon a strong anti-Armenian sentiment.

6. *Rwandan Genocide (1994) – 500,000 to 1 Million*

The Rwandan Genocide witnessed the death of nearly 500,000 to 1,000,000 Rwandans, accounting for nearly 20% of the country's population and 70% of the country's Tutsi populace. The genocide took place over a period of 100 days from April 7th through mid-July of 1994. The massacre was initiated by the Rwandan administration comprising a Hutu-led government against the Tutsis during the Rwandan Civil War in response to the rebellion by the Tutsi-led Rwandan Patriotic Front.

7. *Circassian Genocide (1941 to 1945) – 357,000 to 600,000*

The Circassian Genocide occurred between 1941 and 1945. During this time, anywhere between 357,000 to 600,000 Circassians, people native to the Circassia region of the North Caucasus, lost their lives in the Russo-Circassian War. The genocide was termed an example of ethnic cleansing.

8. *Croatian Ustasha Genocide (1941 to 1945) – 200,000 to 500,000*

The Croatian Ustasha Genocide, also known as the Holocaust of Croatia, took the form of a massacre of the Jews inhabiting the region during the Second World War. It was committed by the fascist Ustaše regime of the Independent State of Croatia, comprising what today modern-day Croatia, Herzegovina, Bosnia, and parts of Serbia is. The Jews were killed in Ustaše-run concentration camps or handed over to Nazi-run concentration camps for execution.

The foregoing list includes estimates of deaths that directly or indirectly resulted from each genocide, as defined by the UN Convention on Genocide. It excludes other mass killings, which may or may not be referred to as genocides by some scholars. Such atrocities include mass murders, crimes against humanity, politicides (the deliberate physical destruction or elimination of a group whose members share the main characteristic of belonging to a political movement), classicides (the deliberate and systematic destruction, in whole or in part, of a social class through persecution and violence), and war crimes. The genocides described above are only a small number of occurrences of wide-ranging annihilation. History records many more.

It is not the author's intention to deny the fact religious fanatics sometimes instigate and/or participate in deadly and costly conflicts. However, as the aforementioned tabulation of genocides reveals, nonreligious autocrats and oppressors were answerable for the majority of history's most devastating wars. Marxism, Leninism and Communism are philosophies that supposedly address ethical, social, political, and economic concerns to the unconcealed exclusion of religious representation. Marxists, Leninists, and Communists, over past centuries, were at the forefront of the unmitigated slaughter of countless millions of people who dared to disagree with their governmental and constitutional policies and decrees.

Bill Maher's remark about "religion-inspired nuclear terrorism" could not be more asinine. If nuclear devastation in the future is to be feared, history suggests it will not be engineered by religionists but by people who do not subscribe to the existence of God. The tally of victims of history's genocides and other mass killings delineated in the preceding paragraph runs into scores of millions. Does the method of annihilation, i.e., nuclear or non-nuclear, really matter?

Richard Dawkins, in his best-selling book *The God Delusion* (2006), brazenly postulates that post-Darwinian scientific advances made any belief in God or a supernatural creator irrational and unnecessary. He refers to religious doctrines as crude and fallacy-ridden attempts by religionists to account for nature and the presence and operation of physical laws and phenomena.

Dawkins' penchant for plunging into rancorous diatribes and nonintellectual reflection is brought to the fore by the following contemptuous statement about people of religious faith.

Do we know of any...examples where stupid ideas have been known to spread like an epidemic? Yes, by God! Religious ideas are irrational. Religious beliefs are dumb and dumber: super dumb. Religion drives otherwise sensible people into celibate monasteries or crashing into New York skyscrapers. Religion motivates people to whip their own backs, to set fire to themselves or their daughters, to denounce their own grandmothers as witches, or, in less extreme cases, simply to stand or kneel, week after week, through ceremonies of stupefying boredom.
11

Dawkins' intimation that all religious people are stupid is puerile and lacks even minimal common sense. His diatribe is misinformed, not to mention revoltingly irreverent. All religions or belief systems are not the same, and doctrines and ideologies differ, sometimes diametrically. It is, therefore, logical to presume adherents of diverse faiths or worldviews would conform to dissimilar types of behavior. It is unfair to cluster them together. It is unfair to condemn them collectively. Even then, there are people who, in contradiction to the teachings of their religions, adopt certain customs and resort to violence and bloodshed. There are foolish religious people, just as there are foolish nonreligious people.

Incidentally, evolutionary theory, which Richard Dawkins and very many of his colleagues around the world hold to be irrefutable truth, is a premise riddled with inconsistencies and is anything but scientific fact. The precept has been imposed on an unwary global audience for over a century and a half and must rank as one of history's greatest hoaxes. Evolutionists believe the universe just happened into existence, and all life proceeded from inanimate material and developed unguided over billions of years into the multitudinous forms present today. Evolutionists deride the idea of the existence of God or a supernatural creator and designer of life and the cosmos – this notwithstanding the fact many of the world's greatest scientific minds, including Isaac Newton, Michael Faraday, Galileo Galilei, Gregor Mendel, Louis Pasteur, George W. Carver, Carl Linnaeus, Johannes Kepler and Wernher von Braun among others, were devout Christians. See Chapter Nineteen – *Evolutionism* for more on the controversial theory.

Christopher Hitchens was one of the New Atheism movement's most prominent advocates. He was also an unrepentant Marxist, even though he loathed totalitarian oppression. Marxism traditionally leads to totalitarian oppression.

In 2017, Hitchens published an acerbic attack on religion titled *God Is Not Great: How Religion Poisons Everything*. Inasmuch as the work was nauseatingly disdainful and farcical, Hitchens' book debuted at number two on Amazon and, after a couple of weeks, catapulted to the top of the New York Times best-seller list. The following was among the numerous polemical outbursts contained in the book.

> *Violent, irrational, intolerant, allied to racism and tribalism and bigotry, invested in ignorance and hostile to free inquiry, contemptuous of women, and coercive toward children: organized religion ought to have a great deal on its conscience.* [12]

Hitchens, like most atheists, including many who cajole themselves into believing they are intellectually superior to other people and possess superior powers of reasoning, repeated in his book the oft-committed blunder of generalizing that all or most religions or faiths are similar in precept and practice. While there exist commonalities among disparate religious belief systems, core doctrines about spirituality and the afterlife often differ diametrically.

Hitchens also chose to ignore the fact that in most instances where religionists gravitate to violence and bloodshed, such people invariably act in divergence from or in nonconformity with the teachings of their respective faiths. The Christian faith, for instance, more than any other major religious worldview, proscribes hatred and hostility against others, including its enemies. Hitchens was sorely mistaken in his thinking. Religion does not poison people. Wicked, misguided people poison religion.

The late socio-political critic (Hitchens died in December 2011) had to be aware of the fact that Marxists, Leninists, Communists, and other non-religionists have been responsible throughout the centuries for the mindless killing of many millions of innocent people. Yet, he conveniently evaded the mention of such barbarism.

The truth remains the truth always. Anger, opinion, hatred, belligerence, or distortion do not transform fact into fiction or truth into untruth.

In the final analysis, the issue comes full circle, i.e., atheist, agnostic, or religionist - if any such individual does not repent of his or her sins and acknowledge Jesus Christ's sacrifice on the cross as atonement for his or her sins, he or she will be consigned to an eternity of damnation and separation from Almighty God.

CHAPTER TWELVE

CHRISTIANITY COMPARED WITH MAJOR RELIGIONS & PHILOSOPHIES - BUDDHISM

BUDDHISM'S BEGINNINGS

The term "Buddha" means "The Enlightened One," Siddhartha Gautama, who lived from 563 to 483 B.C., founded the Buddhist religion. Gautama was born into a wealthy Hindu family and lived in the hill country bordering modern-day India and Nepal.

According to one version of the story about Siddhartha Guatama's early life, he lived luxuriously with little exposure to the outside world. His parents apparently wanted to shield him from the influence of philosophy and religion and sought to protect their son from the pain and suffering of everyday life.

Gautama, the story goes, had visions of an aged man, a sick man, and a corpse. His fourth vision was of a peaceful ascetic monk, i.e., one who denies luxury and comfort. Seeing the monk's peacefulness, he decided to become an ascetic himself. He abandoned his life of wealth and affluence to pursue enlightenment through austerity. He became skilled at this sort of self-mortification and intense meditation. Legend has it Gautama later sat beneath a fig tree (also called the Bodhi tree) in the Gaya region in the state

271

of Bihar in India to meditate till he either reached "enlightenment" or died trying. Despite the temptations and difficulties he encountered, the story goes Gautama achieved enlightenment after 40 days. Thus, he became known as the 'enlightened one' or the 'Buddha.'

Another version of Gautama's early experiences states he lived a sheltered life as a child and young man. One day, after he had married and had fathered a son, he ventured out into the outside world. What Gautama saw – the sick, the suffering, the dying – had such a profound impact on him he decided to leave his wife and young son and wealthy means of existence and embark on a life of asceticism. He sought a means of release from the suffering and pain of the temporal world. Gautama labored for six years, by which time he had been reduced to a severely emaciated physical state, to achieve liberation from the ravages of pain and anguish that accompanied one's existence in the physical world. During this phase of deep meditation, he achieved "enlightenment" and became the Buddha.

Buddha re-entered the world and began teaching about the meaning of life and his way to nirvana or enlightenment. He founded the *Sangha*, an order of monks. By the time he died, some 45 years later, many thousands of people had adopted his teachings. [1]

Buddhists today number close to 500 million people or about 7% of the world's population. It is the world's fourth-largest religion. [2]

The Foundational Teachings Of Buddhism

Buddhism revolves around the following "Four Noble Truths."

1. Life is suffering.

2. Suffering proceeds from desire.

3. The absence of desire eliminates suffering.

4. Eliminating desire comes from adhering to "The Middle Way" between the extremes of sensuousness and asceticism. [3]

The "Middle Way" can be achieved via the "Eightfold Path," which combines the knowledge of the Four Noble Truths with moral practice, thought, and meditation. The "Eightfold Path," in turn, embodies the following "Right" attitudes and actions. [4]

1. Right View.

2. Right Resolve.

3. Right Speech.

4. Right Action.

5. Right Livelihood.

6. Right Effort.

7. Right Concentration.

8. Right Ecstasy.

Buddhist teaching further explains "Right" thoughts and actions in the following ways.

- *Right View* relates to an understanding of the Four Noble Truths.

- *Right Resolve* is purposing to follow and observe the Four Noble Truths.

- 3-5. *Right Speech, Right Action,* and *Right Livelihood* revolve around avoiding the desires of this life that lead to suffering.

- *Right Effort* is spiritual in nature and involves emptying one's mind and directing one's attention toward final liberation from worldly suffering and pain.

- *Right Concentration*, also spiritual in nature, alludes to advanced states of mind and body control.

- *Right Ecstasy* refers to a state of Nirvana, or a spiritual state of complete liberation from sense experiences and the inclination toward worldly desire. Universal knowledge reaches a zenith, and the cycle of reincarnation (a tortuous sequence of death and rebirth) ends. The believer becomes one with the Impersonal, loses his or her individuality, and merges into "nothingness." Buddha taught that one attains true peace at this point but becomes bereft of a soul or personality.

The goal of human existence, Buddha declared, is to free oneself from the law of "Karma," or the cause and effect of good and bad actions and omissions. In this way, one reaches a nirvanic state in which desires cease and suffering ends.

The Main Schools Of Buddhism

Buddhism falls into two major categorizations – *Theravada Buddhism* and *Mahayana Buddhism*. Other forms or branches of Buddhist philosophy are (a) *Vajrayana Buddhism*, a variant of Mahayana Buddhism; (b) *Zen Buddhism*, another offshoot of the Mahayana branch of the philosophy; and

(c) *Pure Land Buddhism* or *Amidism*, a specific interpretation of the Mahayana school.

Theravada Buddhism

Theravada Buddhism is the more conservative of the two major schools of Buddhist spirituality. The other, slightly more popular school is Mahayana Buddhism. Theravada Buddhism is prevalent in Sri Lanka, Laos, Vietnam, Cambodia, and Thailand. Theravada Buddhism differs from Mahayana Buddhism mostly by its adherence to a particular set of written texts as its doctrinal authority. Theravada adherents number about two fifths of all Buddhists. Many of the differences between Theravada Buddhism and other branches of philosophy relate to concepts and practices that complement, instead of those that detract from or oppose what is taught in more conservative Buddhist traditions.

A key characteristic of Theravada Buddhism is its relatively narrow acceptance of certain Buddhist scriptures. Such texts, written in the Pali language and held in high regard, are among the oldest of all known Buddhist writings. The Pali or Magadhan language is a widely studied Middle Indo-Aryan tongue native to the Indian subcontinent. It is the language of the Pāli Canon or Tipiṭaka and is the sacred language of some religious texts of Hinduism and all texts of Theravāda Buddhism.

The earliest archaeological evidence of the existence of canonical Pali comes from Pyu city-state inscriptions found in Burma and dated to the mid-5th to mid-6th century A.D. [5]

Buddhist missionaries who brought their faith from India to Sri Lanka created the writings in the island nation. The writings themselves originated from centuries-old oral traditions. Unlike the sacred texts of faiths such as Christianity and Islam, the sacred texts of Theravada Buddhism are not considered to be infallible by adherents of the religion.

Another major difference between Theravada and other Buddhist schools takes the form of upholding the monastic lifestyle as the best way of achieving enlightenment. Theravada doctrine acknowledges in theory that laymen are capable of spiritual advancement. However, only those committed to the monastic lifestyle have any reasonable hope of actually achieving "Buddha-hood." Theravada Buddhism alludes to a much wider divide between the monk's praxis and the layman's than do other Buddhist traditions.

According to Theravada Buddhism, one is only a "true" Buddhist when he desires to follow the Buddha (meaning both the figure of Gautama Buddha and the practitioner's inner potential for enlightenment), commits himself to follow the guidance of the Sangha (the worldwide family of Buddhist monks and nuns), and resolves to follow the Dhamma (the teachings of Buddha). Compared to the Mahayana school, Theravada Buddhism places much more emphasis on the importance of the traditions of monks than it does on the conceivable enlightenment of laymen or those not affiliated with a monastic lifestyle.

Theravada doctrine integrates the core aspects of Buddhism, such as the Four Noble Truths and the Eightfold Path, to produce seven nucleic stages of spiritual purification. The phases encompass such undertakings as finding the correct teacher, developing one's meditation ability, and growing one's understanding of Buddhist truths. Much of what Theravada Buddhism teaches has parallels in Mahayana schools of thought. The opposite is not necessarily true.

Mahayana Buddhism

Mahayana Buddhism is one of the two major branches of Buddhist philosophy, the other being Theravada Buddhism. Mahayana Buddhism is most popular in Japan, Korea, China, Indonesia, and Tibet and is the philosophy to which about three fifths of the world's Buddhists subscribe.

It is difficult to delineate the exact boundaries of Mahayana belief as, similar to most Eastern religions, such borders are invariably imprecise. There are a few conventions, however, which distinguish it from other approaches to Buddhist philosophy. Three such standards are as follows.

Bodhisattva - After Buddhas, the most important beings in Mahayana iconography are bodhisattvas. The word *bodhisattva* means "enlightenment being." Very simply, bodhisattvas are *beings* who work for the enlightenment of all beings, not just themselves. [6] The highest ideal in Mahayana Buddhism is the path of the bodhisattva. Buddhism generally teaches that those who attain true enlightenment cease to reincarnate, thereby breaking the cycle of suffering and reincarnation. The bodhisattva, however, chooses to delay his entry into the state of nirvana so he can lead others to the same understanding.

According to Mahayana, each individual should aspire to the example of the bodhisattva. This is a major difference between the Mahayana and

Theravada schools. Theravada also upholds the bodhisattva as the greatest possible aspiration, but its pursuit is for a smaller, more elite group. Mahayana holds that all people should seek to follow the path of the bodhisattva. Theravada considers such efforts admirable but not obligatory.

In order to pursue the path of the bodhisattva, the Mahayana adherent must practice the "Six Perfections," i.e., giving, self-control, patience, diligence, meditation, and wisdom.

Bodhicitta - The basic definition of *bodhicitta* is "the desire to realize enlightenment for the sake of others." [7] Buddhist philosophy refers to those who desire to become bodhicittas and free others from the cycle of reincarnation as believers who attain an "awakened mind."

Upaya – Translated as "skillful means" or "expedient means," *upaya* is any activity that helps others realize enlightenment.[8] Mahayana places a strong emphasis on the concept of upaya. In general terms, the practice of upaya translates to "whatever works." The hypothesis is unusually lax or permissive from the standpoint of religious introspection in that virtually any practice, belief, or action is allowable, so long as it is not explicitly condemned by Buddhist thinking and so long as it leads to greater spiritual growth.

In practice, a Buddhist guru could justify anything as upaya, no matter how violent, bizarre, or wanton it is, so long as it benefits someone's spiritual maturity. The idea is borne out in Buddhist history, which includes countless instances of "crazy wisdom," whereby a master receives credit for outrageous actions "beyond" the limited understanding of his students.

While classical or traditional Buddhism is mainly philosophical, Mahayana Buddhism is typically "religious," i.e., it attributes worship to specific deities. Mahayana frequently teaches there were many Buddhas - many enlightened ones - who were spiritual projections of an ultimate power, also referred to as "Buddha." Following this belief, practitioners of Mahayana simultaneously worship Buddha and maintain a non-theistic worldview. The "deity" of Mahayana Buddhism is not a personal entity but an impersonal, all-encompassing force.

Certain sub-schools of Mahayana also teach an interesting concept regarding the "Buddha Nature." The Buddha Nature theory is analogous to the Christian notion of the sinful character of humankind, although it accommodates the involvement of all living things. The Bible teaches that people are inherently evil, and salvation is available to those who admit to their transgressions and accept Christ's sacrifice on the cross as atonement for their sins. Mahayana's view of the "Buddha Nature" is that all sentient beings are inherently connected to the Buddha, the ultimate source of everything, but this Buddha Nature encompasses the attachments and sufferings of life, so, in order to be set free, one must "uncover" this hidden inner truth by attaining a state of nirvanic enlightenment.

Mahayana Buddhism exemplifies a benevolent interpretation of Buddhism, one very similar to other world religions that focus on the worship of a deity or deities. Similar to most Eastern belief systems, the philosophy also comprises several widely varied sub-schools. Consequently, beyond the fundamentals of Buddhism and the general outlines of the Mahayana school of thought and practice, such diversity or multiplicity makes it difficult to presume exactly what any particular Mahayana Buddhist might believe.

Buddhism & Idolatry

Buddhists are essentially atheists. Buddhism calls itself a "non-theistic" religion. The historical Buddha (Siddhartha Gautama) taught that believing in and worshipping gods was not useful for those seeking to realize enlightenment. Due to this, many Buddhists consider themselves to be atheists. [9]

Siddhartha Gautama was, in fact, a Hindu from birth; it was never his intention to devise and/or develop a religion. His goal was to reform Hinduism, which he felt had wandered from its true purpose by incorporating manifold gods, indeed thousands of them, in the worldview – all represented by idols. In actuality, Buddha did not subscribe to the notion of the existence of God and believed the very concept of God or gods was a hindrance to people freeing themselves from the entrapment of karma, suffering, and pain that hallmarked the temporal world.

Idolatry, a practice the founder of Buddhism condemned, is today an indispensable aspect of the religion. There are innumerable shrines and statues of Buddha around the world, most of them in Southeast Asia, where adherents of the worldview live and worship. The Shwe Dagon or Golden Pagoda in Rangoon, Burma, probably the largest Buddhist temple/pagoda in the world, houses over 3,500 idols of Buddha.

It is lamentable that a man who did not believe in God and who sought to restructure a belief system he thought had gone haywire is today himself

280

worshipped as a god. The following statement by Ron Carlson, President of *Christian Ministries International,* and Ed Decker, founder and International Director of Saints Alive in Jesus, two foremost lecturers on cults and Christian apologetics, lays bare the unbelievable level to which the abysmal practice of idol worship can consign naïve and misinformed people.

> *In the hill country of Sri Lanka, where the majority of the world's blue sapphires are mined, Ron lectured several years ago in the city of Kandy. Kandy is the home of the famous Temple of the Tooth – which has a tooth of Buddha. Yes, Buddha's tooth! Here Ron watched as people brought flowers and rice as offerings and bowed down to worship and pray to a gold box encrusted with jewels. Once a year, in a large festival, they bring out the box, open it, and reveal the sacred tooth of the Buddha for all to worship.* [10]

The Holy Bible is unequivocal in its condemnation of idolatry and warns of the dreadful consequences in store for those who participate in the abominable practice.

> *Professing to be wise, they became fools, and changed the glory of the incorruptible God into an image made like corruptible man – and birds and four-footed beasts and creeping things.* (Romans 1:22,23, NKJV)

> *For the practices of the people are worthless; they cut a tree out of the forest, and a craftsman shapes it with his chisel. They adorn it with silver and gold; they fasten it with hammer and nails so it will not totter. Like a scarecrow in a cucumber field, their idols cannot speak;*

they must be carried because they cannot walk. Do not fear them; they can do no harm nor can they do any good. (Jeremiah 10:3-5, NIV)

They are all senseless and foolish; they are taught by worthless wooden idols. Hammered silver is brought from Tarshish and gold from Uphaz. What the craftsman and goldsmith have made is then dressed in blue and purple—all made by skilled workers. But the Lord is the true God; he is the living God, the eternal King. When he is angry, the earth trembles; the nations cannot endure his wrath. (Jeremiah 10:8-10, NIV)

Everyone is senseless and without knowledge; every goldsmith is shamed by his idols. The images he makes are a fraud; they have no breath in them. They are worthless, the objects of mockery; when their judgment comes, they will perish. (Jeremiah 10:14-15, NIV)

Buddhism's Paradoxical Teachings About Karma And Sin

"Karma" means action, work, or deed.[11] The term also refers to the spiritual principle of cause and effect, where the intent and actions of an individual influence the future of that individual.[12] Good intent and good deeds contribute to good karma and future happiness, while bad intent and bad deeds contribute to bad karma and future suffering. [13, 14]

The philosophy of karma aligns closely with the idea of rebirth in Buddhist philosophy, whereby karma affects one in the current life, as well as in his or her future life - one's saṃsāra. [15, 16]

Karmic teaching infiltrates the lives of millions of people around the world, including many who do not subscribe to the tenets of Eastern religious philosophy. The exhortation, sans the inference of spirituality and ceaseless progressive and/or regressive rebirths (reincarnation), is straightforward and seemingly defensible - good intentions and good actions represent *good karma* and ensuing happiness, while bad intentions and bad actions represent *bad karma* and resultant suffering.

The standard or norm relating to karma may appeal to some people only as far as it constitutes upfront advice or encouragement for people to engage in proper or principled thought and conduct, especially from a Western or non-Eastern perspective where Buddhist religious precept and practice may not be apparent. In Buddhism, karma represents nature's balance. Subsequently, the philosophy does not advocate or enforce the performance of good or bad deeds. Nature is not moral; therefore, karma is not a moral code, and ultimately sin is not immoral.

In Buddhist philosophy, sin is essentially ignorance and seen as a "moral error." The idea of committed sin falling outside the precincts of willful wrongdoing, however, serves to distort the true meaning of "evil" and "good" thoughts and actions. Buddhist thought implies one's errors are not a moral issue since they are ultimately impersonal mistakes, not interpersonal violations. The consequence of such indulgence can be devastating. To the Buddhist, sin is more of an ethical blunder than a transgression against the nature of a holy God. Such an understanding of sin is not in accord with man's innate moral awareness of possible condemnation because of his trespasses before a holy God – a situation that the Bible says can be corrected only by embracing Jesus Christ and his message of salvation unto eternal life!

Since, according to Buddhist precept, sin is a depersonalized and humanly fixable error, Buddhist philosophy does not address the doctrine of depravity, a basic teaching of Christianity. The Bible tells us humankind's sinful temperament is a problem of eternal and infinite consequence, and Jesus Christ is the only means of rescue from eternal damnation. Buddhism teaches there is no need for a Savior to rescue people from their damning sins because, as mentioned earlier, sin is simply a moral misstep and can be rectified through human effort. As far as Buddhist thinking goes, there is only ethical living and meditative appeals to nebulous, ill-defined exalted beings in the hope of perhaps achieving enlightenment and ultimate Nirvana. The understanding is that an individual more than likely will have to go through a number of reincarnations to pay off his or her vast accumulation of karmic debt.

Buddhism is essentially a philosophy of morality and ethics, encapsulated within a life of renunciation of one's self. In Buddhism, reality is impersonal and non-relational; therefore, it is not loving. Not only is God seen as illusory, but in dissolving sin into non-moral error and by rejecting all material reality as Maya ("illusion"), man loses his very personality, which itself becomes an illusion.

The intimation that the doctrine of karma mandates any kind of preternatural outcome over time, especially in response to people's behavioral tendencies, particularly without the believer's allegiance to an identifiable divine overseer, is beyond commonsensical analysis and deduction. The Buddhist, as well as Hindu, Jainist and Sikh familiarity with the dogma of reincarnation hardly impacts the understanding of the individual who is less religiously disposed. An individual such as the latter likely would only be interested in whether someone is moral or unethical.

The incongruous or paradoxical nature of karmic doctrine, and consequently, the teaching's confounding revelation, is borne out in the following extract from the book *Fast Facts on False Teachings* by Ron Carlson and Ed Decker referenced above, which recounts a very troubling situation in Thailand during the years following the Cambodian massacres under the despotic ruler Pol Pot and the Khmer Rouge (the Communist Party of Kampuchea (CPK)) in the mid-1970s, and the subsequent invasion of Vietnam at the end of the same decade.

Over 300,000 refugees were caught in a no-man's-land along the Cambodian border. One of the most fascinating things about these refugee camps was the realization of who was caring for the refugees. Here, in this Buddhist country of Thailand, with Buddhist refugees coming from Cambodia and Laos, there were no Buddhists taking care of their Buddhist brothers. There were also no Hindus or Muslims taking care of those people. The only people there taking care of these 300,000 refugees were Christians from Christian mission organizations and Christian relief organizations!

A man heading up one of the relief efforts had lived in Thailand for over 20 years. Ron (Carlson) asked him, "Why, in a Buddhist country with Buddhist refugees, are there no Buddhists here taking care of their Buddhist brothers?" Ron will never forget the man's answer: "Ron, have you ever seen what Buddhism does to a nation or people? Buddha taught that each man is an island unto himself. Buddha said, 'If someone is suffering, that is his karma.' You are not to interfere with another person's karma because he is purging himself through suffering and reincarnation! Buddha said, 'You are an island unto yourself.' "

The leader of the relief effort continued, "Ron, the only people that have a reason to be here today taking care of these 300,000 refugees are Christians. It is only in Christianity that people have a basis for human values and that people are important enough to educate and care for. For Christians, these people are of ultimate value, created in the image of God, so valuable that Jesus Christ died for each and every one of them. You find that value in no other religion, in no other philosophy, but in Jesus Christ!" [17]

Buddha Vs. Jesus Christ

Siddhartha Gautama, as mentioned earlier, did not believe in the existence of God. His objective was to restore Hinduism, which he felt had degenerated from a religion of multitudinous, false gods to a perceived authentic belief system. Buddha considered himself to be a 'way-shower' for others. His followers, however, exalted him to the status of a god after his death. It is ironic that idolatry, a practice Buddha abhorred and sought to eradicate, is today an elemental feature of the religion he founded. It is even more absurd that the countless idols to which Buddhists bow down are idols of Buddha himself.

The Christian Gospel states unequivocally that Jesus is the Son of God. The Gospel of Matthew, for instance, says, "And a voice from heaven said, 'This is my Son, whom I love; with him I am well pleased.'" (Matthew 3:17, NIV). Further, the Gospel of John repeats Jesus' own words claiming that he is God, i.e., "I and the Father are one." (John 10:30, NIV). One cannot rightfully or truthfully profess he or she is a Christian without acknowledging Jesus as God.

Jesus taught that he is the way and not simply one who showed the way. Such an affirmation appears in the Gospel and reads, "I am the way and the truth and the life. No one comes to the Father except through me." (John 14:6, NIV).

When asked how the world began and who or what created the universe, the Buddha is said to have kept silent because, in Buddhism, there is no beginning and no end. Instead, there is an endless circle of birth and death. One would have to ask what kind of originator or maker created people to live, endure so much pain and suffering, and then die over and over again?

The Bible says God sent his Son to die for humankind so people do not have to suffer for eternity. He sent his Son to let people know they are not alone and that he loves them. Christians know there is more to life than suffering and dying. Scripture makes it clear, "…but it has now been revealed through the appearing of our Savior, Christ Jesus, who has destroyed death and has brought life and immortality to light through the gospel." (2 Timothy1:10, NIV). The Christian Gospel speaks about a definitive, merciful God who encourages his wayward children to approach his Throne of Grace and choose eternal life by accepting Jesus as their Redeemer and committing themselves to live for him.

The God of the Bible is a personal God. He is a God of compassion and does not seek to punish and/or alienate his children, and welcomes all who repent of their sins and follow him. There is no interminable cycle of birth and death (reincarnation) whereby the individual, primarily through his or her own means, may achieve a state of enlightenment or *nirvana*, which is the highest level of consciousness, i.e., a state in which one supposedly gains release from the pain and suffering that pervades the physical world.

The concept of nirvana is irrational and, therefore, evades proper explication. Jesus' teaching on heaven, in contrast, was quite specific. He said people's physical bodies die, but the souls of his followers ascend to be with him in heaven. The Gospel of Mark says, "When the dead rise, they will neither marry nor be given in marriage; they will be like the angels in heaven." (Mark 12:25, NIV).

Buddha claimed people do not have individual souls, i.e., the individual self or ego is an illusion. Consequently, Buddhist philosophy avers there is no merciful Father (God) in heaven who sent his Son (Jesus) to die for people's sins, grant them salvation, and provide the way for them to share in God's glory...and thereby escape the damnation of a place called hell!

CHAPTER THIRTEEN

CHRISTIANITY COMPARED WITH MAJOR RELIGIONS & PHILOSOPHIES – HINDUISM, YOGA & REINCARNATION

HINDUISM - ITS ENCROACHMENT INTO AMERICA & EUROPE

Proponents of Western humanistic philosophy, the latter an agglomeration of various attempts at providing answers to life's questions without acknowledgment of the participation or involvement of a supernatural or divine player, perennially find themselves wandering in a sea of uncertainty and confusion. Humanistic philosophy, in the main, rejects supernaturalism and stresses an individual's dignity, worth and capacity for self-realization through reason.

Western humanists, as far back as the 1970s, courted Hinduism, an Eastern belief system or worldview with a clear majority of its adherents on the Indian sub-continent, as a probable alternative to mainstream Christianity. Although Hinduism, like other perceived solutions to the lack of secular answers to people's questions about life and its various ramifications, never impacted a Western and European populace to the extent Western humanists anticipated it would, many of its teachings nevertheless became entrenched in the minds of a fair number of Americans and Europeans.

Eastern religious philosophy, of which Hinduism (discussed in the immediate chapter) and Buddhism (see Chapter Twelve) are prime examples, is attractive to Western humanists for three chief reasons.

Firstly, Eastern philosophy allows an individual the wherewithal, without the use of chemicals or drugs like LSD (*Lysergic acid diethylamide*, a hallucinogenic drug also known as acid)[1] to experience a subjective, so-called reality occurrence. In other words, one endeavors to alter or change the nature or level of his or her consciousness through the practice of Yoga or other forms of Hindu meditation, such as the Transcendental Meditation program introduced by the Indian guru Maharishi Mahesh Yogi in India in the 1950's.

Secondly, Hinduism and Buddhism infer parallelism between evolutionary humanism as delineated by Darwinian scholarship and Eastern religious contemplation that suggests a transmigration of the human soul over innumerable cycles of rebirth called reincarnation. Evolutionary theory, as proposed by secular science, teaches that humankind, once a glob of lifeless protoplasm, underwent an absurdly illogical progression along a path of biological mutations and became what it is today after billions of years.

Reincarnation is the philosophical or religious concept that the non-physical essence (soul) of a living being starts a new life in a different physical form or body after biological death. It is also called rebirth or transmigration and is a part of the Saṃsāra doctrine of cyclic existence or the cycle of death and rebirth. [2]

Thirdly, to many people, Eastern philosophy, including Hinduism and Buddhism, seems to provide a rationale for preserving the environment, even though the Hindu or Buddhist approaches the issue from a perspective that might be different from the outlook of the individual who is not religiously inclined. A central theme of Eastern philosophy is monism, or the Hindu Vedanta postulation that "all is one." The Vedanta or *Uttara Mīmāṃsā* is one of the six orthodox schools of Hindu philosophy.

Monist doctrine declares that man is one with nature, one with the universe, and one with all living things. The cosmos is an intertwined or unified whole with no independent parts. Everyone and everything share a cosmic Oneness that envelopes all that exists.

Humanists, in general, view themselves as replacing a god figure or overseer. They see affiliation with Hinduism, including where it encompasses preserving the environment, as an endeavor to save themselves and to acknowledge the pantheistic message of Eastern philosophy.

The Pantheistic belief that "all is God" parallels the monist Hindu Vedanta philosophy of "all is One." Consequently, in a microcosmic sense Eastern philosophy alleges man is one with the universe (monism), but the universe is God (pantheism). According to Eastern philosophy, then, man is one with God and is in fact, God! The forgoing doctrine notwithstanding, Hinduism perplexingly fosters the idea that "God" or "the universe" is really "impersonal enlightenment."

Hinduism's Scriptures, Gods & Goals

Hinduism is one of the world's oldest organized religions. Its sacred writings date as far back as 1400 to 1500 B.C. The worldview is also one of the most diverse and complex, with its adherents paying homage to millions of deities. Hindus have a wide variety of core beliefs and Hinduism represents many different sects. Hinduism is the third-largest religion in the world, with 1.1 billion followers. The majority of the world's Hindus exist in India and Nepal. [3]

The main texts of Hinduism are the Vedas, considered the most important, Upanishads, the Mahabharata, and the Ramayana. These writings contain hymns, incantations, philosophies, rituals, poems, and stories on which Hindus base their beliefs. Other texts used in Hinduism include the Brahmanas, the Sutras, and the Aranyakas.

Hinduism is often understood as being polytheistic, supposedly recognizing as many as 33 million gods, but the belief system also has one "god" that is supreme—Brahman (see below). The "impersonal enlightenment" referred to in the preceding sub-section represents the Brahmaic entity, which is both unknowable and featureless and sometimes believed to exist in three separate forms collectively known as the Trimurti. The Trimurti comprises Brahma (the Creator), Vishnu (the Preserver), and Shiva (the Destroyer). Each of the Brahmaic constituents is also known through many other specific incarnations. It is difficult to summarize Hindu theology since the various Hindu schools contain elements of many other theological systems. Hinduism, as mentioned earlier, can be Monistic or Pantheistic.

Brahma and Brahman are two characters in Hindu religion and philosophy. While Brahma refers to the four-faced god described in the religious texts of Hinduism, Brahman is the Supreme entity described in the Upanishads and manifests itself into the universe.

According to Hindu philosophy, Brahma is the god of creation. He creates living beings. He is also the writer of the destinies of people and is the originator of the four Vedas. He lives in a separate world called the Satyaloka. Saraswati is his wife or consort, and Sage Narada is his son, who is a staunch devotee of Vishnu.

Brahman is an impersonal entity believed to inhabit every portion of reality and existence throughout the entire universe. Brahman is invisible to the naked eye. It, not he, can only be experienced. Brahman is supposedly all-pervasive and omnipresent. Those who experience the Brahman become realized souls. All individual souls are parts of the Supreme Brahman. After gaining liberation from human bodies, individual souls become one with the Brahman. Death relates only to one's body and not to one's soul. Upanishads extol Brahman and say it is indestructible. Brahman cannot be burnt, made wet, or blown away.

According to Advaita Vedanta, a school of Hindu philosophy and religious practice and one of the classic Indian paths to spiritual realization, [4] Brahman has neither shape nor color. It cannot be seen and cannot be smelled, either. Brahman dwells in every living being, according to Advaita. It resides in human beings, animals, birds, trees, nature, objects, and virtually everywhere.

Panentheistic Hinduism and Theistic Hinduism are two additional forms of the Hindu worldview. According to Panentheistic Hinduism, the world is a part of God, the latter who is viewed as the soul of the universe and the universal spirit present everywhere, which at the same time "transcends" all things created.

While pantheism asserts that "all is God," panentheism claims God is greater than the universe. Some versions of panentheism suggest the universe is nothing more than the manifestation of God. In addition, some forms of philosophy claim the universe exists within God.[5] Panentheism and Pantheism characterize much of Hindu and Buddhist thought and philosophy. [6]

Theistic Hinduism teaches there is only one God, distinct from Creation. While the Vedas, the earliest Hindu scriptures, are for the most part henotheistic, i.e., they advocate the belief in the supremacy of one god without denying the existence of others, the notion of one supreme entity or self becomes more prominent in the Upanishads, the culmination of the Vedas.

One who realizes the Supreme Brahman becomes an individual of self-realization. Such an individual acknowledges the necessity of all the pairs of opposites, such as heat and cold, happiness and sorrow, profit and loss, victory and defeat, and failure and success. He or she is not disturbed by failures and insults. He or she purportedly is in total control of his or her mind, sees Brahman everywhere and remains liberated. Brahman is the supreme controller.[7]

The supreme self or Brahman, in addition to its immanence in constituting the basis of all things, is also the essence of non-being. It therefore retains a sense of ineffability. In other words, Brahman is incapable of being expressed or described in words and/or is not to be spoken of because of its inexpressible sacredness.

Some schools of Hinduism may be atheistic, deistic, or even nihilistic. The diversity of doctrines heaped under the Hinduism worldview is perplexing. One consequently is at a loss to determine what makes a philosophy "Hindu" in the first place. Some scholars of comparative religion seem to think if a belief system recognizes the Vedas (classical Hinduism's most important text) as sacred, then it is classified as Hindu dogma. If a belief system does not acknowledge the Vedas as sacred, then it is not Hindu philosophy.

The Vedas are more than theological texts. They contain a rich and colorful "theo-mythology," i.e., a religious mythology that interweaves myth, theology, and history to establish a foundational religious anecdote. Such "theo-mythology" burrows so deeply into India's history and culture that to snub the Vedas is to express opposition to the country itself. Consequently, Hinduism rejects a belief system if it does not embrace Indian culture to some extent. A philosophy that accepts Indian culture and its theo-mythical history easily qualifies as "Hindu" even if its theology is theistic, nihilistic, or atheistic. Such ready contradiction in Eastern philosophical texts may be problematic for Westerners who seek logical constancy and rational defensibility in their religious views. The Hindu may see the inconsistency as a genuine logical contradiction. The Christian would likely consider the conflict simple hypocrisy or indifference to truth.

Hinduism views mankind as divine. Since Brahman is everything, Hinduism asserts everyone is divine. Atman, or self, is one with Brahman. All of reality outside of Brahman is theoretically a mere illusion. The spiritual goal of a Hindu is to become one with Brahman, thus ceasing to exist in an illusory form of "individual self." Hindus and Buddhists refer to this state of Enlightenment by various names - Moksha, Samadhi, Kaivalya (Hindus), Nirvana (Buddhists), and Satori (Zen Buddhists). In Western countries, people refer to this ostensibly enlightened state as "Cosmic Consciousness," "Unified Field of Creative Intelligence," "Absolute Bliss," and "One with Self."

The freedom from self or material existence is referred to as "moksha." The Hindu believes until he or she achieves moksha he or she will be repeatedly reincarnated in order to work towards self-realization of the truth - the truth being that only Brahman exists, nothing else. Karma, which is a principle of cause and effect governed by nature's balance, determines the mechanics of reincarnation. What one did in the past affects and corresponds with what happens in the present. Present behavior, in turn, determines what takes place in one's life in the future. The reincarnation cycle, as intimated before, is supposedly spread over multitudinous deaths and rebirths.

The Hindu Trimurti

Hinduism is a complicated religion with many gods, some of whom may or may not be avatars or envoys of the tasks delegated by a single supreme lord. Different sects within Hinduism emphasize the worship of

296

different gods based on proclivity, leading, and needs, and different Hindu teachers interpret the same writings from different standpoints and consequently arrive at different meanings.

Hindu philosophy, in some instances, unites three of the prominent Hindu gods to form the "Trimurti," a triple deity of supreme divinity in Hinduism, [8, 9] through which the cosmic functions of creation, maintenance, and destruction are personified. Typically, the "Trimurti' consists of Brahma (not Brahman), the creator. Vishnu, the preserver, and Shiva, the destroyer. [10]

Vishnu and Shiva are two significant avatars or representations of the supreme lord (generally held to be Brahman), who has three manifestations, according to the Rigveda (1700–1100 BC). The Maitri Upanishad (800–400 BC) has a note, quite likely a subsequent addendum, about the combination of Brahma, Vishnu, and Shiva. The first mention of the Trimurti itself, however, was in the poem "Birth of the War-god," written in the 4th or 5th century AD. It wasn't until the time of the Puranas (AD 300) that Hindu scholars brought the members of the Trimurti together and defined their roles in caring for the cosmos.

"The Birth of the War-god" is an epic poem in seventeen cantos. It consists of 1096 stanzas or about 4400 lines of verse. The subject, a story taken from old mythology, is about the marriage of the god Shiva, the birth of his son, and the victory of this son over a powerful demon. [11]

Brahma creates and gives life force to creation. One of his main aspects is knowledge and the dissemination of knowledge. He does not command worship as a separate entity today and has only a handful of temples in India.

Brahma committed a sin and, depending on the story, was (a) too lenient and blessed demons, (b) tried to seduce his daughter, or (c) lied. He has to work under the supervision of Vishnu or Shiva. Brahma, the god, is not to be confused with Brahman, meaning "absolute, supreme reality or the manifestation thereof" or Brahmin, which is the Hindu caste of priests.

Vishnu maintains all the worlds under his jurisdiction. He was a minor god in the early days of Hinduism, and even now, some of his incarnations, such as Lord Rama and Lord Krishna, are the recipients of more adulation than him. Hindus generally claim Buddha is another incarnation of Vishnu, but Buddhists, who believe in enlightened humans instead of gods, disagree. Vishnu exemplifies kingship and military power and enforces order through physical force.

Shiva (or Rudra-Siva) is the destroyer or absorber god. He and Vishnu often competed for the title of "Supreme Lord." Shiva is prone to fits of anger, and his destructive inclination comes from his desire to see the world as newer and purer. Like Vishnu, his incarnations receive more adulation than he does. Shiva is the god of male fertility and also of asceticism or temperance as well. Self-denial, i.e., abstemiousness or abstinence, supposedly increases a man's "ascetic heat" and makes him more attractive to women.

The Trimurti, while it is a complement of Hindu literature, does not seem to represent a significant aspect of Hinduism as practiced, but more of an explanation of the workings of the cosmos. The Trimurti, in essence, addresses the interests and capabilities of the three gods, i.e., Brahma,

Vishnu, and Shiva, with the intent to transform them into a consolidated focus on creation, maintenance, and destruction.

One theory is that the concept of the Trimurti emerged in order to bring worshipers from different Hindu sects into a more cohesive group. Vaishnavites who worshiped Vishnu and Saivites who revered Shiva could join in worshiping a single supreme lord who oversaw a maintainer (Vishnu) and destroyer (Shiva) with the addition of a creator, Brahma, while still adhering to the dictates of their particular sect or faction. When all three deities of the Trimurti incarnate into a single avatar, the avatar is known as Dattatreya.[12] Other Hindu sects combine different gods to form the "Trimurti" triad and choose groupings from the deities Brahma, Vishnu, Bhava, Shiva, and Krishna.

While the defined concept of the Trimurti is a relatively new addition to Hinduism, the importance of the number three (3) is not. Hinduism advocates three layers of nature, three states of being, three divisions of both time and the day, and three phases of life and self-realization, to name a few. It is not surprising the supreme lord would systematize the cosmos in accordance with the characteristics of three of his chiefest avatars.

The Hindu Trimurti is not like the Christian Trinity. The Christian Trinity is one God in three co-equal, co-eternal Persons, i.e., God the Father, God the Son, and God the Holy Spirit. Many Hindus reject the concept of the Trimurti, and even those who accept the Trimurti see the triad as three Hindu gods appearing as avatars, manifestations, or modes of the supreme lord, not as separate entities.

Peculiar Characteristics Of The Hindu Mindset

Hinduism AND THE Loss OF Personality

Hinduism, via its premises of monism and pantheism, which teach that "all is one," all is God," and "all is impersonal," does a dreadful disservice to the principles concomitant with human value and meaning. If everyone and everything represent the impersonal God, as the foregoing precepts claim, then man is as much a god as he is a cockroach. Monism and pantheism declare an animal is the impersonal God, a tree is the impersonal God, and dirt is the impersonal God; therefore, man is the same as an animal, a tree, or dirt.

Hinduism suffers from the perennial problem of being unable to lift the level of nature to the level of humanity. It instead devalues human beings and equates them to the lowest level of nature. Hindu doctrine proposes to destroy individual personality and identity as it teaches that human beings, animals, and nature are nothing more than fragmented elements lost in an impersonal whole.

Hinduism and the Loss of Personal Characteristics

An impersonal universe, if such a thing exists, contributes to the obliteration of human personality and all the unique characteristics attendant to the human state. The following human conditions or propensities cannot exist in an impersonal universe.

Love and Compassion – Love and compassion are two of the foremost expressions of human emotions and temperament. Such states of mind are

300

absent in an impersonal universe. There is no commitment to love or no tendency to be compassionate, as such emotions have no basis in an impersonal environment. An individual will is lost in a morass of perplexing relationships with faceless, depersonalized constituents.

Hindu and Buddhist cultures in places where the worldviews are predominant, i.e., India, Indonesia, Southeast Asia, and East Asia, consider the establishment of hospitals and schools inconsequential. This is because Hinduism and Buddhism teach that human values, like other aspects of the temporal world, are "Maya" or illusory and hardly of any importance. It is interesting to note people in the abovementioned regions generally consider a Hindu "swami" (a Hindu ascetic or religious teacher) a "parasite," as they do a Buddhist monk. Swamis and monks, apart from divulging their religious teachings, do nothing for anyone. Instead, they subsist by begging and living off other people's generosity while renouncing the material world.

Moral Choice – There is no basis for moral precept and practice in an impersonal universe. If "all is one" and "all is impersonal," then there is no line of demarcation between good and evil. The all-encompassing *one-or-all* environment contains both good and evil, with no means of distinguishing between the two mentalities since personality and the physical world are illusions. Eastern religious philosophy essentially says there is no difference between loving someone and killing him or her.

Human Will & Freedom of Choice – An impersonal or featureless universe abandons the wherewithal or means of human will and freedom of choice. According to Hinduism (and Buddhism), an individual's lot or station in life is the result of his or her karma in a past life. Karma, as explained earlier, is the teaching that actions in one's present life determine what his or her destiny will be in the next cycle of life. The forgoing karmic belief helps foster a fatalistic mindset in Hindus and Buddhists in places like India and Southeast Asia, among other locations. Fatalism teaches that fate predetermines the incidents or events in one's life in such a way that he or she is incapable of effecting any change whatsoever. The approach nullifies any desire for human achievement in life since everything has been determined in advance.

Hinduism and the Marginalization of Science and Technology

Science is a body of knowledge and a method of inquiry based on observation and experimentation. Scientific discoveries and advances, aided and abetted by technological expertise, serve to ameliorate the existence of people in numerous ways, including saving and prolonging their lives.

Modern science progressed to its present stage because past scientists and other pioneers of empirical knowledge acknowledged the reality of the material and physical world, and many felt an intelligent Creator brought it into existence. Such a premise prompted the expectation that the results of their work would be reliable and provide logical and intelligent answers to inquiries in the fields of healthcare, medicine, agriculture, and industry, among other ventures.

The Hindu viewpoint that the temporal, material world is "Maya" or an illusion becomes a problematical issue when one considers the reality and

302

importance of science and technology in the lives of people and other living things. How do people undertake scientific research and conduct experiments if everything and everyone are illusions? Hindu philosophy is one of the core reasons scientific precept and practice never developed past a certain level in India – there was never a philosophical footing or foundation for the pursuit of progressive or even nominal technology. As a result, the standards of living in places like India and Southeast Asia invariably left much to be desired.

Thankfully, India today is home to many able scientists and engineers. The introduction of Western philosophy and education within a Judeo-Christian framework by the British in the eighteenth century marked a turning point for India as the country chose to pursue opportunities in science and technology. The source of such learning lay not in the ambit of Hindu philosophy but in the educational programs of schools and universities founded by Christian missionaries.

Hinduism's Caste System

Hinduism's caste system, an inextricable component of the religious worldview, is undergirded by an extraordinarily vile and mortifying mindset that relegates a certain social class of people to a plateau of incomprehensible cruelty and cold-heartedness.

Historians opine that India's caste system, which splits up Hindus into different societal groups according to their work and birth, goes back some 3,000 years. According to the caste system, Hindus are divided up into four classes based on the principle of "varna," which literally means "color" - the Brahmins (the priestly class); the Kshatriyas (the ruling, administrative and warrior class); the Vaishyas (the class of artisans, tradesmen, farmers and merchants); and the Shudras (manual workers). There are also people who fall outside the system, including tribal people and the Dalits, previously known as "untouchables," although the term is somewhat contentious.

Dalits are a group of people historically considered outcasts in societies from South Asia (India, Nepal, Sri Lanka, Pakistan, and Bangladesh) and Eastern Africa (Somalia). Such disenfranchised people adopted the appellation "Dalit" as a means of somehow overcoming the ghettoization imposed by the caste system.

The Dalit social status carries with it the stigma of "untouchability" because it is associated with menial, degrading tasks immediately connected with their traditional occupations, which include unclogging sewers, disposing of dead bodies, and cleaning latrines (toilets). Additionally, Dalits suffer various forms of discrimination, many of them debasing and inhumane, such as the following.

- The caste system forbids Dalits from engaging in cultural and social activities with the rest of the community, including entering temples, sitting in the main spaces of villages, taking part in religious programs, and eating with the rest of the community during village ceremonies.

- The caste system forbids Dalits from using the same items as non-Dalits in the communities; they cannot rent or even enter the homes of non-Dalits, use the same wells, or eat and drink from the same dishes.

- In schools, Dalit children have to sit separately from the rest of the students during the midday meal and are the only ones asked to clean latrines in the schools.

- Dalits cannot marry members of other castes.

- Dalits may not contest for office in elections.

- Dalits may not hoist the national flag during Independence Day or Republic Day.

- Dalits have to vote or not vote for certain candidates during elections.

- Dalits face social boycotts by dominant castes if they refuse to perform their "duties."

Despite more or less recent laws that aim to create equality among Hindus and Indians in general, the caste system in India continues to have a strong impact on society. It is a form of social and religious inequity that refuses to go away.

Yoga - More Than Exercising & Posturing

Yoga as a religious discipline has its roots in the work of Patanjali, a notable Hindu scholar of the Samkhya school of Hindu philosophy. Scholars generally agree Patanjali lived between the 2nd century B.C. and 4th century A.D.. [13, 14] Patanjali was the compiler of the Yoga sūtras, a text on Yoga theory and practice. The Yogasutras comprise one of the most important texts in the Hindu tradition and in the foundation of classical Yoga. [15]

Yoga is an eight-step process called "Astanga Yoga" (Astanga means "eight steps" in Sanskrit). Its central objective is to help an individual transcend or liberate himself or herself from the physical and personal existence in this world and reach a state of enlightenment. The Sanskrit phrase "cittavritta-mrodha," which means "the stoppage of the mental and physical processes," enunciates the philosophy's goal.

Scholars refer to the first five steps of Yoga as "Hatha Yoga." Hatha Yoga is representative of the external, physical disciplines that supposedly precede the transcendence to the peak Hindu state of "Moksha" or enlightenment. Hatha Yoga involves disciplining the body and mind through isometrics and breathing exercises with the objective of detaching one's mind from the sense organs until he or she loses awareness of the physical world.

"Raja Yoga" encompasses the last three steps of Yoga practice. This final phase consists of internal meditative techniques for final transcendence. The first step of Raja Yoga is "dharama," or concentration. According to the scholar Patanjali, "dharma" involves holding one's mind within a center of spiritual consciousness in one's body or focusing on some divine figure or entity either within one's body or outside it. Such activity often takes the form of a mantra, i.e., a mystical formula of invocation or incantation.

The second phase of Raja Yoga is called "dhyana," or meditation. "Dhyana" relates to continual and unbroken thought directed toward the object of concentration or divine entity addressed in the mantra undertaken in the first step mentioned earlier. Hindu philosophy says the yoga practitioner achieves oneness with the universe at this stage, even though there remains a sense of personal existence.

The third or final stage of Raja Yoga is "Samadhi," or absorption, whereby the practitioner purportedly achieves unity with the universe without the sense of individual existence. Hindu doctrine claims "Samadhi" is the point in the yogi's life where he or she transcends the physical, personal, intellectual, and tactile levels of life and diffuses into or blends with the Impersonal Universe. He or she dispenses with every aspect of his or her personality and becomes one with Brahmin.

Many people in the West, including many professed Christians, are not familiar with the history of yogic philosophy and practice and possess an uninformed, superficial understanding of the practice. They feel yoga is simply a means of physical exercise that strengthens and improves the flexibility of the muscles and that eventually attains a semblance of emotional calmness or peace of mind.

The philosophy behind yoga, however, is much more than physically improving oneself. It is an ancient Indian practice believed to be the path to spiritual growth and enlightenment. Since Hinduism presumes everything is God, and yogic philosophy is inseparably linked to this worldview, yoga makes no distinction between humankind and God and, therefore, is little more than self-worship disguised as a form of spirituality.

Yoga, An Anti-Christian, Soul-Damning Philosophy

Yoga, from its inception, was a blatantly anti-Christian philosophy, and such thinking remains unchanged. It teaches one to focus on oneself instead of the one true God. Yogic philosophy encourages its followers to seek the answers to life's difficult questions within their own consciousness instead of through the Holy Bible or the Word of God. Yogis traverse a path they misguidedly believe to be one that leads to true spiritual growth and optimal enlightenment.

The likelihood of yogic practice encompassing maleficent supernatural activity in its later stages ought to be a cause for deep concern. Paranormal or otherworldly goings-on that does not proceed from Biblical import is evil and damning, no matter what the religion or worldview in question. Whoever participates in such a pursuit endangers his or her soul and exposes himself or herself to the very real possibility of eternal damnation.

The following extracts from the Holy Bible caution people about Satan, his demons, and their agenda of continuous cunning and inveiglement in trying to confuse people and lead them astray. Such subterfuge includes the devil's and his minions' capacity to impersonate the so-called gods and deities of myriad religions and philosophies (see "The Kali Puja Ceremony" below). Their primary objective is to prevent as many people as possible from approaching God's Throne of Grace and accepting Jesus Christ and his atoning sacrifice of the cross as a means of obtaining everlasting life in a place called heaven. The alternative, i.e., rejecting Christ, is a frightening proposition and the most regrettable mistake one can make.

Be alert and of sober mind. Your enemy the devil prowls around like a roaring lion looking for someone to devour. (1 Peter 5:8, NIV)

For such people are false apostles, deceitful workers, masquerading as apostles of Christ. And no wonder, for Satan himself masquerades as an angel of light. It is not surprising, then, if his servants also masquerade as servants of righteousness. Their end will be what their actions deserve. (2 Corinthians 11:13-15, NIV)

Dear friends, do not believe every spirit, but test the spirits to see whether they are from God, because many false prophets have gone out into the world. (1 John 4:1, NIV)

See to it that no one takes you captive through hollow and deceptive philosophy, which depends on human tradition and the elemental spiritual forces of this world rather than on Christ. For in Christ all the fullness of the Deity lives in bodily form and in Christ you have been brought to fullness. He is the head over every power and authority. (Colossians 2:8-10, NIV)

The next two Biblical passages warn against the damning rituals of witchcraft, occultism, and spiritism. The Gospel of Matthew extract brings to the fore the danger of the yogic practice of emptying one's mind and compromising one's awareness of the temporal world in an effort to enhance his or her proclivity toward attaining an optimal state of enlightenment. Demons seize any and every opportunity to invade and/or occupy an individual's mind and mislead him or her to think an envisioned, wholesome deity or divine entity seeks to indwell his or her being.

When you enter the land the Lord your God is giving you, do not learn to imitate the detestable ways of the nations there. Let no one be found among you who sacrifices their son or daughter in the fire, who practices divination or sorcery, interprets omens, engages in witchcraft, or casts spells, or who is a medium or spiritist or who

309

consults the dead. Anyone who does these things is detestable to the Lord; because of these same detestable practices the Lord your God will drive out those nations before you. You must be blameless before the Lord your God. (Deuteronomy 18: 9-13, NIV)

When an impure spirit comes out of a person, it goes through arid places seeking rest and does not find it. Then it says, 'I will return to the house I left.' When it arrives, it finds the house unoccupied, swept clean and put in order. Then it goes and takes with it seven other spirits more wicked than itself, and they go in and live there. And the final condition of that person is worse than the first. That is how it will be with this wicked generation. (Matthew 12:43-45, NIV)

The Kali Puja Ceremony

The following first-person story lends credence to the earlier inference that Satan and his demons sometimes pretend to be so-called gods and deities of false religions in order to confuse people and lead them astray. The author was a firsthand witness to the *Kali Puja* ceremony described below, which took place in his native Guyana, South America, many years ago.

Kali Puja, also known as Shyama Puja or Mahanisha Puja,[16] is a festival originating from the Indian subcontinent and dedicated to the Hindu goddess Kali. It is celebrated in the main by the Bengali, Chittagonian, Sylheti, Rangpuri, Odia, Assamese, and Maithili sects. [17]

I distinctly recall attending, as an onlooker, a Kali Puja ceremony in rural Guyana in the early nineteen-seventies. The ceremony took place during the night and there were a great many people present. I witnessed select individuals being beaten mercilessly in attempts to rid them of demons. I saw with my own eyes a man who had red-hot coals put into his mouth retain the burning embers for an extended period of time. He apparently felt nothing. I saw men and women dancing furiously to the beat of drums for hours on end without tiring. I knew some of the participants personally. Stored away somewhere in the recesses of one of our former homes, if they were not distributed or discarded years ago, are pictures we took of individuals dancing and taking part otherwise in the unusual proceedings that evening many years ago.

I remember the wild, trance-like look on the faces of the people involved in the exorcisms. The whole affair was loud and frightening at times. I purposed never to again attend a gathering like the one I joined that night.

In retrospect, I look to the Holy Scriptures and the wisdom they impart in an attempt to put the matter into proper perspective. The following biblical extract about Jesus encountering and exorcising a demon appears in the Gospel of Luke.

Once when He was in the synagogue, a man possessed by a demon began shouting at Jesus. 'Go away! Why are you bothering us, Jesus of Nazareth? Have you come to destroy us? I know who you are – the Holy One sent from God.'

Jesus cut him short. 'Be silent!' He told the demon. 'Come out of the man!' The demon threw the man to the floor as the crowd watched, and then it left him without hurting him further.

311

Amazed, the people exclaimed, "What authority and power this man's words possess? Even evil spirits obey Him and flee at His command!"

(Luke 4:33-36, NLT).

In the foregoing Scriptures, the Son of God himself commands an evil spirit to leave the body of a man it had taken over. Jesus has power and dominion over the devil and all of his demons, and one day, as Almighty God's divine plan of redemption for humankind reaches the appropriate stage, Satan and his fallen angels will be dispatched to a place of eternal punishment.

The Bible shares a story about certain men who were not followers of Jesus attempting to cast out demons. They even used his Holy Name to misrepresent themselves. The demons knew the exorcists were not vested with proper or sufficient authority to perform exorcisms and severely chastised them and chased them away. (Acts 19:13-16)

At the aforementioned "exorcism" ceremony, there was a young man whom I knew personally. We were fairly good friends. He was one of the main attractions at the festival if the gathering could warrant such a description. The young man would hear the distinctive beat of the drums from miles away, and he would begin to dance wherever he was, regardless of the surroundings. I lost contact with him many years ago. I knew him to be a most pleasant person. Wherever he is now, whatever he is doing, I hope he is dancing to the beat of a different drum - one ringing out the message of the Gospel of Jesus Christ!

The attendees at the Kali Puja ceremony, most of them at least, felt they were witnessing the power of the goddess Kali that evening. Little did they know the goddess itself and its helpers were demons and not divine beings. The Holy Bible, as intimated earlier, affirms that the gods and goddesses of false religions are non-existent, and Satan and his demons often impersonate such "deities" in their endeavors to confound people and steer them away from approaching the true Savior and Redeemer of lost humankind – Jesus Christ! [18]

Reincarnation

Reincarnation, or "transmigration," as taught in Eastern philosophy, i.e., Hinduism and Buddhism, views history or time as cyclical. People undergo an endless cycle of rebirths according to karmic determinants, with the expectation of eventually transcending the material or so-called illusory world and attaining Brahmic enlightenment or a *Oneness* with the cosmos.

The law of karma says one's good or bad deeds determine in what form or station he or she will return in the next life. Should one fail to observe the Hindu or Buddhist principles by which to live and renounce the physical world, the latter which is supposedly an illusion, one may come back as a lower life form. An instinctive reaction by most Hindus and Buddhists to the forgoing credo is to accord selected measures of sacrosanctity to certain non-human lifeforms. Consequently, the possibility of a human being returning as a cow or rat has made both animals sacred in India and Southeast Asia, among other places. After all, a cow, as well as a rat, may be a reincarnated human being. People do not kill cows and rats in India. Such actions are philosophically taboo and formally outlawed. The United Nations estimates rats outnumber India's human population, i.e., 1.35

billion [19] by about three to one. The rodents consume close to one-fourth of the country's grain crops.

Scholars use the term "transmigration" interchangeably with "reincarnation," even though the latter expression resonates better with Westerners because they are led to believe an individual can only be reincarnated as another human being instead of a rat, a frog, or a snail, as taught by transmigration. An Indian ascetic named Swami Vivekananda introduced "transmigration" in 1891 at the World's Fair on Religions in Chicago, USA. The swami substituted the term "reincarnation" for "transmigration" to allay the fears of his Western audience, who abhorred the idea of returning to a subsequent life as a lower animal or creature. The doctrines, however, are essentially the same.

A central problem with transmigration or reincarnation and its inference of a cyclical existence is the unavoidability of a life determined by impersonal fate whereby people are helpless to effect any positive change in their lives. Instead, they resign themselves to a fatalistic mindset that dictates they probably will have to traverse thousands of deaths and rebirths until they achieve "moksha" or liberation from "the present world of illusion." Their ultimate expectation is to rise above worldly circumstances and achieve a state of impersonal nothingness. Meaning and purpose in life become nonexistent.

Invalidating Reincarnation

The following essential considerations help invalidate the alleged authenticity of the reincarnation premise. The reflections proceed from the Holy Bible and constitute timeless, indispensable truths.

The Personality of God - People who believe in reincarnation deny the existence and sovereignty of a personal Creator. Such people consider themselves to be part of an impersonal universe. The Holy Bible's doctrine about God abrogates the argument for reincarnation.

According to the Bible, God is personal. He created humans as individual beings, revealed himself to them and made it possible for them to have a personal relationship with him. Reincarnation and transmigration are unsubstantiated and pointless presumptions.

The Atoning Sacrifice of Jesus Christ – Christ's sacrifice on the cross when he covered all of humankind's sins with his shed blood was the ultimate payment on behalf of each and every one of his children. Such a selfless deed was a one-time ransom for the souls of people everywhere, for all time. The Bible says, "And by that will, we have been made holy through the sacrifice of the body of Jesus Christ once for all." (Hebrews 10:10, NIV). Christ did for sinful humankind what it could not do for itself. He is the eternal Lamb of God who died for everyone's sins. Only his divine and pure blood could accomplish such an undertaking.

The Resurrection of Jesus Christ – Jesus Christ died on the cross for God's entire human creation and then rose from the dead three days later. He overcame death and is today the living Redeemer and Savior. Christ's victory over death puts to naught any requirement for a man to die more than once, especially countless times, in order to attain a so-called perfect, nirvanic, or optimally enlightened state of existence.

The Resurrection of the Believer – Christ's resurrection ensures the resurrection of the Christian believer. The Gospel of John states, "I am the resurrection and the life. The one who believes in me will live, even though they die; and whoever lives by believing in me will never die." (John 11:25-26, NLV).

Believers who put their faith and trust in Jesus Christ as their personal Savior and Lord will never die. This is because Christ makes his resurrection power available to them. He defeated death and is the living Savior. He is the eternal God, and he gives the gift of eternal life to his followers. The apostle Paul says, "For to me, to live is Christ and to die is gain." (Philippians 1:21, ESV) It is gain because to be absent from the body after death is to be in heaven with the Lord. Christians, unlike adherents of other faiths and belief systems, are the only people who can laugh at death. They know where they are heading. Death holds no fear for them.

God's Judgement of Humankind – The Book of Hebrews plainly says, "Just as people are destined to die once, and after that to face judgment." (Hebrews 9:27, NIV) The foregoing scriptural statement asserts that everyone dies once and faces an eventual judgment by Almighty God. There is no such thing as reincarnation or cyclic rebirth. One fateful day all of humankind will stand before God and will have to answer the question of all questions - What did you say to Christ's offer of salvation unto eternal life?"

The concept of reincarnation is completely at odds with the teachings of Christianity. The Bible never mentions people having repeated chances at life or coming back as different people or animals. Jesus told the criminal on the cross, "I assure you, today you will be with me in paradise." (Luke 23:43, NLT)

Hinduism Vs. Christianity

The following considerations help summarize the main differences between Hinduism and Christianity.

Christianity has one God who is both personal and knowable.

The Book of Deuteronomy - *"Love the Lord your God with all your heart and with all your soul and with all your strength."*(Deuteronomy 6:5, NIV).

The Book of Corinthians - *"... yet for us there is but one God, the Father, from whom all things came and for whom we live; and there is but one Lord, Jesus Christ, through whom all things came and through whom we live."* (1 Corinthians 8:6, NIV)

Christianity has one set of Scriptures that proclaims God's message of salvation.

The Book of Timothy - *"All scripture is given by inspiration of God, and is profitable for doctrine, for reproof, for correction, for instruction in righteousness."* (2 Timothy 3:16, KJV)

The Book of Romans - *"For whatsoever things were written aforetime were written for our learning, that we through patience and comfort of the scriptures might have hope."* (Romans 15:4, KJV)

The Book of Romans - *For I am not ashamed of the gospel of Christ: for it is the power of God unto salvation to everyone that believeth; to the Jew first, and also to the Greek (Gentile).* (Romans 1:16, KJV)

The Gospel of John - *"Search the scriptures; for in them ye think ye have eternal life: and they are they which testify of me."* (John 5:39, KJV)

The Gospel of Mark– *And Jesus answering said unto them, "Do ye not therefore err, because ye know not the scriptures, neither the power of God?"* (Mark 12:24, KJV)

Christianity teaches that God created the earth and all who live upon it.

The Book of Genesis - *"In the beginning God created the heavens and the earth."* (Genesis 1:1, NIV)

The Book of Hebrews - *"By faith we understand that the universe was formed at God's command, so that what is seen was not made out of what was visible."* (Hebrews 11:3, NIV)

Christians believe that man was created in God's image and lives only once.

The Book of Genesis - *"So God created mankind in his own image, in the image of God he created them; male and female he created them."* (Genesis 1:27, NIV)

The Book of Hebrews - *"Just as people are destined to die once, and after that to face judgment, so Christ was sacrificed once to take away the sins of many; and he will appear a second time, not to bear sin, but to bring salvation to those who are waiting for him."* (Hebrews 9:27-28, NIV)

Christianity teaches that salvation is through Jesus Christ alone.

The Gospel of John - *"For God so loved the world that he gave his one and only Son, that whoever believes in him shall not perish but have eternal life."* (John 3:16, NIV)

The Gospel of John - *"No one can come to me unless the Father who sent me draws them, and I will raise them up at the last day."* (John 6:44, NIV)

The Gospel of John - *"Jesus answered, "I am the way and the truth and the life. No one comes to the Father except through me."* (John 14:6, NIV)

The Book of Acts of the Apostles – *"Salvation is found in no one else (only Jesus Christ), for there is no other name under heaven given to mankind by which we must be saved."* (Acts 4:12, NIV)

Hindus generally regard Jesus Christ as an incarnation of the god Vishnu, one of Hinduism's three main deities that form the Hindu Trimurti (see earlier). According to Hindu mythology, Vishnu is periodically incarnated in the world – in various forms, including a human being. [20] Some Hindus consider Jesus an avatar and, more specifically, the reincarnation of Krishna. In Hinduism, an avatar is the bodily incarnation of a deity on earth. Avatars are most often associated with the god Vishnu. [21]

Hinduism's failure to recognize Jesus Christ as the uniquely incarnated God-Man and Savior i.e., the one solely sufficient source of salvation for humanity - like any other belief system that ignores or jettisons such an all-important truth, leaves its adherents exposed to the heart-wrenching threat of facing an eternity of permanent anguish and torment.

CHAPTER FOURTEEN

CHRISTIANITY COMPARED WITH MAJOR RELIGIONS & PHILOSOPHIES – ISLAM

THE SIX BELIEFS OF ISLAM

Islam endorses six fundamental beliefs described as "Articles of Faith," which form the foundation of the Islamic worldview. [1]

1. *God* – There is one true God, whose name is Allah.

2. *Angels* – Angels are the servants of God, through whom he reveals his will. The greatest angel is Gabriel, who appeared to Muhammad. Everyone is appointed two "recording angels": one who records his or her good deeds and one who records his or her bad deeds.

3. *The Prophets* – Allah has spoken through many prophets, but the final and greatest prophet is Muhammad. Other prophets include Noah, Moses, and Jesus.

4. *The Holy Books* – The Qur'an or Koran is the holiest book of Islam, believed to be Allah's final revelation to man. It supersedes all previous revelations, including the Bible. It contains Allah's word as passed on orally to Muhammad by the angel Gabriel. The

Koran contains 114 chapters or Surahs. Muslims also recognize the Law of Moses (the Torah), the Psalms (Zabur), and the Gospels (the Injil or the New Testament) but consider them to be corrupted.

5. *The Day of Judgement* – A fateful day when each individual's good and bad deeds will be balanced to determine where he or she will spend eternity.

6. *The Decree of God* - Allah ordains the fate of all. Muslims are fatalistic. "If Allah wills it" is the comment of a devout Muslim regarding almost every situation or decision he or she faces.

THE FIVE PILLARS OF ISLAM

The Five Pillars of Islam ("pillars of the religion") are five basic facets of Islam, considered mandatory by believers, and are the foundation of Muslim life. They are summarized in the famous hadith of Gabriel. [2]

1. *Affirmation* (Shahada) – "There is no God but Allah, and Muhammad is his messenger." Devout Muslims recite this affirmation constantly.

2. *Prayer* (As-Salah) – A Muslim must pray five times a day, kneeling and facing Mecca.*

3. *Almsgiving* (Zakah) – A worthy Muslim must give 2.5 percent of his or her income to the poor.

322

4. *The Fast* (Siyam) – Faithful Muslims fast from dawn to dusk every day during the ninth month of the Islamic lunar calendar, i.e., Ramadan, which is a sacred period.

5. *The Pilgrimage* (Al-Hajj) – A Muslim should journey to Mecca at least once in his or her lifetime.*

*These two Pillars of Faith were purloined from Saudi Arabian culture by Muhammad and incorporated into Islamic philosophy. The practices were already being widely observed long before the founder of Islam was born.

Some Islamists add a sixth Pillar of Faith, known as *The Holy War* (Jihad), to the forgoing list. History records the Islamic intent to spread the worldview by force, especially in instances where people refuse to accept the Quranic message. The Koran claims Islam is the only true religion and Allah is the only true God - a doctrine of exclusivity common to most monotheistic faiths – except Islam encourages and condones the extermination of non-Muslims as part of an agenda geared toward worldwide subjugation. Islamic fundamentalists utilize Jihad, or holy war, to help achieve such an objective.

The Prophet Muhammad

Muhammad, the founder of Islam, was born in Mecca in A.D. 570 and died at age 62 in A.D. 632. Mecca is a city in the Hejazi region of the Arabian Peninsula and the plain of Tihamah in Saudi Arabia. At the time of Muhammad's birth, Mecca was the center of trade and religious activity in the region. Muhammad was a camel driver until the age of 25 when he met and married Khadija bint Khuwaylid, a wealthy woman who was 15 years his senior. In another narration, it is reported that she was 28 years old [3] and had four children with Muhammad after their marriage. [4]

When Muhammad was 40 years old, he claimed to have had divine revelations after retreating to a cave normally occasioned by other so-called seekers of truth who would go there to pray and meditate. The cave, called "Hira," lay about two miles north of Mecca in Saudi Arabia.

There are four conflicting versions of the Quran (the Muslim holy book) as to who or what ministered to Muhammad during his visits to the cave. Muslims today claim it was the angel Gabriel who spoke to Muhammad, and conclude such interaction proves he was a prophet to the Arabs. For several years, Muhammad thought he was the victim of attacks by a demon. Once his wife convinced him otherwise, he began to preach what he claimed he heard.

During the supposedly angelic visitations, which continued for about 23 years until Muhammad's death, the angel purportedly revealed to him advice and instructions from Allah (the Arabic word for "God" used by Muslims). Legend has it that Muhammad endured epileptic fits during the revelations. He would shake, perspire, and foam at the mouth. Dissenting religious scholars, including many non-Muslim theologians, opine a demon-possessed Muhammad during the so-called fitful attacks. Muhammad, for his part, claimed his revelations were from an "angel of light." It is interesting to note the Quran does not record the incidence of any witness or witnesses to any of Muhammad's numerous experiences in the cave.

324

Muhammad claimed the revelations from the angel Gabriel authorized him to impart the following teachings to mankind.

1. There is no god but Allah, and he is the one true god who created everything.

2. Man is God's slave, and it is his first duty to submit to God and obey him. The term "Islam" means "submission" in Arabic, and a Muslim is an individual who submits to Allah's will.

3. There will be a day of judgment when God will raise the dead to life and judge all and reward or condemn them according to their deeds. The good doer goes to heaven and the wicked to hell.

The Meccans rejected Muhammad's message and essentially proscribed him from their environment. The self-designated prophet fled to Medina, a city in the Hejazi region of the Arabian Peninsula, about 210 miles north of Mecca. Scholars refer to the migration or journey of Muhammad and his followers in A.D. 622 from Mecca to Medina (formerly Yathrib) as the "Hegira." [5] The Hegira fundamentally marks the beginning of the Islamic calendar.

While in Medina, Muhammad presented himself as a prophet and apostle to the Jews and Christians who lived there. They rejected his advances, and he subsequently turned his attention to non-Jews and non-Christians and encouraged them to pray to Allah, a tribal deity Muhammad himself worshipped.

Muhammad supposedly received additional revelations in Medina that directed him to attack caravans passing through the region, loot them, and kill the men. History records Muhammad participating in scores of battles during which very many people died. The Muslim prophet also allegedly received a revelation in which he was told to kill and banish all Jews.

Muhammad and his followers beheaded some 800 prisoners from the Banu Qurayza tribe.* It is an episode that is not only completely at odds with the idea that Islam is a peaceful religion but also refutes the claim that the worldview supersedes Christianity since even the latter religion's most dedicated critics could hardly imagine Jesus and his disciples doing such a thing. [6]

While Muslim apologists usually engage in deception in dealing with the challenges posed by the Banu Qurayza incident, the fate of the Qurayza people is only the first of many such massacres followers of Islam perpetrated over the centuries. Whether it be the 4,000 Jews at Granada in 1066, the 100,000 Hindus on a single day in 1399, or the millions of Christian Armenians in the early 1900s, untold numbers of innocent people perished in mass executions at the hands of Islam's crazed disciples. [7]

*The Banu Qurayza was a Jewish tribe that lived in northern Arabia, at the oasis of Yathrib (now known as Medina), until the 7th century, when their conflict with Muhammad led to their massacre.

The Quran contains at least 109 verses that speak of war with nonbelievers, usually on the basis of their status as non-Muslims. Some are quite graphic, with commands to chop off heads and fingers and kill infidels wherever they may be hiding. Muslims who do not join the fight are called 'hypocrites' and warned that Allah will send them to hell if they do not join in the extermination of infidels. [8]

Muslim scholars maintain Muhammad had a revelation in A.D. 628 that decreed Islam should be exalted above all other religions, including Christianity and Judaism. In A.D. 629, Muhammad gathered an army of 10,000 men, revisited Mecca, his birthplace, and conquered the region. He subsequently imposed Islam on the rest of the Arabian tribes. The prophet died in A.D. 632, having subjugated much of the Arabian Peninsula. Muslims eventually spread Islam by the sword across North Africa.

Today, Islam numbers around 1.8 billion followers worldwide and is the second-largest belief system in the world. [9]

The Qur'an (Koran)

The Qur'an, often spelled as *Quran* or *Koran*, is the primary holy text of the Islamic faith. According to Muslim belief, the angel Gabriel dictated the words of the Qur'an to Muhammad, who relayed them orally to his followers. Historians generally suggest Muhammad was illiterate, much to the consternation of die-hard Muslim theologians. The term Qur'an literally means "the recitation." Muslim scholars produced the Koran about 800 years after the Christian Gospel came into existence.

Islam considers the Qur'an to be the perfect, eternal message of Allah and obligatory confirmation of Muhammad's status as a prophet. The words of the Qur'an existed in purely oral form until after Muhammad's death. Several early Islamic leaders subsequently assembled the texts into writing. The Qur'an is shorter than the New Testament of the Bible, and according to Islamic theology, it can only be truly understood when read in its original Arabic dialect. The majority of Muslims are incapable of reading and understanding the Arabic language. Hence, the entrenched authority of Imams or Muslim community leaders who lead prayers and services and offer spiritual advice, and by default, should be conversant with the Arabic language.

Muhammad's followers memorized his sayings, maintaining an entirely oral record of the Qur'an. Muslim scholars inscribed minor portions on leaves, rocks, and bones. The central message of the Qur'an is that mankind drifted from the truths that Allah presented to men like Noah, Abraham, Moses, and Jesus. Per Muhammad, man corrupted the words and message of Allah. The Qur'an or "recitation" is meant to be the final, authoritative statement from Allah to humankind. The Qur'an also commands Muslims to follow Allah's instructions and to employ various methods of "struggle," including jihad or war, to spread the Qur'anic message worldwide.

While the Judeo-Christian Scriptures include a large amount of history as well as theology, the Qur'an is overwhelmingly theological. Most of the book's content relates to statements about the nature of Allah, creation, mankind's obligations, and the afterlife. Historical corroboration, including the incidence of archaeological substantiation that would enhance the authenticity of Islam, or any other religious worldview for that matter, is woefully absent.

Recording the Koran

Following Muhammad's death, Islamic leaders undertook the task of recording the Qur'an in written form. The process involved utilizing the memories of the Hafiz (men committed to memorizing the Qur'an) and collecting various written fragments. The result was a single manuscript kept by the leader of Islam, Caliph Abu Bakr (A.D. 573 – A.D. 634), one of Muhammad's fathers-in-law and former companions.

As Islam continued to spread, however, variations within the Qur'an began to arise. This was due to continued oral memorization, alternate writings on leaves and bones, and differences of opinion among Muslims about what Muhammad said and/or meant. A later Caliph, Uthman ibn Affan (A.D. 579 – A.D. 656), a son-in-law and former companion of Muhammad, ordered the collection of all written copies of the Qur'an, including scraps. Uthman had a panel of scholars determine the "correct" words and pronunciations of the gathered material. He subsequently sent a single copy of the revised Qur'an to each of the major regions of the Empire and ordered the destruction of all prior copies in all forms.

The assemblage of the Qur'an stands in stark contrast to the compilation of the New Testament. Muslim scholars selectively compiled the Qur'an - at least twice - after Muhammad's death. Neither endeavor produced a large number of physical copies. The exercises took place entirely under the direction and discretion of the leaders of the Islamic Empire, who resolutely destroyed all prior records after the second compilation. Essentially, this means the Qur'an seen today resulted from a tightly controlled process that fell under the jurisdiction of a group of very few people very soon after its initial production. There is no way to know if or to what extent the information changed from the original.

The New Testament, on the other hand, resulted from the work of various authors at various times and places. Religious sages produced the original texts in the first century of the Christian Era in Greek, which became the common language of Eastern Mediterranean people after the conquests of Alexander the Great (335–323 BC). Scholars believe all of the works eventually incorporated into the New Testament date to no later than around 120 AD. [10]

Religionists copied New Testament texts freely, independently, and often. There was no central control and no restrictions. The end result is the wealth of information present today, i.e., thousands and thousands of surviving manuscripts from an extremely broad geography. The advantage to this is that no one group, church, or government ever had the ability to dictate what those manuscripts expressed. As a matter of fact, scholars estimate that there exist 5,686 Greek New Testament manuscripts today, with an internal consistency of about 99.5% - an astonishing measure of accuracy. [11]

Where there exist multitudinous versions of a manuscript and there are copyist errors or changes, they stand out clearly. Biblical manuscripts had been in circulation for centuries by the time the Roman Empire focused its attention on the Bible. At that point, some three hundred years after the production of the first documents, it was impossible to replace the texts with any kind of controlled version. Effectively, it means it is far more reasonable to assert the current text of the Bible represents the original words of the authors than it is to volunteer a similar contention that the modern Qur'an represents the original words of Muhammad, the validity or truthfulness of his utterances notwithstanding.

Structural Composition of the Qur'an

The Qur'an consists of 114 chapters, or surahs. It is much shorter than either the Old Testament or New Testament used by Christians. Each individual chapter is typically given a name for easier identification based on its content. Rather than being arranged chronologically, Quranic chapters appear in order of length, from longest to shortest. Those with more verses, or more *ayat*, are generally the earlier chapters, while the shorter ones come later. Not only are the Qur'an's chapters presented in non-chronological order, but the topics under discussion from one verse to the next are often dissimilar.

The Qur'an can be divided into two major categories of content: Meccan and Medinan. Such classifications correspond to the two major phases of Muhammad's ministry, the first in the city of Mecca and the second in the city of Medina. The character of Islam, Muhammad's message, and the words of the Qur'an demonstrate a noticeable change after Muhammad left Mecca for Medina.

In Mecca, Muhammad was a relatively powerless, persecuted figure. Meccan surah(s) tend to emphasize coexistence, non-coercion, and peace. These are the ayat most often cited by Muslim scholars who promote Islam as a religion of peace. However, after moving to Medina, Muhammad became a powerful warlord. The Medinan suwar, pertaining to the time from the end of Muhammad's life to the early days of the Islamic Empire, is notably more aggressive in composition. These form the bulk of verses cited by those who believe Islam endorses belligerence and violence, and probably accurately so, as Medinan Islam depicts many of the prophet's later reworked religious principles, including the jihadist approach (see below) toward the subjugation of non-believers.

The term "Jihadism" (also "jihadist movement" and "jihadi movement") is a 21st-century neologism found in Western languages to describe Islamist militant movements perceived as military movements "rooted in Islam" and "existentially threatening" to the West. [12]

Interestingly, Islam teaches a concept known as abrogation or "replacement." According to this premise, a surah or ayah later considered more authoritative than an earlier surah or ayat, replaces and overrides the former. Scholars often address abrogation in discussions on contradictions within the Qur'an, especially with regard to the difference in tone or outlook between the earlier Meccan and later Medinan texts. Muslim academic Farooq Ibrahim decries the application of the *abrogation* principle in Quranic scholarship.

> *In conclusion, for many Muslims, this concept that Allah as the absolute sovereign can alter his commands and replace them at will appears in harmony with their view of God. To them, the Will of God is paramount. While I respect their thoughts and opinions, this was at odds with my view of an all-knowing and all-wise God. It seems to me that a man like myself is limited and needs to learn from his mistakes and therefore, needs to provide better commands after earlier*

commands have not worked. It is not self-evident to me that the creator and sustainer of the universe is like that. Hence, I reached a point where I could no longer defend the Quran as we have it today as the true and complete revelation of Allah. This cast doubts on the credibility of the current Arabic Quran's claim that it is the perfect and final revelation of Allah. [13]

Interpretation and Use of the Qur'an

Interpretation of the Qur'an is more complex than researching and analyzing other religious texts. Most Muslims cannot engage in deep study of the Arabic Qur'an, just as most Christians cannot engage in professional-level studies of the original Hebrew and Greek manuscripts of the Bible. As mentioned earlier, the vast majority of Muslims worldwide cannot speak or read the Arabic language. Christians have access to translations of the Bible. However, Islamic theology teaches the words of the Qur'an can be fully understood only in their original Arabic vernacular.

Muslims envisage the miracle of the Qur'an in its supposedly perfect language and structure. According to Islam, therefore, translating the Qur'an into any other language is unworkable and forbidden. Any "changing" of the text, even in a realistic or viable manner, is akin to an interpretation of the original meaning or intent, which is unacceptable. The forgoing adamant and inflexible position against researching and analyzing the text of the Qur'an puts most non-Muslims at odds with the perceived miracle of the words of Allah.

The short length and primarily oral nature of the early Qur'an encouraged the development of Hadith (also Ahadith) or oral traditions. Hadith is the record of the words, actions, and silent approval of the Islamic prophet Muhammad. Within Islam, the authority of Ḥadīth as a source of religious law and moral guidance ranks second only to that of the Qur'an. The comments are generally from Muhammad's wives, lieutenants, or close associates. Not all Muslims believe hadith accounts proceed from divine revelation. Muhammad's followers did not create Hadith material immediately after his death but several generations later when scholars collected, collated, and compiled them into a great corpus of Islamic literature.

Independent collections of Ahadith lend to distinctive branches of the Islamic faith. A small minority of Muslims called Quranists reject all Ḥadīth. [14]

The language barrier, the chaotic nature of the text, and the existence of the hadith make the Qur'an significantly more abstruse and incomprehensible than the Christian Bible. The average Muslim does not have access to all of the thousands and thousands of variant collections of oral traditions that form the hadith. The Qur'an, it follows, although it is the most important Islamic religious text, is not the religion's sole source of reference and guidance. As a result, most Muslims rely heavily on some form of interpretation-commentary in order to understand and apply the Qur'an. Such commentaries, or *tafsirs*, generally combine explanations of context with the opinions of various Islamic scholars.

Tafsir is the Arabic word for "exegesis" or the critical explanation of the text, usually of the Qur'an. An author of a tafsir is a mufassir. A Qur'anic tafsir attempts to provide elucidation, explanation, interpretation, and context or commentary for a clear understanding and conviction of God's will. [15]

Principally, a tafsir deals with the issues of linguistics, jurisprudence, and theology. In terms of perspective and approach, tafsirs can be broadly divided into two categories, namely *tafsir bi-al-ma'thur* (lit. received tafsir), which the prophet Muhammad and his companions transmitted during the early days of Islam and *tafsir bi-al-ra'y* (lit. tafsir by opinion), which derives through personal reflection or independent rational thinking. [16]

The Qur'an And The Bible Compared

Islam has a complex relationship with the Bible, in no small part because of statements made in the Qur'an. In theory, Muslims believe that Allah (God) gave written revelations to men like Moses, David, and Jesus. They refer to Jesus as Isa. The Qur'an seems to contradict itself by suggesting the revelations given to the aforementioned prophets and others ought to be studied while also inferring such information is corrupt. Qur'anic teaching also suggests Christians worship a trinity of God, Jesus, and Mary - a gross misunderstanding of Christian doctrine.

In short, the Bible stands as the strongest empirical evidence against the validity of the Qur'an. There are copies of the Bible, available in museums today, written centuries before the birth of Muhammad. The claim that the text of the Bible changed cannot be sustained. Recall the earlier mention of there being around 5,686 New Testament manuscripts in Greek in existence today, with an internal consistency of 99.5 percent. Yet the text of the Bible does not agree with or mirror the text of the Qur'an or the Qur'an's assertions about the Christian Holy Book.

While the Qur'an is held in high esteem by Muslims, it does not occupy exactly the same position within the Islamic faith as the Bible does within Christianity. Its composition, character, and history are extremely different from those of the Bible, and ultimately, the validity of the Qur'an simply cannot survive a protracted comparison with the Christian Scriptures.

Islam's History

The pre-Islamic world in which Muhammad lived was one governed by animism, i.e., the belief that all things have a spirit or soul, including animals, plants, rivers, mountains, stars, the moon, and the sun. Each being is a spirit that can offer help or harm to humans. As such, spirits must either be worshiped or appeased. [17] Arab tribes worshipped so-called sacred magic stones they believed possessed powers of protection and blessing. They housed such stones in the Kaaba, a building at the center of Islam's most important mosque in the Hejazi city of Mecca in Saudi Arabia.

Muhammad's own tribe set down a black stone in the Kaaba. It was probably part of an asteroid or meteorite, which worshippers nevertheless view to this day as being divine. In Muhammad's time, a major religion was Sabianism, which advocated the worship of celestial bodies. Believers viewed the moon as a male deity and used a lunar calendar. Fasting, a pagan rite, followed the appearance of the crescent moon and was a fixture in Arab

336

religious practice long before Muhammad was even born. Muslims later adopted the practice as one of Islam's five pillars of faith.

Unbeknownst to probably the majority of Muslims, the use of the crescent moon and star as Islamic symbols actually pre-dates Islam by several thousand years. Most sources agree these ancient celestial symbols were in use by the peoples of Central Asia and Siberia in their worship of sun, moon and sky gods. [18]

Muslims incorrectly claim Allah is the same God Christians worship, just under another name. As a matter of fact, Allah was a deity known to pre-Islamic Arabs. Allah was the moon God of Muhammad's tribe and took the form of a black stone that allegedly fell from heaven.

Pre-Islamic Arabs in Arabia worshiped Allah, the moon god (male) and the sun god (female), who married each other. The two gods produced three goddesses called the Daughters of Allah. The goddesses stood at the top of the pantheon of 360 Arabian deities housed in the Kaaba. Muhammad, after he assumed control of Mecca, destroyed all the idols in the Kaaba except the stone deity, Allah.

The crescent moon in the Islamic symbol actually denoted reverence to the moon god, Allah, in pre-Islamic culture in the Middle East. The crescent moon remains on every flag of every Islamic nation. The crescent moon adorns the dome of every mosque around the world – yet the majority of Muslims know nothing about its origin and meaning.

Islam & Gender Parity

Islamic Schools of Legal Premise

A widespread consensus of opinion among many religious scholars is that Islam, like a number of other theocratic and autocratic religious worldviews, encourages the inequitable treatment of their womenfolk.

Scholars of comparative religion generally agree that at the onset of Islam in the early 600s A.D., Muhammad, the founder of the worldview, instituted expansions of women's rights to encompass inheritance, property, and marriage rights. It was a daring and progressive undertaking during a time when women held few, if any, rights. Over the centuries following the establishment of Islam as a pervasive belief system, *Sunni* Islamic scholars introduced conflicting views as to how to interpret the Quran and the sayings of the Prophet Muhammad's sayings, which gave rise to four prominent schools of legal premise.

The four prominent schools of Islamic law are named after their founders and are called the Hanafiyya, the Malikiyya, the Shafiyya, and the Hanbaliyya schools of religious law. Most Muslims regard these four schools as equally valid interpretations of the religious law of Islam.

Sunni Islam (/ˈsuːni, ˈsʊni/) is the largest branch of Islam, followed by 85–90% of the world's Muslims, and simultaneously the largest religious denomination in the world. Its name comes from the word Sunnah, referring to the tradition of Muhammad.. The differences between *Sunni* and *Shia* Muslims arose from a disagreement over the succession to Muhammad and

338

subsequently acquired broader political significance, as well as theological and juridical dimensions.

The strictest of the above schools is known as the Hanbaliyya institution, which forms the basis of hardline inclinations or trends in Islamic thought, including Saudi's ultra-conservative Wahhabism and variants of Salafism. It is this trend of thinking that has further isolated women in the eyes of the law in states where Islamic law is practiced or enshrined. [19]

However, that hasn't stopped activists, civil society actors and even governments from trying to elevate the legal status of women with regards to Islamic jurisprudence.

Making Inroads to Fair Treatment of Women

Mauritania, officially the Islamic Republic of Mauritania, is a sovereign country in Northwest Africa. Labeled as an exporter of conservative Islamic thought, women's rights have long been subjugated to the status of men, a legacy that was underwritten by the Hanbali school's influence in the region. The Mauritanian government, however, is seeking to remedy such a situation.

Early in 2020, the governmental administration supported proposed legislation to "remove prejudice and discriminatory attitudes towards women and girls." The draft law's main objective is to better protect women from violence and provide a legal avenue to bring charges against perpetrators, oftentimes family members such as husbands or fathers. It specifically designates violence against women as a crime.

The proposed legislation, as expected, has triggered controversy among conservative scholars and leaders, who see it as an affront to men's status. They argue that the draft legislation violates Islamic law, and as such cannot be granted legitimacy through parliamentary backing.

Similar efforts to effect women's rights in Mauritania failed in 2018 for analogous reasons. Currently, the country does not have adequate laws on rape and other forms of sexual violence, according to Human Rights Watch (HRW), an international non-governmental organization headquartered in New York City that conducts research and advocacy on human rights.

Religious Lobbying & Blurred Advocacy

Saad Eddin al-Hilali, professor of comparative law at Cairo's al-Azhar University, considered the seat of Sunni thought, said those who tend to voice opposition against women's rights in the name of Islam make up a "religious lobby."

Al-Hilali said that the lobby often comprises "senior religious scholars who appear in the media to influence public opinion … regardless of whether an opinion is religiously permissible or forbidden."

In Islam, each legal school of thought and practice has particularized ways to establish a sound opinion on a matter. However, al-Hilali believes that few are adhering to the criteria, and instead are opting to express their personal views on important issues.

"Everyone cannot pretend that his personal opinion comes directly from God," al-Hilali said. "For, in principle, all jurisprudence can contain right and wrong — even if it is expressed from the highest authority."

Marwa Sharafeldin, Egyptian activist and owner of an Oxford University doctorate, agreed, saying the use of religion as a means to prevent legal protections for women is clearly unacceptable, even in Islam.

Sharafeldin said such reasoning could be used to justify violence against women within Islam, a notion she considers fundamentally incompatible with the religion's values. As a result, the distinction between jurisprudence and religion is often deliberately blurred by proponents of hardline interpretations.

"Some representatives of political Islam are trying to distinguish themselves at the expense of women," Sharafeldin said.

An Uphill Battle

Musawah, a movement centered on equality in the Muslim family, recently launched a campaign to "build support at the national, regional, and global levels for the urgency of reform towards equality and justice for women living in Muslim contexts."

The movement has identified at least 45 countries that have Muslim family laws that discriminate against women and girls. Musawah said, "Not only do these family laws fail to fulfill the Sharia requirements of justice, but they are also being used to deny women rights and dignified choices in life."

Even in Egypt, long considered a bastion of moderate religious practice, women's legal rights have been eroded and have come under threat from conservative lawmakers who have facilitated delays to much-needed revisions to the country's family law. Musawah opponents say the latest proposals would weaken men's status by strengthening women's legal claims.

For activists, civil society groups, and even governments, ensuring that women and girls are accorded equal rights with their male counterparts remains an uphill battle.

"For women and girls, there can be no equality in society without equality in the family," said Musawah. "Religion, ideology, culture or tradition can no longer be used to justify discrimination against women and girls."

Evaluating Islam

Compared to Christianity, Islam has some similarities, but there are significant differences. Like Christianity, Islam is monotheistic. However, Muslims reject the Trinity, i.e., the revelation of God as the Father, Son, and Holy Spirit.

Muslims claim Jesus was one of the most important prophets but not God's Son. Islam asserts that Jesus, though born of a virgin, was created like Adam. Muslims do not believe Jesus died on the cross. They do not understand why Allah would allow his prophet Isa (the Islamic word for "Jesus") to die a torturous death. Yet the Bible shows how the death of the perfect Son of God was essential to pay for the sins of the world (Isaiah 53:5-6; John 3:16; 14:6; 1 Peter 2:24).

Islamists contend the Qur'an is the final authority and the last revelation of Allah. Christian sages, however, completed the Bible in the first century with the Book of Revelation. The Bible warns against anyone adding to or subtracting from God's Word (Deuteronomy 4:2; Proverbs 30:6; Galatians 1:6-12; Revelation 22:18). The Qur'an, as a claimed addition to God's Word, directly disobeys God's command.

Muslims believe paradise can be earned through observing the Five Pillars. The Bible, in contrast, reveals sinful man can never measure up to God's holy standards (Romans 3:23; 6:23). Only by God's grace may sinners be saved through repentant faith in Jesus (Acts 20:21; Ephesians 2:8-9).

As a result of the forgoing essential differences and contradictions, Islam and Christianity cannot both be true. The Bible and the Qur'an cannot both be God's Word. The truth has eternal consequences, i.e., an eternity of a joyous existence in the company of Almighty God and his Redeemer Son, Jesus Christ, *or* eternal damnation and estrangement from them.

The following passage from the Holy Bible advises all of humankind:

Dear friends, do not believe every spirit, but test the spirits to see whether they are from God, because many false prophets have gone out into the world. This is how you can recognize the Spirit of God: Every spirit that acknowledges that Jesus Christ has come in the flesh is from God, but every spirit that does not acknowledge Jesus is not from God. This is the spirit of the antichrist, which you have heard is coming and even now is already in the world. (1 John 4:1-4, NIV).

PART FIVE

CHRISTIANITY COMPARED WITH NEW
RELIGIONS, PHILOSOPHIES & CULTS

CHAPTER FIFTEEN

CHRISTIANITY COMPARED WITH NEW RELIGIONS, PHILOSOPHIES & CULTS - JEHOVAH'S WITNESSES: THE WATCHTOWER BIBLE & TRACT SOCIETY

JEHOVAH WITNESSES (JW) – AN OVERVIEW

The sect known today as the Jehovah's Witnesses started out in Pennsylvania in 1870 as a Bible class led by Charles Taze Russell, the organization's founding father. Russell grew up in a Protestant church but did not agree with Biblical teachings dealing with subjects such as eternal judgment, hell, and the Trinity or Triune Godhead.

Russell, even though he was not a known religious scholar, developed his own theology. He published a six-book religious series called *Studies in the Scriptures*, which he described as "practically the Bible itself." [1] Russel claimed to know the Greek alphabet but, under examination, could not read Greek letters. [2] He appeared in court in 1912 after being charged with perjury.

In 1879, Russell launched the *Watchtower* magazine. He incorporated his organization as the Watchtower Bible & Tract Society (WTBTS) in Pennsylvania in 1884 and later relocated its headquarters to Brooklyn, New York, USA.

Russell considered himself a religious seer and prophesied Jesus Christ would return in 1874. He changed the date for Christ's return to 1914 after the first prophecy went unfulfilled. Russell's second prediction about Christ's return did not materialize either. Undaunted, he redefined the second coming of Christ to mean Jesus Christ indeed came back in 1914, in spirit form, to help set up the Jehovah's Witnesses organization. Charles Russell died a failed prophet in 1916.

Joseph Franklin Rutherford assumed leadership of the Watchtower organization after Charles Russell's demise. Rutherford galvanized the Jehovah Witnesses (a name he coined) organization into the formidable theocratic "kingdom" it is today. Jehovah Witnesses claim their church is God's government on earth, and all other governments proceed from Satan. The organization's doctrine denies that Jesus Christ is God and the Holy Spirit is God. Jehovah alone, Jehovah Witnesses profess, is God.

Joseph Rutherford, like Charles Russell before him, considered himself a prophet._He set 1925 as the new date for Armageddon. Rutherford advertised the prophecy widely across the United States, especially in the *Watchtower* magazine, as a prediction not of man but of God and "absolutely and unqualifiedly correct." [3] The year 1925 came, and there was no Armageddon. Rutherford claimed Jehovah's Witnesses, who anticipated the end of the world, "misunderstood" him and that the 1925 Armageddon prophecy did not originate from God.

In the late 1930's, Rutherford, known for his contemptuous denouncements of traditional Christianity, insisted Armageddon was "coming soon," although he refrained from predicting any revised date for the event. In 1941, the organization stated, "There were just a few remaining months before Armageddon." [4] Franklin Rutherford died in 1942, and Armageddon still had not taken place. Rutherford, like Charles Russell before him, was a failed prophet.

Nathan H. Knorr took over the Watchtower Bible & Tract Society in 1942. Knorr was the architect behind the organization's resilient missionary outreach around the world. Knorr also spearheaded the Watchtower organization's re-translation of the Holy Bible, which led to the creation of *The New World Translation of the Christian Greek Scriptures.* Notwithstanding claims by Jehovah's Witnesses that Greek scholars carried out the translation of the Bible from the Greek, scholars were able to identify gross errors in their work. Experts thought the exercise was a deliberate attempt to produce a book that accommodated preconceived Witness theology.

As is wont of so many self-designated religious seers, Knorr, like his predecessors Charles Russell and Joseph Rutherford, sought to establish himself as a charismatic leader with prophetic powers. He prophesied via the *Watchtower* and *Awake* magazines in 1966 that the present age would come to an end in 1975, the latter the "absolutely final" date for

Armageddon.[5] The world did not end in 1975. Armageddon did not occur either. Knorr died in 1977, another failed Jehovah's Witnesses prophet.

More than a million Jehovah's Witnesses left the Watchtower organization in 1976 and 1977, disillusioned with a church that claimed to be the voice of God on earth but which had repeatedly shown itself to be rooted in duplicity and falsehood.

Succeeding leaders of the Watchtower Bible & Tract Society organization after Nathan Knorr were Frederick Franz, the church's leading theologian for over 60 years, who died in 1992 at the age of 98, and Milton Henschel, who served up to 2001. As of 2018, Jehovah's Witnesses reported a monthly average membership of approximately 8.36 million actively involved in preaching, with a peak number of 8.58 million adherents. [6]

Organizational Sovereignty

Jehovah's Witnesses hold fast to the following five fundamental tenets about the Watchtower Organization's sovereignty.

Jehovah's Witnesses:

1. Acknowledge the Watchtower Organization to be God's prophet.

2. Accept the Organization as God's sole channel for his truth.

3. Believe rejection of the Organization is a rejection of God.

4. Believe only the Organization can interpret the Bible, as they are incapable of doing so as individuals.

5. Believe the *Watchtower* magazine contains God's truth, directed by him through the organization.

Jehovah's Witnesses - Teachings At Odds With Christianity

Jehovah's Witnesses and the Watchtower Organization proclaim the following teachings, which are in manifest contradiction with mainstream Christianity.

1. Jesus Christ is a created being, not an eternal God.

2. Jesus is actually Michael the Archangel.

3. Jesus was not resurrected bodily but as a spirit being.

4. Jesus returned invisibly and secretly to earth in 1914 to help form the Watchtower Organization.

5. Jesus was only a man when on earth, not "the Word become flesh."

6. The Holy Spirit is only an active force, not the Person of God.

7. Hell is simply the grave.

8. Heaven's doors are open to only 144,000 people.

9. The majority of Witnesses must remain on earth.

10. Salvation can be maintained only by energetic works for the Organization until the end, when one may then merit eternal life on paradisial earth.

11. Satan is the author of the doctrine of the Trinity.

12. Jesus should not be accorded worship, only honor as Jehovah's first creation.

Denial of Essential Christian Tenets

Jehovah's Witnesses deny the following basic tenets of mainstream Christianity.

1. The Trinity.

2. The deity of Jesus Christ.

3. The bodily resurrection of Christ.

4. The visible return of Christ.

5. The Person of God the Holy Spirit.

6. The promise of Heaven to all believers.

7. The necessity of the new birth for all believers.

8. The Lord's Supper for all believers.

9. The eternal security of all believers.

10. The conscious eternal punishment of the lost.

Rebutting Jehovah's Witnesses (The Watchtower Organization's) Heresy

Following are rebuttals to the above statements of denial of and disagreement with the teachings of the Holy Bible by Jehovah's Witnesses. The Bible, i.e., the Old Testament (written during a period that stretched

350

from the 1660's B. C. to 400s B.C.)[7] and the New Testament (written during the period 35 A.D. to 95 A.D.) [8] has withstood multitudinous attacks on its authenticity over the many centuries since its inception yet essentially stands irrefutable. The sources of the refutation of the claims by Jehovah's Witnesses proceed from the Bible, the same book Jehovah's Witnesses endeavored to distort in their shameful and reprehensible agenda of misinformation. The Bible is unlike any other text on religion or philosophy. Christian apologist Dr. Jason Lisle of *Answers in Genesis* volunteers the following observation.

> *The truth of the Bible is obvious to anyone willing to fairly investigate it. The Bible is uniquely self-consistent and extraordinarily authentic. It has changed the lives of millions of people who have placed their faith in Christ. It has been confirmed countless times by archaeology and other sciences. It possesses divine insight into the nature of the universe and has made correct predictions about distant future events with perfect accuracy. When Christians read the Bible, they cannot help but recognize the voice of their Creator. The Bible claims to be the Word of God, and it demonstrates this claim by making knowledge possible. It is the standard of standards. The proof of the Bible is that unless its truth is presupposed, we couldn't prove anything at all.* [9]

Many scholars of comparative religion view *The New World Translation*, the Jehovah's Witnesses Bible – produced a mere 150 years or so ago by disgruntled, self-appointed "Christian" prophets – as the product of an exercise in shameless manipulation and heresy. As theologian and philosopher Douglas Beaumont (Ph.D. Theology; M.A. Christian Apologetics) opines:

> *Jehovah's Witnesses (JW's) have their own version of the Bible that contains several key changes to the English text in order to lend support for their heretical doctrines. The New World Translation (NWT) is defined by the Jehovah's Witnesses' parent organization (The Watchtower Society) as "a translation of the Holy Scriptures made directly from Hebrew, Aramaic, and Greek into modern-day English by a committee of anointed witnesses of Jehovah" (Reasoning from the Scriptures, 276). The NWT is the anonymous work of the "New World Bible Translation Committee." Jehovah's Witnesses claim that the anonymity is in place so that the credit for the work will go to God. Of course this has the added benefit of keeping the translators from any accountability for their errors and prevents real scholars from checking their academic credentials.* [10]

Detailed Rebuttals to Jehovah's Witnesses Heresy

1. God exists in a Trinity of three eternal and co-equal persons.

As the following passages from the Bible indicate, there are three eternal Persons, Father, Son, and Holy Spirit, within the nature of the one God.

Father:

To all in Rome who are loved by God and called to be his holy people: Grace and peace to you from God our Father and from the Lord Jesus Christ. (Romans 1:7, NIV)

Son:

Thomas said to him, "My Lord and my God!" (John 20:28, NIV)

Holy Spirit:

Peter said, "Ananias, how is it that Satan has so filled your heart that you have lied to the Holy Spirit and have kept for yourself some of the money you received for the land? Didn't it belong to you before it was sold? And after it was sold, wasn't the money at your disposal? What made you think of doing such a thing? You have not lied just to human beings but to God." (Acts 5:3-4, NIV)

2. **Jesus is no less than God in human flesh.**

   For in Christ, all the fullness of the Deity lives in bodily form. (Colossians 2:9, NIV)

3. **God, the Holy Spirit, is the third member of the Holy Trinity.**

   Go and make followers of all the nations. Baptize them in the name of the Father and of the Son and of the Holy Spirit. (Matthew 28:19, NLV)

   While they were serving the Lord and fasting, the Holy Spirit said to them, "Set apart for me, Barnabas and Saul, to do the work to which I have called them." (Acts 13:2, GNT)

4. **Jesus Christ rose bodily from the grave.**

"What!" they exclaimed. "It has taken forty-six years to build this Temple, and you can rebuild it in three days?" But when Jesus said, "this temple," he meant his own body. (John 2:20-21, NLT)

Look at my hands and my feet. It is I myself! Touch me and see; a ghost does not have flesh and bones, as you see I have. (Luke 24:39, NIV)

5. Jesus is visibly coming again to set up his kingdom on earth.

Then the sign of the Son of Man will appear in heaven, and then all the tribes of the earth will mourn, and they will see 'the Son of Man coming on the clouds of heaven' with power and great glory. (Matthew 24:30, NRSV)

But you will receive power when the Holy Spirit has come upon you, and you will be my witnesses in Jerusalem, in all Judea and Samaria, and to the ends of the earth. (Acts 1:8, NRSV)

Behold, He is coming with clouds, and every eye will see Him, even they who pierced Him. And all the tribes of the earth will mourn because of Him. Even so, Amen. Revelation 1:7, NKJV)

6. Salvation is in the Person of Jesus Christ and comes through faith in him.

Believe in the Lord Jesus Christ, and you will be saved – you and your household. (Acts 16:31, NKJV)

For by grace you have been saved through faith, and that not of yourselves; it is the gift of God, not of works, lest anyone should boast. (Ephesians 2:8-9, NKJV)

7. **It is the work of God for man, not a work of man for God.**

But when the kindness and love of God our Savior appeared, he saved us, not because of righteous things we had done, but because of his mercy. He saved us through the washing of rebirth and renewal by the Holy Spirit, whom he poured out on us generously through Jesus Christ our Savior...(Titus 3:4-6, NIV)

8. **Jesus was worshiped and should be worshiped.**

A week later, his disciples were in the house again, and Thomas was with them. Though the doors were locked, Jesus came and stood among them and said, "Peace be with you!" Then he said to Thomas, "Put your finger here; see my hands. Reach out your hand and put it into my side. Stop doubting and believe." Thomas said to him, "My Lord and my God!"(John 20:26-28, NIV)

When they saw the star, they were overjoyed. On coming to the house, they saw the child with his mother, Mary, and they bowed down and worshiped him. Then they opened their treasures and presented him with gifts of gold and of incense and of myrrh. And having been warned in a dream not to go back to Herod, they returned to their country by another route. (Matthew 2:10-12, NIV)

Then those who were in the boat worshiped him, saying, "Truly you are the Son of God." (Matthew 14:33, NIV)

The Heaven-Bound 144,000 Believers

One of the Watchtower Organization's more contentious doctrines revolves around the declaration that only 144,000 people will go to heaven. The suggestion is a preposterous one and in utter contradiction of legitimate Biblical scholarship.

Jehovah's Witnesses believe 144,000 people will merit residence in heaven, while believers who will not be included in this elite group will live on earth forever in a newly created paradise. Where did Jehovah's Witnesses get such an idea? They got it from no other than the failed prophet Franklin Rutherford, who distorted the meaning of Biblical passages in Revelation 7:4 (NIV) and Revelation 14.4 (NIV), which mention a select number of 144,000 people God will set aside for special service in his kingdom.

Rutherford, after he became president of the Watchtower Organization in 1917, prophesied that the great Battle of Armageddon was impending and the world would soon come to an end. In an effort to increase the organization's membership, Rutherford proclaimed only 144,000 people would be taken to heaven.

Jehovah's Witnesses intensified their door-to-door visits to prospective converts and informed them they had better join the Watchtower Organization before it became too late. Armageddon was imminent, and the 144,000-member ceiling was fast approaching fulfillment. Jehovah's Witnesses preached the forgoing message for many years and recruited many new members. Then, in 1935, they found themselves in an embarrassing predicament. The organization's membership surpassed

144,000 adherents, which theoretically meant heaven could hold no more residents. Also, Armageddon had yet to take place!

What would happen to all the extra Witnesses? Where would they go at the end of time after Judgement Day?

Joseph Rutherford had an answer! He conveniently received another revelation from God. The message this time was that everyone who became a Jehovah's Witness before 1935 would go to heaven, while everyone who became a Jehovah's Witness after 1935 would remain on earth and live in a new paradise.[11] Most Jehovah's Witnesses today are convinced they have no hope of ever going to heaven. They believe such bewildering nonsense because Joseph Rutherford told them so.

It is meet to tarry a short while on the issue of the 144,000 heaven-bound Jehovah's Witnesses in order to shed some light on Joseph Rutherford's and, accordingly, the Watchtower Organization's misguided position on the matter.

A few passages of scriptures relative to the 144,000 residents of heaven are as follows.

Then I heard the number of those who were sealed: 144,000 from all the tribes of Israel. (Revelation 7:4, NIV)

These are those who did not defile themselves with women, for they remained virgins. They follow the Lamb wherever he goes. They were purchased from among mankind and offered as first fruits to God and the Lamb. (Revelation 14:4, NIV)

357

After this, I looked, and there before me was a great multitude that no one could count, from every nation, tribe, people, and language, standing before the throne and before the Lamb. They were wearing white robes and were holding palm branches in their hands. (Revelation 7:9, NIV)

Misinterpreting The Scriptures

If the 144,000 souls mentioned in the Book of Revelation of the New Testament represent all, who would end up in heaven, then, according to the Watchtower Organization's presumption, no one who was not of the actual twelve tribes of Israel would be in heaven (see below).

Heaven's sole residents would therefore exclude Abraham, Isaac, and Jacob — who were never members of the tribes of Israel. Such a postulation conflicts with Jesus' affirmation that Abraham, Isaac, and Jacob will be in the kingdom of heaven (Matthew 8:11).

Further, if only 144,000 Israelites, and no one else, will end up in heaven, then not one Gentile has the hope of entering the kingdom of heaven. Such an allusion, however, runs afoul of Christ's promise that says, "I say to you that many will come from the east and the west, and will take their places at the feast with Abraham, Isaac, and Jacob in the kingdom of heaven." (Matthew 8:11, NIV) Jesus plainly referred to Gentiles, among others, when he made the foregoing declaration.

Chapter 7 of the Book of Revelation, which lists the Israelite tribes to which the 144,000 people sealed for God's services belong, interestingly omits the tribe of Ephraim and the tribe of Dan, as the following biblical extract confirms.

From the tribe of Judah, 12,000 were sealed,

from the tribe of Reuben 12,000,

from the tribe of Gad 12,000,

from the tribe of Asher 12,000,

from the tribe of Naphtali 12,000,

from the tribe of Manasseh 12,000,

from the tribe of Simeon 12,000,

from the tribe of Levi 12,000,

from the tribe of Issachar 12,000,

from the tribe of Zebulun 12,000,

from the tribe of Joseph 12,000,

from the tribe of Benjamin 12,000.

(Revelation 7:5-8, NIV)

Were the Watchtower Organization's supposition that the 144,000 sealed residents chosen for special service in God's kingdom an accurate count of heaven's total residents, then no one from either of the Ephraim or Dan tribes will go to heaven because neither tribe appears in the list in Revelation 7:5-8. Consequently, it would mean Old Testament heroes like Joshua (from Ephraim) and Samson (from Dan) will not go to heaven. As a matter of fact, mention of the "tribe of Joseph" (7:8), which was not a tribe at all in a literal sense, is evidence of a kind of symbolism attendant to the scriptural passages about the 144,000 residents of heaven – an allegorical intimation that escapes the *soi-disant* erudition of Jehovah Witnesses scholars.

Jehovah's Witnesses exclude the "great multitude" mentioned in Revelation 7:9 in heaven. The Biblical excerpt reads, *"After this I looked, and there before me was a great multitude that no one could count, from every nation, tribe, people and language, standing before the throne and before the Lamb.'* (Revelation 7:9, NIV). This group, the Witnesses allege, represents the "earthly class." Such an interpretation is amiss for the following reasons.

a) The Apostle John describes the multitude as "standing before the throne" (7:9), which is in heaven (Revelation 1:4; 4:2-10).

b) Furthermore, these saints "before the throne" are serving God in "his temple" (Revelation 7:15).

c) John says, "The temple of God ... is in heaven" (Revelation 11:19).

Should a consistent, literal scheme of interpretation as undertaken by the Watchtower Organization be pursued, the following conclusions would emerge.

a) Only men will be in heaven, hence, Hannah, Mary, Dorcas, Esther, Ruth and women of like faith would be excluded from citizenship in paradise.

b) Only unmarried men who are virgins would obtain residence in heaven. Individuals like Abraham, Moses, Peter, and a host of other Biblical notables would spend eternity estranged from God.

c) Such deliberations are an insult to Biblical scholarship and the auspices of a just and merciful God.

Jehovah's Witnesses Encapsulated - A Religion Mired In Falsehood & Misrepresentation

Close scrutiny of the Watchtower Organization's doctrinal position on such subjects as the deity of Christ, salvation, the Trinity, the Holy Spirit, and atonement for sin through Christ's sacrifice on the cross shows beyond a doubt that Jehovah's Witnesses do not hold to orthodox Christian positions on these issues.

The New World Translation (NWT), the re-translated Bible used by Jehovah's Witnesses, went through numerous editions as religious leaders discovered more and more Scriptures that contradicted their teachings. Unfortunately, the NWT's message is full of distortions, deceptions, and false doctrines. The Watchtower Organization, for instance, gets wrong one of the most important of all religious questions: *Who is Jesus Christ?* Jehovah's Witnesses maintain Jesus Christ is actually the first creation of Jehovah God, not God incarnate as the Bible clearly teaches (Titus 2:13; Colossians 2:9). In doing so, they place Christ in the category of a created creature and neglect to accord him his rightful place as Creator of all things (Colossians 1:16-17; John 1:1-3).

The late Dr. Bruce Metzger (1914 – 2007), a well-known Christian scholar whose works are representative of seminary theological standards, used the following adjectives when describing the *New World Translation*: "a frightful mistranslation," "erroneous," "pernicious," and "reprehensible." British Bible scholar H.H. Rowley (1890 -1969) said the NWT is "a shining example of how the Bible should not be translated." He also referred to the NWT as "an insult to the Word of God." Dr. William Barclay (1907 – 1978), former Professor of Divinity and Biblical Criticism at the University of Glasgow, Scotland, remarked about Jehovah's Witnesses - "It is abundantly clear that a sect which can translate the New Testament like that is intellectually dishonest." [12]

A further reason to reject the claims of the Watchtower Organization is its long track record of engaging in false prophecy. The Watchtower Society, on numerous occasions, predicted in print the end of the world, the most recent dates being in 1946, 1950, and 1975. Even more pitiable is the Jehovah's Witnesses practice of glossing over their misrepresentation of the true scriptures when prophecies fail to materialize and substituting them with further "revelations" as they claim to be "the true prophetic mouthpiece for God on earth." The Watchtower Organization's history of false prophecy stands in glaring contrast to the standard for a true prophet as laid out in the Holy Scriptures, i.e., "If a prophet speaks in the name of the Lord and what he says does not come true, then it is not the Lord's message. That prophet has spoken on his own authority, and you are not to fear him." (Deuteronomy 18:22, GNT)

Moreover, the Watchtower Organization persists in indoctrinating its members to decline to enlist for military service, to shun the celebration of holidays, and to refuse to salute the nation's flag. The impetus for these restrictions finds its root in Jehovah's Witnesses' false claim to be the exclusive, organized collection of God's people. Jehovah's Witnesses see the entire "World system," i.e., any activity not connected with the Watchtower Organization, as connected to Satan and thus prohibited. Such practices include blood transfusions, which the Watchtower Organization wrongly believes to be proscribed by Scripture. The organization says a blood transfusion "may result in the immediate and very temporary prolongation of life, but at the cost of eternal life for a dedicated Christian."[13] The Society irrationally assumes the biblical prohibition against eating blood (Genesis 9:4; Acts 15:28-29) extends all the way to the modern procedure of blood transfusions. Such illogicality and ignorance have led to the loss of the lives of many Jehovah's Witnesses and even their children.

Despite a track record of repeated false prophecies, cultic isolation of their own people, and a flagrant mistranslation of the Bible to justify their own theology, the Watchtower Organization continues to gain unsuspecting converts every year. Biblically faithful Christians must shoulder the responsibility of refuting Jehovah Witnesses errors in connection with sound doctrine (Titus 1:9). As the Book of Jude tells us, we must "contend for the faith that was once for all entrusted to God's holy people." (Jude 1:3 NIV)

Jehovah's Witnesses, like adherents of all iniquitous, fabricated doctrines that contradict the teachings of orthodox Christianity, put their very souls at risk every second they remain alienated from the saving grace of Jesus Christ, who paid a one-time ransom for all humankind over two thousand years ago when he suffered and died on the cross and then rose from the dead three days after his burial.

Christ went to his death willingly so people everywhere can make the most important decision of their lives – choosing where to spend eternity!

CHAPTER SIXTEEN

CHRISTIANITY COMPARED WITH NEW RELIGIONS, PHILOSOPHIES & CULTS – MORMONISM: THE CHURCH OF JESUS CHRIST OF LATTER-DAY SAINTS

A BRIEF HISTORY OF MORMONISM

The Apostle Paul, in the first chapter of his epistle to the Galatians, made the following incisive statement about the Gospel of Jesus Christ.

I am astonished that you are so quickly deserting him who called you in the grace of Christ and are turning to a different gospel— not that there is another one, but there are some who trouble you and want to distort the gospel of Christ. But even if we or an angel from heaven should preach to you a gospel contrary to the one we preached to you, let him be accursed. As we have said before, so now I say again: If anyone is preaching to you a gospel contrary to the one you received, let him be accursed. (Galatians 1:6-9, ESV)

Paul, as early as during the formative years of the Christian faith, a belief system that today numbers a following of more than one-third of the world's population, recognized the danger inherent in the proclivity by devious, misguided prophets of falsehood to distort and/or misrepresent

365

Christ's Gospel to serve wicked and selfish ends. Among the numerous cults and sects over the centuries guilty of fostering fallacious and counterfeit religious doctrines, Mormonism stands out as one of the chief transgressors.

How It Began – Joseph Smith

On the night of September 21, 1823, young Joseph Smith, Jr., of New York allegedly received a visit from an angelic personage named Moroni, who pronounced himself "a messenger sent from the presence of God" and who further stated that the god whom he represented chose him (Joseph Smith) to undertake a special assignment. Smith, known as a treasure hunter, occultist, "peep stone gazer,' and "seer," also claimed he received a personal visit from God the Father and Jesus Christ [1,] who told him that all churches and their creeds were an abomination. [2] Joseph Smith then set out to "restore true Christianity" and claimed his church to be the "only true church on earth." [3] God, Smith contended, anointed him a prophet in order to pen a revised revelation of the Holy Scriptures – a version known today as The Book of Mormon.

Joseph Smith, after a supposed threefold visit from the "angel" Moroni and under so-called angelic guidance, unearthed a number of "golden plates" that purportedly contained information inscribed in "Reformed Egyptian Hieroglyphics," an unfamiliar language, the latter which conveniently made it difficult for anyone to challenge the authenticity of Smith's claims. The "angel" also directed Smith to a mysterious pair of Urim and Thummim "spectacles," which, when the "prophet" gazed through them, he was able

366

to translate the "Reformed Egyptian Hieroglyphics" into English and use the translated information to produce The Book of Mormon. [4]

Early Opposition to Mormonism

The Church of Jesus Christ of Latter-Day Saints (the Mormon Church) officially came into existence on April 6, 1830, in Fayette, New York, with a membership of thirty believers. By the end of 1831, the new church numbered several hundred members and shortly thereafter relocated to Kirtland, Ohio. Church leaders soon sent missionaries to Jackson County, Missouri, the envisaged location of the great City of Zion, according to the interpretation of Mormonic "prophecy" at the time. However, in 1833, the Mormons had to flee Jackson County, having offended the populace with their religious precepts and practices. Mormon refugees relocated to Clay County, Missouri, but increasing opposition to their presence resulted in their expulsion in 1839. Moving to Quincy, Illinois, in 1839, the Mormons built the city of Nauvoo in Hancock County, and with the help of a charter granted to them by the State Legislature, they erected well over 2,000 homes, a temple, and many other edifices.

The Mormons experienced a period of constancy and growth during the next five years or so until 1844, when a number of apostate Mormons founded a newspaper called "The Nauvoo Expositor," in which they vigorously criticized the "Prophet" or "General Smith," as the organization's leader had become fond of being called. Smith, in retaliation, ordered an attack on the newspaper offices, which resulted in the destruction of the presses. The authorities found Smith guilty of orchestrating the crime and sentenced him to prison in June of 1844 in Carthage, Illinois.

On June 27, 1844, a violent assault on the jail led to a shoot-out between Joseph Smith and his supporters and an irate mob. Smith and his brother, Hyrum, both died. Mormons preposterously recorded Joseph Smith's demise as unarmed martyrdom in which he went like a "lamb to the slaughter" and likened his death to that of Christ at Calvary! Reports to the contrary indicated Smith died fighting, using a six-shooter smuggled to him, and he succeeded in killing at least two of his assailants. [5]

Brigham Young (1801 – 1877) assumed the presidency of the Mormon Church or The Church of Jesus Christ of Latter-day Saints (LDS Church) after Joseph Smith's death. As could be imagined, there developed tremendous friction between the Mormons at Nauvoo and the general populace of Illinois. The Mormons abandoned Nauvoo in 1846 and migrated across the Midwest to Iowa, and eventually arrived on July 24, 1847, to form Salt Lake City in Utah where, under the able leadership and creative energy of Brigham Young, they eked out a fruitful existence in the desert. Mormonism flourished in the Salt Lake Valley. as did polygamy, which Joseph Smith instituted in Nauvoo, and the hierarchy of the Mormon Church practiced freely. The tradition gradually passed down through the ranks until it became commonplace. Brigham Young himself was a polygamist and had 55 wives.

Young instituted a church ban against conferring the priesthood on men of black African descent and also led the church during the Utah War against the United States. [6] Brigham Young died in 1877, and John Taylor, a close associate of Joseph Smith who himself had been wounded during the Carthage, Illinois, skirmish during which Smith died, assumed the presidency of the LDS organization. John Taylor died in 1887, and Wilford Woodruff succeeded him to the presidency.

Wilford Woodruff issued a manifesto in 1890 abolishing the practice of polygamy among Mormons. The edict was more an institutional stratagem than a pseudo-religious redirection, as the Supreme Court of the United States outlawed plural marriage in 1884. Polygamy was a chief reason authorities denied Utah statehood at least six times, and government pressure threatened the very existence of all Mormon temples. [7] The Federal Government, after the enactment of a polygamy law in 1904, imprisoned over a thousand Mormons, disincorporated the Church of Jesus Christ of Latter Day Saints, confiscated its property, and imposed other penalties against the organization.

Mormon Violence

Mormonism's history is rife with incidents of violence, although Mormons refer to their participation in aggression and hostility as a response to the "persecution of the Latter-Day Saints." Mormons were party to rebellion against the United States of America sporadically during LDS history. They were guilty of the 1857 massacre of 150 non-Mormon immigrants (men, women, and children) at Mountain Meadows by a band of Mormons and Indians led by Mormon Bishop John D. Lee. [8] Twenty years after committing this heinous crime, John D. Lee confessed and admitted he acted under direct orders from "Prophet" Brigham Young, the then president of the Mormon organization. The Government of the United States imprisoned, tried, convicted, and eventually executed Lee. [9]

Mormonism Today

The Mormon establishment of today is a far cry from its early configurations. Mormonism in the modern age is a well-organized, smoothly run, religio-economic empire that features in the top fifty USA companies. The organization figures prominently in the sugar beet industry of the United States and owns vast areas of real estate in the State of Utah and elsewhere. Headquartered in Utah, the Mormon Church continues to grow at a phenomenal rate and boasts of affiliation with many high-profile political and economic luminaries in the USA and abroad.

The 2022 Statistical Report for a 2023 April Conference for Mormons held in Salt Lake City, Utah, showed a membership count of 17 million, with 411 missions in operation around the world. [10]

Mormon Religious Texts

Mormons believe there are four sources of divinely inspired information. The four sources are:

1. *The Bible*, "as far as it is translated correctly" (8th Article of Faith). It is not always clear which verses are incorrect.

2. *The Book of Mormon,* which Joseph Smith "translated" and published in 1830. Smith claimed it is the "most correct book" on earth. An individual can get closer to God by following the precepts in *The Book of Mormon* more than those of any other book. [11]

3. *Doctrine and Covenants*, containing a collection of modern revelations regarding the "Church of Jesus Christ as it has been restored."

4. *The Pearl of Great Price*, which Mormons say "clarifies" doctrines and teachings lost from the Bible.[12] The Pearl of Great Price contains its own version of the earth's creation.

Core Beliefs – Mormonism Vs. Christianity

The following are Mormon beliefs about God.

1. God was not always the Supreme Being of the universe (Mormon Doctrine, p. 321) but attained that status through righteous living and persistent effort.[13] Mormons believe God the Father has a "body of flesh and bones as tangible as man's."[14] Brigham Young taught that Adam actually was God and the father of Jesus Christ—although modern Mormon leaders do not subscribe to such teaching.

In contrast, Christians know the following facts about God. There is only one true God (Deuteronomy 6:4; Isaiah 43:10; 44:6–8). He always has existed and always will exist (Deuteronomy 33:27; Psalm 90:2; 1 Timothy 1:17). He was not created but is the Creator (Genesis 1; Psalm 24:1; Isaiah 37:16). He is perfect, and no one else is equal to Him (Psalm 86:8; Isaiah 40:25). God the Father is not a man, nor was He ever a man (Numbers 23:19; 1 Samuel 15:29;

Hosea 11:9). He is Spirit (John 4:24), and Spirit is not made of flesh and bone (Luke 24:39).

2. Mormons believe there are different levels or kingdoms in the afterlife, i.e., the celestial kingdom, the terrestrial kingdom, the telestial kingdom, and outer darkness.[15] Where people will end up depends on what they believe and do in this life. [16]

In contrast, the Bible says after death, believers go to heaven or hell based on whether or not they had faith in Jesus Christ as their Lord and Savior. To be absent from one's body means, as a believer, he or she is with the Lord (2 Corinthians 5:6–8). Unbelievers will be sent to hell (Luke 16:22–23). When Jesus comes the second time, believers will receive resurrected, glorified bodies (1 Corinthians 15:50–54). There will be a new heaven and new earth for believers (Revelation 21:1), and unbelievers will be thrown into an everlasting lake of fire (Revelation 20:11–15). There is no second chance for redemption after death (Hebrews 9:27).

3. Mormons claim Jesus' incarnation was the result of a physical relationship between God the Father and Mary.[17] Mormons say Jesus is a god, but that any human can also become a god [18] Mormons believe salvation can be earned by a combination of faith and good works.[19]

Christianity teaches that no one can achieve the status of God—only he is holy and perfect (1 Samuel 2:2). One can only be made holy in God's sight through faith in him (1 Corinthians 1:2). Jesus is the only begotten Son of God (John 3:16), is the only one who ever lived a sinless life, and now has the highest place of honor in heaven (Hebrews 7:26). Jesus and God are one in essence, Jesus being the only man who existed before physical birth (John 1:1–8; 8:56). Jesus gave himself to humankind as a sacrifice, God raised him from the dead, and one day everyone will confess that Jesus Christ is Lord (Philippians 2:6–11). Jesus taught it is impossible for man to get to heaven by his own works and that only through faith in him is such attainment possible (Matthew 19:26). Everyone deserves eternal punishment for his or her sins, but God's infinite love and grace allow him or her a way out. "For the wages of sin is death, but the gift of God is eternal life in Christ Jesus our Lord." (Romans 6:23, NIV)

Mormonism's Law Of Eternal Progression

Mormonism touts as one of its major maxims a theological postulation that militates against all that is truly Biblical and holy, i.e., the doctrine of the law of eternal progression. To embrace and propagate such a philosophy is to separate oneself from Christian orthodoxy to such an extent the unrepentant individual jeopardizes his or her very soul and courts entry into a Christless eternity - an everlasting period of unimaginable pain and torment.

Christians oppose in no uncertain terms the Mormonic teaching about the nature of God and man. The Bible consistently affirms there is only one eternal God. Joseph Smith, however, introduced the doctrine that God progressed from a mortal state to the position of a god.

The preceding dictum proceeds from the Mormonic belief that there exist throughout the universe multitudinous planets, over which countless exalted men-gods who once were human beings exercise dominion. While the forgoing scenario may seem unduly bizarre or far-fetched to most people, it undergirds the entire spectrum of Mormon theology. Mormons fixatedly subscribe to the actuality of a meticulously structured agenda that encompasses every aspect of their lives as they pursue exaltation and godhood and eventual jurisdiction over their own individual planets, the latter scattered across the vastness of outer space.

Mormonism, by way of extrapolation of the doctrine of the law of eternal progression, weaves an irrational story of a distant past...and a mystifying present. The story is perplexing and troublingly irreverent. The following information appears in *Fast Facts on False Teachings* by Ron Carlson & Ed Decker, two prominent Christian theologians. Incidentally, Ed Decker is a former Mormon. The narrative takes an enumerated form. [20]

4. Mormonism teaches there are trillions of planets scattered throughout the cosmos. Countless gods who were once human beings ruled these planets.

5. Elohim was a spirit child born to an unidentified god and one of his goddess wives. Human parents later gave the spirit child a physical body.

6. Elohim, through obedience to Mormon teaching and as a result of his death and resurrection, was able to attain godhood.

7. Mormons believe Elohim is their heavenly Father and lives with his many wives on a planet near a mysterious star called Kolob. Elohim and his wives, via some sort of endless, inexplicable celestial sexual interaction, produced billions of spirit children.

8. Elohim called a great heavenly council meeting to decide on a plan for the future. Elohim's two eldest sons i.e., Jesus and Lucifer, were in attendance.

9. The decision was taken to build planet Earth where the spirit children would be sent to take on mortal bodies. The council rejected Lucifer's alternative scheme to force everyone to become gods, with him as the savior, and approved the Mormon Jesus' plan to allow people to be moral agents. Jesus, instead of Lucifer, would become the savior of planet Earth.

10. An enraged Lucifer persuaded one-third of the spirits destined for Earth to revolt with him. Lucifer became the devil and his followers became demons. The council banished them to Earth in spirit form, forever to be denied bodies of flesh and bone.

11. Spirits who remained neutral in the battle were cursed to be born on Earth with black skin – the Mormon explanation for the Negro race. The spirits who fought against Lucifer would be born into Mormon families on Earth and would be lighter-skinned or as the Book of Mormon describes them, "white and delightsome."

12. Early Mormon prophets taught that Elohim and one of his goddesses visited the earth to start the human race as Adam and Eve. Thousands of years later Elohim revisited earth to have sexual

relations with the Virgin Mary in order to provide Jesus with a physical body.

13. Mormon Apostle Orson Hyde says Jesus Christ had at least three wives i.e., Mary, Martha, and Mary Magdalene. He fathered a number of children, one of whom was Mormon founder Joseph Smith (see below).

14. The Book of Mormon says Jesus Christ came to the Americas to preach to the Indians, who the Mormons believe are really Israelites. Jesus therefore established his church in the Americas, as he had in Palestine. Dark-skinned Israelites, or Lamanites, fought against the white-skinned Nephites, and conquered all of them by A.D. 421. Moroni, the last surviving Nephite, buried records of the Nephites, inscribed on a set of golden plates, in the Hill Cumorah.

15. About 1400 years later, one Joseph Smith, (see above) supposedly uncovered the aforementioned golden plates near his home in upstate New York, USA. He claimed he received divine authority to organize the Mormon Church as all current Christian creeds were an abomination. Smith originated most of the peculiar doctrines that millions of Mormons today believe to be true.

16. Mormons employ a rigid code of financial and moral requirements, and combine such praxis with the performance of secret temple rituals for the dead and themselves. Their ultimate objective is to prove themselves worthy of becoming gods. Mormons say there

will be a final judgement, with Joseph Smith, the Mormon Jesus, and Elohim holding court.

17. Mormons sealed in the eternal marriage ceremony in Latter Day Saints temples anticipate becoming Mormon gods or goddesses in the Celestial Kingdom, ruling over other planets and spawning new families throughout eternity.

18. Mormons revere Joseph Smith, who claimed he did more for humankind than any other man, including Jesus Christ. They consider Smith a martyr for shedding his blood for humankind so its members can become gods.

The forgoing encapsulated information is an account of a religion that began about 190 years ago i.e., the Church of Jesus Christ of Latter Day Saints (the Mormon Church), which became official on April 6, 1830. Mormons, however, quickly declare they subscribe to the same religion Adam and Eve practiced (see 9. above), which makes their religion about 6,000 years old. Such a claim is hardly true.

Mormonism is in reality a recently contrived philosophy that borrows parts of an irreproachable, time-honored belief system i.e., mainstream or Biblical Christianity, and cunningly and conveniently interweaves such extractions with groundless and debased fantasy.

Refuting Mormon Doctrines About Jesus Christ

According to Mormonic teaching, Jesus was an elder brother who showed people the way to eventual salvation but was not the Way to salvation as Christians understand it.

Mormonism claims Jesus was the god of the Old Testament. Once he assumed a physical form, however, he fell under the obligation to earn his own spiritual salvation through his works while in the flesh, in just the same way Mormon doctrine dictates other humans must do.

The Mormon religion says Jesus suffered for humankind's sins in the Garden of Gethsemane, thereby providing *personal* salvation, which may mean exaltation to godhood. Such spiritual progression, however, is contingent upon obedience to the laws and ordinances of the LDS gospel. Jesus' crucifixion provided a *general* salvation whereby all members of humankind will be resurrected and judged for their works.

No one, according to Mormon philosophy, may attain any kind of godhood, or granted godhood, through divine grace. Godhood must be obtained via works, which contradicts the Biblical message of salvation through God's grace. The Mormon concept of eternity, as espoused earlier, is diametrically different than eternity from a Christian perspective.

The fact that Mormons preach about a salvation that hinges on good works, and neglect to acknowledge the importance of God's grace via Christ's sacrifice on the cross in the process, leads them to disregard or lessen the significance of the cross. Consequently, there are no crosses on Mormon churches. Mormons are unable to deal with the subject of the cross' or God's gift of grace.

Mormons also use water instead of wine or red-colored liquid for communion. It is another way of minimizing or abating Jesus's role as Savior and Redeemer of humankind. Essentially, by substituting water for wine or another red liquid in the Sacrament of Holy Communion, Mormons detract from the symbolism of Christ's atonement for sinners through his shed blood at Calvary.

Clearly, there is only one way to receive salvation and that is to know God and His Son, Jesus (John 17:3). Obtaining salvation is not realized through works but through faith (Romans 1:17; 3:28). Anyone can receive this gift no matter who he or she is or how sinful he or she might be (Romans 3:22). "Salvation is found in no one else, for there is no other name under heaven given to mankind by which we must be saved." (Acts 4:12, (NIV)

Refuting Mormon Doctrines About God

There are four ensconced perspectives about the God or deity that Mormons worship.

Firstly, God the Father has a body of flesh and bone as tangible as a man's. Secondly, God evolved from mortal man over a long period of time and is now a man-God. He is an exalted being of flesh and bone and is ruler over planet Earth.

Thirdly, Mormons advocate the doctrine of polytheism i.e., the belief in the existence of multiple gods. According to Mormonic teaching, there are literally millions of gods of various lineages and descents – father gods, mother gods, grandfather and grandmother gods, great-grandfather and great-grandmother gods, and gods who are uncles and aunts, among others. Fourthly, every male Mormon, by convention, pursues a position of godhood.

The following excerpts from various leading Mormon publications propagandize the LDS notion of God, his attributes and his history. The ideas represent rooted Mormon doctrine and theology upon which multiple millions of Mormon believers base their decision as to where they will spend eternity. It is a very serious issue, more so because Mormons, like adherents of any other religion or philosophy besides mainstream Biblical Christianity, court an afterlife of unmitigated suffering and alienation from Almighty God and his Redeemer Son Jesus Christ.

God was once as we are now, an exalted man and sits enthroned in yonder heavens. I say if you were to see him today you would see him like a man in form like yourselves and all the person and image of man. I am going to tell you how God came to be God. We have imagined that God was God from all eternity. I will refute that idea and take away the veil. God was once a man like us and dwelt on an earth, the same as Jesus Christ did, and you have got to learn to be gods yourselves the same as all gods before you. Namely by going from one small degree to another, from a small capacity to a great one. [21]

The Lord created you and me for the purpose of becoming gods like himself. We are created to become gods like unto our Father in heaven. [22]

Gods exist, and we had better strive to become one with them...A plurality of gods exist, indeed this doctrine of plurality of gods is comprehensive and glorious that it reaches out and embraces every exalted personage. Those who attain exaltation are gods. [23]

What does the Holy Bible say about the nature and history of God in contrast with the teachings of the Mormons, who among other things, claim God the Father has a body of flesh and bone as tangible as a man's?"

Jesus Christ, who would know God the Father more thoroughly than anybody else, made the following statement about God's nature.

You Samaritans worship what you do not know; we worship what we do know, for salvation is from the Jews. Yet a time is coming and has now come when the true worshipers will worship the Father in the Spirit and in truth, for they are the kind of worshipers the Father seeks. God is spirit, and his worshipers must worship in the Spirit and in truth. (John 4:22-24, NIV)

Jesus said unequivocally in the above statement that "God is spirit." He defined what a spirit is and allayed the fears of his terrified disciples who saw him after his resurrection.

But they were terrified and affrighted, and supposed that they had seen a spirit. And he said unto them, "Why are ye troubled? And why do thoughts arise in your hearts? Behold my hands and my feet, that it is I myself: handle me, and see; for a spirit hath not flesh and bones, as ye see me have. And when he had thus spoken, he shewed them his hands and his feet." (Luke 24:37-40, KJV)

The Gospel of Matthew provides further evidence that God is a spirit and does not have a body of flesh and bone. Jesus asked the disciple Simon Peter who people say he (Jesus) was, and Simon Peter answered:

"You are the Christ, the Son of the living God." And Jesus answered him, "Blessed are you, Simon Bar-Jonah! For flesh and blood has not revealed this to you, but my Father who is in heaven." (Matthew 16:16-17, ESV)

Jesus' statement in response to Simon Peter's declaration that he (Jesus) was the Christ, the Son of the living God, affirmed the fact that his Father, who revealed the answer to Jesus' question to Simon Peter, was spirit and not flesh and blood, or flesh and bone.

Mormons teach about a God who evolved from mortal man. Mortals of flesh and bone, they advocate, are continuously changing and slowly transforming themselves into gods, depending on whether they live according to doctrines of the Church of Jesus Christ of Latter Day Saints. Does the Christian Gospel support or confirm the forgoing Mormonic concept of God? The following scriptural extracts tender an unambiguous *No*!

God is not human, that he should lie, not a human being, that he should change his mind. Does he speak and then not act? Does he promise and not fulfill? (Numbers 23:19, NIV)

I will not carry out my fierce anger, nor will I devastate Ephraim again. For I am God, and not a man—the Holy One among you. (Hosea 11:9, NIV)

The following passage from Psalm 90 of the Holy Bible puts to naught the Mormon teaching (enunciated in the speech given by Joseph Smith shown earlier and recorded in the Mormon text *Times & Seasons*, volume 5) that God is not eternal but was once a mortal man.

382

Before the mountains were born or you brought forth the whole world,
from everlasting to everlasting you are God. (Psalm 90:2, NIV)

The finite man of flesh and bone Mormons worship is not god at all.
Indeed, such a god is non-existent. The Bible proclaims an eternal, infinite,
immutable God and discredits imagined and made up deities like the
Mormon god.

Although they claimed to be wise, they became fools and exchanged the
glory of the immortal God for images made to look like a mortal human
being and birds and animals and reptiles. (Romans 1:22-23, 25, NIV)

They exchanged the truth about God for a lie, and worshiped and
served created things rather than the Creator—who is forever praised.
Amen. (Romans 1:25, NIV)

A fundamental aspect of Mormon theology is polytheism – the belief
in the existence of multiple gods. Mormons claim the universe houses many
millions of gods on its countless planets. The Holy Bible refutes the forging
lie in no uncertain manner, as the following scriptures from the Book of
Isaiah demonstrate.

Thus saith the Lord the King of Israel, and his redeemer the Lord of
hosts; I am the first, and I am the last; and beside me, there is no God.
(Isaiah 44:6, KJV)

I am the Lord, and there is no other; apart from me, there is no God.
(Isaiah 45:5, NIV)

Turn to me and be saved, all you ends of the earth, for I am God, and
there is no other. (Isaiah 45:22, NIV)

Remember the former things, those of long ago; I am God, and there is no other; I   am God, and there is none like me. (Isaiah 46:9, NIV)

God abhors polytheism! He is a holy and righteous God and reserves the right to condemn and chastise those who teach and practice polytheism. God justly destroyed the nations around Israel because of their polytheistic traditions. He chastised Israel and sent it into exile in 722 B.C. and did the same to Judah in 580 B.C.

And Joseph Smith?

Mormonism predicts Joseph Smith, the religion's endorsed founder, will return at the end of time, and along with Jesus Christ and the Mormon god Elohim, judge all of humankind. Smith, if what the Mormons advocate is true, is already a god-man and will only gain higher deific acclamation by the time he returns as a judge.

According to historian Dennis Michael Quinn, a former professor of history at Brigham Young University, Joseph Smith was heavily involved in the occult before he ever received revelations from his "messengers of light." Quinn's *Early Mormonism and the Magic World View* is an exhaustive recounting of the role of 19th-century New England folk magic lore in Joseph Smith's early visions and in the development of the Book of Mormon. Quinn argues Smith's early religious experiences were inextricably intermingled with ritual, supernaturalism, and white magic. [24]

Smith said he went into the woods near his home to pray and enquire of God as to which Christian church was genuine so he could become a member. The LDS church today considers Smith's story Scriptural truth. It

384

also forms part of *The Pearl of Great Price*, a standard text of the Mormon Church.

According to Smith, a powerful force took hold of him, thick darkness gathered around him and he could not speak. He began to sink into despair and was about to give up to this *actual being from the unseen world who had such marvelous powers*, when there appeared over his head a pillar of light in which were two personages. Smith inquired of the personages as to which Christian church was genuine. Following is the response Smith claims the two personages gave him.

I was answered that I must join none of them, for they were all wrong, and the Personage who addressed me said that all of their creeds were an abomination in his sight, and that all their teachers were corrupt. **25**

It behooves the serious enquirer to question the identity of the "personage of light" who told Joseph Smith in 1820 all of Christianity's doctrines were an abomination. Thankfully, the answer can be found in the Apostle Paul's letter to the Corinthians in which he warns members of the nascent Christian church there to be on the lookout for messengers of evil and falsehood.

For such people are false apostles, deceitful workers, masquerading as apostles of Christ. And no wonder, for Satan himself masquerades as an angel of light. It is not surprising, then, if his servants also masquerade as servants of righteousness. Their end will be what their actions deserve. (2 Corinthians 11:13 -15, NIV)

While the inference of demonic involvement in the facilitation of religious falsehood is undeniable, especially from a standpoint of Christian circumspection, the character and temperament of principal participants in the formation and development of a counterfeit worldview is troublingly significant. In such a regard, it is meet to provide a few more informative, and disquieting, details about Mormonism's "prophet of God."

Joseph Smith had, at an early age, earned an unflattering reputation, to say the least, and he is best understood in the light of the statement made by those who knew him best, his neighbors:

"... by reason of the extravagancies of his statement, his word was received with the least confidence by those who knew him best. He could utter the most palpable exaggeration or marvelous absurdity with the utmost apparent gravity" [26]

Some sixty-two residents of Palmyra, New York (where Joseph Smith lived for some time) signed the following statement:

We, the undersigned, have been acquainted with the Smith family for a number of years, while they resided near this place. We have no hesitation in saying that we consider them destitute of that moral character which ought to entitle them to the confidence of any community. They were particularly famous for visionary projects; spent much of their time in digging for money which they pretended was hid in the earth, and a large excavation may be seen in the earth not far from their residence where they used to spend their time in digging for hidden treasures. Joseph Smith, Sr., and his son, Joseph, were, in particular, considered entirely destitute of moral character and addicted to vicious habits. [27]

Like the adherents of many belief systems, including the major faiths, i.e., Islam, Hinduism, and Buddhism, and lesser religions and philosophies like Jehovah's Witnesses, the New Age Movement, Freemasonry, and the Masonic Lodge, Mormons exhibit a zeal to serve God. Consequently, Christians should endeavor to share, directly and indirectly, the truth about Christ's Gospel of eternal life with these misguided souls. Such an essential task should be undertaken with love and compassion.

There is one infinite and eternal God, and there is one Savior, i.e., Jesus Christ, who carried with him to the cross on which he was crucified all the laws and ordinances that prevented humankind from obtaining salvation. To neglect Jesus' offer of everlasting life through acceptance of his atoning death at Calvary and his subsequent resurrection from the dead is to jeopardize one's soul and risk an eternity of estrangement from Almighty God and his Redeemer Son.

CHAPTER SEVENTEEN

CHRISTIANITY COMPARED WITH NEW RELIGIONS, PHILOSOPHIES & CULTS – SEVENTH DAY ADVENTISM

AN OVERVIEW OF THE SEVENTH DAY ADVENTIST (SDA) CHURCH

There exist many questions with reference to the Seventh Day Adventist (SDA) Church. Is the Church an evangelical organization, or is it an extremist, avant-garde establishment that could be regarded as a cult?

The SDA Church, from a number of prominent perspectives, recognizes the authenticity of the historic Christian faith. The Church believes in Christ's imminent bodily return and acknowledges the inspiration and authority of the Bible. Seventh-Day Adventists accept the Biblical teaching that believers are saved by Christ's righteousness rather than their own. Amid that truth, though, there are some disquieting and perilous doctrines of falsehood..

The Seventh-Day Adventist Church had its beginning in the mid-1800s under the headship of William Miller (1782-1849), a farmer and Baptist preacher who lived in upstate New York. Originally a Deist, Miller converted to Christianity and became a steadfast Baptist lay leader.[1] He undertook years of intensive Bible study and concluded that the Second Coming of Jesus Christ was fast approaching.

Miller analyzed a passage from Daniel 8:14, in which angels said, "It will take 2,300 evenings and mornings; then the Temple will be made right again," and presumed the term "evenings and mornings" referred to "years." Starting with the year 457 BC, Miller added 2,300 years and came up with the period between March 1843 and March 1844 as the period during which Christ would return to earth. He published a book in 1836 titled *Evidences from Scripture and History of the Second Coming of Christ about the Year 1843.*[2]

The year 1843 passed without incident, and so did 1844. The nonevent was called The Great Disappointment, and many disillusioned followers abandoned the religious group. Miller subsequently withdrew from the Church's leadership. He died in 1849.

The Great Disappointment

Those who had embraced Miller's Adventist preaching experienced great grief and sorrow—they had truly believed that they would be transported to Heaven in 1844, but it didn't happen. Instead, their lives went on as before. The nonevent became known as "the Great Disappointment."

The Great Disappointment could have been avoided if only William Miller and his followers were prudent enough to acknowledge a critical Biblical fact. The scriptures exhort followers of Christ to live in confident expectation of the Lord's return at any moment (Titus 2:13). Additionally, Revelation 22, the last chapter in the Bible, reassures believers that Jesus

Christ is coming soon. William Miller was correct about Jesus' impending return, but for all his study of Scripture, he missed a vital truth. The expectation of Christ's Second Coming is to be tempered with a pronouncement that Jesus himself made very clear: "But about that day or hour no one knows, not even the angels in heaven, nor the Son, but only the Father" (Matthew 24:36). God specifically chose not to reveal the day or time of Christ's return, and no one, but no one, can circumvent such a declaration.

Many of the Millerites; named thus after William Miller, or Adventists, as they subsequently called themselves, banded together in Washington, New Hampshire. The assemblage included Baptists, Methodists, Presbyterians, and Congregationalists.

Ellen White (1827-1915), an American author, her husband James, and Joseph Bates emerged as leaders of the movement, which was incorporated as the Seventh-day Adventist (SDA) Church in May 1863.

Ellen White and her family moved to Michigan and made trips to California to spread the Adventist faith. After her husband's death, White traveled to England, Germany, France, Italy, Denmark, Norway, Sweden, and Australia and encouraged missionaries to join the SDA organization.

Ellen White, incessantly active in the church, claimed to have had more than 2,000 visions from God [3] and became a prolific writer. During her lifetime, she produced more than 5,000 magazine articles and 40 books, and her 50,000 manuscript pages are still being collected and published. The Seventh-day Adventist Church accorded her prophetess status, and members continue to study her writings today.

390

Because of White's interest in health and spirituality, the church began building hospitals and clinics. It also founded thousands of schools and colleges throughout the world. Higher education and healthy diets are greatly valued by Adventists.

In the latter part of the 20th century, advanced technology enabled Adventists to look for new ways to convert those who would join the organization. The church today uses enhanced high-tech means to add new converts, including a satellite broadcast system with 14,000 downlink sites, a 24-hour global TV network, The Hope Channel, radio stations, printed matter, and the Internet,

Since its meager beginnings over 150 years ago, the Seventh-day Adventist Church membership has grown exponentially; today claiming more than 22 million followers and maintaining a missionary presence in over 215 countries and territories.

Seventh-Day Adventist Doctrines & Practices That Contradict Biblical Erudition

Predicting the Second Coming of Jesus Christ

Following William Miller's failed prophecy about Christ's return to earth in 1843 or 1844, many Adventists disbanded in dismay. The nonevent, as mentioned earlier, became known as the "Great Disappointment." The failure of Miller's prophecy notwithstanding, some Adventists persisted with the SDA's erstwhile leader's prediction and volunteered a perplexing explanation as to what really happened.

A handful of Miller's followers claimed to have had visions that served to accommodate reasons for the failed prophecy. Instead of coming to earth, Miller's disciples said, Christ had entered the heavenly temple in 1844 - thus, the prediction about his return indeed took place – except Miller's prophecy had a spiritual fulfillment instead of a physical one.

There are a number of cardinal inconsistencies between the inclination to predict the return of Jesus Christ to earth and authentic Biblical scholarship.

Firstly, the prophecy about Christ's return to earth in 1843 or 1844 by William Miller, in addition to its abject failure, was an attempt to circumvent a salient Biblical pronouncement. The Gospels of Matthew and Mark record Jesus' answer to his disciples after they asked him when he would return as the conquering King of the universe. The information presented in the remainder of this subsection is repeated for the reader's benefit.

But about that day or hour no one knows, not even the angels in heaven, nor the Son, but only the Father.

(Matthew 24-36, NIV)

However, no one knows the day or hour when these things will happen, not even the angels in heaven or the Son himself. Only the Father knows. And since you don't know when that time will come, be on guard! Stay alert!

(Mark 13:32-33 (NIV)

Christ effectively cautioned his followers to be ready for his return. It is possible that Jesus, still in human form when he spoke the forgoing words to his disciples, really did not know the day or hour of his return. Or maybe because no mortal, past or present, was or is endowed with the capability to foretell the exact time of Christ's return, he voluntarily constrained his own knowledge on the issue. Jesus' actions were part of his submission to his Father (see John 5:30 (NLT), John 6:38 (NIV), and John 8:28-29 (ESV) below) and his delegacy to live a human life.

I can do nothing on my own. I judge as God tells me. Therefore, my judgment is just, because I carry out the will of the one who sent me, not my own will. (John 5:30 (NLT)

For I have come down from heaven not to do my will but to do the will of him who sent me. (John 6:38 (NIV)

When you lift up the Son of Man, then you will know that I am He, and I do nothing on My own initiative, but I speak these things as the Father taught Me. And He who sent Me is with Me; He has not left Me alone, for I always do the things that are pleasing to Him. (John 8:28-29 (ESV).

If no one, including the angels in heaven and even the incarnate Son of God (Jesus Christ) himself, knew the time of the Messiah's return to earth, how could the leaders of a dubious religious movement, i.e., Seventh-Day Adventism's William Miller and Ellen White, purport to possess such knowledge? Miller and White not only claimed to be privy to information known only to God, they sought to sully the very Word of God by intimating that it was inaccurate and inauthentic, and that they instead knew he truth.

It is highly likely that Jesus, now in his glorified state, is aware of the day and hour of his imminent return to earth. Just before his ascension to heaven after his resurrection, Jesus reminded his disciples, "It is not for you to know the times or dates the Father has set by his own authority." Acts 1:7 (NIV). None of God's children knows, or will ever know, the day and hour of Christ's return. It becomes imperative, therefore, for believers always to be ready, every day, for the return of the Savior.

Jesus emphasizes the need for believers to pay attention at all times, stay awake, and be ready at a moment's notice. Mark 13 (NLT) contains multiple exhortations for watchfulness and vigilance. Many so-called sages and prophets have tried to predict the day of Christ's return and have failed. The Holy Scriptures are straightforward – no one knows the day or the hour of the Lord's return. Jesus himself admonishes those who would seek to circumvent Biblical doctrine and claim preternatural or divine wisdom, i.e., privileged knowledge about his Second Coming. Revelation 16:15 (NLT) and 1 John 2:28 (NLT) repeat Christ's direct advice for believers everywhere.

Look, I will come as unexpectedly as a thief! Blessed are all who are watching for me, who keep their clothing ready so they will not have to walk around naked and ashamed. (Revelation 16:15 (NLT).

And now, dear children, remain in fellowship with Christ so that when he returns, you will be full of courage and not shrink back from him in shame. (1 John 2:28 (NLT).

Investigative Judgment

The Investigative Judgment teaching is a proposition born of failed prophecy. Seventh-Day Adventists, lending credence to their organization's prophetess Ellen G. White's contrivance of an explanation as to why Jesus Christ did not return to earth in 1843 or 1844, hold fast to a bewildering claim. White concocted what she felt was an expedient excuse for Christ's non-appearance during an event that was supposed to be a concrete testament to Biblical scholarship.

The Investigative Judgment doctrine states that instead of returning visibly to earth in 1843 or 1844, Christ entered the tabernacle of Heaven in order to engage in a work of final atonement. Such an undertaking would erase a believer's sins only after a procedure of *investigative judgment* determined whether he or she merited salvation and eternal life in a paradisial location, i.e., Heaven.

The Investigative Judgment teaching is in stark contradiction to one of the Holy Bible's most salient pronouncements, i.e., Christ's death on the cross and his subsequent resurrection encompassed the full atonement of a believer's sins. Consequently, an accompanying or concomitant occurrence, i.e., an investigative judgment exercise, is totally unnecessary to complete the process of pardoning one's transgressions and assigning him or her a place in God's eternal kingdom.

Additionally, the Investigative Judgment precept effectively disparages and mocks the words of the Savior from the Cross on which he hung as he died for the sins of humankind.

*When he had received the drink, Jesus said, "**IT IS FINISHED.**" With that, he bowed his head and gave up his spirit.* John 19:30 (NIV)

*But He, having offered **ONE sacrifice** for sins **FOR ALL TIME**, sat down at the right hand of God.* Hebrews 10:12 (NASB)

CHRISTOPHER H. K. PERSAUD

Jesus Christ paid fully for humankind's sins through his death and resurrection. His selfless sacrifice on the Cross atoned for such transgressions in their entirety. Any religious or philosophical teaching that says otherwise is steeped in falsehood.

SDA's Arian Heretical Teaching – Christ and the Archangel Michael are One and the Same

Seventh-Day Adventists allegedly acknowledge the full deity of Jesus Christ i.e., He is truly and fully God, and indeed He is. The SDA Church is in full agreement with historical Christianity on the forgoing, prominent doctrine. However, the SDA Church also endorses the centuries-old Arian heresy, which teaches that Jesus Christ is, in reality, the Archangel Michael, and sometimes called as such in heaven.

The Arian controversy (the term "Arian" is not to be confused with the term "Aryan," which refers to Indo-Europeans) was a discourse that occurred in the Christian church of the 4th century CE, which threatened to upend the meaning and mission of the church itself.

The Christian church, like the Judaic church before it, was committed to monotheism: all the Abrahamic religions say there is only one God. Arius (256–336 CE), a fairly obscure scholar and presbyter at Alexandria and originally from Libya, is said to have argued that the incarnation of Jesus Christ threatened the monotheistic status of the Christian church because he was not of the same substance as God, but instead, a creature made by God and so capable of vice.[4]

The Council of Nicea (Nicaea), held in 325 CE in Bithynia (Modern Turkey), sought to resolve the issue. The Trinitarian Bishops prevailed at the council, and the Trinity was established as a core tenet of the Christian church.[5]

The name of the Archangel Michael appears in three books of the Holy Bible i.e., Daniel, Jude, and Revelation. In Daniel 10:13 (NIV) it reads:

But the prince of the Persian kingdom resisted me twenty-one days. Then Michael, ONE of the chief princes, came to help me, because I was detained there with the king of Persia.

The forgoing scriptural extract impresses upon the reader that the Archangel Michael, as high up as he is in the angelic hierarchy, is merely one of the chief princes. He is a created being and is not Jesus Christ. The inference in the aforementioned Biblical passage, if Christ is indeed Michael as the SDA Church claims, is that there may be many Christs or Saviors, of which Jesus is only one.

Seventh-Day Adventists profess that the scriptural passage in Jude 9 (see below) makes reference to Christ, even though it clearly identifies Michael as an Archangel or "chief of the Angels," a translation Adventists claim is incorrect.

But even the archangel Michael, when he was disputing with the devil about the body of Moses, did not himself dare to condemn him for slander but said, "The Lord rebuke you!" (Jude 9, NIV)

The forgoing Biblical excerpt states that Michael did not dare rebuke Satan. Jesus, on the other hand, repeatedly reprimanded Satan (Matthew

17:18, Mark 9:25). It follows that the Archangel Michael, who is mentioned in Jude 9, cannot be Christ.

Hebrews 1:6 (NLT) reads as follows.

And when he brought his supreme Son into the world, God said, "Let all of God's angels worship him." (Hebrews 1:6, NLT).

In the above scriptural verse, God commands all the angels to worship His Son Jesus. God would hardly decree that angels should worship another angel. There exists no Biblical statement that says Jesus and Michael are one and the same individual. Additionally, the contexts of the above scriptures about the Archangel Michael distinctly show that Jesus Christ is not Michael.

Who Bears Humankind's Sins?

Who bears humankind's sins? The Holy Bible provides an unequivocal answer to the forgoing inquiry in 1 Peter 2:24 (NLT), which reads as follows.

He personally carried our sins in his body on the cross so that we can be dead to sin and live for what is right. By his wounds you are healed.

2 Corinthians 5:21 (NLT) emphasizes the profound truth that God made his Son Jesus Christ to be an offering for humankind's sins. In other words, Christ bore the sins of everyone and became a conduit through which people's transgressions could be forgiven and their spiritual record made clean.

For God made Christ, who never sinned, to be the offering for our sin, so that we could be made right with God through Christ.

In spite of the aforementioned scriptural pronouncements, Seventh-Day Adventists submit an alternative, befuddling rejoinder to the question of who bears humankind's sins. They venture to say that Christ will lay everyone's sins on Satan i.e., He will make the devil a scapegoat [6] Such a concept is unsupported by Scriptural teaching.

The idea of Satan being made a scapegoat that shoulders the sins of all people proceeds from a peculiar interpretation by Adventists of Leviticus, Chapter 16. which pertains to an Old Testament ceremony whereby the Israelites petitioned Almighty God during a *Day of Atonement* to seek pardon for their wickedness and rebellion. The ritual involved the putative transfer of committed sins to a goat selected for the purpose and that was presented to God. The goat or scapegoat (or Satan, according to Seventh-Day Adventism) was sent into the wilderness to make atonement for the sins of the Israelites,

Leviticus Chapter 16:7-10 and 16:20-22 read as follows.

Then he is to take the two goats and present them before the LORD at the entrance to the tent of meeting. He is to cast lots for the two goats— one lot for the LORD and the other for the scapegoat. Aaron shall bring the goat whose lot falls to the LORD and sacrifice it for a sin offering. But the goat chosen by lot as the scapegoat shall be presented alive before the LORD to be used for making atonement by sending it into the wilderness as a scapegoat. (Leviticus 16:7-10, NIV)

When Aaron has finished making atonement for the Most Holy Place, the tent of meeting and the altar, he shall bring forward the live goat He is to lay both hands on the head of the live goat and confess over it all the wickedness and rebellion of the Israelites—all their sins—and put them on the goat's head. He shall send the goat away into the wilderness in the care of someone appointed for the task. The goat will carry on itself all their sins to a remote place; and the man shall release it in the wilderness.

(Leviticus 16: 20-22, NIV)

Any attempt to tarnish Jesus' role as Savior and Redeemer, which includes his unparalleled capacity to forgive the acknowledged sins of believers and remove such transgressions from their spiritual records, must obviously be viewed as a damning, pejorative undertaking.

An obvious failing of the contention by Adventists that Satan becomes the bearer of people's sins is that the ludicrous notion maculates the all-important truth about Jesus as a sin-bearer. Even more importantly, assigning Satan as sin-bearer essentially adds to Christ's finished work of Atonement. This is a fundamental contravention of the Christian Gospel that, if true, would render Christ's message of salvation and eternal life null and void.

Not only is the SDA's construction of the aforementioned Leviticus chapter 16 narrative about the Old Testament Day of Atonement ritual an embarrassing exercise in religious perspicacity, but the Adventists' persistent inclination to accord little or no relevance to the demarcations among Christianity's covenantal history places the SDA belief system at odds with Biblical truthfulness.

Ellen G. White (1827 - 1915), SDA's co-founder and acknowledged prophetess, and essentially the individual whose idiosyncratic ideas constitute many of the religious and philosophical pillars upon which the Seventh-Day Adventist church pivots, seemingly was oblivious to the significance of Christianity's five covenants. Such covenants pertain to separate eras of Christendom's history. The five Biblical covenants are as follows.

1. The Covenant with Noah and all Creation.[7]

2. The Abrahamic Covenant [7]

3. The Mosaic Covenant [7]

4. The Davidic Covenant [7]

5. The New Covenant (Instituted by Jesus Christ) [7]

Even a marginally astute scholar of comparative religion would readily acknowledge that the forgoing covenants, although they comprise a single belief system, would harbor distinctive features and/or changes from previous ones, especially as they relate to different time periods.

Ellen White harbored a penchant, either via honest scholarship or misdirected goal-setting, for neglecting to delineate among the essential features of discrete covenants as listed above. Observance of the Christian Sabbath (see below) is a prominent example. White sought vigorously and wrote at length to establish Saturday as the day when Adventists observed the Sabbath. The New Covenant initiated by Jesus Christ and that supersedes the Mosaic Covenant advocates Sunday as the Sabbath.

White perused Chapter 16 of the Old Testament Book of Leviticus, which contains a narrative about a Day of Atonement ceremony in which *"...all the iniquities and rebellious acts of the Israelites in regard to all their sins"* were transferred to a scapegoat and sent into the wilderness, and decided that the scapegoat was actually Satan. The foolhardiness of such an interpretation was discussed above. Additionally, Ellen White and other SDA principals abandoned the prerogative to conduct adequate research, which would have alerted them to the fact that the Day of Atonement ritual mentioned in Leviticus 16 referred to Jewish or Israeli practices that existed under the Mosaic Covenant.

While in Jesus - the promised seed of Abraham (Gal. 3:16), the anticipated "prophet like Moses" (Matt. 17:5; cf. Deut. 18:15), King David's greater son (Matt. 22:41–46), and the mediator of the new covenant (Heb. 8:6) - God's covenant promises for both Israel and the nations have come to fruition, the ultimate expression of God's creative and redemptive goal awaits fulfillment in the eschatological reality of the new creation. Only then will the hope expressed in the covenant formula be most fully experienced (Rev. 21:3), for "the throne of God and of the Lamb will be in the city, and his servants will serve him, And they will reign for ever and ever" (Rev. 22:3–5).

The Saturday Sabbath

A foremost tenet of Seventh-Day Adventism philosophy revolves around the observance of Saturday (instead of Sunday) as the Sabbath i.e., sunset Friday to sunset Saturday. Ellen G. White, the acknowledged prophetess of the SDA Church strongly felt that Christians should observe the Jewish Sabbath, going so far as declaring that those who refused to keep the Jewish Sabbath would receive the Mark of the Beast! Essentially, White's diktat is a condition for obtaining salvation, thus adding to the atoning work of Christ and suggesting the believer must earn salvation. Such a requirement militates against the incontrovertible Biblical doctrine that teaches the Christian attains redemption through God's dispensation of grace and through no other means.

It should be noted that the Christian Gospel does not mandate the observance of the Sabbath on either Saturday or Sunday. Believers who wish to worship on either Sunday or Saturday are free to do so. They commit no infraction of scriptural protocol. It would be helpful to analyze briefly what the Bible teaches in connection with observation of the Sabbath.

The Sabbath was given as a token of the Covenant between God and the nation of Israel (Exodus 31:16-17). Adherence to Sabbath keeping was never a directive for Gentiles or non-Jews. The Book of Colossians imparts the following directive about observing the Sabbath and settling any dispute that arose in the early church.

Therefore do not let anyone judge you by what you eat or drink, or with regard to a religious festival, a New Moon celebration or a Sabbath day. (Colossians 2:16-17, NIV)

The early Christians preached on the Jewish Sabbath because the Jews gathered in the synagogue on that day (Acts 17:2-4), but Christians always got together on the first day of the week i.e., Sunday, the day of Christ's resurrection, as disclosed below.

> *On the first day of the week we came together to break bread. Paul spoke to the people and, because he intended to leave the next day, kept on talking until midnight.* (Acts 20:7, NIV)

The Sabbath was given to Israel, not the church. The Sabbath is still Saturday, not Sunday, and has never been changed. The Sabbath is part of the Old Testament Law, and Christians are free from the bondage of the law [8] (Galatians 4:1–26; Romans 6:14).

Seventh-Day Adventists & The Vegetarian Diet

Another practice upon which Seventh-Day Adventists place much importance and that bears considerable doctrinal clout surrounds the adherence to a strict vegetarian diet. Ellen White wrote in one if her books, "…if we subsist upon the flesh of dead animals, we shall partake of their nature." [9] The Holy Bible does not advocate such bewildering nonsense.

Christ Himself ate fish and lamb. As a matter of fact, Jews customarily eat lamb to help celebrate the Passover (*Pesach* in Hebrew) - one of the Jewish religion's most sacred and widely observed holidays. In Judaism, Passover commemorates the story of the Israelites' departure from ancient Egypt, which appears in the Hebrew Bible's books of Exodus, Numbers and Deuteronomy, among other texts. Passover is so named because God decreed it to be so.

Diet has no bearing on a Christian's salvation. The following Biblical extract brings to the fore, the secondary level of import or significance relative to diet and its implications from a spiritual standpoint.

Accept the one whose faith is weak, without quarreling over disputable matters. One person's faith allows them to eat anything, but another, whose faith is weak, eats only vegetables. The one who eats everything must not treat with contempt the one who does not, and the one who does not eat everything must not judge the one who does, for God has accepted them. (Romans 14:1-3, NIV)

Soul Sleep

Seventh-Day Adventists, along with Jehovah's Witnesses, Christadelphians, and other ill-advised derivatives of Christianity, unequivocally deny the existence of a real hell, notwithstanding Christ's clear declaration in Matthew 25:46,[10] which says:

And these will go away into eternal punishment, but the righteous into eternal life. (Matthew 25:46, ESV)

The identical Greek word for "eternal" is used both times in the forgoing statement. Consequently, if one were to deny the reality of eternal punishment, he or she must also deny the reality of eternal life. "Soul sleep" refers to the belief that after someone dies, his or her soul "sleeps" until the resurrection and final judgment. The concept of "soul sleep" is unbiblical.

Seventh-Day Adventists subscribe to the "soul sleep" construct and thereby contradict the Bible's teaching about what happens after an individual dies. When the Bible describes a person "sleeping" in relation to death (Luke 8:52) and (1 Corinthians 15:6), it does not address literal sleep, but in all likelihood utilizes the term "sleep" because a dead body appears to be asleep.

The moment someone dies, he or she is subjected to the judgment of God (Hebrews 9:27).

For believers, to be absent from the body is to be present with the Lord (2 Corinthians 5:6-8), (Philippians 1:23). For unbelievers, rejection of Jesus Christ's atoning sacrifice on the Cross, death means everlasting punishment in hell (Luke 16:22-23)

Prior to the final resurrection, though, there is a temporary heaven - *paradise* (Luke 23-43), 2 Corinthians 12:24) and a temporary hell – *Hades* (Revelation 1:18; 20:13-14). As revealed in (Luke 16: 19-31), people are not asleep in either *Paradise* or *Hades*. It could be said, however, that a person's body is "sleeping" while his or her soul resides in *Paradise* or *Hades*.[11]

At the resurrection, a "sleeping" body is "awakened" and transformed into an everlasting body an individual will possess for eternity, whether in heaven or hell. The occupants of *paradise* will be sent to the new heavens and new earth (Revelation 21:1). The occupants of Hades will be cast into the lake of fire (Revelation 2:11-15). Heaven and the lake of fire become the final eternal destinations of all people – based on whether an individual trusted Jesus Christ for salvation or did not.

Annihilationism or the Denial of Hell

Annihilationism is the belief that people who reject Jesus Christ's sacrifice on the Cross as an unprecedented expression of atonement for sin will not experience an eternity of suffering in hell, but instead will be destroyed permanently or annihilated after death.

Many people consider annihilation as a more or less attractive concept because of the dreadfulness of the idea of people spending eternity in hell where punishment would be never-ending.

Although the Holy Bible contains a few passages that seem to present a case for annihilationism, a comprehensive analysis of what God's Word says about the destiny of the wicked and unrepentant people reveals that punishment in a location called hell is eternal. Belief in annihilationism proceeds from a misunderstanding of one or more of the following doctrines i.e., (1) the nature of hell (2) the consequences of sin, and (3) the justice of God.

The Nature of Hell

Annihilationists misunderstand the meaning of the lake of fire and what its nature portends. A common interpretation about what would take place in a lake of burning lava if a human being is cast into the flames is that he or she would be consumed almost immediately. The lake of fire about which the scriptures speak, however, constitutes both a physical and spiritual complexion. A body that is cast into the lake of fire is a human's body, soul and spirit. A spiritual nature cannot be consumed by physical fire. It seems that unsaved individuals would be resurrected with a body prepared for eternity just as the saved would be (Revelation 20:13; Acts 24:15). Such bodies are prepared to exist throughout eternity and withstand the consequences of their fate – good or bad.

Annihilationists seem to be unable to grasp the nuance or gradation of the term *eternity*. While annihilationists correctly presume the Greek word *aionion*, which is usually translated "eternal," does not by definition mean "eternal," but may refer to an "age" or "eon" i.e., a specific period of time, it sometimes is used to refer to an eternal length of time [12], as in Revelation 20:10, which says.

> *And the devil, who deceived them, was thrown into the lake of burning sulfur, where the beast and the false prophet had been thrown. They will be tormented day and night for ever and ever.* (Revelation 20;10, NIV)

It becomes obvious that the devil, the beast, and the false prophet are not annihilated or destroyed after they are thrown into the lake of fire. It follows that the fate of the unsaved would not be any different i.e., they will not die but experience eternal suffering, as disclosed by (Revelation 20:14-15).

> *Then death and Hades were thrown into the lake of fire. The lake of fire is the second death. Anyone whose name was not found written in the book of life was thrown into the lake of fire.* (Revelation 20:14-15, NIV)

A further hypothesis about the eternity of hell is given in Matthew 25:46., which reads as follows.

Then they (those who are unsaved) will go away to eternal punishment, but the righteous to eternal life. Matthew 25:46, (NIV)

In the above verse, the writer used the same Greek word to refer to the destiny of the wicked or unsaved and the destiny of the righteous. If the wicked and lost are tormented only for an "age," then the righteous will experience joy and happiness in heaven only for an "age." Alternatively, if believers will live in heaven forever, then unbelievers will live in hell forever.

The Consequences of Sin

Annihilationists take offense to the conformist or orthodox Biblical teaching that unbelievers will be punished in hell for eternity for a finite measure of sin or wrongdoing. How could it be fair for God to condemn an individual who lived for 70 years to unmitigated punishment in hell for all of eternity, the frequency and magnitude of such a person's transgressions notwithstanding?

A markedly contemplative answer to such an inquiry would be that a sin perpetrated by an individual bears an eternal consequence because it is committed against an eternal God. When King David committed the sins of adultery and murder, he wailed, "Against you, you only, have I sinned and done what is evil in your sight; so you are right in your verdict and justified when you judge." (Psalm 51:4, NIV). Even though David sinned against Bathsheba and her husband Uriah, he claimed to have sinned only against God. How could David neglect to mention that he wronged Bathsheba and Uriah?

David understood that all sin is ultimately against God. God is an eternal and infinite entity. As a result, all sin against Him is worthy of eternal punishment. It does not matter how many sins one commits or the enormity of such sins, it is the fact that he or she sins against a God of superlative and peerless character.

Annihilationism & The Justice of God

Another aspect of annihilationism that dissuades prospective SDA believers and serves towards an inclination to reject the notion of an eternal hell and punishment, revolves around the situation whereby believers in heaven will be separated from family and friends who are sent to hell. The Biblical assertion that unsaved people consigned to hell will suffer for all eternity understandably discomfits their relatives who expect to spend eternity in heaven or paradise.

Revelation 21:4, however, encourages believers to realize that when they arrive in heaven, they will not have occasion to complain or be sad about anything. The following biblical passage assures Christians of such a prearrangement.

He will wipe every tear from their eyes. There will be no more death' or mourning or crying or pain, for the old order of things has passed away. (Revelation 21:4, NIV)

If some members of one's family do not obtain entry into heaven while that person does, a pertinent enquiry would be how could such an individual be happy to know that loved ones are suffering unmitigated and continuous torment in hell. The Scriptures seek to comfort the believer by averring he or she will be preternaturally enabled to understand that his or her loved ones do not belong in paradise and their condemnation to a place of unending torment proceeds from their own volition. It is somewhat difficult to fathom, but believers in paradise will not be saddened by the absence of their loved ones who would be sentenced to an eternity in hell.

Also, one must remember that an omniscient, omnipotent and omnipresent God is in charge and will always be in control. He is capable of engineering awesome and incomprehensible marvels. He is a God who is able to suspend or shelve the mindfulness of the passage of time and its portents. Eternity may well be experienced as a protracted, continuous stretch of time that is essentially imperceptible – simply because the need to track the course of time is unnecessary. Further, in addition to the preternatural enablement (mentioned above) with which believers will be blessed so they will readily acquiesce to the realization that their loved ones in hell cannot share their company and are more or less deserving of their consignment to a place of suffering, believers in heaven essentially will be able to expunge the memories of their loved ones from whom they have been separated.

The following two scriptural passages express God's love for all his children and the wherewithal for justice, especially divine justice, to be served.

For God so loved the world that he gave his one and only Son, that whoever believes in him shall not perish but have eternal life. (John 3:16 (NIV)

411

Jesus answered, "I am the way and the truth and the life. No one comes to the Father except through me. (John 14:6, NIV)

The Christian's focus should not be to try to determine how he or she would enjoy the blessings of heaven without his or her loved ones, but on how he or she can encourage them to embrace Jesus Christ while on earth and so help them ensure they will get to heaven.

Looking at the issue from another perspective, one may say that hell is perhaps a primary reason for God sending his Son Jesus to pay the penalty for humankind's sins. Annihilation or extermination after death is hardly a fate to dread when compared with everlastingness in hell. Christ's death was an infinite event, which paid for humankind's sin debt so that people would not have to pay it in hell for eternity. (2 Corinthians 5:21).

When an individual places his or her trust in Jesus, he or she becomes saved, forgiven, cleansed, and promised an eternal home in heaven. If an individual rejects God's gift of eternal life through his Son's atoning sacrifice on the Cross, such a person faces the eternal consequences of his or her disobedience.

A Word on Ellen G. White

The Adventist Ministry Magazine of October 1981 contained a number of acutely disquieting statements, including the following declaration.

We believe the revelation and inspiration of both the Bible and Ellen White's writings to be of equal quality. The superintendence of the Holy Spirit was just as carefully and thorough in one case as in the other. [13]

412

Ellen White herself made the following preposterous proclamation.

The atonement was not completed at the cross. This fact may startle you.[14]

Donald McAdams, president of the SDA Southwest Union College, concedes there exists a more or less urgent problem in connection with the perception of the SDA organization by third parties that requires a solution. McAdams bares his concern in the following statement.

Do we use Ellen White in such a way to give her control over the interpretation of Scripture in much the same way as the Catholics of Martin Luther's day gave the Church the right to interpret Scripture? The answer for most Adventists is, "Yes, we do...!"

If we grant Ellen White hermeneutical control over the Scriptures, we will blunt, perhaps destroy, our witness. We will be seen as a cult that makes the Bible say what we want it to say." [15]

Many Christians share the sentiments echoed in Donald McAdams' affirmation. It behooves all honest Seventh-Day Adventists to read the book *"The White Lie"* [16] (by Walter Rea) contemplatively and objectively. Rea was an SDA minister for 33 years and the organization's foremost expert on the writings of Ellen G. White. Rea has challenged Adventists to prove that White's work is original and not plagiarized from other people's writings. The former long-serving SDA minister opines that at least 80% of Ellen White's writings was stolen from other authors and religious scholars.

Honest seekers of the truth are likely to reach only one conclusion, namely that Ellen G. White fails to live up to the high office of prophetess accorded her by the Seventh-Day Adventist organization.

The Seventh-Day Adventist Church - In Conclusion

The Seventh-Day Adventist Church – Christian Church or Religious Cult?

Notwithstanding the Seventh-Day Adventist Church's adherence to a number of salient of Biblical or Christian tenets i.e., (1) belief in Christ's imminent bodily return (2) acknowledgment of the inspiration and authority of the Holy Bible (3) the teaching that people are saved by Jesus' righteousness rather than their own works, there exist a number of dangerous, false teachings that hold sway. Following is a list of SDA doctrines and beliefs that contradict true Christian precept and practice.

1. Strict adherence to the observance of a Saturday Sabbath

2. Investigative Judgement of believers (In a heavenly Sanctuary)

3. Soul Sleep

4. Annihilationism & the denial of hell and eternal punishment

5. The Arian heresy that says Christ and Micheal the Archangel are one and the same.

6. Strict adherence to a vegetarian diet.

The forgoing recalcitrant and intractable SDA teachings and traditions militate against mainstream or evangelical Christianity, and effectively relegate the Seventh-Day Adventist Church to the status of a cult rather than a legitimate Christian denomination.

CHAPTER EIGHTEEN

CHRISTIANITY COMPARED WITH NEW RELIGIONS, PHILOSOPHIES & CULTS – THE NEW AGE MOVEMENT

THE NEW AGE MOVEMENT - AN OVERVIEW

The New Age Movement (NAM) is reflective of a smorgasbord of notions and practices that spring from an assortment of religions, philosophies and cultures, some dating back to ancient times. Many NAM beliefs are incongruent with the Christian faith, and even at odds with one another within the wide spectrum of New Age pseudo-religious components. NAM's lack of formal structure or organization and the absence of an interconnected doctrinal framework make it difficult to define the New Age Movement in any distinctive manner.

Russell Chandler, former religion journalist for the Los Angeles Times, noted that "New Age is not a sect or cult, per *se.*" [1] John Gordon Melton, American religious scholar and Distinguished Professor of American Religious History with the Institute for Studies of Religion at Baylor University in Waco, Texas, says the following about the New Age Movement:

...the Nam is a worldview that claims to offer a new way of thinking. Despite a lack of formal structure and organization, millions of New Age activists hope to transform society by bringing about a reawakening that will emphasize self-discovery, spiritual growth and enlightenment. [2]

An important characteristic of the New Age Movement revolves around the worldview's detachment from traditional religious doctrine and dogma, even though many of its philosophies and practices proceed from the teachings of major world religions i.e., Buddhism, Hinduism, Islam, Judaism and Christianity. Additionally, NAM philosophies and practices derive strong influences from East Asian religions. However, the extractions from the various belief systems that help form the New Age Movement are more or less disparate and do not comprise any kind of unified framework or organizational unanimity. The NAM is essentially a mixture of various discrete ideas and a quasi-platform for leaders and principals who do not necessarily share similar beliefs and convictions. The lack of cohesion among the various NAM philosophies and practices and the absence of an overall goal or objective places the individual adherent at a loss to pinpoint any one belief system to which he or she might subscribe. At best, he or she may simply be seeking "the truth," wherever it may be found.

The worldview includes elements of older spiritual and religious traditions ranging from atheism and monotheism through classical pantheism, naturalistic pantheism, and panentheism to polytheism combined with science and Gaia philosophy (see below). In many ways, elements of psychology and philosophy, particularly existential philosophy

417

and Jungian psychology (see below), play a major role in NAM belief systems.

Additionally, the New Age Movement combines aspects of cosmology, astrology, esotericism, alternative medicine, music and several other ideas and phenomena of modern origin as well. NAM, for instance, includes the acknowledgment of unidentified flying objects (UFOs), extraterrestrial intelligence, and psychokinesis (bending metal into different shapes by applying the mind).[3]

New Age Beliefs And Practices

Following is a list of some of the NAM's major beliefs and practices, many of them drawn from assorted religions and cultures.

Theism – This is a general and abstract idea of God, which may be understood in many ways. Some see God as both transcendent (an outside force or entity) and immanent (an inner force or entity).

The Afterlife – The *afterlife* is the belief that consciousness persists after death as life in different forms. Some think the afterlife exists for further learning through the form of a spirit, reincarnation and/or near-death experiences.

The Law of Attraction - This spiritual law says humans attract joy or sadness, success or failure, love or non-love by asking for it and therefore attracting it into their lives.

The Concept of Karma – Taken from Buddhist and Hindu belief systems, karma is the "lesson plan" that accumulates as a result of good and bad choices people make. Bad choices must be reconciled to achieve higher levels of consciousness.

The Age of Aquarius Era – Some astrologers think the current time period is the dawning of the Age of Aquarius, which correlates to various changes in the world. Some claim the early 1960s was the actual beginning of the Age of Aquarius, though this claim is highly contentious. Common developments associated with the Age of Aquarius include, but are not limited to, human rights, democracy, innovative technology, electricity, computers, and aviation. Esoteric elements related to the Age of Aquarius include a rise in consciousness.

Gaia philosophy (named after Gaia, Greek goddess of the Earth) - Gaia philosophy is a broadly inclusive term for concepts about living organisms on a planet affecting the nature of their environment and making the environment more suitable for life.

Jungian Philosophy - Carl Gustav Jung was a Swiss psychiatrist and psychoanalyst who founded analytical psychology. Jung's work was influential in the fields of psychiatry, anthropology, archaeology, literature, philosophy, and religious studies.

Existentialism - The philosophical study about the human subject—not merely the thinking subject, but the acting, feeling, living human individual.[4] dates back to certain 19th and 20th-century European philosophers who, despite profound doctrinal differences,[5] shared a belief in the importance of existentialist thinking.

Enlightenment - Taken from Hindu and Buddhist beliefs, enlightenment is the concept of a transcendence of one's self. It is central to many New Age beliefs. For instance, the higher self is able to take over from the lower self and no longer needs to identify with the idea of a separate personality or identity.

Egotism - In New Age thinking, the ego is a false view of oneself as a body or personality, which must be transcended to achieve the stage of enlightenment in this life.

Astrology – Astrologers utilize Horoscopes and the Zodiac in attempts at understanding, interpreting, and organizing information about personality, human affairs, and other terrestrial matters.

Teleology – *Teleology* is the idea that everything shares a universal connection with God and participates via a common energy. There is a cosmic goal and a belief that all entities are (knowingly or unknowingly) cooperating towards this goal.

Optimism – *Optimism* teaches that positive thinking supported by affirmations will achieve success in anything. Humans have a responsibility to take part in positive creative activity and to work to heal themselves, each other and the planet.

Human Potential Movement – New Agers believe the human mind has much greater potential than commonly believed, and is even capable of overriding physical reality.

Spiritual Healing – Spiritual healing relates to the belief humans possess potential healing powers, such as therapeutic touch, which they can develop to heal others through touch or from a distance.

The forgoing list is not exhaustive and represents only some of the numerous New Age beliefs and practices. The heterogeneous nature of the NAM makes it difficult to attempt an accurate or comprehensive definition of a New Ager. Some adherents subscribe to individual aspects of the movement, while others accept the worldview's teachings *en masse* in an endeavor to develop what they consider a useful and meaningful approach to life.

Origin & Development Of The New Age Movement

The New Age Movement emerged as a prevalent lifestyle during the late 1960's through the early 1970's, although elements of the movement may be traced back to the 19th and early 20th centuries. The hippie counter culture movement of the 1960's and 1970's, with its emphasis on the use of psychedelic drugs, became heavily involved with New Age philosophy and spiritual thought. The attitude concomitant with religious and spiritual contemplation and experimentation of the era contributed in no small measure to people's openness to adopting new approaches to finding God and spirituality.

The aforementioned observances notwithstanding, the New Age phenomenon, as intimated earlier, is difficult to define, with much scholarly disagreement as to its scope. The scholars Steven J. Sutcliffe and Ingvild Sælid Gilhus suggested it remains "among the most disputed of categories in the study of religion."[6] The historian of religion Olav Hammer termed it "a common denominator for a variety of quite divergent contemporary popular practices and beliefs" that emerged in the late 1970s and are "largely united by historical links, a shared discourse and an air de famille."[7]

The sociologist of religion, Michael York, described NAM as "an umbrella term that includes a great variety of groups and identities," united by their "expectation of a major and universal change being primarily founded on the individual and collective development of human potential." [8]

William Blake, the English poet, painter and printmaker, alluded to the New Age Movement as early as 1809 when he addressed a spiritual and artistic "New Age" in his preface to *"Milton: A Poem."* H. G. Wells, George Bernard Shaw, D.H. Lawrence and William Butler Yeats also influenced the development of the movement.

Elements of New Age precepts and practices appeared in 19th century metaphysical movements e.g. Spiritualism, Theosophy, naturopathy, and alternative medicine and chiropractic undertakings. These campaigns in turn proceeded directly or indirectly from disciplines such as Transcendentalism, Mesmerism, Swedenborgianism, and various earlier Western esoteric or occult traditions like the hermetic arts of astrology, magic, alchemy, and Kabbalah.

In the early to mid-1900's, American mystic, theologian and founder of the Association for Research and Enlightenment, Edgar Cayce, played a swaying role in developing what would later become the New Age

Movement. Cayce was a prominent practitioner of channeling, or the practice of professedly entering a meditative or trancelike state in order to convey messages from a spirit guide.

Carl Gustav Jung, the renowned Swiss psychiatrist and psychoanalyst, was an early proponent of the Age of Aquarius, which supposedly began in the early 1940's, and heralded advancements in human rights, democracy, innovative technology, electricity, computers, aviation, and a rise in consciousness.

The Harmonic Convergence was the name given to one of the world's first globally synchronized meditation events, which occurred on August 16–17, 1987. The occasion coincided closely with an exceptional alignment of planets in the Solar System.[9] Many people saw the event as one spawning an alternative spiritual subculture that buttressed the New Age Movement and included practices such as meditation, channeling, crystal healing, astral projection, psychic experience, holistic health, and environmentalism. Environmentalism is the belief in phenomena like Earth mysteries, ancient astronauts, extraterrestrial life, unidentified flying objects, crop circles, and reincarnation.

Several significant events during the late 1960's through the 1980's helped raise public awareness of the New Age Movement. They included (a) the publication of Linda Goodman's bestselling astrology books *Sun Signs* (1968) and *Love Signs* (1978), (b) the American Tribal Love-Rock musical *Hair* (1967) with the opening song "Aquarius" and its signature line, "This is the dawning of the Age of Aquarius," (c) the broadcast of

Shirley MacLaine's television mini-series *Out on a Limb* (1987), and (d) the Harmonic Convergence (1987) event mentioned above.

New Age Movement Statistics

The New Age Movement's manifold elements lend to a problem when one undertakes to estimate the number of people who are New Agers in America and around the world. New Agers, after all, do not maintain membership rosters like the Mormons and Jehovah's Witnesses. Moreover, as noted previously, not all who hold a New Age worldview actually subscribe to every tenet of the overall philosophy. Some, therefore, do not even consider themselves New Agers.

During the early '90s, around 12 million Americans were active participants in the NAM, with another 30 million avidly interested in one or more aspects of the movement. A recent Gallup poll revealed 32 percent of Americans believe in some sort of paranormal activity. The statistic holds true for even graduating college seniors and college professors. Meanwhile, 28 percent of Americans believe people can communicate with the dead. Among teenagers, some 73 percent have participated in psychic activities. Four out of five teenagers have had their horoscopes read by an astrologer. Seven million people claim to have personally encountered a spirit being, such as an angel or a supernatural entity. Two million people profess to have psychic powers. Such facts reveal that the New Age movement has broadly penetrated American culture. [10]

The New Age Movement's Fallacious, Damning Philosophies

Dr. Neil Anderson, Biblical Scholar and Founder & President of Freedom in Christ Ministries, writes in his book, *Walking Through the Darkness - Discerning God's Guidance in the New Age*:

> *The New Age movement is not seen as a religion but a new way to think and understand reality. It's very attractive to the natural man who has become disillusioned with organized religion and Western rationalism. He desires spiritual reality but doesn't want to give up materialism, deal with his moral problems, or come under authority.* [11]

Among the more maleficent and condemning philosophies of the New Age Movement are the following:

The New Age Movement (NAM) advocates Monism - New Age thinking promotes the belief that all is one and one is all i.e., everyone and everything is divine. Monism is a philosophical worldview in which all of reality can be reduced to one "thing" or "substance." This view is opposed to *dualism*, in which all of reality is reducible to two substances, e.g., good and evil, light and darkness, form and matter, and body and soul; and *pluralism*, whereby reality consists of multiple substances.

The Holy Bible declares history is about the story of humanity's fall into sin and its restoration by God's saving grace through the involvement of his Redeemer Son, Jesus Christ. The New Age Movement, on the contrary, essentially says humanity's fall into ignorance and wickedness can be restored by gradual ascent into enlightenment through various avenues of pseudo-spiritual and moral endeavor without the involvement of God. New Agers do not identify God as a specific, supreme entity.

NAM promotes Pantheism - New Agers completely reject the existence of a personal God who revealed himself in the Bible, and in Jesus Christ. God, to the pantheist, is impersonal, so the New Ager doesn't believe he or she has to serve a god. God, to such people, is an "it," not a "He."

Pantheists, including New Agers, harbor the view God is everything and everyone and everyone and everything is God. Pantheism is similar to polytheism (the belief in many gods), but goes beyond polytheism to teach that everything is God. A tree is God, a rock is God, an animal is God, the sky is God, the sun is God, and man is God. Pantheism is a cardinal tenet of many cults and religions e.g. Hinduism and Buddhism, the various unity and unification cults, and "mother nature" worshippers.

Christianity does not teach pantheism. What some people confusingly regard as pantheism is the doctrine of God's omnipresence.

Where can I go from your Spirit? Where can I flee from your presence? If I go up to the heavens, you are there; if I make my bed in the depths, you are there. (Psalm 139.7-8, (NIV)

God's omnipresence means he is present everywhere. There is no place in the universe where God is not present. This is not the same thing as pantheism. God is everywhere, but he is not everything. Yes, God is "present" inside a tree and inside a person, but that does not make that tree or person God. Pantheism is not at all a biblical belief.

426

The clearest biblical arguments against pantheism are the countless commands against idolatry. The Bible forbids the worship of idols, angels, celestial objects and items in nature, among other things. If pantheism were true, it would not be wrong to worship such an object, because such an object would, in fact, be God. If pantheism were true, worshipping a rock or an animal would have just as much validity as worshipping God as an invisible and spiritual being. The Bible's clear and consistent denunciation of idolatry is a conclusive argument against pantheism.

There is a change in consciousness – New Agers become engrossed in a so-called renewed awareness or consciousness. If humans are gods, they need to know they are gods. They must become conscious, enlightened, or attuned to the cosmic consciousness. Some who reach this enlightened status claim to be "born again" and attempt to equate such a state with Christian conversion. This, however, is an example of counterfeit biblical doctrine. The essential issue is not whether one believes or meditates, but in whom he or she believes, and upon what he or she meditates. Looking to Christ is the ultimate objective. He said that he is the way, the truth and the life, and no one comes to the Father except through him (John 14:6).

NAM teaches a cosmic evolutionary optimism – New Agers envision the coming of a New Age and a new world order. There will be a new government, they say, which will be perfectly equipped to govern the world's people, who in turn will readily acquiesce to every facet of the new government's inspectorate. New Age thinkers believe there will eventually be a progressive unification of world consciousness, with everyone a willing

427

participant in a global agenda that caters to the diverse pursuits of the movement's multitudinous adherents.

The aforementioned utopian new age, as fascinating as it seems, is a mockery of the truth. It is, according to Biblical precepts, a phony kingdom led by Satan himself. Christ is head of the true universal kingdom, and one day he will rule the universe with peace for all who accept him as Savior and King (Revelation 5:13).

New Agers endeavor to create their own reality – New Agers believe they can create reality by changing what they believe. There are no moral boundaries. There are no absolutes because there is no distinction between good and evil. Everything is relative. Each individual determines what spiritual and/or philosophical path he or she will follow, with envisioned absolution or release from accountability for his or her actions or omissions. New Agers immerse themselves in a sea of self-deception and plunge headlong into a world of spiritual and moral ambiguity.

If, as New Agers suppose, finite man can create truth, society is in desperate trouble. It is eminently foolhardy to presume humankind is capable of exercising unencumbered jurisdiction over what constitutes moral and immoral, or evil and good behavior. Unless men and women acknowledge there are absolutes – temporal and eternal – established by Almighty God, they hasten toward sure destruction, and even more terrifyingly, risk eternal damnation.

New Agers accost the kingdom of darkness – Many New Age Movement adherents participate in occult activities, thereby exposing themselves to demonic endangerment. New Agers surreptitiously refer to spiritual mediums as "channelers' and demons as "spirit guides." Such smokescreens do not detract from the reality of the soul-damning nature of these cryptic pursuits.

The kingdom of darkness in which New Agers and others find themselves ensnared, many through impudence and fatalistic dare, has no other than Satan himself as its head. Those involved in this kind of activity become players in a world totally opposed to the kingdom God revealed to us in Jesus Christ, who has already defeated and condemned Satan and his demons (Matthew 4:1–11; Colossians 2:15; Hebrews 2:14–18).

Refutation Of New Age Objections To Christianity

In this sub section the author purposes to refute a number of popular New Age protestations or objections against the Christian faith. It is the author's steadfast opinion that adherents of the New Age Movement, in the main, object to Christianity because such demurrals provide excuses for them to live however they want without any measure of moral and/or spiritual accountability for their actions and/or omissions.

Objection – *Religion is bad because it divides and separates people.*

Response – It is true that religion, which in a basic sense is a set of rules and regulations that supposedly reflect particular ideas and doctrines, can lead to division and often hatred among people, especially where dogma and philosophy differ. This is not to say an absence of religion guarantees peace and agreement among people as a whole. Human beings are moral agents and there will always be those who agree and disagree with one another. While disagreement does not necessarily constitute hatred or resentment, differences of opinion, even within belief systems, can result in strife and dissension.

A salient difference between the Christian faith and other belief systems is that Christianity is not a religion, *per se*. Religion, by definition, relates to humankind's attempt to reach God through works or personal endeavor in order to attain a perceived moral and/or spiritual zenith. While engaging in principled or moral conduct is an important Christian requirement, such activity only evidences a saved condition. It is entirely through a forgiving God's grace that the Christian believer obtains salvation unto eternal life.

Essentially therefore, Christianity is not a religion or morass of rules, regulations and observances, but a unique relationship with God, his Son Jesus Christ and the Holy Spirit.

Objection – *Jesus Christ was moral and good man – if everyone followed his teachings, there would be world peace.*

Response – People generally acknowledge Jesus as one of history's greatest moral teachers who taught men and women to love and show concern for one another. New Agers consequently presume if people followed Jesus' teachings, there would be universal peace.

The problem with the forgoing observation is Jesus Christ was much more than a moral teacher. His teachings encompassed infinitely more than the exhortation to do good and live ethical lives. Christ, unlike all of history's upright and honorable teachers, claimed he was God's Son, without whom humankind could not attain eternal life. To separate Jesus' offer of salvation unto everlasting life in a place called heaven from his

430

moral advocacy is to attempt to negate all his teachings. His appeal to humankind to live good and decent lives is inextricably intertwined with his encouragement to approach God's Throne of Grace so that men and women everywhere could live forever in paradise.

Universal peace and goodwill in the earthly realm is meaningless if people neglect to address the afterlife about which Jesus taught, and that includes *heaven*, a place of unending peace and joy, and *hell*, a place of ceaseless anguish and torment.

One cannot truly follow Jesus' teachings – the full complement of his doctrines – without the help of God's Holy Spirit. Jesus commands everyone to love God with all of his or her heart, soul and strength, and to love his or her neighbor as he or she loves himself or herself. The New Ager is incapable of doing so, simply because he or she does not believe in God. Also, the New Ager cannot effectively follow Christ's teachings without first accepting him through faith as the Savior of the world. (See Chapter Two: *Jesus Christ – Who Is He?*)

Objection – *Hell is not a real place.*

Response – The renowned Christian evangelist Billy Graham once said one of the devil's foremost accomplishments is persuading people to think he does not exist. A spinoff consequence of such a mindset is that hell does not exist either. The forgoing is one of the leading spiritual deceptions of all time.

If people were to subscribe to the notion there is no hell and it's really a false concept, then no one would feel he or she should be accountable for his or her actions and/or omissions. Further, the absence of accountability dispenses with the requirement to follow or observe God's commandments. New Agers thrive on such duplicity. Effectively, New Agers say people may live their lives as they wish, do whatever they want, and uninhibitedly pursue what they consider to be happiness.

The Holy Bible says humankind breaks God's commandments by thinking and doing evil. Jesus equates hating with murdering, and lusting with committing adultery. God's standards are high, holy and just, and he will judge people against such laws.

Hell does exist and even though one sins, no matter how deeply, and he or she acknowledges Jesus' atoning sacrifice of the cross for humankind's sins and accepts him as Savior, he or she will receive forgiveness by a merciful and righteous God and be spared the horrors of an eternity estranged from him. (See Chapter Three: *The Devil, or Satan – Is He Real?* and Chapter Five: *Is There a Hell?)*

Objection – *If there is a God, why is there so much suffering in the world.*

Response - There is indeed much suffering the world – sickness, disease, starvation, wars, and natural disasters. The question is – whose fault is it? Who is to be blamed for the sad state of affairs in the world today?

God created a perfect world and placed the forerunners of the human race, Adam and Eve, in a paradisial location called the Garden of Eden. God gave specific instructions to the man and woman he birthed and expected them to be obedient in order to enjoy the wonderful blessings in store for them.

Adam and Eve chose to disobey God and sinned. They allowed Satan to tempt them to defy their Creator. Adam and Eve became moral agents from that time on with the prerogative to choose between good and evil, and between obedience and rebellion. God also granted Satan limited jurisdiction, albeit temporary, over the earth. By allowing the devil to do what he wants in the earthly realm, God provides men and women with the choice either to follow him, or to follow the enemy. It is part of his divine plan to facilitate his wayward children's return to his fold, through their own accord.

New Agers and adherents of other false religions surely err in blaming God for the world's ills when errant, disobedient humankind is really at fault. They err in an even greater sense by influencing others to follow their lead and reject the one true God of the universe; the God of the Holy Bible, who one day will restore the world to its original sin-free state. Satan, although he presently wields control over the earth and entices flawed humankind to serve him, will eventually face God's supreme wrath and be condemned to everlasting damnation.

Objection – *Why would God create a system, with the possibility of most of its members going to hell?*

Response – God created a perfect universe. The Bible says there was no evil or suffering in the world. Adam and his wife Eve lived in unblemished harmony. The reason there is so much suffering in the world today is because Adam and Eve committed sin in contravention of God's implicit directions. Ever since then sin has plagued humankind.

God did not create the world in order to send people to hell. Sinful humankind is responsible for such a probability. A merciful and loving God provides an opportunity for his children, tainted with inherent sin because of the foolish actions of the first human beings, to escape eternal damnation through his Son Jesus Christ.

It is likely very many people will end up in hell, but it would be because they would have chosen a path that leads there. Men and women, after Adam and Eve's original sin, became moral agents with the wherewithal to choose everlasting life or unceasing suffering by accepting or rejecting Jesus' sacrifice on the cross as atonement for their sins. No one can really be forced to select either path!

Objection – *What about people of different religions or belief systems? Where do they go after death?*

Response – Everyone who sins does so against God and needs to seek his forgiveness and pardon. Should a sinner approach another god i.e., an idol or a non-existent entity, and apologize for his or her wrongdoing, then much would be amiss. Yet, this is what everyone who worships a false god or subscribes to an untruthful philosophy does.

The most telling mistake anyone can commit is rejecting Jesus' paying the price for all of humankind's sins – past, present and future – through his death on the cross. Christ's act of unprecedented love and concern at Calvary for a creation gone astray allows every human being the opportunity for God forgive him or her and wash away his or her sins. The individual who makes a genuine decision for Christ has no reason to fear death, because he or she enjoys the guarantee of an eternity in the presence of Almighty God and his Redeemer Son.

In spite of all the evil and wickedness for which rebellious men and women are responsible, a merciful God implemented a plan to redeem lost humankind and accommodate its repentant members in his everlasting Kingdom. All one has to do is repent, accept Christ's sacrifice as atonement for his or her sins, welcome him as Savior of his or her life and purpose to live a godly life.

The New Age Movement – Veiled Deception & Evil

Sponsors of the New Age Movement promote their organization as a means of escape from the cares and troubles of a tumultuous world. Belief systems like the NAM, however, are the very vehicle by which the world is traveling swiftly along a path to final judgment whereby a just God will deservingly condemn the rebellious members of his creation to an eternity of agony and torment. The biblically attuned individual would see the New Age Movement's predispositions as no surprise since, as the Book of 2 Timothy reminds everyone.

For the time will come when people will not put up with sound doctrine. Instead, to suit their own desires, they will gather around them a great number of teachers to say what their itching ears want to hear. They will turn their ears away from the truth and turn aside to myths. (2 Timothy 4:3-4, NIV)

Further, the Book of Romans puts into proper perspective, the besmirched and ungodly mentality that pervades the current, sin-ridden world where people, including followers of the New Age Movement, debase God's Holy Word and defy his mandates for purposeful and principled living. The biblical extract is somewhat lengthy, but provides undeniable proof of the sorry state of affairs in the world today. It also serves as a guide for those who earnestly and honestly hunger for the truth.

For although they knew God, they neither glorified him as God nor gave thanks to him, but their thinking became futile and their foolish hearts were darkened. Although they claimed to be wise, they became fools and exchanged the glory of the immortal God for images made to look like a mortal human being and birds and animals and reptiles.

Therefore God gave them over to the sinful desires of their hearts to sexual impurity for the degrading of their bodies with one another. They exchanged the truth about God for a lie, and worshiped and served created things rather than the Creator—who is forever praised. Amen.

Because of this, God gave them over to shameful lusts. Even their women exchanged natural sexual relations for unnatural ones. In the same way the men also abandoned natural relations with women and were inflamed with lust for one another. Men committed shameful acts with other men, and received in themselves the due penalty for their error.

Furthermore, just as they did not think it worthwhile to retain the knowledge of God, so God gave them over to a depraved mind, so that they do what ought not to be done. They have become filled with every kind of wickedness, evil, greed and depravity. They are full of envy, murder, strife, deceit and malice. They are gossips, slanderers, God-haters, insolent, arrogant and boastful; they invent ways of doing evil; they disobey their parents; they have no understanding, no fidelity, no love, no mercy. Although they know God's righteous decree that those who do such things deserve death, they not only continue to do these very things but also approve of those who practice them. (Romans 1:21- 32, NIV)

New Agers, in their zeal to normalize every conceivable pseudo-moral and pseudo-spiritual pursuit, and to dispense with the involvement of God in the affairs of men and women, entice very many unwary people to traverse a path that leads to eternal damnation. Young children even, fall prey to indoctrination via the auspices of so-called legitimate educational systems around the world. Educators present gay, lesbian and transgender practices to kids with impressionable minds as comprising normal and acceptable lifestyles. New Age oriented education is becoming increasingly popular in secular institutions of learning. Children as young as those in first grade receive instruction in practicing visualization, guided imagery, Yoga, and meditation. Instructors encourage innocent little boys and girls to engage in cryptic and puzzling practices in order to "reach within themselves and tap their divine energy."

Celebrities from various disciplines openly proclaim their departure from traditional lifestyles and promote the New Age Movement, both from personal and professional perspectives. Same-sex liaisons among luminaries today are fashionable instead of taboo.

Among the numerous notable people (past and present) from different walks of life who have embraced New Age philosophies are Shirley MacLaine, the Beatles, Oprah Winfrey, Clint Eastwood, Mary Tyler Moore, Linda Evans, Levar Burton, George Lucas, Lisa Bonet, Sharon Glass and Stephanie Kramer. Western spiritual leaders affiliated with the New Age movement are Ken Wilbur, Werner Erhard, Carlos Castaneda, John Lilly, Charles Tart, Robert Muller, and Robert Leightman.

Many environmental and ecological establishments increasingly adopt New Age precepts and practices. The New Age Movement attaches a motherhood persona to the earth, and because humankind allegedly evolved out of the earth and is one with it, its members must undertake to preserve and save it in order to save and preserve themselves – from both a physical and spiritual standpoint. No God; no Jesus Christ!

In Summary

New Age principals capitalize on the world's present chaotic state of affairs and blame organized religion, among other things, for humankind's sufferings and fears. They proceed to offer confused and troubled people a solution to their predicament by leading them to think they are God and can enhance their lives through their own efforts and undertakings. God is therefore unnecessary, and humankind does not need a Savior. Nothing is further from the truth!

The New Age movement is a counterfeit philosophy that appeals to the presentiments of men and women everywhere. The reality is that human beings are born, grow up, live a while on planet Earth, and die. Men and women are finite. They can never be God.

Humankind needs someone great and powerful enough through whom its members can obtain forgiveness for their iniquities and receive the promise of eternal life. Jesus Christ alone, the very Son of God, through his death and bodily resurrection, provides these unprecedented blessings - forgiveness from God, a life of purpose and meaning in this life, and eternal life beyond the grave in a paradisial location called heaven.

CHAPTER NINETEEN

CHRISTIANITY COMPARED WITH NEW RELIGIONS, PHILOSOPHIES & CULTS - EVOLUTIONISM

A BRIEF OUTLINE OF EVOLUTIONISM

Evolutionism, also called Darwinism, is a pseudo-scientific philosophy based on the English naturalist Charles Darwin's (1809 – 1882) premise that all life forms evolved from a common ancestor. Evolutionary thought dates back to the time of ancient Greek philosophers. Darwin popularized the concept in his 1859 book *The Origin of the Species by Means of Natural Selection.* Notwithstanding widespread acceptance back then and even today, mostly by a misinformed, unwary global audience, evolutionism, or evolutionary theory, is anything but scientific fact.

Darwin basically tried to use science to confirm the worldview of naturalism i.e., nature is all there is and God does not exist. Evolutionism from such a perspective is a type of religion, particularly among secular scientists who look upon the concepts of a supernatural God and the creation of life as anathema. As Charles Colson, former politician turned evangelical Christian, and founder of Prison Fellow International opined, "Naturalism may parade as science, martialing facts and figures, but it is a religion." [1]

Darwin's theory of natural selection proposes that plants and animals compete with others of similar genuses in an effort to survive in their attendant environments. Some plants and animals, through mutational processes, develop new characteristics, capacities or features that enable them to survive and adapt to their surroundings while other plants and animals perish. As the changes and competences become permanent, new species evolve. Darwin said a small number of simple original life forms produced every species of animal that ever existed through natural selection or a process whereby only the fittest forms survived under competitive circumstances. The naturalist of course was incapable of presenting any objective proof of simple life forms evolving into higher ones. Darwin's theory nevertheless impacted society dramatically, as many people who, for one reason or another, felt disenchanted with the concept of God, embraced evolutionism as a "scientific" reason to jettison belief in God's existence and subsequently in the "myth" of creation.

The irrationality of evolutionary thought and woeful lack of legitimate scientific corroboration notwithstanding, Darwin's theory gained in popularity and acceptance and grew leaps and bounds in the latter part of the nineteenth century and well into the twentieth century. Even though many Christian leaders fervidly rejected the theory and resiliently defended biblical scholarship, the juggernaut that was the secular scientific establishment, buoyed by a newfound confidence availed by Darwin's misguided predispositions, eventually assumed control of the global educational infrastructure. People everywhere, with exceptions in profoundly Christian and moralistic spheres of thought, gravitated to the pervasive influence of evolutionist doctrine. Some professed Christians even, falling prey to the trappings of ostensive scholastic sophistication or misled into actually believing Darwin's theory, sought to accommodate their religious beliefs within an evolutionist milieu, referring to themselves as "theistic evolutionists."

In due course, the secular academic establishment adopted an imperious and intolerant attitude towards any philosophy or discipline besides evolutionary theory that exhibited any semblance of authority or challenged the newly established scientific status quo. [2] Naturalistic evolution became the reigning scientific "orthodoxy" in education around the world, and remains so today.

Evolutionist Precepts & Practices

In 1995, the National Association of Biology Teachers (USA), in deciding on an approach to educate high school students about the origin of life, concluded that life resulted from "an unsupervised, impersonal, unpredictable, and natural process." [3] Widespread protests by people offended by the NABT's reckless disregard for alternative theories about the origin of life, including those pertaining to divine accommodation, led the organization to delete the words "unsupervised and impersonal" from its incautious and judgmental statement. Many observers nevertheless felt the words "unpredictable and natural" carried a meaning similar to "unsupervised and impersonal."

Notwithstanding its demonstrable lack of scientific corroboration, secular educators impart evolutionary theory as confirmed scientific fact in institutions of learning around the world. Additionally, evolutionists spare

442

no effort in making known their aversion to theological or religious dogma. A typical declaration in college textbooks about evolutionism reads as follows: "By coupling undirected, purposeless variation to the blind uncaring process of natural selection, Darwin made theological or spiritual explanations of the life processes superfluous." [4]

Lamentably, the forgoing observations point to a global educational system that falls under the jurisdiction of people who, guided by flawed and unrepresentative scientific precept and practice, spread untruth and misinformation. They promote the gargantuan lie that life is the outcome of purely happenstance events that incomprehensibly progressed over millions of years to produce the multitudinous creatures, including human beings, which exist today. These prophets of disinformation also allege life, which in itself is an incomprehensibly astounding process, emerged from inanimate matter or from nothing. God, to such people, is absent or non-existent, and did not create the universe or life. Consequently, humankind does not need God or his morals. Biologists William Provine and Philip Johnson echo such dismaying sentiments when they say, "No life after death; no ultimate foundation for ethics; no ultimate meaning for life; no free will." [5]

Charles Darwin himself was unsure how the first crude lifeform came into being, but was reluctant to say it came from nowhere or nothing. At the end of his book, *The Origin of the Species by Means of Natural Selection*, Darwin intimated life could have "been originally breathed by the Creator into a few forms or into one." [6] However, after evolutionist scientists and secular humanists obdurately decided to traverse a path that acknowledged naturalistic evolution as the only explanation for the origin of life, they arbitrarily plugged any loopholes Darwin might have left open with suppositions that augmented their version of the already implausible theory.

Naturalistic or biological evolutionists, utilizing markedly subjective language, propose that the universe began about 3 or 4 billion years ago with a "Big Bang," and planet Earth emerged under conditions perfectly suited for life. "Big Bang" theorists presume a tiny, infinitely hot, and dense point called a *singularity* exploded and gave rise to the universe with its galaxies, planets, and other celestial bodies. Life resulted from a series of random, unguided processes that combined certain chemicals and some form of energy, i.e., lightning. An alternative evolutionist theory about the origin of life is that it proceeded from non-life in a "prebiotic soup" ("prebiotic" means "pre-life") of various chemicals in the early Earth's oceans. Over a very long period of time, some of these chemicals gradually came together and formed molecular chains, which eventually produced the first primitive life form. The initial life form somehow survived against all odds and reproduced itself over and over until a complete cell emerged.

The first living cell continued to reproduce itself and evolved through millions of years through natural means alone, i.e., natural selection and genetic mutation, and eventually developed into firstly, simple organisms, then into animals and plants, then fish, then amphibians, then reptiles, then into mammals. Mammals later produced the primates – monkeys, apes, and finally, man. [7]

Darwin inferred that mutational changes, prompted by natural selection, took place in small, gradational stages, not by leaps and bounds. Creationists and evolutionists alike acknowledge the actuality of small changes in species of living things, i.e., the process of macroevolution or horizontal evolution – evolution within species. Darwin went further, however, in an attempt to validate his outlandish theory by saying that over billions of years, microevolution resulted in macroevolution or vertical evolution, i.e., evolution from species to species.

Christian scientists and other scientifically inclined scholars as well, rebuffed Charles Darwin's evolutionary theory and other evolutionist concepts for many decades. They did so not solely on the premise of theological or religious convictions but primarily because of the lack of evidence for the British naturalist's suppositions, including mutational changes and macroevolution, the latter of which has never taken place (in the laboratory or in nature), irrational claims about the fossil record, and spurious theories about the awesome, living cell.

The claims about genetic mutations and their effect on the living cell are two of evolutionism's most contentious issues, and along with implications of the fossil record, represent major stumbling blocks for proponents of the controversial theory.

According to evolutionism, environmental conduciveness and consequent favorable mutational changes, in as much as beneficial genetic mutations are extremely rare, most of them over inordinately lengthy periods of time, enabled fitter organisms to survive while species less adaptable to change died. It is mathematically impossible for enough beneficial genetic mutations to occur and result, especially unguided, in an improved or progressively complex cellular system, not to mention the unbelievably lengthy time required for such changes to take place. Genetic mutations in general are extremely rare occurrences, and the clear majority of such modifications are harmful to the organisms in question.

The noted geneticist Dr. Lane Lester, Professor of Biology at Emmanuel College in Franklin Springs, Georgia, USA and Dr. Raymond Bohlin, a population biologist with a Ph.D. in Molecular and Cell Biology from the University of Texas at Dallas, USA, in their work, *The Natural Limits to Biological Change*, make the following insightful observation.

The overall factor that has come up again and again is that mutation remains the ultimate source of all genetic variation in any evolutionary model. Being unsatisfied with the prospects of accumulating small point mutations, many are turning to macromutations to explain the origin of evolutionary novelties. Goldschmidt's* hopeful monsters have indeed returned. However, though macromutations of many varieties produce drastic changes, the vast majority will be incapable of survival, let alone show the marks of increasing complexity.

If structural gene mutations are inadequate because of their inability to produce significant enough changes, then regulatory and developmental mutations appear even less useful because of the greater likelihood of nonadaptive or even destructive consequences...But one thing seems certain: at present, the thesis that mutations, whether great or small, are capable of producing limitless biological change is more an article of faith than fact. [8]

A nucleotide is one of the structural components, or building blocks, of DNA (deoxyribonucleic acid). A nucleotide consists of a base, i.e., one of four chemicals: adenine, thymine, guanine, and cytosine, plus a molecule of sugar and one of phosphoric acid. DNA is an essential component of the living cell and resides in the cell's nucleus.

I. L. Cohen, a well-known mathematician member of the New York Academy of Sciences and an official of the Archaeological Institute of America, writes about the mathematical impossibility of the accidental formation of nucleotides.

Based on probability factors...any viable DNA strand having over 84 nucleotides cannot be the result of haphazard mutations. At that stage, the probabilities are 1 in 4.8 x 1050. Such a number, if written out, would read 480,000,000,000,000,000,000,000,000,000,000,000,000,000,000,000.

Mathematicians agree that any requisite number beyond 1050 has, statistically, a zero probability of occurrence (and even that gives it the 'benefit of the doubt).' Any species known to us, including 'the smallest single-cell bacteria,' has enormously larger numbers of nucleotides than 100 or 1,000. In fact, single-cell bacteria display about 3,000,000 nucleotides aligned in a very special sequence. This means that there is no mathematical probability whatever for any known species to have been the product of a random occurrence - random mutations (to use the evolutionist's favorite expression) [9]

Professor Michael Behe (1952 -), the noted American biochemist, Intelligent Design advocate, and Professor of Biochemistry at Lehigh University in Pennsylvania, USA, sheds light on the total unlikelihood of a

447

single cell developing out of a so-called "pre-biotic soup" and eventually evolving into man, as evolutionist scholars maintained happened. Behe explains how the "irreducible complexity of molecular mechanisms" makes it virtually impossible for even a lone cell, with its numerous interconnected parts, to have been built up gradually, step by tiny step, over a long period of time. Behe opines Charles Darwin knew very little about the composition of the living cell and how it worked. Behe's work in cell structure and function is recognized throughout the global scientific community. [10]

The myriad concerns over the subjectivity of evolutionary time spans utilized by evolutionists in their attempts to explain the origin of life leave them in a quandary. Critics of Darwin's theory feel evolutionist scholars conveniently invented the vast time periods to complement their far-fetched suppositions about a multi-billion-year-old universe and the primordial beginnings of the earliest life forms. As expected, evolutionists proposed new or alternative evolutionary theories to supplement and/or supplant previous hypotheses in an effort to lend some semblance of logic and believability to Darwin's postulations. One such assumption was the *punctuated equilibrium* theory introduced by Stephen Jay Gould (1941 – 2002), former Professor of Geology and Paleontology at Harvard University and committed evolutionist. Gould suggested evolution could have taken place in extremely short time frames.

Genome evolution (change) is a relatively recent discovery that evolutionists theorize might have been involved in the origin and development of life. Genome evolution or modification is the process by which a genome changes in structure (sequence) or size over time. The study

448

of genome evolution involves multiple fields, such as structural analysis of the genome, the study of genomic parasites, gene and so-called ancient genome duplications, polyploidy, and comparative genomics. In the fields of molecular biology and genetics, a genome is the genetic material of an organism and consists of DNA (or RNA in RNA viruses). The genome includes both the genes (the coding regions) and the noncoding DNA, [11] as well as mitochondrial DNA[12] and chloroplast DNA. The intimation or insistence by evolutionists that genome change is in any way proof of Darwinian evolution is ambitious conjecture, at best.

The author directs the reader to the next sub-section, *Twenty Arguments That Show Evolutionary Theory Falls Outside The Realm of Real Science,* for more on the incommodious dilemmas surrounding genetic mutations, macroevolution, the fossil record, and other dilemmas that confront evolutionists.

Twenty Arguments That Show Evolutionary Theory Falls Outside The Precinct Of Real Science

Limited space allows the author to list only twenty arguments that show evolutionary theory falls outside the realm of real science. There exist innumerable other arguments against evolutionism, one of the greatest hoaxes ever visited on a largely uninformed global audience.

1. If the theory of evolution were true, there should be millions upon millions of transitional fossils evidencing the development of one genus into another species. There is not one such fossil in existence. Over the years, evolutionists produced a number of so-

called "intermediary fossils," which supposedly confirmed evolutionary theory. Among such "confirmations" were (a) the Peking man (b) the Nebraska man (c) the Java man (d) the Piltdown man (see 13. below), (e) the Neanderthal man (f) the Nutcracker man (g) the Lucy fossil and (h) the Ida skull. Level-headed scientists and researchers exposed every single one of the above "proofs" of evolution as a misrepresentation of the truth. Some were deliberate fabrications.

2. Stephen Jay Gould, former Professor of Geology and Paleontology at Harvard University and staunch evolutionist, made a surprising remark about the lack of transitional fossils - "The (human) family trees which adorn our (science) textbooks are based on inference, however reasonable, not the evidence of fossils." [13]

3. If "evolution" were taking place right now, as evolution scientists infer it is, there would be millions of living creatures out there with partially developed features and organs. Not a single such creature can be identified.

4. Addressed from an evolutionary perspective, the sudden appearance of complex life in the fossil record is unexplainable, as is the absence of intermediary life forms. Even Richard Dawkins, the notoriously irreverent evolutionist admits:

It is as though they [fossils] were just planted there, without any evolutionary history. Needless to say this appearance of sudden

450

planting has delighted creationists. Both schools of evolutionary thought (Punctuationists and Gradualists) despise so-called scientific creationists equally, and both agree that the major gaps are real, that they are true imperfections in the fossil record. The only alternative explanation of the sudden appearance of so many complex animal types in the Cambrian era is divine creation and both reject this alternative. [14]

5. Macroevolutionary or biological changes across species have never been observed in the laboratory or in nature. In other words, no one has ever observed one kind of creature turn into another kind of creature. The entire theory of evolution hinges on blind faith – exponentially more faith than it takes to believe in God and a created universe and life.

6. Evolutionist Jeffrey Schwartz, a professor of anthropology at the University of Pittsburgh, openly admits that "the formation of a new species, by any mechanism, has never been observed." [15]

7. Evolutionary theory is actually a deeply pagan religious philosophy traceable to thousands of years ago. Its origins may not be scientific at all, as the following observations reveal.

    Greek Philosophers: The fragments of Anaximander (c. 610–546 BC) taught that 'humans originally resembled another type of animal, namely fish.[16] Democritus (c.460–370 BC) taught that primitive people began to speak with 'confused' and 'unintelligible' sounds but 'gradually they articulated words.' [17] Epicurus (341–270 BC) said there was no need of a God or gods, for the Universe came about by a chance movement of atoms.[18] After them, the Roman naturalist Pliny the Elder (AD23–79) said, "... we are so subject to chance that *Chance* herself takes the place of God; she proves that God is uncertain." [19]

Egyptians, Babylonians, & Hindus: The Greeks borrowed some of the forgoing ideas from the Babylonians, Egyptians, and Hindus, whose philosophies extended back centuries before. For example, one Hindu belief was Brahman (the Universe) spontaneously evolved by itself like a seed, which expanded and formed all that exists about 4.3 billion years ago.[20] These Hindus believed in an eternal Universe that had cycles of rebirth, destruction, and dormancy, known as 'kalpas,' rather like oscillating big bang theories. One also reads in the Hindu Bhagavad Gita that the god Krishna says, 'I am the source from which all creatures evolve.' [21] Some Babylonians claimed they had astronomical inscriptions on clay tablets for 730,000 years; others, like Berosus, the Chaldean priest and author (flourished 290 c. B.C.), suggested the inscriptions were 490,000 years old.[22] The Egyptians claimed they were familiar with astronomy for more than 100,000 years. [23]

The early Christian Church Fathers constantly argued with the pagans about the age of the earth, or about the age of civilization. They unanimously agreed God created the earth less than 6,000 years before their time.[24] The renowned Church Father Augustine (AD 354-430) and Theophilus (AD 115–181), Bishop of Antioch, were irrepressible advocates of a biblical or creationist explanation of the origin of the universe and of life, while taking to task, paganish thinkers like Plato (428/427 – 348/347 BC), the Athenian philosopher, and Apollonius of Tyana (AD 15-100), the Greek Neopythagorean scholar, for their reckless and misinformed conjectures.

8. Any fossil or artifact more than 250,000 years old should have no radiocarbon in it whatsoever. Yet, radiocarbon is present in everything evolutionists dig up, including dinosaur bones, which are supposedly multiple millions of years old. Such a fact is manifest confirmation the "millions of years" theory about bones and fossils that represent evidence of evolution is false and even laughable.

9. The odds of even a single sell "assembling itself" by chance are infinitesimal, or so low that even mentioning the possibility of such a process taking place is an insult to true scientific precept. The following is an excerpt from the globally recognized author and researcher Jonathan Gray's book, "The Forbidden Secret."

Even the simplest cell you can conceive of would require no less than 100,000 DNA base pairs and a minimum of about 10,000 amino acids to form the essential protein chain. Not to mention the other things that would also be necessary for the first cell.

Bear in mind that every single base pair in the DNA chain has to have the same molecular orientation ("left-hand" or "right hand")? As well as that, virtually all the amino acids must have the opposite orientation, and everyone must be without error. To randomly obtain those correct orientations, do you know your chances? It would be 1 chance in 2110,000, or 1 chance in 1033,113!

To put it another way, if you attempted a trillion, trillion, trillion combinations every second for 15 billion years, the odds you would achieve all the correct orientations would still only be one chance in a trillion, trillion, trillion, trillion ... and the trillions would continue 2755 times! It would be like winning more than 4700 state lotteries in a row with a single ticket purchased for each. In other words,...impossible! [25]

10. In 2007, fishermen caught a very rare creature known as a "coelacanth." Evolutionists originally said this "living fossil" evolved into roughly its current form approximately 400 million years ago.[26] Scientists long considered the coelacanth a "living fossil" because they thought it was the sole remaining member of a taxon otherwise known only from fossils, with no close living

relations.[27] However, several recent studies revealed coelacanth body shapes are much more diverse than previously thought. [28] Scientists today acknowledge the coelacanth is not a living fossil at all.

11. According to evolutionists, the Ancient Greenling Damselfly last showed up in the fossil record about 300 million years ago. Evolutionary precepts indicate 300 million years ought to be more than enough time for mutations to occur in the damselfly and for natural selection to weed out the unfit traits and generate a new living form. [29] The Ancient Greenling Damselfly still exists today in its previous shape and form. So why did it not evolve at all over 300 million years?

12. Darwinists claim the human brain developed without the assistance of any designer. The notion is so preposterous, it is mind-boggling any sane individual believes it. Following are well-informed statements and facts about the human brain.

    The human brain is the most complicated structure in the known universe. [30] The human brain contains over 100 billion cells, each with over 50,000 neuron connections to other brain cells. [31]

    This structure (the human brain) receives over 100 million separate signals from the total human body every second. If we learned something new every second of our lives, it would take three million years to exhaust the capacity of the human brain. [32]

In addition to conscious thought, people can actually reason, anticipate consequences, and devise plans - all without knowing they are doing so. [33]

13. The Piltdown Man was a paleoanthropological fraud in which conniving evolutionists presented bone fragments as the fossilized remains of a previously unknown early human. The falsity of the hoax came to light in 1953. An extensive scientific review in 2016 established amateur archaeologist Charles Dawson as its likely perpetrator. [34]

The Piltdown fossil was discovered in 1912 in England by Charles Dawson, an anthropologist, and comprised of portions of a modern-looking skull attached to a distinctly ape-like jaw. Evolutionary scientists immediately hailed the "find" as a genuine "missing link." The New York Times proudly published a headline that read "Darwin Theory Proved True." The evolutionary propaganda machine promoted the discovery as proof of evolution and pro-evolution publishers featured the news in textbooks and encyclopedias around the world. Over the next four decades, evolutionists touted the Piltdown Man as evolution's premier showpiece, and gullible, uninformed people everywhere swallowed the lie hook, line and sinker.

In 1953, the scientific community, in one of its most embarrassing and ego-shattering admissions, confirmed the Piltdown Man fossil was, no, not a mistake, but a downright forgery. The

456

perpetrators of the fraud, from all indications entirely prejudiced against creationism and blindly loyal to evolutionary speculation and who had the gall to call themselves scientists, had cunningly put together a modern human skull and the jaw of a recent orangutan and stained the ensemble to make it appear aged. They filed the teeth down to make them resemble those of a human being.

14. If the neutron were not about 1.001 times the mass of the proton, all protons would have decayed into neutrons, or all neutrons would have decayed into protons, and life, therefore, would not be possible. Evolutionists cannot explain how such a situation could emerge through happenstance events.

15. If gravity were stronger or weaker by the slimmest of margins, then life-sustaining stars like the sun could not exist. This would also make life impossible. Evolutionists are at a loss to explain how such conditions could result from chance events.

16. Evolutionists allege the ancestors of birds developed hollow bones over thousands of generations so that they would eventually be light enough to fly. Of course, no evidence exists for such a patently ridiculous suggestion.

17. The term *irreducible complexity* refers to a system or arrangement in which numerous, well-matched, efficiently interacting components or parts contribute to a fundamental or basic function and where the absence or elimination of any one of the

constituents or parts effectively leads to a malfunctioning or the closing down of the system or structure.

Professor Michael Behe (1952 -), the noted American biochemist and Intelligent Design advocate, introduced the theory of the irreducible complexity of cellular structures. Dr. Behe is Professor of Biochemistry at Lehigh University in Pennsylvania, USA and is a senior fellow of the Discovery Institute's Center for Science and Culture. Dr. Behe, while not a creationist in the strict sense of the term, argues some cellular structures are too complex at the biochemical level to have resulted from evolutionary mechanisms. Organs or structures such as the human eye, the ear, the heart and the brain are all irreducibly complex and could not have developed through evolutionary processes.

18. If dinosaurs really are tens of millions of years old, why have scientists found dinosaur bones with soft tissue still in them? The following is from an NBC News report about one of these discoveries.

For more than a century, the study of dinosaurs has been limited to fossilized bones. Now, researchers have recovered 70 million-year-old soft tissue, including what may be blood vessels and cells, from a Tyrannosaurus rex. [35]

Clearly, evolutionists grossly overstate the ages of fossils to lend credence to the outlandish time periods required in order for evolutionism to be considered even remotely credible.

19. DNA (deoxyribonucleic acid) is so incredibly complex it is absolutely illogical to suggest that such a language system could have "evolved" all by itself by accident. The very existence of DNA invalidates evolutionary thought. Following is an excerpt from an *Answers in Genesis* article about the wonders of the DNA language.

When it comes to storing massive amounts of information, nothing comes close to the efficiency of DNA. A single strand of DNA is thousands of times thinner than a strand of human hair. One pinhead of DNA could hold enough information to fill a stack of books stretching from the earth to the moon 500 times.

Although DNA is wound into tight coils, your cells can quickly access, copy, and translate the information stored in DNA. DNA even has a built-in proofreader and spell-checker that ensure precise copying. Only about one mistake slips through for every 10 billion nucleotides that are copied. [36]

Today, almost 160 years after Charles Darwin's introduction of evolutionary theory, scientific scholarship confirms that the living cell, viewed through the primitive microscopes of Darwin's day, appeared to be but a simple blob of jelly or uncomplicated protoplasm. Today, scientists acknowledge the presence of a virtual chemical universe inside the living cell.

When Charles Darwin published his book *On the Origin of Species* in 1859, life appeared much simpler. "It was once expected," writes Professor Behe, "that the basis of life would be exceedingly simple. That expectation has been smashed. Vision, motion, and other biological functions have proven to be no less sophisticated than television cameras and automobiles. Science has made enormous progress in understanding how the chemistry of life works, but the elegance and complexity of biological systems at the molecular level have paralyzed science's attempt to explain their origins." [37]

Michael Denton, the British-Australian scientist and a Senior Fellow at the Discovery Institute's Center for Science and Culture, conclusively says, "Ultimately, the Darwinian theory of evolution is no more nor less than the great cosmogenic myth of the twentieth century." [38]

Phillip E. Johnson, (1940 – 2019), former UC Berkeley law professor and co-founder of the Discovery Institute's Center for Science and Culture (CSC), made the following astute remark.

Every history of the twentieth century lists three thinkers as preeminent in influence: Darwin, Marx, and Freud. All three were regarded as 'scientific' (and supposedly more reliable than anything 'religious') in their heyday. Yet Marx and Freud have fallen, and even their dwindling bands of followers no longer claim that their insights were based on any methodology remotely comparable to that of experimental science. I am convinced that

Darwin is next on the block. His fall will be by far the mightiest of the three. [39]

20. Evolutionists are unable to explain why planet Earth is so perfectly suited to support life. Creationists can! A supreme Designer and Creator brought the universe and all life into existence.

Stuart Clark of New Scientist magazine recently asked the question, "How come Earth got all the good stuff?" Of all the planets in our solar system that allegedly formed naturalistically "from the same cloud of gas and dust that surrounded the sun more than 4.5 billion years ago," why is "Earth...so suitable for life?" [40]

Clark acknowledged:

We know that its distance from the sun provides the right amount of heat and light to make the planet habitable, but that alone is not enough. Without the unique mix of carbon, hydrogen, nitrogen, oxygen, phosphorus and sulphur that makes up living things, and without liquid water on the planet's surface, life as we know it could not have evolved. Chemically speaking, Earth is simply better set up for life than its neighbors. So how come we got all the good stuff? [41]

The forgoing examples are but a small sample of what must be an inexhaustible number of reasons why evolutionism is an audacious attempt at prostituting real scientific precept and practice. The theory is an assault on people's inborn intelligence and constitutes a shameless, derisive condemnation of their religious beliefs. Evolutionary theory, peddled as scientific truth, actually is incomprehensibly far-fetched. Dr. Harry Rimmer (1890-1952), scientist, archaeologist and Christian author, allegedly was one of only a dozen men around 1940 competent enough to understand Albert Einstein's theory of relativity. Dr. Rimmer made the following astute statement about the farcicality of evolutionism in his book, "The Magnificence of Jesus."

> *I fail to see how the natural man can scoff at the faith of a Christian who believes in one miracle of creation when the unbeliever accepts multiplied millions of miracles to justify his violation of every known law of biology and every evidence of paleontology, and to cling to the exploded myth of evolution.* [42]

Key Differences Between Evolutionism And Christianity

Chance vs. Design – Secular scientists claim naturalistic evolution resulted from pure chance and required no supervision. The Bible says a supreme and living God created the universe, the earth and all living creatures that exist (Genesis 1:1-31; Psalm 24:1; Romans 1:18-20).

Purpose & Meaning of Life – According to naturalistic evolution, there is no purpose or meaning to life, which resulted from a blind combination of time, chance and matter. Biblical Christianity, on the contrary, teaches that (a) God created life (Psalms 33:6-9; Isaiah 45:18), (b) creation clearly reveals the glory of God (Psalm 19:1-4; Romans 1:18-20), (c) Jesus Christ is eternal and existed from the beginning (John 1:1-5; Colossians 1:16-18) and (d) instead of meaninglessness in this life and nothingness afterwards, God offers eternal life and the opportunity to belong to him forever (John 1:10-12; 3:15,16; 1 Corinthians 8:6).

Value of Humanity – Evolutionist thought implies humans, although more advanced biologically and genetically, are similar to lower animals and are not unique or special. Christianity says God created man in his image and likeness (Genesis 1:26, 27; 5:1; James 3:9). Furthermore, Genesis 1:28; Psalm 8:4-8; and Matthew 6:26; 12:11,12 speak about the value of human beings to God, and their dominion over animals and the rest of creation.

Moral Agency – Evolutionary theorists allege humans are constrained by their environment and genetic diktats due to an evolutionary path littered with chance mutational adaptations. Human beings, therefore, are not free to exercise any kind of far-reaching moral agency. The Bible, which contradicts evolutionist thought, declares that humans are moral agents under God's inspectorate and bear the consequences of the decisions they make (Genesis 2:17; Deuteronomy 30:19; Joshua 24:15; 1 Kings 18:21; Mark 8:36; Luke 15; Romans 6:23).

Universal Morality & Divine Law – The evolutionary premise of natural selection (survival of the fittest) negates the requirement that humans adhere to universal moral values based on any kind of divine law. Biblical doctrine says otherwise, and emphasizes that sinful humankind should not attempt to dictate what constitutes moral practice. (Exodus 21:1-17; Matthew 22:37-40). Law and authority proceed from God alone (Deuteronomy 6:25; John 19:11; Romans 13:1; 1 John 3:4).

Sin and Salvation – An undeniably salient difference between naturalistic evolutionism and biblical Christianity revolves around the concepts of sin and salvation. Evolutionism suggests that "Human beings did not fall from perfection into sin as the Church had taught for centuries; we were evolving, and indeed are still evolving into higher levels of consciousness."

Christian scholarship rejects a despoiled opinion such as the forgoing, and stresses that sinful humankind's only hope of redemption is salvation provided by God through Jesus Christ, not through any other means (Matthew 9:13; John 3:16,17; Romans 10:13; 1 Timothy 2:4; Titus 2:11; 1 John 3:18).

Evolutionism is falsehood. Life did not evolve, nor did the universe appear out of nothingness. After death and judgement by a righteous God, the souls of human beings go either to heaven or hell.

CHAPTER TWENTY

CHRISTIANITY COMPARED WITH NEW RELIGIONS, PHILOSOPHIES & CULTS – SATANISM & THE OCCULT

WHAT IS SATANISM?

Satanism is not easily defined, as the term may encompass several connotations. In contrast to discourse among Christians, Satanists disagree on very fundamental principles about the worldview. Satanists debate among themselves whether Satan even exists and whether they are worshiping him or themselves. In essence, they are a confused group bound by lies. The following biblical passage may well apply to Satanists.

> *You belong to your father the devil, and you want to carry out your father's desire. He was a murderer from the beginning, not holding to the truth, for there is no truth in him. When he lies, he speaks his native language, for he is a liar and the father of lies.* (John 8:44, NIV)

It is because of these lies and untruths there is a plethora of ideologies within Satanism. Some of Satanism's practices are constant, and Satanists' unity is found more in rituals than in an underlying belief system. Many Satanists robotically participate in certain activities without harboring any deep seated commitment to the meanings of such undertakings.

Most Satanists, devil worshipers, diabolists, Luciferians, and members of the Church of Satan claim to have roots in LaVeyan Satanism, named after Anton Szandor LaVey, the author of the Satanic Bible and founder of the First Church of Satan. LaVey, born Howard Stanton Levey (1930 – 1997), was an American author, musician, and occultist. [1] He founded the Church of Satan in 1966 and pioneered the religion of LaVeyan Satanism.

The Church of Satan ironically professes to be atheistic. In their belief system, the only god is oneself. The only sacraments are to please oneself in any way imaginable. The only commandment is to do whatever makes you happy. Curiously, however, in their private rituals, they constantly invoke Satan's name. [2] All forms of Satanism claim life is about consumption and that selfishness is a virtue. Some Satanists hold that the only existence they will ever know is here on Earth. Thus, devil worshippers live for the moment and their creed revolves around debauchery and gluttony .

Satanism pledges its allegiance to Satan, although some in the Church of Satan believe no God or devil exists. Most members of the Church of Satan also believe there is no redeemer or savior for themselves, or anyone else. Each person is fully responsible for the path of his own life. Still, they pray to Satan in rituals, asking for his sovereign hand to be manifest in their lives. Such an approach reveals the influence of lies and deceptions in their convoluted philosophy and the resultant uncertainty that holds sway in their lives. It matters not to the devil himself whether professed Satanists really acknowledge his existence. The end result is the same—their souls are held in bondage to him, and, unless God's grace intervenes, Satanists, like all

466

people who reject Jesus Christ as their Savior and Redeemer, are sure to experience eternity in hell.

While Satanism may or may not involve actually worshiping Satan, it is a conscious effort to refrain from worshipping the one true God. The Book of Romans allows a cogent look into the heart and motives of a Satanist.

And since they did not see fit to acknowledge God, God gave them up to a debased mind to do what ought not to be done. They were filled with all manner of unrighteousness, evil, covetousness, malice. (Romans 1:28-29, ESV)

People misled by Satan into a lifestyle of selfishness and incertitude find it difficult to understand God's concept of grace and freedom. Instead, they live for the moment and take unbridled chances at dangerous pursuits.

What Is Occultism?

Occultism relates to hidden, secret and mysterious inclinations, particularly those pertaining to the supernatural. Among occult practices are astrology, witchcraft (Wicca), the black arts, fortune telling, magic (both black and white), Ouija boards, Tarot cards, spiritism, parapsychology, and not unexpectedly, Satanism. Occult practices and psychic phenomena captivate millions of people worldwide, and this is not limited to the ignorant or uneducated, but includes very many learned individuals willing to embrace the fearsome and unknown. Several factors make the occult fascinating to people, even in today's age of technological and scientific advances.

467

Occult practices, for instance, appeal to an individual's natural curiosity. Many people who become involved in the occult begin with seemingly harmless practices such as playing with a Ouija board. Many who experiment in this way find themselves delving deeper and deeper into the occult. Unfortunately, this type of involvement is akin to gambling - easy to get into and difficult to leave. Participants anticipate improved results each time they "take a chance." Another fascination of the occult is that it appears to offer quick and easy answers to life's questions. The astrologer gladly charts one's future, the Ouija board and Tarot cards give one direction, and the psychic allows one to contact a departed relation who says all is fine in the afterlife. Unbeknownst to such hapless seekers of truth and plenty, demons direct and control occult practices and they provide just enough information to keep their victims intrigued while exerting more and more control over their gullible minds.

The danger of occult practices cannot be overstated. God strictly warned the Israelites against being involved with the occult (Leviticus 20:6). The pagan nations surrounding Israel engaged in uninhibited divination, sorcery, witchcraft, and spiritism, and this is one reason why God gave his people the authority to drive them out of the land (Deuteronomy 18:9–14). The New Testament says the rise of interest in the occult is a sign of the end of the age: "The [Holy] Spirit clearly says that in later times some will abandon the faith and follow deceiving spirits and things taught by demons." (1 Timothy 4:1, NIV)

How does one recognize occultism and those who practice and promote it? An incident involving Paul and Barnabas in the early days of the church

468

is a good place to start. The Book of Acts of the Apostles contains the following edifying passage of Scripture:

> *They traveled through the whole island until they came to Paphos. There they met a Jewish sorcerer and false prophet named Bar-Jesus, who was an attendant of the proconsul, Sergius Paulus. The proconsul, an intelligent man, sent for Barnabas and Saul because he wanted to hear the word of God. But Elymas the sorcerer (for that is what his name means) opposed them and tried to turn the proconsul from the faith. Then Saul, who was also called Paul, filled with the Holy Spirit, looked straight at Elymas and said, "You are a child of the devil and an enemy of everything that is right! You are full of all kinds of deceit and trickery. Will you never stop perverting the right ways of the Lord?*
> (Acts 13:6-10, NIV)

This account reveals several characteristics of those involved in occultism. Firstly there are the false prophets (in verse 6) who deny the basic doctrines of Christianity i.e., the deity of Christ, the fall of humankind into sin, heaven, hell, salvation and the atoning work of Jesus on the cross. Secondly, the prophets seek to influence other people, particularly those in positions of power, to turn them from the faith (verses 6-7). Thirdly, they do everything in their power to keep the true Gospel of Christ from being spread, opposing his ministers at every turn (verse 8). Satan and his demons rejoice any time anyone inhibits, waters down, or rejects the truth of the Christian Gospel.

The New Testament Book of Ephesians provides invaluable advice on how to stand against and extinguish the "flaming arrows" of the devil and his minions.

Finally, be strong in the Lord and in his mighty power. Put on the full armor of God, so that you can take your stand against the devil's schemes. For our struggle is not against flesh and blood, but against the rulers, against the authorities, against the powers of this dark world and against the spiritual forces of evil in the heavenly realms. Therefore put on the full armor of God, so that when the day of evil comes, you may be able to stand your ground, and after you have done everything, to stand. Stand firm then, with the belt of truth buckled around your waist, with the breastplate of righteousness in place, and with your feet fitted with the readiness that comes from the gospel of peace. In addition to all this, take up the shield of faith, with which you can extinguish all the flaming arrows of the evil one. Take the helmet of salvation and the sword of the Spirit, which is the word of God.

And pray in the Spirit on all occasions with all kinds of prayers and requests. With this in mind, be alert and always keep on praying for all the Lord's people. (Ephesians 6:10-18, NIV)

The Upsurge In Satanism & Occultism

Few Americans took notice that in a 2010 U.S. census, *witchcraft* had become the fourth largest religion in the United States. As shocking as that may be, *Satanism* was just as popular. Zachary King, a renowned former Satanist who converted to the Catholic Church, made these observations in an interview with *Crusade Magazine*.[3] According to the 2010 census, there were more people involved in the occult in America than there were Muslims or Jehovah's Witnesses. Compare this estimate to polls conducted in 1980 when the people who affiliated themselves with the occult were so statistically small that no specific data was assigned to them. Statisticians, at the time, grouped occultists with Muslims, Buddhists, Unitarians and others and arrived at a tally of only 2% of Americans. [4]

The total number of Satanists is somewhat more difficult to determine. According to Zachary King, there are about 4 million Satanists in the United States and about 10 million worldwide. One reason why it's impossible to have hard figures on the number of Satanists in America is because of the secrecy. The Church of Satan, founded by Anton La Vey, was the first of its kind to establish itself officially as a non-profit religious organization with the U.S. government on September 20, 1971, in California. [5]

Scores of millions of Americans read their horoscopes every morning in order to determine what they should do during the day. Horoscopes appear in virtually every newspaper across the USA and in countless periodicals around the world. The forecasts are an indispensable feature in most daily newspapers and in the lives of innumerable eager readers as well.

Young people today seem entranced by occult jewelry, such as earrings or medallions of the inverted pentagram and the upside down five-pointed star with a goat's head in the center, the latter a symbol that is unmistakably satanic. The peace symbol, or the inverted broken cross, is a popular piece of jewelry for Satanists. They see the overturned cross as a sign of the defeat of Christianity.

Movies, Television & Video Games

People's unprecedented interest in the occult and Satanism is aided and abetted in no small measure by Hollywood and the film industry. Shown below are names of movies that revolve around the damning precepts and practices of Satanism, devil worship, exorcism, and the occult, and with which very many people easily become obsessed. The selections are but a small sample of hundreds of similar movies that serve to beguile unwary people into adopting lifestyles that reek of moral bankruptcy, and worse, embracing supernatural evil.

Movies about satanic cults: Rosemary's Baby (1968), Drive Angry (2011), Prince of Darkness (1987), Devil's Due (2014), Rosemary's Baby (2014), Scary Tales: Last Stop (2015), Wild Honey (1972), Mind, Body & Soul (1992), Race with the Devil (1975), Black Candles (1982).

Movies about devil worship: Chilling Adventures of Sabrina (2018), The Omen (2006), Midnight Offerings (1981), Inquisition (1977), Good Against Evil (1977), Vengeance of the Zombies (1973), The Masque of the Red Death (1964), South of Hell (2015), Pyewacket (2017), Devil's *Kiss (1976)*.

Movies about exorcism: Supernatural (2005), Constantine (2014), The Exorcist (1973), The Conjuring (2013), The Vatican Tapes (2015), Blue Exorcist (2011), Exorcist: The Beginning (2004), When the Lights Went Out (2012), Legion (1990), The Rite (2011).

Movies about Satanism: Borderland (2007), The Possession of Michael King (2014), The Mephisto Waltz (1971), Beyond the Door (1974), To the Devil a Daughter (1976), The Satanic Rites of Dracula (1973), Atomic Hotel Erotica (2014), Evil Bong 666 (2017), The Devil Rides Out (1968), End of Days (1999).

Movies about the occult: A Dark Song (2016), The Ninth Gate (1999), Blood Creek (2009), The Skeleton Key (2005), Noroi: The Curse (2005), Amityville Dollhouse (1996), Devour (2005), [REC] 4: Apocalypse (2014), The Possession of Michael King (2014), The Wicker Man (2006). [6]

Jesus himself warned incautious people about what to expect in *the last days* before his Second Coming.

The (Holy) Spirit clearly says that in later times some will abandon the faith and follow deceiving spirits and things taught by demons. (1 Timothy 4:1, NIV)

Television also plays a significant role in luring vast numbers of people into the realms of Satanism and the occult. Among the more popular television shows/series over recent times that endorsed occult and satanic overtones were the following. (a) Twin Peaks (1990 – 1991), (b) Sabrina the Teenage Witch (1996), (c) Charmed (1998), (d) Buffy the Vampire Slayer (1997-2003), (e) True Blood (2008 – 2014), (f) American Horror Story (2011 onwards), (g) Penny Dreadful (2014 – 2016), (h) True Detective (2014 onwards), (h) Ash vs. The Evil Dead (2015 -2018), (j) Dark (2017 onwards) and (k), The Haunting of Hill House (2018).

Television cartoons too carry occult and satanic themes. Shows like "The Smurfs," "Pokemon," "Yu-Gi-Oh," and even "Scooby Doo" all contain some measure of occult content. "The Smurfs" is deceptively alluring to children and young audiences in general. First published back in 1958, and animated in 1981, the Smurfs are charming little blue characters that practice the occult. They habitually prepare caldrons of magic potions, cast spells and put hexes on people.

Movies and television shows with occult and satanic themes continue to saturate the public and entrap unsuspecting audiences into perfunctory acceptance. People are so desensitized to the veiled agenda of evil, they are numb to the reality of the danger posed by satanic and occult movies and shows.

Video Games represent yet another channel through which Satanism and the occult infiltrate the minds of people, especially younger folks. The following video games are decidedly occult. (a) Taboo: The Sixth Sense (b) Xenogears (c) Silent Hill (d) DmC – Devil May Cry (e) Dante's Inferno (f) Diablo III (g) Deus Ex: Human Revolution (g) Assassin's Creed (h) BioShock Infinite, and (i) Shin Megami Tensei: Nocturne.

Dungeons & Dragons (D&D), another popular video game, is one of the bestselling games for high school and college students in the USA and abroad. Audiences generally acknowledge D&D's publication as the beginning of modern role-playing games and the role-playing game industry. D&D is a role-playing game in which a player lives out innumerable decadent and perverse desires in a fantasy world. The player can summon a plethora of occult characters i.e., witches, wizards, demons,

474

and demigods, to assist him or her to experience various forms of immoral behavior.

Yet sometimes, it is difficult to demarcate between fantasy and reality, with tragic consequences. Ron Carlson, the president of Christian Ministries International and prominent expert on cults and Christian apologetics, and Ed Decker, the founder and International Director of Saints Alive in Jesus, a counter-cults ministry, reported in their book Fast *Facts on False Teachings*:

> *Dr. Thomas Radke, a practicing psychiatrist and a professor at the University of Denver, documented 123 cases where Dungeons & Dragons had played a specific role in either murder or suicide among young people.*[7]

Satan, as mentioned earlier, does not approach people dressed in red, sporting a pair of horns, a tail, and armed with a pitchfork. The Bible says, "And no wonder, for Satan himself masquerades as an angel of light." (2 Corinthians 11:14, NIV) The Book of 1 Peter warns all to "...be alert and of sober mind. Your enemy the devil prowls around like a roaring lion looking for someone to devour." (1 Peter 5-8, NIV)

Satan does not always terrorize or antagonize his intended victims. He sometimes offers them wisdom, knowledge and power - of course the wrong kind for the wrong reasons! Satan's gifting of wisdom, knowledge and power to his victims overwhelms them and they hardly ever realize the devil's aim is to pilfer their souls in return. It is a trap from which many cannot escape.

Heavy Metal Music

Deep involvement with heavy metal music is a demonstrable indication someone is dabbling with Satanism or the occult. Heavy metal music is unlike traditional rock and roll and its staid offshoots in which the music and lyrics span acceptable parameters of decency and presentation. A few classic rock and roll groups, however, did play a part in ushering heavy metal music and its concomitant occult strains during the 1960's and 1970's, even though heavy metal was not their earmarked genre.

The Beatles, for instance, a seminal rock and roll group considered a comparatively pure musical innovator, showcased sinister occult guru Aleister Crowley on their "Sgt. Pepper Lonely Hearts Club Band" album cover in 1967. Mick Jagger and the Rolling Stones took a cue from the Beatles and in the same year and depicted themselves as witches on the cover of their album "Their Satanic Majesty's Request." Additionally, the cover of the Rolling Stones' 1973 album "Goat's Head Soup" displays a cauldron of boiling liquid with a goat's head floating in it. A goat's head is generally symbolic of satanic or occult activity.

Heavy metal entered the realm of mainstream music on February 13th of 1970 when the British group Black Sabbath released their eponymous album. The impact of Black Sabbath's foray into the occult and Satanism via their shockingly loud music, explicit lyrics, and lurid exhibitionism discomfited even hardened, liberally indulgent music fans. The dark, diabolical and damning pursuit known as heavy metal music evolved through the decades into the frightening state of occult music in the 21st century via prominent practitioners like AC/DC, Iron Maiden, Merciful

476

Fate, Led Zeppelin, Slayer, Motley Crue, Anthrax, Danzig, Exodus, Grim Reaper, Halloween, Megadeth, Metal Church, Metallica, Celtic Force, Satan, Sodom, and Possessed. Witchfinder General, Pentagram, Saint Vitus, and Reverend Bizarre were other groups that helped pioneer the heavy metal genre in one way or another.

Among today's heavy metal exponents are ensembles such as Ghost, Purson, Uncle Acid & the Deadbeats, Blood Ceremony, Orchid, Sabbath Assembly, Jess & the Ancient Ones, Mount Salem, Avatarium, The Skull, Jex Thoth, Witch Mountain and Lucifer.

Typical lyrics of many heavy metal songs are very disquieting to the time-honored, moral psyche. The group Slayer's song "Altar of Sacrifice" for instance, contains the following lines.

...waiting the hour destined to die here on the table of hell, a figure in the white unknown by man approaching the alter of death. High priest awaiting, dagger in hand, spilling the pure virgin blood. Satan slaughters ceremonial death, answer his every command...Learn the sacred words of praise hail Satan, hail Satan, hail Satan

Young people in many parts of the world today habitually listen to such lyrics, which saturate their very existence. Heavy metal music, in the main, is not about fun and games or love and romance. The lyrics address dreadful subjects such as death and unbridled evil. The group Slayer's album "South of Heaven" features a song titled "Mandatory Suicide," which endorses self-destruction. Teenagers and young people commit suicide thinking it is somehow a means of attaining power and escaping from a world's with which they have become disenchanted.

The Holy Bible relays in no uncertain terms, God's directive to avoid any type of involvement in occultism and Satanism.

There shall not be found among you anyone who makes his son or his daughter pass through the fire, or one who practices witchcraft, or a soothsayer, or one who interprets omens, or a sorcerer, or one who conjures spells, or a medium, or a spiritist, or one who calls up the dead. (Deuteronomy 18:10-11, NKJV)

Advanced Entrapment

In addition to the ramifications of spiritual imperilment, embracing occultism often emboldens the participant to experiment with psychotropic drugs that affect his or her mental state, or with consciousness-expanding techniques such as Yoga and Transcendental Meditation (TM). The participant consequently exposes himself or herself to psychotic experiences (PEs) or worse, demonic possession.

Psychotic experiences (PEs) are hallucinatory and delusion-like experiences that occur in the absence of a psychotic disorder. People who report these phenomena are vulnerable to a range of current and later mental health outcomes, including an increased risk of depression, anxiety, psychosis, substance abuse, and poorer functioning in daily life.[8]

Some practitioners steeped deeply in occultism and Satanism misguidedly think they have the authority and wherewithal to manipulate people's minds and bodies, including their own, for the good of all involved. Such perverted ratiocination often results in dubious ethical practices, seduction, rape, physical abuse, and torture and mutilation of animals, and even of human beings in extreme instances.

The occultist's desire for power sooner or later scales even boundaries of the atypical and bizarre. He or she eventually enters an arena where Satan bares his true agenda of deception and evil and ensnares yet another ill-fated disciple. Sociopathic and iniquitous behavior become the norm. The occultist or Satanist loses all self-control and fully acquiesces to his or her inner demons who direct him or her to harm and destroy. Individuals like Jeffrey Dahmer, Charles Manson, Richard Ramirez and David Berkowitz were occultists and/or Satanists who gave themselves over to the devil, and wreaked unprecedented havoc. Providentially, the law caught up with them. The capture and conviction of these men notwithstanding, they represent just a small percentage of the many disciples of satanic enslavement who roam society. They imperil their own souls and seek also to endanger the souls of multitudinous prospective victims of supernatural inveiglement.

The Various Areas Of Occultic Activity

Mantic Behavior

Mantic behavior comprises a popular facet of occultic activity. Mantic activity relates to the practice of divination or seeking to foretell the future through the use of astrology, tarot cards, palmistry, numerology, crystal balls, and tea leaves.

Television, the Internet and various types of digital media abound with the means to access so-called fortune tellers, astrologers and psychics for updated readings of one's horoscope and fortune.

Black & White Magic

The practice of magic is another principal element of occultism. The term "magic" as used here does not refer to traditional sleight-of-hand tricks or illusions, but magic in its classical definition.

Occultists allude to both white and black magic. White magic, also known as white witchcraft, teaches there is only one universal source of power. Black magic acknowledges both a good source and an evil source of power. The primary objective of both white and black magic practitioners is to access a source of power that enables them to exercise control over their own lives and the lives of other people.

New Age adherents routinely advocate the existence of a universal power source that parades the cosmos. They are correct in a sense, but either knowingly or unknowingly, they deny the reality of the one true God, and by pursuing an unknown universal "force," they court the alliance of demons and deceitful spirits.

Many young people, via the auspices of television and the Internet, believe they can tap into a universal force and obtain spiritual power. Further, they believe witchcraft is not evil, but good, and it harbors benefits available to all who would dispense with moral and spiritual responsibilities coexistent with a traditionally religious point of view. Christianity especially, they suppose, is irrelevant and unnecessary.

Satanism

Satanism itself is another central area of occultism. The subject of Satanism encompasses, in the main, the story of the fallen angel Lucifer

(Satan) and the fallen angels; all finite created beings, whom Almighty God cast out of heaven after they rebelled against him. Satan and his demons are bent on deceiving humankind and leading its members away from Jesus Christ, the latter who is the only way through whom lost sinners can be reconciled with Almighty God.

The author directs the reader to the sub section titled *What is Satanism?* At the beginning of this chapter and Chapter Three - *The Devil, or Satan – Is He Real?* for more on Satanism.

Astrology

Astrology is the most extensive area of the occult. The discipline revolves around the study of the supposed 12 houses of the zodiac. There are 12 astrological or zodiac signs, which derive from the times people are born. Astrologists refer to the position of the planets, stars, the sun, and the moon at the time of an individual's birth to forecast and/or determine future events and cycles of good and bad in his or her life.

There is not a modicum of logical or scientific validity to astrology. The practice is also one of the oldest pagan pursuits known to humankind. God explicitly condemns astrology as an abomination and as the Book of Deuteronomy of the Bible says, people are to avoid embracing the practice at all costs.

And when you look up to the sky and see the sun, the moon and the stars—all the heavenly array—do not be enticed into bowing down to them and worshiping things the Lord your God has apportioned to all the nations under heaven. (Deuteronomy 4:19, NIV)

481

If a man or woman living among you in one of the towns the Lord gives you is found doing evil in the eyes of the Lord your God in violation of his covenant, and contrary to my command has worshiped other gods, bowing down to them or to the sun or the moon or the stars in the sky, and this has been brought to your attention, then you must investigate it thoroughly. If it is true and it has been proved that this detestable thing has been done in Israel, take the man or woman who has done this evil deed to your city gate and stone that person to death. (Deuteronomy 17:2-5, NIV)

In olden Israel, people found guilty of practicing astrology were to be put to death. Today, people are not killed because they become involved in astrology or any other occult activity, especially in America and other Western nations. This is because the majority of today's societies are democracies, and not theocracies. Such an observation notwithstanding, Christian scholarship emphasizes that occultism, including astrology, runs afoul of a Holy God's dictates for righteous living.

Spiritism

Spiritism is another prevalent facet of occultism. Spiritism relates to the channeling of advice or so-called New Age wisdom by a spirit being via a human channeler. The Bible states very lucidly that the practice of spiritism contradicts the edicts of a pure and holy God.

Do not turn to mediums or seek out spiritists, for you will be defiled by them.

I am the Lord your God. (Leviticus 19:31, NIV)

I will set my face against anyone who turns to mediums and spiritists to prostitute themselves by following them, and I will cut them off from their people. (Leviticus 20:6, NIV)

A man or woman who is a medium or spiritist among you must be put to death. You are to stone them; their blood will be on their own heads. (Leviticus 20:27, NIV)

While the Christian Gospel, which exemplifies God's covenant with His children today, does not advocate stoning people to death, it does consider spiritism a heinous sin and forbids its practice.

Fortune – Telling (Prophesying)

Fortune-telling or prophesying is an undeniable component of occultism. Modern-day prophets and prophetesses rush to forecast events in people's lives, and also occurrences from national and international perspectives. The Bible condemns fortune-telling and false prophesying in unmistakable terms.

God instructs His children to utilize two tests in order to determine whether a prophet is an authentic disseminator of truth. Firstly, one must test the prophecy. Secondly, one must test the teaching. The Book of Deuteronomy describes the first test.

But a prophet who presumes to speak in my name anything I have not commanded, or a prophet who speaks in the name of other gods, is to be put to death.

You may say to yourselves, "How can we know when a message has not been spoken by the Lord?" If what a prophet proclaims in the name of the Lord does not take place or come true, that is a message the Lord has not spoken. That prophet has spoken presumptuously, so do not be alarmed. (Deuteronomy 18:20-22, NIV)

If the prophecy does not materialize or come to pass, the prophet is not of God. The Hebrew prophets of the Old Testament had to be 100 percent accurate in their predictions or they paid with their lives. Claiming to be a prophet of God entails the adoption of serious responsibility. The claimant must be sure God is the author of the prophecies being spoken and that they do not proceed from his or her own mind or imagination.

The second test to determine if a prophet is of God requires the source of the teaching to be analyzed. Does the teaching lead one to worship the true and living God, or does the teaching lead one away from God? Also, is the teaching contrary to God's Holy Word? The prerequisites that the prophecy or teaching should lead people to the true and living God, and not be dissimilar to God's Word must be satisfied in order to pass the second test. The Book of Second Timothy says:

All Scripture is God-breathed and is useful for teaching, rebuking, correcting and training in righteousness, so that the servant of God may be thoroughly equipped for every good work. (2 Timothy 3:16-17, NIV)

Satanism And The Occult – Forbidden By God

The Bible sounds a dire warning against assenting to Satanism or any other belief system besides Christianity and the one true God:

These people are springs without water and mists driven by a storm. Blackest darkness is reserved for them. For they mouth empty, boastful words and, by appealing to the lustful desires of the flesh, they entice people who are just escaping from those who live in error. They promise them freedom, while they themselves are slaves of depravity. (2 Peter 2:17-19, NIV)

Likewise, the occult in any of its forms should be avoided at all costs. As God's Word cautions the Christian believer, he or she must, "Be alert and of sober mind. Your enemy the devil prowls around like a roaring lion looking for someone to devour." (1 Peter 5:8, NIV). Christians need to be aware of Satan's schemes and not become enticed or entrapped by occult phenomena or practices. The devil's ultimate goal is the damnation of people's souls for eternity.

485

CHAPTER TWENTY-ONE

CHRISTIANITY COMPARED WITH NEW RELIGIONS, PHILOSOPHIES & CULTS - OTHER NON-CHRISTIAN/ANTI-CHRISTIAN RELIGIONS & PHILOSOPHIES

The Christian faith has been assailed, criticized, and subjected to countless attempts to undermine it since the first century, or shortly after the worldview emerged as a revolutionary and unique belief system during a time when much of the civilized world fell under the inspectorate of a ruthless Roman dictatorship.

Adversaries of Christianity take offense to the faith's affirmation that its founder, Jesus Christ, the second Person of the Trinity, is the Savior and Redeemer of all people through whom they may obtain salvation from their sins and secure for themselves a place in God's kingdom for all eternity. Some of Christianity's enemies come from within its ranks, even though their gripes may assume disputations that are dissimilar to those advanced by others resolutely opposed to the worldview's principal tenets.

Biblical Christian churches and organizations constitute an environment conducive to infiltration by cultists and other new age or extremist groups on the lookout for Christians who may not truly understand their own religious ideology and who seek avenues of fulfillment for certain unmet needs. Many such cults or groups exist in today's multidimensional societies and new ones constantly seem to arise.

Following are some of the more familiar pseudo-religious philosophies that challenge, attack, and endeavor to undermine the Christian Gospel. Some of them simply differ from biblical Christianity. Limited space allows only short descriptions of the groups, but the author attempts to provide rounded analyses that touch upon the origins, history, beliefs and practices of the worldviews, while he simultaneously compares them with biblical Christianity.

The Baha'i Faith

The Baha'i faith is a movement started by an Iranian businessman and Shi'ite Muslim with the objective of reforming Islam. For centuries following the death of the Islamic prophet Mohammed in 632 AD, many Muslims awaited a successor to the religion's founder. In 1844, wool merchant Mirza Ali Mohammed announced that he was the precursor to the promised successor. Mohammed became known as "The Bab" (pronounced "bob," meaning "a gate leading to a new era for man") and his followers were called Babists (or *Bobis*). Muslim zealots who disagreed with the Bab's teachings and rejected the notion of restructuring the Islamic religion executed him along with many of his followers in 1850. [1]

In 1863, some 1,230 years after the Islamic prophet Mohammed died, one of The Bab's followers, Mirza Husayn Ali (1817-1892), assumed the name "Baha'u'llah" and declared himself Mohammed's long-awaited successor. Baha'u'llah named the new movement "Baha'i." He proceeded to develop his own religious doctrines and prepared an estimated 100 to 200 books and documents, which his followers eventually considered divinely inspired. One of Baha'u'llah's most significant texts is *The Most Holy Book*, which contains the laws that govern the Baha'i religion.[2]

Baha'u'llah died in 1892, and his son Abdu'l Baha' (1844-1921) took up leadership of the organization. Abdu'l Baha' successfully introduced Baha'i to the United States in 1893. He was an adept teacher and able interpreter of his father's teachings, and was vehicular in the construction of a $2.5 million Baha'i temple in Wilmette, Illinois, north of Chicago, USA. Abdu'l Baha died in 1921, and his Oxford-educated grandson, Shoghi Effendi, ascended to the position of the Baha'i organization's Guardian of the Faith. Effendi died in 1957. No one succeeded him.

The first Baha'i Universal House of Justice, a nine-person governing board, emerged in 1963. The board, considered infallible, oversees the affairs of the world's five to seven million Baha'i Faith members from the organization's headquarters in Haifa, Israel. [3]

Baha'i Teachings And Practices

Baha'i sees no contradiction among the world's major belief systems and hold all to be equally truthful. Judaism, Islam, Buddhism, Christianity and Hinduism are essentially all in agreement, with only minor, inconsequential differences. Baha'i philosophy teaches that Adam, Abraham, Moses, Krishna, Buddha, Jesus and Mohammed were all manifestations of God, each a genuine prophet and each divine, sinless and flawless. [4]

Baha'i doctrines revolve, in the main, around the teachings and claims of Baha'u'llah, who supposedly superseded all other prophets and manifestations of God, including Jesus Christ. Baha'u'llah instituted stringent rules about daily worship, which included the requirement that believers wash their faces and hands three times a day, turn toward his (Baha'u'llah's) tomb and recite obligatory prayers. Baha'i followers also must repeat on a daily basis, the words "Allah-u-Abha" (God of highest glory). Every March, Baha'is must fast from sunup to sundown for 19 days.

Obligatory Bahá'í prayers are daily prayers said by Bahai's according to a fixed form decreed by Bahá'u'lláh. Prayers in the Bahá'í Faith are reverent words addressed to God, Prayer & Worship, [5] and refer to two distinct concepts; obligatory prayer and devotional prayer (general prayer). The act of prayer is one of the most important Bahá'í laws for individual discipline. Along with fasting, obligatory prayer is one of the greatest obligations of a Bahá'í. [6]

One of the major goals of Baha'i is to foster the unity of humankind. There are certain implications, however, with such a pursuit. A unified humankind will have to accommodate an international political empire in which Baha'ism would be the state religion. Baha'i expectations are that all nations would give up national sovereignty and allow the Baha'i global government to rule. Specifically, every human being on Earth would fall under the jurisdiction of the Baha'i World Parliament. [7]

BAHA'I vs. CHRISTIANITY

Baha'i differs from Christianity in many ways. Following are some of the more significant dissimilarities.

View of God – Baha'is are supposedly firmly monotheistic and like the followers of Judaism and Islam, claim that God is one, period. However, the Baha'i belief that all major religions, including, Judaism, Islam, Christianity, Buddhism and Hinduism all represent religious truth and point to the same universal God, and that Adam, Abraham, Moses, Krishna, Buddha, Jesus and Mohammed were all manifestations of God, each a genuine prophet and each divine, sinless and infallible, makes the Baha'i faith's advocacy of its monotheistic nature distinctly problematical.

Biblical Christianity teaches about a plurality of personhoods, i.e., the Father, Son, and Holy Spirit, that constitutes a single Triune God. See Old Testament references (Genesis 1:26; 3:22; 11:7; Isaiah 6:8), and New Testament references (Matthew 28:19; John 14:6; 15:26; 2 Corinthians 13:14; 1 Peter 1:2). The Christian faith, in effect, promotes the idea of one God, not many gods. Further, the worldview is not syncretistic like the Baha'i religion, which maintains that God is one, yet perplexingly alleges that all major religions, the members of which revere different deities or gods, are the same.

View of Jesus Christ and *the Holy Spirit* – Baha'is look upon Jesus as a prophet whose status as a manifestation of God ended after Mohammed founded Islam in the seventh century.[8] Baha'i scholars firmly disagree with the Biblical doctrines about the Trinity, Jesus' incarnation, his bodily resurrection from death, and the need for Jesus' sacrificial atonement for humankind's sins. [9]

According to the Holy Bible, Christ is the second Person of the Trinity. Christianity also imparts unequivocally that Christ's death and resurrection are necessary as atonement for humankind's sins, a feat human works are incapable of accomplishing. Refusal to accept Jesus as Savior and Redeemer and acknowledge his sacrifice on the cross sentences an individual to an eternity of everlasting suffering and torment (Matthew 1:23; 3:16,17; 28:19; Mark 16:1-6; John 1:1-5; Romans 3:24-26; 1 Corinthians 15:12-15; 1 John 2:2; 4:10).

Baha'is believe Baha'u'llah was the fulfillment of Christ's promise of the Holy Spirit. Baha'u'llah taught that he replaced Jesus as a more recent and greater manifestation of God. [10] Contrary to Baha'i teaching, the Gospel of John (14:1-9) records Christ asserting his permanent, unchanging divinity. Further, in John 14:16-18 and 16:12-15 Christ plainly states the Spirit of truth or the Holy Spirit will come to glorify him and help the Christian believer.

Baha'i scholars do not share the biblical affirmation that Christ is the only way to God. Baha'is feel religious truth is relative, not absolute, and revelation is continuous and never final. [11, 12] The Gospel of John in the New Testament teaches in no uncertain manner Jesus Christ is the source of life and truth (John 1:14; 14:6; 18:37).

In Summary

The Baha'i faith differs from the Christian faith in many ways, but perhaps the most pronounced dissimilarity is Baha'i's syncretism – a monist doctrine that says all religions are one and the same and the gods are more or less collectively singular. Baha'u'llah's teachings, of course, endorse him as the final and foremost manifestation of God.

Also, the rejection of Jesus Christ as humankind's Savior and Redeemer by Baha'is, and their belief people must rely on themselves and good works to attain what they perceive to be a kind of salvation from their sins, expose adherents of the worldview to the very real danger of languishing for eternity in a dreadful place called hell, where they will forever be alienated from God.

Christian Science

The Origin Of Christian Science

Scholars of comparative religion generally regard Christian Science as the premier religion of its type, from which other mind science belief systems, including many New Age groups, sprouted over the years since the late 19th century. [1] An Encyclopedia Britannica article about Christian Science reads as follows:

Christian Science emerged in late 19th-century America when Darwinism, biblical criticism, and other secularizing influences weakened the supernaturalist structure of Protestant orthodoxy. Troubled Christians, divided between what Eddy (Mary Baker Eddy

(1821-1910), credited with establishing the worldview, called a "stern Protestantism" and a "doubtful liberalism," were drawn to Christian Science because of the practice of spiritual healing and the promise of renewed faith. [2]

Eddy's teachings bear heavily on her association with Phineas Parkhurst Quimby (1802-1866). Quimby, who treated Eddy for "spinal inflammation," was an American spiritual teacher, magnetizer, mesmerist, and inventor. Scholars generally recognize his work as leading to the New Thought movement. [3]

Although generally acknowledged as the founder of Christian Science, Mary Baker Eddy was a somewhat controversial figure. Some scholars rejected her claims to originality and truthfulness and accused her of plagiarism. For instance, Eddy's book *Science and Health with Key to the Scriptures*, considered Christian Science's central text, contains passages almost verbatim from one of Phineas Parkhurst Quimby's own books. [4] Additionally, historians determined Eddy used the works of other authors while neglecting to accord them credit. [5] Furthermore, Mary Baker Eddy's physician, Dr. Alvin M. Cushing, discredited her story that after being severely injured in a fall and approaching death, she read the Bible and returned to complete health on the third day. [6]

The foregoing reflections notwithstanding, Mary Baker Eddy was a resilient leader and creative strategist. She founded the Church of Christ, Scientist in Boston, Massachusetts, USA, in 1879. The mission of the church was "to commemorate the word and works of Jesus Christ" and "reinstate primitive Christianity and its lost element of healing." At the time of Eddy's death in 1910, the Church of Christ Scientist boasted about 1 million members worldwide. Today, the church does not officially report membership and recent estimates as to worldwide membership range between about 400,000 to less than 100,000.

Christian Science - Teachings & Practices

Christian Science and other mind science philosophies seek to discredit the indubitable biblical teaching that God, the sovereign head and creator of the universe and of life, is infinite, personal, good, and signally discrete from his creation. Christian Scientists maintain God "is not a person, but a principle," the principle of Impersonal Mind. [7]

Science & Health with Key to the Scriptures (1875), Mary Baker Eddy's pioneering Christian Science text, teaches "there is no life, truth, intelligence, or substance in matter. All is Infinite Mind and its infinite manifestation, for God is all in all...man is not material; he is spiritual." [8] Christian Science philosophy proposes that evil, sin, disease, sickness, and death are "illusions of the mortal mind," and the physical realm is really non-existent. [9]

Christian Scientists, in presuming the physical world is illusory and intangible, promote a doctrine that parallels the ceaselessly perplexing premise of Hindu or Buddhist pantheism and relegates God to a status of an impersonal force or idea. In projecting the notion that sin, sickness, suffering, and evil are objectively non-existent, they consequently trivialize

494

the need for material medicine. Scientific and medical methods of preserving and prolonging life, therefore, serve no purpose. [10]

Mary Baker Eddy is known to have said, "The sick are not healed merely by declaring there is no sickness, but by knowing that there is none." [11]

Contrary to Eddy's bewildering analysis, biblical Christianity avers sickness – physical and spiritual – is very real, and Jesus Christ is the ultimate Physician (Matthew 4:23, 24; Luke 4:40).

Biblical Christianity informs humankind about an infinite and personal God who created the physical universe and physical life, both of which are real, and were originally perfect (Genesis 1:4.10,12,18,21,25,31). The Bible declares evil, sin, sickness and death are the consequences of humankind's disobedience, or Fall from God's grace in the Garden of Eden where he placed them after he created them (Genesis 3; Romans 3:10-23; 5:12-21; 6;23). Christian Science's denial of the validity of science and medicine contradicts the biblical acknowledgment of the importance of progressive medical science, which is invaluable in treating the physical causes of many human ailments and diseases and in healing people around the world.

Key Differences Between Christian Science And Biblical Christianity

Interpreting the Scriptures – Christian Science advocates interpreting the Bible via the revelations and principles enunciated in Mary Baker Eddy's *Science and Health with Key to the Scriptures*. [12] Deuteronomy 4:2;

2 Timothy 3:16; Hebrews 1:1, 2; and Jude 3 say the Holy Bible proceeds from divine inspiration. Christian scholarship forbids the interpretation of God's Holy Word through any means that would detract from its original and true intent.

Christian Science Healings - Christian Scientists trumpet healing through their worldview's methods as proof of their religion's genuineness. The Bible, in Exodus 7:11, 12, 22 and Matthew 7:22, 23, reveals Satan may enable false prophets to perform miracles and therefore lead people away from God.

Jesus Christ and the Trinity - Christian Science makes the following claim: "The theory of three persons in one God (that is, a personal Trinity or Triunity) suggests polytheism, rather than the one ever-present I AM. Jesus Christ is not God, as Jesus himself declared, but is the Son of God." [13] The Bible, on the contrary, affirms that Jesus is God. The doctrine of the Trinity dispels any contradiction between referring to Jesus as God or as the Son of God (John 1:1, 2; 5:19; 8:58; 14:6-9; 2 Peter 2:1).

God and Humankind – According to Christian Science philosophy, "God is the principle of man; and the principle of man remaining perfect, its idea or reflection – man remains perfect." [14] The Bible says otherwise, i.e., God created man and woman, who are by essence and ascendancy different from God and are far from perfect (Genesis 1:26, 27; 2:7; Romans 3:9-23; 5:12-21).

Jesus' Crucifixion and Resurrection - Christian Science disputes biblical Christianity's central, all-pervasive tenet, i.e., Christ's sacrifice on the cross and his subsequent resurrection. Adherents of the worldview tender the following misinformed statement: "...the material blood of Jesus was no more efficacious to cleanse from sin when it was shed upon 'the accursed tree' than when it was flowing through His veins. Jesus' students...learned that he had not died." [15] The Bible, in refutation of Christian Science, clearly enunciates the importance of Jesus' atonement on the cross through the shedding of his precious blood and his resurrection and emphasizes the need for all who would seek forgiveness of their sins and entry into paradise to embrace him as Lord and Savior. (Matthew 27:50-60; Romans 10:9; 1 Corinthians 15:1-4)

Means of Salvation – Christian Science believers abide by the following doctrines. "...the sinner makes his own hell by doing evil, and the saint his own heaven by doing right..." [16] and "Man as God's idea is already saved with an everlasting salvation." [17] Biblical erudition, in strong dissensus to Christian Science philosophy, cautions those who would entertain the idea they can earn salvation on their own through good works. Sin leads to death and separation from God. No one is "already saved," but all who would be saved must turn to Christ who, through His death and resurrection, is able to redeem humankind from sin and ensure for them an eternity in heaven. Jesus warns everyone about a real hell where suffering never ends (Romans 3:23; 6:23; Matthew 8:12).

The Holy Spirit - Christian Scientists rebuff the biblical doctrine that the Holy Spirit is the third "person" of the Trinity since God, they say, is impersonal. [18] The Bible affirms in no uncertain manner that the Holy

Spirit, sent by God the Father and Christ, dwells in the hearts of believers (John 14:15-18, 26, 27; 15:26; 16:7-14).

The Importance of Prayer - Christian Science offers the following incomprehensible excuse for denying the importance of prayer: "The mere habit of pleading with the divine Mind, as one pleads with a human being, perpetuates the belief in God as humanly circumscribed – an error which impedes spiritual growth." [19] Biblical Christian practice requires believers to pray always about everything. A personal, benevolent God desires that his children communicate with him as often as possible (1 Chronicles 16:11; Matthew 7:7; 26:41; Luke 18:1; John 16:24; Philippians 4:6; 1 Thessalonians 5:17). Such a practice enhances spiritual growth, not hinder it.

In Summary

Christian Science, of all the so-called Christian cults in existence, is the most inaccurately named. The worldview is neither Christian nor based on science. It denies all the core truths of what makes a belief system "Christian." Christian Science is, in fact, opposed to science and points to mystical new-age spirituality as the path to physical and spiritual healing. Followers of the worldview, unless they seek salvation through acceptance of Jesus' atoning sacrifice on the cross and his subsequent resurrection and victory over death, expose their very souls to eternal damnation.

Cultural Relativism

Cultural relativism is the position there is no universal standard by which to measure cultures and that all social, educational, and philosophical values and beliefs must be understood relative to their cultural context and not judged based on outside norms and values. Proponents of cultural relativism also tend to argue that the norms and values of one culture should not be evaluated using the norms and values of another.[1]

Cultural relativism is widely accepted in modern anthropology. Cultural relativists believe that all cultures are worthy in their own right and are of equal value. Diversity of cultures, even those with conflicting moral beliefs, is not to be considered in terms of right and wrong or good and bad. A prevailing anthropological mindset considers all cultures to be equally legitimate expressions of human existence, to be studied from a purely neutral perspective.

Anthropology is the scientific study of humanity, concerned with human behavior, human biology, cultures, societies, and linguistics in both the present and past, including archaic humans. [2] *Social anthropology* studies patterns of behavior, while cultural anthropology studies cultural meaning, including norms and values.[3] The term *sociocultural anthropology* is commonly used today. *Linguistic anthropology* studies how language influences social life. *Biological or physical anthropology* studies the biological development of humans.[4]

Cultural relativism is closely related to *ethical relativism*, which views truth or uprightness as variable and not confirmable or restrained. What constitutes right and wrong is determined firstly by the individual and, secondly, by society at large. Since truth is not considered to be objective, there can be no objective standard that applies to all cultures or lifestyles.

Essentially, no one can say if someone else is right or wrong. It is a matter of personal opinion. Similarly, no society can condemn another society.

Ethical relativism (often reformulated as relativist ethics or relativist morality) is also called *moral relativism* and is used to describe several philosophical positions concerned with the differences in moral judgments across different peoples and cultures. An advocate of such ideas is often referred to as a relativist.[5]

Cultural relativism sees nothing inherently wrongand nothing inherently good with any cultural expression. Accordingly, the ancient Mayan practices of self-mutilation and human sacrifice are neither good nor bad; they are simply cultural distinctives akin to the American custom of shooting fireworks on the Fourth of July. Human sacrifice and fireworks— both are simply products of discrete societal norms.

In the aftermath of the September 9th, 2001, attacks by terrorists on the World Trade Center buildings in New York, USA, when President George Bush referred to terrorist nations as an "axis of evil," cultural relativists were mortified and deeply chagrined. That any society would call another society "evil" is anathema to the relativist. The cultural relativist believes Westerners should not impose their ideas on residents of other nations, terrorist or not, including the idea that the suicide bombing of civilians is evil. Relativists proclaim that Islamic belief in the necessity of jihad is just as valid as any belief in Western civilization. Americans, they say, were as much to blame for the heinous attacks in New York, USA, on September 9th, 2001, as were the terrorists.

Cultural relativists are generally opposed to missionary work. When the Gospel penetrates hearts and changes lives, some cultural change always follows. For example, when Don and Carol Richardson evangelized the Sawi tribe of the Netherlands New Guinea in 1962, the Sawi changed; specifically, they gave up their long-held customs of cannibalism and immolating widows on their husband's funeral pyres. Cultural relativists may want to accuse the Richardsons of cultural imperialism (see below), but most people would agree that ending cannibalism or prohibiting the practice of burning women on their husbands' funeral pyres are honorable undertakings.

(For the complete story of the Sawis' conversion to Christianity as well as an exposition of cultural reform as it relates to missions, see Don Richardson's book "Peace Child.")

Cultural imperialism (also referred to as cultural colonialism) encompasses the cultural dimensions of imperialism. The word "imperialism" describes practices in which a country engages culture (language, tradition, ritual, politics, economics) to create and maintain unequal social and economic relationships among social groups. Cultural imperialism often uses wealth, media power, and violence to implement the system of cultural hegemony that legitimizes imperialism.

Although the Oxford English Dictionary has a 1921 reference to the "cultural imperialism of the Russians," John Tomlinson, in his book on the subject, writes that the term emerged in the 1960s [6] and has been a focus of research since at least the 1970s.

Regardless of the unconventionalities that might appertain to a *cultural relativism* or *cultural imperialism* hypothesis, discontinuing the abhorrent traditions of immolating women and consuming the flesh of human beings (cannibalism) can only be praiseworthy endeavors.

Christians value all people, regardless of culture, because they recognize that all people are created in the image of God (Genesis 1:27). They also recognize that diversity of culture is a beautiful thing, and differences in food, clothing, language, etc., should be preserved and appreciated. At the same time, Christians know that because of sin, not all beliefs and practices within a culture are godly or culturally beneficial. Truth is not subjective (John 17:17); truth is absolute, and there does exist a moral standard to which all people of every culture will eventually be held accountable (Revelation 20:11-12).

The goal of Christian missionaries is not to Westernize the world. Rather, it is to bring the good news of salvation in Christ to the world. The gospel message will kindle social reform to the extent that any society whose practices are out of step with God's moral standard will change. Idolatry, polygamy, and slavery, for example, will come to an end as the Word of God prevails (see Acts 19). In issues that may encompass amoral distinctive, missionaries seek to preserve and honor the culture of the people they serve.

The Illuminati Conspiracy

The Illuminati conspiracy is a theory about international machination whereby a society of global principals is either in control of the world or is seeking to take control of the world. As with most conspiracy theories, beliefs regarding the Illuminati conspiracy vary widely, so it is virtually impossible to volunteer a synopsis of the scheme. The Illuminati conspiracy has been popularized in books and movies so much so as to the attain a "cult fiction" status.

Doctors, politicians, actors, and musicians purportedly are members of the shadowy group known as the Illuminati. Although most of the rumors about an Illuminati conspiracy are fiction, the original group was real, even though its influence was hardly as extensive and enduring as modern conspiracists allege.

The Order of the Illuminati was a secret assemblage of individuals founded in 18th century Bavaria, Germany, in 1776 by Adam Weishaupt (1748 – 1830), a German philosopher, professor of civil law, and later canon law. Weishaupt believed "the monarchy and the church were repressing freedom of thought." [1] In a historical sense, the term "Illuminati" refers to the Bavarian Illuminati, a secret society that operated for only a decade, from 1776 to 1785.[2]

Weishaupt sought to develop another form of "illumination," a set of ideas and practices that could be applied to change radically, the way the European states were run." He based his society on the operational etiquette of the Freemasons, complete with a hierarchy of strange rituals, and named it the Order of Illuminati to reflect the enlightened ideals of its educated members.

Weishaupt wanted to educate Illuminati members about reason, philanthropy, and other secular values so that they could influence political decisions when they came to power.[3]

The Illuminati are alleged to be the primary motivational forces encouraging global governance, a one-world religious ethic, and centralized control of the world's economic systems. Organizations such as the United Nations, the International Monetary Fund, the World Bank, and the International Criminal Court are seen as tentacles of the Illuminati. According to the Illuminati conspiracy, the Illuminati are the driving force behind efforts to brainwash the gullible masses through thought control and manipulation of beliefs, through the press, the educational curriculum, and the political leadership of the nations.

The Illuminati supposedly have a private board of elite, interlocking delegates who control the world's major banks. They create inflations, recessions, and depressions and manipulate the world markets, supporting certain leaders and undermining others, in order to achieve their overall goals. The supposed goal behind the Illuminati conspiracy is to create and then manage crises that will eventually convince the masses that globalism, with its centralized economic control and one-world religious ethic, is the necessary solution to the world's woes. This structure, usually known as the "New World Order," will, of course, be ruled by the Illuminati.

US President Joe Biden fanned the flames of the conspiracy in 2022 when he referred to a coming "new world order" in the wake of the Ukraine crisis. The Independent reported that it was clear "he was referring to the

504

shifting sands of geopolitical relations." However, this didn't stop Twitter from lighting up with outlandish ideas.[4]

Does the Illuminati conspiracy have any basis from a Christian/biblical perspective? Perhaps. There are many end-times prophecies in the Bible that are interpreted by most to point to an end-times one-world government, a one-world monetary system, and a one-world religion. Many Bible prophecy interpreters see this New World Order as being controlled by the Antichrist, the end-times false messiah. If the Illuminati conspiracy and the New World Order have any validity and are indeed occurring, there is one fact that Christians must remember: God has sovereignly allowed all these developments, and they are not outside of His overall plan. God is in control, not the Illuminati. No plan or scheme the Illuminati develop could in any way prevent, or even hinder, God's sovereign plan for the world.

If there is indeed some truth to the Illuminati conspiracy, the Illuminati are nothing but pawns in the hands of Satan, tools to be manipulated in his conflict with God. The fate of the Illuminati will be the same as the fate of their lord, Satan/Lucifer, who will be cast into the lake of fire to be tormented day and night, forever and ever (Revelation 20:10). In John 16:33 Jesus declared, "In this world you will have trouble. But take heart! I have overcome the world." Christian believers should not fear the Illuminati conspiracy, having this promise in 1 John 4:4: "You, dear children, are from God and have overcome them, because the One who is in you is greater than the one who is in the world."

Transcendental Meditation

An Indian guru named Maharishi Mahesh Yogi (1918 – 2008), born Mahesh Prasad Varma, developed the Transcendental Meditation (TM) technique in the 1960's. Among his followers were the British musical group the Beatles, who actually visited India and learned the Hindu practice, and the American pop group, the Beach Boys. Maharishi Yogi became the leader of a worldwide organization characterized in multiple ways, including as a new religious movement and also as a non-religious one. [1]

Mahesh Yogi realized he could prosper by offering a "quick means to Enlightenment" called Transcendental Meditation (TM) to spiritually hungry Westerners who were willing to buy a simple form of Hinduism and Raj Yoga (see Chapter Thirteen). The Indian teacher brought his practice to the USA in the 1960's and named it the "Spiritual Regeneration Movement," with the intention of enmeshing it with Western culture. He founded the Maharishi University in Fairfield, Iowa, which is the TM movement's headquarters. Transcendental Meditation subsequently became a worldwide philosophy, even though proponents of the beliefs and practices of the movement today refer to them as "Maharishi Technology of the Unified Field" in an effort to obfuscate its intrinsic Hindu nature.

Statistics reveal the Transcendental Meditation organization had an estimated 900,000 participants worldwide in 1977, [2] a million by the 1980s, [3] and 5 million in more recent years [4] including some notable practitioners.

The Unified Field

The term "Unified Field" is essentially a pseudoscientific tag for the religious philosophy of Hindu monism. Monistic Hinduism teaches "all is One," i.e., the universe, nature, and all living things form a unified whole and share a cosmic Oneness. The inherent Hindu temperament of Transcendental Meditation philosophy is evident in Maharishi's own writings. He wrote in *Transcendental Meditation*:

> *To be is of an impersonal nature, so in order to be one's self it is only necessary to come out of the personal nature, come out of the field of doing and thinking, and be established in the field of Being. The impersonal God is that Being which dwells in the heart of everyone. Every individual in his true nature is the impersonal God.* [5]

Further, Maharishi said:

> *The transcendental state of Being lies beyond all seeing, hearing, touching, smelling, and tasting, beyond all thinking and beyond all feeling. This state of unmanifested, absolute pure consciousness of the Being is the ultimate stage of life. It is easily experienced through the system of Transcendental meditation.* [6]

The primary objective of Transcendental Meditation is for one to experience the "Unified Field," or the impersonal reality of Hindu monism by practicing "Maharishi Technology." In order to experience such "enlightenment" however, one first has to submit to a patently Hindu initiation ceremony.

The Personal Mantra

A central requirement for becoming a practitioner of "Maharishi Technology" is the performance of the initiation ceremony mentioned above, in which an initiate receives a personal "mantra" or scared word on which to meditate. The prospective adherent first pays an initiation fee.

The TM initiate, before he participates in the initiation ceremony, takes off his shoes and goes into a small, dimly lit room. In the middle of the room is an altar with burning candles and incense. A picture of one Guru Dev, the long departed master of Maharishi Mahesh Yogi, sits on the altar. The initiate stands before the altar, and the instructor recites the Puja, the fundamental feature of the initiation ritual. A Puja or *pooja* is a Hindu prayer ritual performed by Hindus in devotional worship of one or more deities, or to host and honor a guest, or to celebrate an event spiritually. [7] A Puja is an essential ritual of Hinduism, and generally takes the form of a Sanskrit hymn of worship, and the offering of a form of light, flowers, and water or food to the divine. The reciting of the Puja is a prelude to imparting the mantra. See Chapter Thirteen: *Hinduism, Yoga & Reincarnation* for the mention of a *Kali Puja*, a Pooja dedicated to the Hindu goddess Kali. The author was a bystander at the function described in Chapter Thirteen.

The English translation of the Puja or Sanskrit hymn contains the following petition.

To Lord Narayana, to lotus-born BRAHMA the Creator...to Shankaracharya the redeemer, hailed as KRISHNA, I bow down. To the glory of the Lord I bow down again and again, at whose door the whole galaxy of gods prays for perfection day and night.

White as camphor, kindness incarnate, the essence of creation garland with BRAHMAN, ever dwelling in the lotus of my heart, the creative impulse of cosmic life, to that, in the form of Guru Dev, I bow down…

Guru in the glory of BRAHMA, Guru in the glory of VISHNU, Guru in the glory of the great LORD SHIVA, Guru in the glory of the personified transcendental fullness of BRAHMAN, to Him, to Shri Guru Dev adorned with glory, I bow down.

Hundreds of thousands of Westerners likely have participated in the TM initiation ceremony and Puja in search of fulfillment and the "ultimate reality." Unbeknownst to most of these misinformed people, the initiation ceremony and Puja are traditions steeped in classical Hinduism. Additionally, the mantra or "sacred word" given to the TM initiate on which he is to meditate is a name of, or a name associated with one or more Hindu gods or goddesses.

The following extracts from writings by Maharishi Mahesh Yogi, and Kenneth W. Morgan (1908 – 2011), an American educator in the field of Asian and other religions, tell about the significance of mantras from a Hindu perspective.

The Vedas (Hindu Scriptures) are a very basic study of the fundamentals of life. That is the reason why, through Vedic hymns, it is possible for those expert in chanting those hymns to produce certain effects here or there. The universe is vast, so many worlds and all that. We do something here according to Vedic rites, particularly, specific

509

chanting to produce an effect in some other world, draw the attention of those higher beings or gods living there. The entire knowledge of the mantra or hymn of the Vedas is devoted to man's connection, to man's communication with the higher beings "in different strata of creation."[8]

A mantra is not a mere formula or a magic spell or a prayer; it is an embodiment in sound of a particular deity. It is the deity itself. And so, when a mantra is repeated, the worshiper makes an effort to identify himself with the worshiped, the power of the deity comes to his help. Human power is thus supplemented by the divine power. [9]

What Biblical Christianity Says

The Bible warns against accosting false gods. The consequences can be devastating morally and spiritually. As Ron Carlson, President of Christian Ministries International, and Ed Decker, founder and International Director of Saints Alive in Jesus, two experts on cults and comparative religion, advise:

Calling upon other gods, chanting their names, and emptying oneself of self will surely bring a person under the headship of whatever god he or she embraces. To embrace a pagan deity is a sure guarantee that you will soon be the surrendered servant of that deity. [10]

There is one true and living God – the God of the Holy Bible. All other gods are either non-existent or impostors who would only lead their followers to everlasting doom. What is not of the true God is of the devil!

510

People who think they can "unite with the cosmos" by emptying themselves of self are really inviting demonic forces into their lives.

People who profess to be Christians and feel they can safely embrace Eastern mystic cults and belief systems like Transcendental Meditation, Yoga, Hinduism and Buddhism, among others, foolishly endanger their souls. The following passages make it clear that the Bible, and the Bible alone imparts God's truth.

Do I mean then that a sacrifice offered to an idol is anything, or that an idol is anything? No, but the sacrifice of pagans are offered to demons, not to God, and I do not want you to be participants with demons. You cannot drink the cup of the Lord and the cup of demons too; you cannot have a part in both the Lord's table and the table of demons. Are we trying to arouse the Lord's jealousy? Are we stronger than he? (1 Corinthians 10:19-22, NIV)

The Spirit clearly says that in later times some will abandon the faith and follow deceiving spirits and things taught by demons. (1 Timothy 4:1, NIV)

Those who claim there is no God or that all people comprise one unified god, yet pay homage to demons in one way or another, need to realize and acknowledge an undeniable fact – demons are deceiving spirits who are aware of the truth about the one true God mentioned in the Bible, but who seek to conceal such truth for their own iniquitous purposes.

Satan and his demons are fallen angels who Almighty God cast out from His presence. Like the devil, demons constantly attempt to lead people away from the one true God, whose Holy Word reveals what eventually happens to such perpetrators of evil.

> *But I am not surprised! Even Satan disguises himself as an angel of light. So it is no wonder that his servants (demons) also disguise themselves as servants of righteousness. In the end they will get the punishment their wicked deeds deserve.* (2 Corinthians 11:14-15, NLT)

Freemasonry

Freemasonry is the largest international *fraternal order* in the world. A fraternal order is an organization with traits that allude to religious, chivalric, or pseudo-chivalric orders, guilds, or secret societies. Freemasonry is a secret society that practices and spreads its traditions through symbolism, rituals, and oaths taken on pain of death if broken.[1] Freemasonry is somewhat unique in that it is diverse in organizational structure, with many discrete branches. There is no single central authority, major text, or even definitions of generally acceptable Freemasonry precepts and practices.[2]

Freemasons allude to a number of ancient biblical connections in an endeavor to establish their religion as an authentic belief system. Masonic legends include the following fantastic claims:

1. The first Masonic aprons (utilized in initiation rites) were the fig leaves Adam and Eve used to cover themselves in the Garden of Eden.[3]

512

2. Freemasonry dates back to the time of the biblical King Solomon, who employed stonemasons to construct Solomon's Temple (the First Temple, the Holy Temple) in ancient Jerusalem. [4]

3. Freemasonry derives in one way or another from biblical accounts of the Tower of Babel (Genesis 11:1-9), Noah, the pre-Flood patriarch (Genesis, Chapters 5-9), and Seth, third son of Adam and Eve (Genesis 4:25). [5]

The first official Masonic Lodge dates back to the one founded in London, England in 1717 by James Anderson, George Payne and Theopholis Desaguliers. Soon after, other lodges surfaced in England and Europe. The first Masonic Lodge in the USA appeared in Boston in 1733. Freemasonry grew leaps and bounds during the 1800's with several thousand lodges emerging in the USA. However, the order experienced a major backlash when a former Freemason named William Morgan (1774 - 1826) disappeared in 1826 after he threatened to expose Masonic secrets.

Many people believed Masons from western New York kidnapped and killed Morgan, a resident of Batavia, New York, even though authorities found no proof of any crime. The incident, however, ignited a powerful movement against the Freemasons and led to a sharp decline in membership. [6] Freemason membership in the USA stood at around 1 million in 2017. It's all time high to date was 4 million in 1959. [7] Famous Freemason Americans were George Washington, John Wayne, Henry Ford and General Douglas MacArthur. [8]

Freemason Precepts & Practices

Freemasonry's central tenets advocate the civic values of brotherliness, charity and mutual aid, [9] and the conviction that all religions acknowledge the same God. [10] The society enmeshes distinctive myths and rituals with elements from other religions, including Christianity, Islam, Judaism and Egyptian belief systems. [11] Joseph Smith, the founder of the Mormon Church, was a Freemason. Mormon and Masonic rituals are very similar. [12]

The Freemasonry society kindles the interest of prospective members by touting itself as a men's fellowship that helps to "make good men better" and that exhibits "no contradictions with Christianity." Freemasonry's fundamental doctrines, however, proceed from ancient Gnostic, esoteric and pagan sources.

At lower or early levels of the worldview, Freemasonry observes the tenets of Deism or Unitarianism, both of which teach (a) God is the creator and worthy of worship, (b) virtue and piety are good, (c) humankind should repent from sin and, (d) in the afterlife there will be rewards and punishments. [13] Freemasonry nevertheless unequivocally rejects the idea that God reveals himself through the history of Israel, the Holy Bible and the Messiah Jesus Christ. Biblical Christians, on the other hand, categorically deny Freemasonry is compatible with the Christian faith. [14]

At higher or later stages in Freemasonry, the worldview's precepts and practices resemble those pertaining to occultism and New Age religions. As an adherent progresses in Masonic practice, he or she becomes increasingly involved in the occult, spiritism, deception and blasphemy against God. [15] Freemasonry, with the penchant by its members to mix and match beliefs that complement their religious idiosyncrasies, is not unlike the New Age movement, the followers of which often choose to construct their own paths to truth and spirituality.

Regrettably, many Christians see Freemasonry simply as an interesting and innocuous vocation that allows well-meaning professionals, businessmen and businesswomen to engage in various humanitarian and other projects to assist the disadvantaged members of society. They fail to recognize the order for what it really is i.e., a religion or philosophy that essentially is in conflict with fundamental Christian truths.

Freemasonry vs. Christianity – Major Contradictions

Authority of the Bible - Freemasons do not consider the Bible the unique Word of God. "The Bible is used among Freemasons as a symbol of the will of God, however it may be expressed. Therefore, whatever…expresses that will may be used as a substitute for the Bible in a Masonic Lodge i.e., (the Qur'an or the Vedas)." [16] Christian doctrine declares in no uncertain manner the Bible is the believer's final, eternal and trustworthy authority for faith and living according to God's will (Psalm 119:105; Isaiah 48; 2 Timothy 3:15, 16; Hebrews 4:12; 2 Peter 1:16-21).

The Identity of God – Freemasonry likens the God of the Bible to other gods, and names him "Jabulon." Other names used by Freemasons for God are "Jah," the Syriac name; "Bel" (Baal), the Chaldean name, and "On," the

Egyptian name.[17] Christian scholarship (see Judges 3:7; 2 Kings17:9-18; Jeremiah 19: 4,5,15) warns that identification of the God of the Bible with pagan deities, including the Freemason god, is blasphemy and those who engage in such a practice falls under divine condemnation.

The Importance of Jesus Christ – Freemasons reject the claim by Christians that Jesus Christ is God the Son and/or the Savior of the world. "Jesus was just a man…one of the great men of the past, but not divine and certainly not the only means of redemption of lost humankind." [18] The Bible, in unconstrained disputation, declares Jesus Christ is uniquely God the Son and Savior of humankind (John 1:1,14; Philippians 2:9-11; Colossians 1:15-17, 2:9).

The Name of Christ – Although Freemasons use the Bible, they omit Jesus' name from Scripture references. Freemasonry doctrine forbids its adherents to mention Jesus' name in Masonic rituals and prayers.[19] The Biblical texts of John 14:13,14; Acts of the Apostles 4:12; and 2 Thessalonians 1:12 underscore in no uncertain manner, the importance of Jesus' name to the Christian.

Regarding Scriptural Truth – Freemasons contend their religion is the world's one true faith and it is capable of lifting spiritual darkness. "Masonry is the universal, eternal, immutable religion, such as God planted in the heart of universal humanity…all (religions) that ever existed have had a basis of truth; and all have overlaid that truth with errors." [20] Christianity affirms the Bible is God's inerrant Word and is the source of real truth. All who deny the authenticity of the Holy Scriptures face divine judgement (John 1:14; 14:6; 18:37; Galatians 1:6-9; 1 John 2:22).

Human Beings Divine? – According to Masonic doctrine, humans are basically good, even divine, and human nature is perfectible. "The perfection is already within. All that is required is to remove the roughness...divesting our hearts and consciences of all vices...to show forth the perfect man and Mason within."[21] The Bible says it is not possible for anyone to be perfect in this life (Titus 2:11-14; 1 John 1:5-10; 3:1-3). Human beings are born into sin and they need salvation from spiritual death (Mark 7:20-23; Galatians 2:15,16; Ephesians 2:1-13). People may obtain redemption from sin only through acceptance of Jesus Christ as Lord and Savior. Rejection of Christ's entreaty is tantamount to courting permanent alienation from God and an eternity in hell.

Hare Krishna

Hare Krishna - A Brief Outline

The Hare Krishna movement, also called Gaudiya Vaishnavism or Chaitanya Vaishnavism, falls under the jurisdiction of the International Society for Krishna Consciousness (ISKCON). Abhay Charan (1896 – 1977), a Hindu from Calcutta, India founded the organization in the United States.

Charan, whose followers gave him the title of Swami Prabhupada (meaning "at whose feet masters sit), established ISKCON centers in numerous major U.S. cities and, by the time of his death at age 82, had published 70 volumes of translation and commentary on the Hindu scriptures, including the *Bhagavad Gita (As It Is)*. Additionally, he organized ISKCON into a global network of *ashrams* (religious communities), schools, temples, and farms. [1]

The Hare Krishna movement grew quickly after its formation in 1965. At the time, many people were questioning Western values and Eastern thought was becoming fashionable. Hare Krishna is a mystical sect of Hinduism and usually classified as a monotheistic form of Hinduism, since Hare Krishnas believe all deities are simply various manifestations of the god Vishnu. Krishna is supposedly the eighth incarnation (avatar) of Vishnu, one of the three deities of Hinduism. The three major deities of the Hindu pantheon of India are Vishnu, Shiva and Brahma.[2] The "monotheism" of Hare Krishna is a little muddled, however, as Sri Krishna has an "eternal consort" named Srimati Radharani; together, Krishna and Radharani comprise the "Divine Couple."

The Hare Krishna movement dates back to the fifteenth century (1486), when its founder, Chaitanya Mahaprabhu, began teaching that Krishna was the supreme Lord above every other god. Mahaprabhu advocated a devotional method of faith in which adherents of Gaudiya Vaishnavism entered into a relationship with Krishna and expressed their adoration for Krishna through dancing and chanting. Mahaprabhu's public displays of adoration gained a large following, in part, due to their sharp contrast with the dispassionate and ascetic expressions common to Hinduism. The sect, however, distinctive as it is in its unique adherence to Krishna, is still quite Hindu, since even Krishna is but a manifestation or *avatar* of Vishnu—one of the classic deities of Hinduism. Moreover, Hare Krishnas use the *Bhagavad Gita*, a principal Hindu Scripture, and abide by the doctrines of reincarnation and karma as well.

ISKCON is an affluent organization today, having gained its wealth largely through soliciting funds and distributing its literature. During the 1960s and 1970s, Hare Krishnas were so prevalent in public places such as airports, authorities enacted laws to prevent them from accosting people with their often aggressive and intimidating demands for money.

Swami Prabhupada, instead of selecting a particular disciple to assume leadership of the Hare Krishna movement after him, assigned control to 11 senior devotees. ISKCON members today number about 1 million worshipers, 2,500 monks and 250,000 lay priests [3] George Harrison (1943 – 2001), a member of the renowned British pop group the Beatles, embraced ISKCON or the Krishna consciousness movement. Harrison dedicated his hit song, "My Sweet Lord" to the Hindu deity. [4]

Teachings And Goals Of Hare Krishnas

The ultimate goal of Hare Krishnas is a transcendental, loving relationship with Lord Krishna. "Hare" refers to "the pleasure potency of Krishna." Due to their mystical devotion expressed in chanting and dancing, the Hare Krishnas superficially resemble Sufi Muslims ("Whirling Dervishes") and adherents of certain mystical expressions of Christianity that emphasize ecstatic experiences and mystical transcendence.

The Hare Krishna organization places heavy demands on its followers. Becoming a member involves choosing a guru and becoming his disciple.

The guru is critical to attaining enlightenment: "Without [the guru] the cultivation of Krishna consciousness is impossible." On the devotee's side, "initiation means that he or she accepts the guru as his spiritual master and agrees to worship him as God." [5]

The Hare Krishna devotee's whole life revolves around Krishna-centered practice and devotion. ISKCON members generally retreat to communes where everything centers on Krishna and Indian/Hindu culture. There are recorded instances whereby ISKCON faced criminal charges alleging illegal and immoral practices, including widespread child abuse, taking place within communes and the movement proper. Also, many ex-members harshly criticize the organization from time to time.

Hare Krishna, like so many cults and non-Christian religions, requires a series of works for salvation. Devotion and relationship are salient components of the belief system, but these are built up from works - from bhakti-yoga to meditation before an altar to soliciting funds. Chanting is a major part of Hare Krishna activities. Devotees generally chant 100,000 holy names every day. They use a mala or a rosary of 108 beads to aid them when they chant. Krishna disciples may not eat meat, nor dine in restaurants, due to the belief that food retains the consciousness of the cook, i.e., ingesting food prepared by an angry chef will make the eater angry. ISKCON philosophy pushes its members to chant more, dance more, and work harder lest they become unable to relieve themselves of residual karmic debt and fail to achieve Krishna consciousness.

Self-denial and sacrifice are also crucial for salvation, according to Hare Krishna ideology. Salvation is thoroughly entwined with the Hindu concept of karma, or retributive justice. The teaching requires belief in reincarnation and/or the transmigration of the soul. One's works, measured and judged after death, determine what he or she becomes in the next life. If one's deeds are good, he or she continues to be reincarnated into higher life forms; if his or her deeds are bad, he or she will assume a lower life form. It is only when an individual's good deeds counterbalance his or her bad deeds can he or she cease the cycles of rebirth and realize oneness with Krishna.

Iskcon's Main Differences With Christianity

ISKCON's Cultic Worldview about Truth - Swami Prabhupada (founder of Hare Krishna) said, "No person or religion can claim absolute truth, since absolute (truth) is beyond man's reasoning powers." [6] Swami Prabhupada's reflection is puzzling as he delegitimizes his own religion, of which he was the founder. The statement is even more perplexing since Prabhupada and his followers felt he possessed the powers and prerogatives of a god, yet he refers to "man's reasoning powers" and not divine reasoning.

The Holy Bible imparts definitive teachings that contradict Swami Prabhupada's bewildering reflection, and says,

The Word became flesh and made his dwelling among us. We have seen his glory, the glory of the one and only Son, who came from the Father, full of grace and truth. (John 1:14, NIV)

Biblical Scriptures also record Christ's profound assertion:

I am the way and the truth and the life. No one comes to the Father except through me. (John 14:6, NIV.) See also John 18:37 and Romans 3:4.

The Subject of Salvation – ISKCON teaches salvation is attainable through a personal relationship with the god Krishna and complete surrender in devotion to him. The Bible teaches salvation can be obtained only through acceptance of Christ's sacrifice on the cross as atonement for humankind's sins, and through God's grace.

But because of his great love for us, God, who is rich in mercy, made us alive with Christ even when we were dead in transgressions—it is by grace you have been saved. And God raised us up with Christ and seated us with him in the heavenly realms in Christ Jesus, in order that in the coming ages he might show the incomparable riches of his grace, expressed in his kindness to us in Christ Jesus. For it is by grace you have been saved, through faith—and this is not from yourselves, it is the gift of God— not by works, so that no one can boast. (Ephesians 2:4-9, NIV) See also Romans 3;24 and Titus 2:11; 3:7.

About Jesus Christ – ISKCON, while it claims to "revere" Jesus Christ, nevertheless considers him to be the son of Krishna and inferior to the Hindu deity, who is "the original Personality of the Godhead himself." [7] Christianity professes a diametrically different and higher view of Jesus.

In the beginning was the Word, and the Word was with God, and the Word was God. He was with God in the beginning. Through him all things were made; without him nothing was made that has been made. In him was life, and that life was the light of all mankind. The light shines in the darkness, and the darkness has not overcome it. (John 1:1-5, NIV) See also John 14:6; Acts 4:12; Colossians 1:15-20.

Prabhupada's Claim of Godhood – Hare Krishna ideology confers the powers and entitlements of a god on Swami Prabhupada. He is supposedly capable of taking the "bad karma" of others upon himself, thus becoming a mediator between the god (Krishna) and the Krishna disciple. Prabhupada, in doing so, claims a Christ-like personality or identity and likens himself to one who is able to absorb the sins of another and make the latter whole. The Holy Bible, on the contrary, clearly teaches Jesus Christ is God and is the only mediator between God and humankind (1 Timothy 2:5).

In Conclusion

Hare Krishna beliefs are typically Hindu and are incompatible with biblical Christianity. ISKCON's view of God is basically pantheistic, meaning Hare Krishnas believe God is all and in all. God is everything, and everything is God to them. The Christian believes God is transcendent, i.e., He is above all that he created. One of the tenets of ISKCON philosophy is that humans can actually achieve relational unity with God. The goal of Hare Krishnas is to reach "Krishna consciousness," a kind of enlightenment. ISKCON, with its Hindu roots, subscribes to a pantheistic view of God and, therefore, teaches man is ultimately identical to God. This is an old lie dating back to the Garden of Eden when Satan told the woman God had created:

For God knows that when you eat from it your eyes will be opened, and you will be like God, knowing good and evil. (Genesis 3:5, NIV)

Krishna, the ISKCON deity, is utterly dissimilar to the compassionate and merciful God of the Bible who "so loved the world that He gave His only begotten Son, that whoever believes in Him should not perish, but have eternal life." (John 3:16, NIV). The Bible clearly says salvation comes by grace through faith in the shed blood of Jesus Christ (Ephesians 2:8-9 (NIV). Further, God's Holy Word declares, "God made him who had no sin (Jesus) to be sin for us, so that in him we might become the righteousness of God." (2 Corinthians 5:21, NIV).

No amount of good deeds can ever earn salvation for anyone. Hare Krishnas, like all members of humanity, have only one hope for eternal life i.e., Jesus Christ, crucified, resurrected, and exalted forever. As the Bible proclaims, all paths besides the one revealed by the Christian Gospel lead to eternal damnation.

Salvation is found in no one else, for there is no other name (Jesus) under heaven given to mankind by which we must be saved. (Acts 4:12, NIV).

Secular Humanism

A Brief Outline

Secular Humanism developed as an identifiable worldview in the first half of the twentieth century. However, the philosophy has its roots in the fourteenth to sixteenth centuries during the Renaissance, and in the seventeenth and eighteenth centuries during the period generally referred to as the Great Enlightenment. The Secular Humanist philosophy endorses the ability and responsibility of human beings to lead personal lives of ethical fulfillment and aspire to contribute to the greater good of humanity, without the acknowledgement of theism (religion) or belief in the supernatural.

Modern science progressed in no small measure as a result of the work of scholars like Galileo Galilei (1564 - 1642) the Italian astronomer, physicist and engineer, sometimes described as a polymath,[1] and Sir Isaac Newton* (1642 – 1726/27), an English mathematician, physicist, astronomer, theologian and author, and widely recognized as one of the most influential scientists of all time. Subsequent to the findings of Galileo and Newton, people in general began to jettison medieval perspectives of the world and nature as they became "enlightened" - hence the birth of the age of modernism.

*Isaac Newton, in addition to his enormous contribution to science and the title "the greatest scientific genius the world has known," was a devout Christian. Many scholars feel Newton's notable scientific discoveries were never meant to dissuade people from pursuing religious truth. According to Charles E. Hummel of *Christianity Today - Christian History*, "For Newton, the world of science was by no means the whole of life. He spent more time on theology than on science; indeed, he wrote about 1.3 million words on biblical subjects. Newton's understanding of God came primarily from the Bible, which he studied for days and weeks at a time. He took special interest in miracles and prophecy, calculating dates of Old Testament books and analyzing their texts to discover their authorship."[2]

The age of Enlightenment brought in its wake, an unprecedented emphasis on humankind as opposed to attention to God. Scientific advances in the eighteenth century impelled a mindset that promoted the power of human reasoning as inexhaustibly self-sufficient. The concept of God and his involvement in the affairs of people became progressively irrelevant to many people.

19th & 20th Century Growth Of Secular Humanism

Disbelief in a supernatural God who created the universe and all life gained increased momentum in the nineteenth and twentieth centuries, due in great part to four major secular campaigns that sought to relegate biblical Christianity to a status of philosophical and logical inconsequence.

Firstly, there was the so-called "higher criticism of the Bible" paradigm, through which anti-Christian scholars sought to analyze biblical texts from a purely nonspiritual standpoint. Proponents of the misguided endeavor capriciously excluded every supernatural attribute of the Scriptures in an attempt to delegitimize the Word of God. Although the undertaking never unearthed anything that detracted from the authenticity of the Christian Gospel, many people chose to relegate the Bible to the status of just another olden mythological book.

The Christian Apologetics Research Ministry (CARM) volunteered the following observation about "higher criticism of the Bible."

Higher criticism, again also known as the historical-critical method, treats the ancient texts of the Bible from an entirely secular perspective. The presupposition of secular necessity to the exclusion of supernatural possibility regarding the origin of the documents means that any texts that have a prophetic nature to them and also seem to find fulfillment in the events must have been written after the events occurred. [3]

Secondly, people eager to discredit biblical Christianity looked to Karl Marx (1818 –1883), the German philosopher, historian, sociologist, political theorist, and socialist revolutionary, and his "atheistic Communism" concept. Many people today still consider Marxian ideology an important socio-political option, and the dogma remains a threat to the spread of the Christian Gospel. As Fr. John A. Hardon S.J. of the Real Presence Eucharistic Education and Adoration Association reflects:

In the light of this contrast between science and religion, it is nothing less than a divine intervention that Russian political Communism died in 1993. But Communism as organized Marxism has not only not died. It is alive in many countries. Communist China is only a tragic example. Our own beloved country has been deeply penetrated by Marxian ideology.

That is why I would like to conclude this conference by paraphrasing what Pope Pius XI told us in his classic encyclical "On Atheistic Communism." He was speaking to professed Christians. Specifically he was addressing "those of our children who are more or less tainted with the Communist plague. We earnestly exhort them to hear the voice of their loving Father. We pray the Lord to enlighten them that they may abandon the slippery path which will precipitate one and all to ruin and catastrophe. We pray that they may recognize that Jesus

Christ our Lord is their only Savior, "for there is no other name in heaven given to man whereby we must be saved." [4]

Thirdly, the British naturalist Charles Darwin (1809 – 1882) and his theory of naturalistic evolution – the supposition that humankind progressively evolved from ape-like creatures, who had evolved from lower life forms that originally proceeded from inanimate matter - took the world by storm. Countless millions of people today accept evolutionism unreservedly as fact even though it is woefully lacking in scientific corroboration.

Darwin's theory of natural selection, also referred to as "survival of the fittest," implied life was the result of happenstance events over multiple billions of years. God did not design and create life. God did not even exist. He was just an unnecessary hypothesis. Evolutionism is in reality a fantastic theory riddled with inconsistencies that place it at odds with true scientific and practice. (See Chapter Nineteen – *Christianity Compared with New Religions, Philosophies & Cults: Evolutionism*).

Fourthly, Sigmund Freud (1856 - 1939), the Austrian neurologist and the founder of psychoanalysis, a clinical method for treating psychopathology through dialogue between a patient and a psychoanalyst, significantly influenced the mindset of many so-called freethinkers and other people averse to the idea of creationism. Even though psychoanalytic theory is no longer widely used, its impact on the field of psychology is undeniable. The concept continues to serve as a foundation on which to build other psychological theories.

Psychoanalytic theory treats God as an illusion, an obviously unbiblical perspective. The superego, or the conscience, is where our old, sinful nature and our new, godly nature engage in battle. Freud thought the superego emerged via social influence. Christians believe morality comes from God. Freedom does not come through self-awareness, but through Christ (John 8:32). Also, Freud's concept of psychological health is rather egocentric and minimizes the importance of loving others. Loving others is, of course, basic to the spiritual health of a Christian (John 13:34). To be truly healthy, one needs Jesus to heal past wounds and make functional changes. The power of the Holy Spirit residing within the individual is what brings health, not projection onto a therapist.

The premise that God does not exist, or more particularly, the belief he never existed and never created the universe and life, became the pillaring motivation behind the emergence of the secular humanism worldview. The American Humanist Association, a non-profit organization in the United States that advances secular humanism, published the *Humanist Manifesto I* in 1933. The opinions expressed in the *Humanist Manifesto I* became the battle cry of secular humanists around the world. Secular humanists published the *Humanist Manifesto II* in 1973 in an attempt to counter criticism of humankind's unprecedented hatred and savagery during World War II (1939 – 1945). Years before, following World War I, many people had also criticized secular humanist philosophy for its insistence that humans are basically good and did not need God in order to rid the world of evil.

Secular Humanism today represents a lingering objection to biblical Christianity and any other belief system expressing belief in a supernatural creator of any kind. Attempts to estimate the number of secular humanists in the world today, like undertakings to number adherents of the New Age Movement and other nebulous worldviews, would be futile because of the difficulties in concretely identifying or demarcating who such people might be - this notwithstanding belligerent persistence by some who insist the belief system is growing rapidly. The American Humanist Association (AHA), a self-designated, non-profit organization, has over 575,000 followers on Facebook and over 42,000 followers on Twitter. [7] The U.S. Internal Revenue Service recognizes the AHA as a nonprofit, tax-exempt, 501(c) (3), publicly supported educational organization. Observers dispute AHA membership numbers, with some claiming it is "definitely fewer than 50,000."[5]

Humanist Manifesto I (American Humanist Association

The *Humanist Manifesto I*, issued in 1933 by the American Humanist Association, endorsed the following philosophical viewpoints.

1. The universe has always existed – it was never created by a "God."[6]

2. In fact, there is no real proof for God - men and women must live as if he does not exist – they must indeed "save themselves."[6]

3. Humankind's chief goal is development of the human personality in this life, which is all there is.[6]

4. There is no objective way to determine morality or what is valuable and useful. The only morality is that which comes out of human experience and experiment. In short, there are no moral absolutes.[6]

Humanist Manifesto II (American Humanist Association)

The *Humanist Manifesto II*, issued in 1973, advocated the following doctrines.[7]

1. Reaffirmed the secular humanist point of view that all moral and ethical truth is relative.[7]

2. Ethics are "autonomous and situational."[7]

3. Reason and intelligence are the most "effective instruments that humankind possesses."[7]

4. Critical intelligence, "infused by a sense of human caring," is the best method humanity has for resolving its problems.[7]

Secular Humanism & Christianity - Major Dissimilarities

The Existence of God – Secular humanists' naturalistic/materialistic worldview is unyieldingly atheistic. It states there is no God. Christians believe in God, the compassionate and supreme creator of the universe and life, to whom all humankind owes thanks and praise (Genesis 1:1; Isaiah 40:28; Hebrews 11:3).

The Source of Truth – Secular humanists claim people discover truth by their own reasoning and logical thinking. Christians believe all truth is of God and all of humankind's discoveries are only part of what God created (Psalm 19:1; Acts 17:24 – 28; Romans 1:20).

Biblical Truth vs. Relativeness – Secular humanists claim where human experience or experiment cannot establish discernible standards in certain areas, all truth is relative. They identify such precincts as philosophy, religion, ethics and morals. In other words, truth is a matter of opinion, which can differ from individual to individual. Christians affirm morals and ethics proceed from God's written Word (Exodus 21:17) and from his living Word, Jesus Christ (John 1:1-14).

Salvation – Secular humanists postulate that while human beings make mistakes, they are not fallen sinners and are able to "save themselves" by taking responsibility for their errors. Christians contend humans are fallen because of sin (Genesis 3, Romans 3:23) and their only hope for salvation unto eternal life is in Jesus Christ (Romans 8:22-27; 1 Peter 1:3-7).

In Conclusion

The secular humanism philosophy is bereft of moral absolutes by which its adherents might be guided. Secular humanists believe moral guidelines are meaningless and unnecessary, since humanists doubt the existence of God and feel accountable to no one for their actions and/or omissions. Such an attitude of non-accountability translates into a *laissez-*

faire approach towards defining ethical behavior. Concepts of right and wrong are nebulous considerations, while the ascendancy of individual rights, regardless of how adherents conduct themselves, is of paramount importance.

Humanist Manifesto II declares people's goodness will enable them to use technology for the good of all by identifying and avoiding harmful and destructive changes.[8] However, humanists, because they do not believe in the existence of God and do not recognize moralistic parameters, find themselves hard-pressed to ascertain who is competent or suitable enough to decide what is really good for humankind. Also, the question arises as to who will enforce the rulings or judgments determined to be beneficial to people. [12]

The secular humanist inclination to deny the importance of absolute moral values is probably its single most ruinous contention. Such a position places humanists in a sea of illogicality and uncertainty. Someone eventually has to lay down the rules. Christians believe God is at the forefront of initiating lifestyles that respect time-honored values of decency, love and compassion. He articulates in the Bible, unadulterated moral values by which his children should live. Secular humanists think humans are capable enough to determine what is moral and good without God's counsel, and subsequently people can live peaceful, happy and productive lives. They deceive themselves, as violence, hatred and evil run rampant everywhere and secular humanism can provide no solution to these quandaries.

A Miscellany Of Additional Non-Christian/Anti-Christian Religions & Philosophies

There are other minor non-Christian religious ideologies, which the author did not address in the preceding sub sections of this chapter, but does so here, albeit in encapsulated form. The author uses the word "minor" in a context of numerical significance as it relates to the number of adherents of each of these belief systems, as well as the universality of each of them. The intention is not to cast aspersion on the worldviews, but to evaluate them from a biblical standpoint in determining whether their followers satisfy the requirements for obtaining redemption from their sins through Jesus Christ and securing a place in God's kingdom for eternity.

The International Churches Of Christ (Formerly The Boston Church Of Christ)

The International Churches of Christ (ICOC) is a body of religiously conservative and racially integrated Christian congregations. The ICOC believes the whole Bible is the inspired Word of God and each adherent gains salvation at the time of baptism by the grace of God, and through faith in Jesus Christ. The ICOC enjoys a presence across some 155 nations. ICOC churches are non-denominational. The organization's structure seeks to avoid two extremes: "overly centralized authority" on the one side and "disconnected autonomy" on the other side. The ICOC boasts a current member count of 112,000 in 690 congregations. [1]

534

The International Churches of Christ places very strong emphasis on discipleship. However, "discipleship" in the ICOC often looks very different from what most other churches practice. Many who left the ICOC reported they experienced high-pressure, intrusive, and borderline abusive treatment, as well as spiritually manipulative therapy at the hands of the disciples under whose jurisdiction they fell. The methodology was similar to that utilized by church leaders who practice heavy shepherding.

Another distinctive ICOC feature is the focus of its evangelism almost exclusively on college students. This suits the ICOC's preferred method of "love-bombing" - suddenly and purposefully surrounding an individual with high amounts of friendly contact, various forms of aid, and an overall sense of being immersed in a community - something first-year college students especially crave. While none of these things, i.e., community, service, and friendliness are not unbiblical, the International Churches of Christ employs these virtues as a façade and manipulative tool to increase membership.

Theologically, the International Church of Christ holds to the basic tenets of Protestant evangelicalism, but with two very important exceptions. First, the group is exclusivist, claiming the church is meant to be united in one association, divided only by geography, and any church that remains outside of this unified system, i.e., not under the ICOC's leadership, is not a part of the "true church." Such claims of exclusivity are indicative of untruth and misrepresentation. Any church or denomination that claims to be the "one true church" while it dismisses all others as counterfeit or insincere is itself an agency of falsehood.

The International Churches of Christ also departs from biblical scholarship in its teaching of baptismal regeneration i.e., the belief that baptism is imperative for salvation. The ICOC believes anyone who is not baptized is not saved and must be "evangelized" and brought into the church as an ICOC disciple. Further, the ICOC claims baptism under the auspices of the ICOC is the only form of baptism that can help ensure one's salvation. No other baptism will do. Such doctrine contradicts the biblical teaching that salvation is by grace through faith, apart from works, the latter that includes the practice of baptism (Ephesians 2:8-9; John 1:12; 3:16).

Biblical Christianity says the method and timing of baptism is open to the believer (Acts 8:38; 9:18). Further, 1 Peter 3:21 says baptism with water is the vivid symbol of the changed life of a Christian who has peace with God. [2]

The Bible (Matthew 16:24 and John 8:31) describes a disciple as someone who follows Jesus' teachings, not someone who submits to the mandates of a more "mature" Christian. Jesus taught His disciples to serve one another instead of "lording it over each other as the rulers of the Gentiles do." (Matthew 20:25-28).

Another significant difference between ICOC philosophy and biblical Christianity revolves around the ICOC's attempts to discourage private interpretation of the Scriptures, attack other churches' traditions or creeds, and limit critical thinking. The Bible, on the contrary, encourages believers to "search the Scriptures for yourself." (Deuteronomy 17:19; John 5:39; Acts 17:11; Romans 15:4).

ICOC philosophy belittles common evangelical phrases it considers biblically thin, such as the appeal to "accept Jesus into your heart." ICOC teachers attack any view of baptism that deviates in any way from the organization's doctrine. Also, devotees must agree to "share" their sins with their assigned spiritual leaders.

The Bible encourages the Christian to confess his or her sins to God, who alone can cleanse and forgive him or her. (1 John 1:5-10) As for "sharing sins," such a practice easily leads to spiritual abuse, especially when church leaders use confidential information for disciplinary purposes in "breaking sessions;" something many ex-members of the ICOC claim they experienced. [3]

Yet another unconventional ICOC teaching says only "disciples" of Christ, who in turn make disciples of other people, will be saved and granted eternal life. Essentially, this directive perverts the Scriptural declaration that says, "For by grace are ye saved through faith; and that not of yourselves: it is the gift of God: Not of works, lest any man should boast." (Ephesians 2:8-9, KJV).

The International Churches of Christ (ICOC) has a strict and invasive power structure that uses manipulation and indoctrination to control its membership. Many people have been hurt by this group. People who allow themselves to fall prey to ICOC's unbiblical teachings about discipleship, baptism, confession and sharing of sins, denominational exclusivity and salvation, expose themselves to emotional, psychological, and spiritual impairment and jeopardize their very souls.

Postmodernism

The Postmodern movement emerged during the twentieth century as professionals from diverse spheres of society i.e., philosophers, theologians, literary critics, historians and others sought to counter the failures of modernism, i.e., secular humanism. Secular humanists (see *Secular Humanism* earlier in this chapter) had envisaged a world of ideal social and political conditions where scientific advancements and humanistic predilections bereft of any kind of divine involvement would guide humankind towards a utopian existence. Instead, the social and pseudo-political environments that resulted from modernistic precepts and practices were oppressive and burdensome and were a far cry from people's expectations. Consequently, some Christian scholars felt the Church was being caught up in a pervasive cultural shift, and society in general was "fast becoming a postmodern culture." [1]

The basic principles of postmodernism may be summarized as follows:

1. No one thinks independently without bias. An individual's culture molds him or her to think in a certain way. [2]

2. One cannot judge, or deem wrong the thoughts, ideas or actions of someone from another culture because his or her idea of reality is different. [2]

3. Each person's reality is in his or her own mind. One can construct his or her own reality. Whatever is real to someone is his or her reality. [2]

538

4. No one can "prove" anything, whether one uses science, history or any other set of facts. [2]

Postmodernism actually broadens the secular humanist assertion that all moral and ethical truth are relative and takes the preposterous stand there is no absolute truth anywhere. Postmodernists contend truth is always changing, whether it is spiritual, moral or even scientific.[3] The postmodernist worldview imparts the notion that all truth is "manufactured," and is a product of the culture in which people live and of the language they use. People are all just "producers of their culture; cogs in a social machine." [4]

A most worrisome and dangerous feature of the postmodern psyche is its absolute acquiescence to the concept of tolerance. It is not tolerance in the conventional sense of the term, whereby the attitude does not necessarily translate into acceptance, and whereby one can be tolerant, yet still be free to voice his or her disapproval of certain actions and/or omissions and encourage change. The postmodernist view of tolerance, a trait of undergirding importance to the worldview's philosophy, and spread today by philosophers, educators and other societal leaders, assigns equal respect to all values and beliefs and casts aspersion on any attempt by anyone to establish a "hierarchy of truth." [5]

In today's increasingly humanistic and profane environment, children in public schools and young people today believe "…what every individual believes or says is equally right, equally valid. So not only does everyone have an equal right to his beliefs, but all beliefs are equal. All values are equal. All lifestyles are equal. All truth claims are equal." [6]

The debased, postmodernist definition of the term "tolerance" explains the perverse and irreverent behavior of many of today's younger and also older people. Consider the following scenarios:

- A daughter, for instance, comes home from college with her boyfriend and expects no protest from her parents when she suggests they sleep together in her bedroom.

- The father or mother who considers homosexuality or lesbianism wrong and immoral is deemed bigoted or self-righteous by his or her son or daughter.

- The young woman who wishes to join a local coven of witches cannot understand why her parents would discourage her from doing so.

Uninhibited, unbridled tolerance encourages people to expect no one to condemn their actions and/or omissions, regardless of the nature and/or extent of their pursuits.

Postmodernist norms question and often contradict mainstream Christian and biblical standards and ethics. Postmodernism sanctions a kind of tolerance that accommodates everything everyone does, except the undertaking by people to conform to the dictates of objective moral absolutes. [7]

The Christian or moralist who, in conformity with his or her religious or ethical principles, would separate the sinner from the sin is looked upon by the Postmodernist with derision. Postmodernism teaches that an individual should love and agree with the sinner *and the sin* – no questions asked, or he or she must be a bigot, a racist or a hatemonger.

Following are the major differences between *Postmodernism* and biblical Christianity.

1. Postmodernists, even if, and when they admit to the existence of God, refer to the "god within" rather than a supreme sovereign creator. [8] Christians believe God exists outside of his creation and that he is personally and constantly involved in the lives of His children (Isaiah 40:28-31; Hebrews 11:3; Acts 17:24-28).

2. Postmodernists say societal practices determine what truth is i.e., there is no absolute truth of any kind. Even scientific truth is not absolute or trustworthy. [9] Additionally, all beliefs and values are "arbitrary social constructs," [10] and one set of ideas, no matter how radical or dangerous, is as good as another. [11] Christians believe ultimate truth proceeds from Christ's teachings and centers around him (John 14:6), and as they know and abide in that truth they become empowered to enjoy life to its fullest (John 8:31,32; 10:7-10).

3. Postmodernists consider "sin" to be (a) the intolerance of the views of others and (b) the use of metanarratives (broad

explanations of reality) regarded as universal truth but that lead to violence, greed, and yearning for power. Postmodernists relegate Christianity to the status of a metanarrative. Christians, however, acknowledge sin, which proceeds from the human heart, to be humankind's fundamental problem (James 4:1; Psalm 51:5).

Lamentably, even many professed Christians today are wont to define truth imprecisely and lend credence to the humanist or postmodernist interpretation of truth as always being relative. They allow themselves to be caught up in the postmodern mind-set that says there are no moral absolutes, even though they claim to follow the teachings of the Bible and trust Jesus Christ as their Savior.

The lack of commitment to the acceptance of unconditional truth and sure morals has led to a fragmented view by many people as to what constitutes a Christian conscience. The element of contingency inherent in the postmodernist view of moral behavior serves to confuse Christians who neglect to focus sufficiently on God's Holy Word. Charles Colson (1931 – 2012), the prominent Christian evangelist and president of Prison Fellowship International noted our conscience has become a "barometer of our emotional state" instead of being a strong monitor of moral choices. [12]

Christians must avoid faltering in living out their faith, and renew their commitment to serve God in honesty and unrestrained loyalty. There is absolute truth in the Word of God. There is absolute morality in the teachings of Scripture. Finally, there is the ultimate absolute behind God's message of salvation unto eternal life for humankind via Jesus Christ, who is the Way, the Truth and the Life!

Postmodernism's Demise

Much akin to imprecise, ill-defined philosophies like secular humanism, the New Age movement and the like, the number of adherents of postmodernism is difficult to quantify. The movement, however, seems to be in the throes of disappearing from public consciousness, notwithstanding the persistence of certain questionable moral paradigms, especially in younger generations. Since the late 1990s there has been a growing feeling both in popular culture and in academia that postmodernism "has gone out of fashion", [13] and arguing from the context of current cultural production, many contend that postmodernism may be dead. [14]

Unification Church (The Moonies)

The Unification Church is a cult founded by Rev. Sun Myung Moon (1920–2012), who started it in Seoul, Korea in 1954. Moon was a Korean religious leader also known for his business ventures and engagement in social and political causes. [1] The official name of the Unification Church is the Family Federation for World Peace and Unification (founded as the Holy Spirit Association for the Unification of World Christianity – HSA-UWC). Hak Ja Han, Moon's widow, is the Unification Church's current leader.

The beliefs of the Unification Church are based on Moon's book *Divine Principle*, which he claimed he produced under divine inspiration, and differ from the teachings of Nicene Christianity in its view of Jesus Christ [2] and the concept of "indemnity." [3] Moon believed the Bible could not be understood without the aid of the doctrines advocated in *Divine Principle*. The Unification Church is well known for its ceremonial funerals [4] and mass weddings. [5] One of the movement's most notorious undertakings was the mass wedding of 3,000 couples in 1992. Moon amassed quite a fortune for himself as the leader of the Unification Church - by the time he died in 2012, he was worth millions.

The Unification Church was strongly criticized and was the subject of numerous controversies, including being branded as a dangerous cult. [6] Jewish and Christian scholars question the organization's beliefs. [7] The Church's involvement in politics, including anti-communism and support for Korean reunification, is the subject of ongoing scrutiny and investigation. [8] The governments of Germany and the other 14 Schengen treaty nations banned Moon and his wife from entering their countries on the grounds they were leaders of a sect that endangered the personal and social development of young people. [9] The Schengen Agreement is a treaty which led to the creation of Europe's *Schengen Area*, in which internal border checks have largely been abolished. It originated on 14 June 1985, near the town of Schengen, Luxembourg, by five of the ten member states of the then European Economic Community. [10]

The Unification Church is not unlike other pseudo-religious organizations that claim tenuous associations with mainstream Christianity. However, even a cursory analysis of the group's philosophies confirms such viewpoints and values and are markedly unlike true biblical precepts and practices.

Firstly, it is meet to compare the life of Sun Myung Moon to what the Bible says about false teachers. According to 1 Timothy 6:3, teaching from God leads to holy and righteous living. Moon, however, faced charges of sexual impurity on numerous occasions. Also, authorities convicted Moon of tax evasion and sentenced him to prison. [11] The apostle Jude warns the church about people who would turn grace into a license for ungodly behavior.

For there are certain men crept in unawares, who were before of old ordained to this condemnation, ungodly men, turning the grace of our God into lasciviousness, and denying the only Lord God, and our Lord Jesus Christ. (Jude 4:4, KJV)

Secondly, the Unification Church preaches false, unbiblical theology. Moon's teaching says man is visible God, and God is the invisible form of man (Hebrews 2:6–8 presents a clear refutation of such a canard). Moon, as a matter of fact, crowned himself the "King of Peace" in 2004 and claimed to be the Messiah and Savior of the world. He also claimed his wife was the Holy Spirit. The purported goal of Unificationism is world peace through the creation of "true families." Rev. Moon and his wife presented themselves as the "True Parents" and the first to have children who were sinless. Unificationism alleges dead people can return to earth for a second chance to atone for their sins.

Thirdly, Unification theology denies the Trinitarian understanding of the Godhead (see Titus 2:13). Furthermore, Unificationism denies Jesus rose physically from the dead (1 Corinthians 15) and rejects the doctrine of his divine nature (Hebrews 1:1–3). Deliverance from sin, according to the Unification Church, proceeds from human effort and making restitution, directly contradicting biblical scholarship that teaches people obtain salvation and have their sins cleansed through the dispensation of God's grace, not by works. (Ephesians 2:8–9 (NIV)

The deceptive tactics and mind-control practices of the Unification Church aside, the movement is dangerous because the theology directly contradicts biblical Scripture. Followers of Sun Myung Moon's teachings trust a false messiah and subscribe to false understandings about God, about Jesus, and about life after death. It is regrettable people attempt to obtain salvation through self-effort when Jesus Christ already paid the complete penalty for their sins on the cross. It is regrettable Moonies follow a self-serving (and dead) leader rather than the self-sacrificial (and risen) Christ.

An exact number of Unification Church members is extremely difficult to obtain. The organization does not publish official statistics for outsiders, explaining that the media may use these statistics to the detriment of believers. Membership is estimated at 1-2 million worldwide, with the largest number of adherents in Korea, and approximately 10 to 30 thousand in the United States.

Unitarian Universalism

Unitarian Universalism (UU) is a liberal religion characterized by a "free and responsible search for truth and meaning." [1] Unitarian Universalists assert no creed, but instead affirm unity by their shared search for spiritual growth. As such, their congregations include many atheists, agnostics, and theists. The roots of Unitarian Universalism lie in liberal Christianity,* (See below). Unitarian Universalists suggest these traditions facilitate a deep regard for intellectual freedom and inclusive love. Congregations and members seek inspiration and derive insight from all major world religions.

*Liberal Christianity, also known as liberal theology, covers diverse philosophically and biblically informed religious movements and ideas within Christianity from the late 18th century onward. Liberal does not refer to progressive Christianity or to political liberalism but to the philosophical and religious thought that developed and grew as a consequence of the Enlightenment Age (generally held to be between 1715 and 1789).

The Unitarian Universalism movement numbers about 199,850 members in the United States, while around 800,000 individuals identify themselves as Unitarian Universalist adherents throughout the world. [2]

The name "Unitarian Universalist" stems from the group's denial of the doctrine of the Trinity of God i.e., God the Father, God the Son, and God the Holy Spirit, and the belief all human beings will eventually obtain salvation. Universalists consider the possibility of anyone being sent to hell incompatible with the character of a loving God. Such a view goes all the way back to the sixteenth century when Unitarian beliefs became popular during the Reformation. Furthermore, there was a merging of Unitarian thought and Universal thought during the late eighteenth century in America during the Age of Reason or Age of Enlightenment. The intellectual elite of the era refused to believe in biblical teachings such as those about total depravity and eternal damnation but rather embraced the idea of a loving God who would never cause someone to suffer.

Adherents of Unitarian Universalism base their beliefs primarily upon their own experiences and do not commit to any one religious system. They believe an individual has the right to decide for himself or herself what to believe, and no one should infringe upon this right. Such a principle in itself is a predictable one, especially in a worldview that does not proclaim a single, identifiable deity but allows subscribers the latitude to choose from a pantheon of gods or to follow none. However, should a religion promote the worship of an exclusive deity, adherents are free to pay homage to it. Of course, if an individual refuses to worship the deity, he or she must be allowed to opt out of the belief system or not join at all.

The forgoing observations notwithstanding, one bears the consequences of his or her choices, and the nature and magnitude of the outcome of certain ventures can be overwhelming. Furthermore, there is a marked difference between asking or encouraging someone to consider making a decision and forcing or coercing him or her to choose a particular course of action.

Unitarian Universalism is mostly about unbridled tolerance. There is no demarcation between right and wrong or between good and bad.

Everyone makes up his or her own rules in an environment of moral and religious plurality. Unitarian Universalists seem to be intolerant only of biblical Christianity. They view the Bible as a book of poetry, myth, and moral teaching, a completely human book and not truly the Word of God. They reject the Bible's portrayal of a Triune God, leaving the concept of God up to each individual's imagination.

The Unitarian Universalist considers Jesus a good moral teacher but nothing more. Jesus is not divine, and every miracle associated with him falls outside the realm of human reason.

Universalists regard most sayings of Jesus recorded in the Bible as embellishments on the part of the authors. Further, Universalists believe Jesus did not die to save humankind from sin, as a human being is not a fallen sinner. Unitarian Universalism places heavy emphasis on humankind's capacity for goodness and claims sin is completely relative. One saves himself or herself through personal improvement, salvation being a purely worldly experience or a "waking up" to the world around oneself. Death is final, and most Unitarian Universalists deny the existence of an afterlife.

Biblical Christianity refutes Universalist falsehoods in no uncertain manner. Jesus does save humankind, the members of which sank into a fallen state after the first humans rebelled against a Holy God in the Garden of Eden and separated themselves from him through their sin (John 10:15; Romans 3:24-25; 5:8; 1 Peter 2:24). Man is not good, but sinful and hopelessly lost. It is only through the grace of God and faith in the shed blood of Christ on the cross that mankind can be reconciled to a holy,

549

transcendent Creator (Genesis 2:16-17; 3:1-19); John 3:36; Romans 3:23; 1 Corinthians 2:14; Ephesians 2:1-3; 1 Timothy 2:13-14; 1 John 1:8).

Unitarian Universalism has nothing in common with biblical Christianity. It is a false gospel, its teachings are contrary to Christian doctrine, and its members strongly oppose traditional, biblical Christian beliefs while purporting to be free of discrimination or prejudice of any kind.

In the final analysis, the incontrovertible truth does not change – Jesus Christ is the only means through which anyone can attain eternal life in a place called heaven, and to reject his offer of salvation is to court eternal destruction in a dreadful location called hell!

PART SIX

TWO DOORS TO ETERNITY

CHAPTER TWENTY-TWO

TWO DOORS TO ETERNITY - MAKING THE MOST IMPORTANT DECISION OF YOUR LIFE

Two Doors to Eternity, up to this point, essentially has been a prologue to its final chapter - a chapter that consolidates the build-up of the reader's wherewithal to *make the most important decision of his or her life!*

Just about every decision in an individual's life relates to choosing between two or from among multiple alternatives. This is so regardless of the nature or magnitude of the issue at hand. The individual bears the consequences of his or her decision. Wise choices generally lead to positive outcomes, while imprudent choices produce adverse results. Where a matter is trivial, the outcome of the selection of a course of action, even if it is an unwise choice, may not be a cause for undue distress. In an important matter, however, a poor choice may engender calamitous repercussions, especially if such consequences stretch into an indefinite time in the future.

The author feels confident the presentations in the preceding chapters of this book about God, Jesus Christ, the devil, heaven, hell, and eternity are thorough and informative, as are the expositions on major world religions, philosophies, cults, and newer belief systems. He also thinks the utilization of Biblical Christianity as a standard for comparison with other worldviews, religious and otherwise, provides the enquiring reader with enough information to enable him or her to determine what course of action to adopt as he or she confronts the inevitable – *deciding where he or she will spend eternity!*

What Happens After Death?

Christians generally subscribe to three versions of what happens to people after death. Some hold that after death, everyone "sleeps" until the final judgment, after which everyone will be sent to heaven or hell. Others believe that at the moment of death, people are instantly judged and sent to their eternal destinations. Still others claim that when people die, their souls/spirits are sent to a "temporary" heaven or hell to await the final resurrection, the final judgment, and the assignment to their eternal destination.

Notwithstanding the above differences in beliefs relative to what takes place after one dies, the doctrine that an individual's destination for eternity is either heaven or hell is confirmative of biblical explication. It is meet to attempt an analysis of what the Bible says happens after death?

First, the Bible says after death the Christian's soul/spirit goes to heaven, because his or her sins are forgiven through having received Christ as Savior (John 3:16, 18, 36). Death, for the believer, is to be "away from the body and at home with the Lord" (2 Corinthians 5:6-8; Philippians 1:23). However, biblical passages such as 1 Corinthians 15:50-54 and 1 Thessalonians 4:13-17 describe believers being resurrected and given glorified bodies. One may ask if believers go to be with Christ immediately after death, what is the purpose of this resurrection? It seems while the

553

souls/spirits of believers go to be with Christ immediately after death, the physical body remains in the grave "sleeping." Furthermore, at the resurrection of believers, a believer's physical body is resurrected, glorified, and then reunited with his or her soul/spirit. This reunited and glorified body-soul-spirit will be the possession of the believer for eternity in the new heaven and new earth (Revelation 21-22).

Second, for those who do not receive Jesus Christ as Savior, death precedes everlasting punishment. However, as in the instance with believers, it seems unbelievers also are sent immediately to a temporary holding place, to await their final resurrection, judgment, and eternal destiny. Luke 16:22-23 describes a rich man being tormented immediately after death. Revelation 20:11-15 tell about the unbelieving dead being resurrected, judged at the great white throne, and then being cast into the lake of fire. Unbelievers or those who do not accept Christ as their Savior do not enter hell immediately after death, but rather exist in a temporary realm of judgment and condemnation. Even though unbelievers do not go to the "lake of fire" instantly, their immediate fate after death is not a pleasant one, as the Gospel of Luke indicates in no uncertain manner.

> *And he cried and said, Father Abraham, have mercy on me, and send Lazarus that he may dip the tip of his finger in water, and cool my tongue; for I am tormented in this flame.* (Luke 16:24, KJV)

At the final resurrection, when the current, temporary realm ceases to exist, a person's eternal destiny will not change. The precise "location" of the eternal destiny is what changes. Believers will eventually gain entrance into the new heaven and/or new earth (Revelation 21:1). Unbelievers will ultimately be banished to the lake of fire (Revelation 20:11-15). These are the final, eternal destinations of all people - based entirely on whether they will have trusted Jesus Christ alone for the salvation of their souls (Matthew 25:46; John 3:36). There is no neutral or middle ground.

The author apologizes if he rouses the emotions of readers by suggesting many peaceful looking, well-dressed corpses that lie in repose at funeral homes or burial sites all over the world are only cadavers whose souls have exited them - souls that have begun to experience unmitigated anguish as they await an eventual sentencing to a place of eternal damnation. These bodies belong to people who neglected to make a decision for Jesus Christ. The observation may be a difficult, and seemingly unpitying one, but sadly, it is indicative of the truth.

Why Christ Alone Is The Means Of Salvation From Sin & Hell

Throughout this book, there has been a singular appeal to all who would approach Almighty God's Throne of Grace in search of an answer as to where they might spend eternity. The author, at the risk of appearing unduly pedestrian, repeats such an exhortation i.e., *embrace Jesus Christ as Lord and Savior!* Christ alone is the means of salvation unto eternal life in a place called heaven. He is the only way to heaven for several reasons.

- Jesus was "chosen by God" to be the Savior (1 Peter 2:4). Jesus is the only One to come down from heaven and return there (John 3:13). He is the only person to live a perfect human life (Hebrews 4:15). He is the only sacrifice for sin (1 John 2:2; Hebrews

10:26). He alone fulfilled the Law and the Prophets (Matthew 5:17). He is the only man to conquer death forever (Hebrews 2:14–15). He is the only Mediator between God and man (1 Timothy 2:5). He is the only man whom God has "exalted . . . to the highest place" (Philippians 2:9).

- Jesus spoke of himself as the only way to heaven in several places in the Bible besides John 14:6. He presented himself as the object of faith in Matthew 7:21–27. He said his words are life (John 6:63). He promised that those who believe in him will have eternal life (John 3:14–15). He is the gate of the sheep (John 10:7), the bread of life (John 6:35), and the resurrection (John 11:25). No one else can rightly claim those titles.

- The apostles' preaching focused on the death and resurrection of Jesus Christ. Peter, speaking to the Sanhedrin, clearly proclaimed Jesus as the only way to heaven: "Salvation is found in no one else, for there is no other name under heaven given to mankind by which we must be saved." (Acts 4:12, NASB). Paul, speaking in the synagogue in Antioch, singled out Jesus as the Savior: "I want you to know that through Jesus the forgiveness of sins is proclaimed to you. Through him everyone who believes is set free from every sin" (Acts 13:38-39, NIV) John, writing to the church at large, specifies the name of Christ as the basis of our forgiveness: "I am writing to you, dear children, because your sins have been forgiven on account of his name." (1 John 2:12, NIV). No one but Jesus forgives sin.

Yes, Jesus is the only way to heaven. Such an exclusive statement may confuse, surprise, or even offend people, but it is true nonetheless. He is not a way, as in one of many; He is the way, as in the one and only. No one, regardless of reputation, achievement, special knowledge, or personal holiness, can approach God the Father except through Jesus the Son.

Eternity With God

The believer's topmost priority should be to contemplate spending eternity in heaven. Heaven's grandeur is beyond anyone's capacity to describe, or even understand, but it befits the Christian to attempt to envision the unparalleled magnificence that awaits the children of God in their eternal abode. Nevertheless, perhaps it is God's will that heaven-bound believers do not comprehend fully what is in store for them, hence the lack of untimely revelation of Heaven's wonders. Christians after all, walk by faith, and not by sight.

Heaven – Unimaginably Wonderful

While biblical scholarship intimates even inspired men are unable to reveal the details of heaven, and concomitantly, much about eternal life with God, believers are to persist in lives of glorious expectancy.

"But just as it is written, 'Things which eye has not seen and ear has not heard, and which have not entered the heart of man, all that God has prepared for those who love Him' " (1 Corinthians 2:9, NASB)

The apostle Paul, probably speaking of himself, knew a man who was:

"caught up into Paradise and heard inexpressible words, which a man is not permitted to speak."(2 Corinthians 12:4, NASB)

Much of what people know about heaven appears in symbolic language. In the Book of Revelation, John paints an unfathomable picture of heaven as a city that's two-thirds the size of the United States, reaching 1,500 miles into the air, and extending hundreds of miles further into space than the International Space Station.* Such a city is impossible for man to build and maintain, making heaven more amazing than anything anyone can imagine from a worldly perspective.

*The International Space Station (ISS) is a space station (habitable artificial satellite) in low Earth orbit. [1]

Heaven - God Will Be There

Imagine living in the presence of God for eternity?

For the believer, one of the most extraordinary experiences would be seeing God and Jesus face to face in heaven, and worshiping them (Rev. 22:4).

No one today is able, or allowed to stand face to face with God because of sin. Moses' face shone from being in the presence of God, and Isaiah could do nothing but prostrate himself when he saw God's throne in a vision. When the believer finally sees God's face, it will be an indescribable experience because no human at the present time can grasp the magnificence of such glory.

No Evil in Heaven

Imagine living in an environment in which there is no evil, temptation, sin, or fear?

Heaven's environment will be a perfect one. Neither Satan, demons, nor evil people will be there. Only those who bring glory to God will be in heaven. There will be nothing unclean, immoral or malevolent, as evident in the present system of things. In heaven, believers will no longer have to struggle against evil, as the following scriptural passages state they do.

For our struggle is not against flesh and blood, but against the rulers, against the authorities, against the powers of this dark world and against the spiritual forces of evil in the heavenly realms. (Ephesians 6:12, NIV).

Be alert and of sober mind. Your enemy the devil prowls around like a roaring lion looking for someone to devour. Resist him, standing firm in the faith, because you know that the family of believers throughout the world is undergoing the same kind of sufferings. And the God of all grace, who called you to his eternal glory in Christ, after you have suffered a little while, will himself restore you and make you strong, firm and steadfast. (1 Peter5:8-10, NIV).

Eternal Rest in Heaven

There will be eternal rest in heaven for believers, as promised in the Bible.

Come to Me, all who are weary and heavy-laden, and I will give you rest. Take My yoke upon you and learn from Me, for I am gentle and humble in heart, and you will find rest for your souls. For My yoke is easy and My burden is light. (Matthew11:28-30, NIV)

Though the Christian finds rest in Jesus while upon earth, he or she still struggles against Satan. However, after the believer dies, he or she will rest from all labors because the struggle will be over.

Then I heard a voice from heaven say, "Write this: Blessed are the dead who die in the Lord from now on." "Yes," says the Spirit, "they will rest from their labor, for their deeds will follow them."(Revelation 14:13, NIV)

For anyone who enters God's rest also rests from their works just as God did from his. Let us, therefore, make every effort to enter that rest, so that no one will perish by following their example of disobedience. (Hebrews 4:10-11, NIV)

Eternity Without God

If the multiple meanings of the term *eternity* (see Chapter Six: *What is Eternity?)* were to be encapsulated within a framework relative to God and eternity, the inferences would be confined to (a) the timeless state following death and (b) the afterlife, and possibly *immortality*. In other words, after death an individual will live forever with God (see the preceding sub section) or without God, or in heaven or hell.

What does an eternity without God or an eternity in hell entail?

560

Eternal Suffering

God's Holy Word warns that after judgment, people who would have rejected Christ's offer of salvation will be cast into the lake of fire to live with the devil.

Then death and Hades were thrown into the lake of fire. This is the second death, the lake of fire. And if anyone's name was not found written in the book of life, he was thrown into the lake of fire. (Revelation 20:14-15, ESV)

Then he will say to those on his left, 'Depart from me, you who are cursed, into the eternal fire prepared for the devil and his angels. (Matthew 25:41, NIV)

Such punishment lasts for eternity, not just for a short while as taught by some misdirected religionists, including some professed Christians. Anyone cast into hell will be there forever. There is no escape from hell, or avoidance of its punishment.

Satan & His Demons

Not only will people in hell have to live with the devil, they will have live with demons and the vilest people who lived on earth, all suffering unspeakable torment together.

As frightful as today's world is, it's a place where God restrains its ruler (Satan). Imagine an environment in which Satan and his demons, although languishing themselves, are free to hound and inflict immeasurable suffering on people cast into the lake of fire for rejecting Jesus Christ.

Eternity with the devil, demons, and the wickedest people on earth - it's not a place where anyone would want to be, even for a second, much less forever!

Eternal Separation from God

People who do not repent of their sins, ask God's forgiveness and accept Jesus Christ as their Lord and Savior will be punished with eternal separation from God. The Bible clearly states:

...dealing out retribution to those who do not know God and to those who do not obey the gospel of our Lord Jesus. These will pay the penalty of eternal destruction, away from the presence of the Lord and from the glory of His power.

(2 Thessalonians 1:8-9, NASB)

Eternal life with the devil is bad enough, but eternal separation from God is worse.

No Goodness, No Love, Only Evil & Uncleanliness

Eternal life without God will be a life where everything will be evil and bad. There will be nothing good. There won't be happiness or joy. No one would feel good about himself or herself. Life will be utter misery.

God is love; Satan is not (1 John 4:8). Eternal life without God will be a life without love. Hell will be a place of wickedness and hatred, not a place of love. There will be widespread uncleanliness and abomination. In heaven, however, there will be "...nothing unclean, and no one who practices abomination and lying, shall ever come into it, but only those whose names are written in the Lamb's book of life." (Revelation 21:27, NASB)

Hell, an environment without God, will be a crowded place of unending, unimaginable torment, horror, and regret. No one, but no one, should want to go there!

Guarding Against Satan's Lies & Deceit

As emphasized elsewhere in this book, Satan, or the devil, and his demons relentlessly pursue prospective victims whom they would lead away from God and into a domain of interminable darkness and ruin.

People who have never heard Christ's Gospel, and those who have, but have yet to make a decision to follow the Galilean miracle-worker, are especially susceptible to Satan's guile and subterfuge. The devil is very evil and very formidable. He is able to lead astray, even some professed Christian believers who are not vigilant in safeguarding their faith.

God, of course, created Satan and his fallen angels, or demons, and God is eminently more powerful than the devil, his minions and all else. As a matter of fact, a holy and just God has already condemned Satan and his underlings to eternal damnation in hell. Satan no doubt is aware of such a sentence and consequently tries to ensnare as many people as possible into sharing a similar fate.

The life of the individual who is not a Christian but who entertains even a remote yearning to become one, must encompass embracing Jesus Christ while simultaneously rebuffing Satan's advances. The committed Christian also, must adopt a similar path of conduct, because the devil never gives up and seeks to inveigle anyone who would backslide or falter in his or her religious convictions. The following are among Satan's more devious contrivances, some of them repeated here for the reader's convenience.

- *God does not exist* - This shameless lie concocted by the devil has become increasingly popular over recent decades. Atheists are outspoken and often egregious in attempts to promote their absence of faith in a superior or supernatural overseer. The falsehood about God being non-existent is more prevalent in affluent societies than penurious ones where people lack the necessities of a comfortable life. Richer people tend to trust in money and other material things and synchronously mislead themselves into thinking they are in control of their lives and are accountable to no one, not even God, whom they doubt exists anyway.

  The proclivities of atheists notwithstanding, recent statistics reveal the overwhelming majority of Americans believe in God or a higher power. A 2017 December Pew Research Survey yielded the following statistics.

  The vast majority of Americans (90%) believe in some kind of higher power.

  In the U.S., Christians are particularly likely (99%) to believe in God or a higher power, with 80% claiming faith in a biblical God.

- *He (Satan) does not exist* – One of Satan's more audacious endeavors is misleading people into thinking he does not exist. As long as people do not acknowledge there is a real spiritual enemy in this world named Satan, they will never recognize the need to resist him or retaliate against what he does in their lives.

  People learn of Satan's existence by reading the Bible, which is the only reliable means of any evidence of such a reality. People who do not believe the Bible is the inspired Word of God are in serious trouble, especially if they look to worldly or alternative literature for the truth. Details about Satan's existence and activities appear in Mark 4:15, Luke 4:8, Luke 13:16 and Acts 26:18, among other biblical sources.

- *There is no such place as hell* – Satan understands if he can persuade people to believe there is no hell, very many of them would throw caution to the wind and sin uninhibitedly. He impresses upon people that a loving God would not condemn members of his own creation to a place of eternal torment. Hell, however, is a real place. Jesus spoke explicitly about hell on numerous occasions.

  John Walvoord (1910 – 2002), the well-known American Christian theologian and pastor, in his contribution to the book *Four Views on Hell* said that when it comes to the doctrine of hell in the Bible, "Jesus himself defined this more specifically and in more instances than any New Testament prophet. All the references to *gehenna*, except James 3:6, are from the lips of Jesus Christ himself..." [3]

- *The earthly life is all there is* – Another favorite lie of the devil is when someone dies, he or she simply ceases to exist. There is no heaven or hell. There is no afterlife during which people will experience never-ending suffering. Satan tells people to live for today, and don't worry about tomorrow. Life, he says, is too short to waste on fairy tales and myths about God, salvation, and judgment.

  The Bible makes it very clear there is an afterlife and that each and every individual will spend eternity in either heaven or hell. The Book of Hebrews says, "And as it is appointed for men to die once, but after this the judgment." (Hebrews 9:27, NKJB). The Book of Romans declares, "For the wages of sin is death, but the free gift of God is eternal life in Christ Jesus our Lord." (Romans 6:23, NIV)

- *Sin isn't really serious. It's enough just be a good person* - Satan deceives people into thinking most sins are not serious offenses. All that really matters is being a "good person" and God will be pleased and will not judge or condemn anyone.

  By contrast, the Christian gospel states that people are broken, spiritually bankrupt souls who stand guilty before God and are in desperate need of a Savior. The Gospel of John says, "If we say we have no sin, we deceive ourselves, and the truth is not in us." (1 John 1:8, ESV). The Book of Romans reminds everyone that "...for all have sinned, and fall short of the glory of God, and all are justified freely by his grace through the redemption that came by Christ Jesus." (Romans 3:23-24, NIV).

566

- *God wants you to be happy, so do what makes you happy, regardless* – While God does want his children to be happy, to presume it is okay for one to do whatever he or she wants without having to answer for any wrongdoing is far too simplistic a mindset. Yet Satan tells people they should do whatever they want to do and not worry about any consequences. He encourages people to rebel against God and everything good and holy. He was, after all, the first and foremost agent of rebellion a long time ago when he led a third of heaven's angels in an attempt to overthrow Almighty God, the latter who subsequently banished them from his presence.

God loves his children more than they could possibly imagine, and his chief concern is what is best for them, always!. Sometimes however, what's best for someone isn't what makes him or her happy, especially in the short run. For example, someone suffers and wonders why God allows such suffering. Later on, he or she looks back and realizes God orchestrated what took place for the good of all.

Contrary to the devil's misleading inference, God isn't trying to prevent his children from enjoying life. He's actually trying to protect and bless them. Believers therefore should trust him in return, even when they don't understand his actions and decisions. The following are three of many verses from God's Holy Word that communicate his promise to do what is best for his children at all times.

But seek first His kingdom and His righteousness, and all these things will be added to you. (Matthew 6:33, ESV) .

You will make known to me the path of life; In Your presence is fullness of joy; In Your right hand there are pleasures forever. (Psalm 16:11, NASB).

The thief comes only to steal and kill and destroy; I came that they may have life, and have it abundantly. (John 10:10, ESV).

"Abundant life" refers to life in its abounding fullness of joy and strength for mind, body, and soul. "Abundant life" signifies a contrast to feelings of lack, emptiness, and dissatisfaction. Such feelings may motivate an individual to search for meaning and a change in his or her life. An abundant life may include tangible, material things, but encompasses much more. It is an existence full of everything one needs to sustain himself or herself in joy and purpose.

- *You can't be saved, you're too sinful* – Yet another misrepresentation of the truth by the devil is some people are too sinful to obtain Christ's pardon and a place in God's everlasting kingdom.

Jesus didn't give up heaven and his Godhood, albeit to a limited extent, to become God incarnate and journey to the cross at Calvary in order to give each individual a one-in-a-million shot at squeezing into heaven. God's grace is real! He longs to save as many people as possible, and if he loves his children, as he does, salvation and heaven is within everyone's reach.

- *A brief comment about "Godliness"* - There is a common misconception that Christians ought to be perfect. Many believers, in consequence, become obsessed with pretending to live faultless lives, and exude confidence and happiness. At times they're ashamed to admit their shortcomings, as though they should not exist. Salvation through Jesus, however, doesn't change the fact that sin is present in a believer's life. When one is born again, God forgives him or her and sees him or her as righteous. Nevertheless, a Christian's battle with sin continues until he or she arrives in heaven.

In fact, striving for perfection actually can be a trap that pulls one away from living a godly life. In other words, trying desperately to be perfect is a form of relying on one's own capability instead of God's. Jesus said he came to heal the spiritually sick because they recognized their weaknesses. An awareness of one's inadequacy lays bare the realization of one's need for the Lord. The world sees successful people as powerful and self-sufficient, but Jesus didn't care about these qualities. Instead, he wants people to be aware of their own brokenness. This is the foundation of godliness.

One should accept his or her neediness and seek God passionately. Doing so allows the following attributes to develop: a hunger for God's Word, faithful service, deepening trust, and decision-making based upon principle rather than preference. Patiently and mercifully, God matures his children.

A believer should be careful not to cover up his or her sins in order to look like a "good Christian." Without recognition and confession of one's sinfulness, he or she is unable to rely fully on God. It is only with this awareness can one passionately seek God, and confess with repentance when he or she falls short.

- *Once you're saved, regardless of how you live, you cannot lose your salvation* – This is a dangerous, unbiblical lie that Satan often uses to confuse people who have made a decision to follow Jesus Christ.

Even though it is impossible for anyone, no matter how righteous and good, to match or outdo Jesus Christ as a sinless individual, the Gospel exhorts Christians to strive to be like the Savior as he was when he graced the earth with his presence. The New Testament is unmistakably clear that God's children are to live holy lives. If people choose to walk according to the flesh, God will reject them. In other words, they jeopardize their salvation and risk being sent to hell. (See 1 Peter. 1:13-16; Galatians 1:6-9; Hebrews 10:24-26)

No one, including the Christian believer, should think he or she can willfully commit sin, especially heinous wrongdoing, repeatedly, and expect to share in God's glorious promise of eternal life in heaven.

Please see the previous brief discussion about "Godliness," which helps demarcate between a pretentious effort to live a godly life and an honest endeavor to petition God's involvement in the process.

- *Diverse philosophical and belief systems prove all religions are valid* – The devil trades on this inexactitude in no small measure. He impresses on the minds of people that most religions and belief systems teach their adherents to love and serve their fellow human beings and perform acts of kindness. Consequently, most religions and philosophies proceed from innate good, and supernatural overseers (God/gods) and are basically the same.

  While it is true there are commonalities in many religions, including where they relate to good works, doctrines about the identity and character of God are poles apart. Such differences are pivotal, especially where they impact issues like sin, salvation and the afterlife. The Bible clearly says good works cannot save an individual and erase his or her sins. It also says Jesus Christ is the only means through which one can inherit eternal life in heaven and escape everlasting torment in hell. All religions are not the same. Only Christianity holds the answer to life's most important question – Where to spend eternity?

- *Evolutionary and Big Bang theories prove there is no God, so man is the master of his own destiny* – The author covered this topic in Chapter Nineteen: *Evolutionism*. Nevertheless, because of the misrepresentation of a premise secular scientists and the liberal, anti-religion/anti-Christian media shamelessly parade as true science, the author revisits the issue in abridgment.

Evolutionary and Big-Bang theories about the origin of life and the universe are primarily guesses contrary to what real science deems *the scientific method*. The theories lack scientific corroboration and are insults to logic and commonsense. Secular educators all over the world promote the theories as scientific truth. The lies are aided and abetted by a recalcitrant liberal media, the proponents of which are not only embarrassingly uninformed about the precepts of true science, but who precipitously repeat rhetoric rooted in misrepresentation and ignorance.

The driving force behind evolutionary and Big-Bang theories is an escapist mindset that abhors accountability for ethical behavior and spiritual answerability. Both theories propose that the universe and life originated and developed over multiple millions of years through chance events without supervision, and encourage people to abandon belief in a Designer and Creator of life. Life, evolutionists say, came about accidentally from inanimate or non-existent matter.

Satan is at the forefront of peddling evolutionary and Big-Bang theories as proof that God does not exist and man is in charge of his own destiny. Consequently, he exposes people's souls to eternal damnation.

- *Saving the planet (Earth), preserving nature and pursuing healthful habits take precedence over acknowledging God's existence and worshiping Him* - Yet another ruse by the devil to belittle the importance of God's intervention in people's lives or even to question his existence, revolves around ostensibly noble and just causes such as saving the earth, preserving nature, and adopting obsessively healthful lifestyles.

The Bible directs human beings to respect, protect and preserve the environment and nature since they are part of God's breathtaking creation. They should not worship God's creation, however, only God himself. When people exalt anyone or anything created, such people or objects tend to supplant whoever or whatever created them. Such an attitude is abomination to God.

The organic food craze, for instance, largely advocated by liberal anti-corporate activists, created a global market worth an estimated $48 billion in 2007, and made a lot of disingenuous people very wealthy. A 2009 study by the London School of Hygiene & Tropical Medicine, published in the *American Journal of Clinical Nutrition,* found that organic food has no nutritional or health benefits over ordinary food.[4] Behind it all, lurk Satan and his demons, who undertake to beguile gullible people into thinking a robust planet, a wholesome environment and healthy living supersede a supernatural overseer (God). Essentially, the devil seeks to trivialize God's involvement in the affairs of men and women.

Apart from the many falsehoods Satan peddles to mostly unsuspecting people everywhere, there are certain truths about himself he does not want people to know. He determinedly tries to keep such facts secret.

a) He cannot be everywhere at once, unlike God. [5]

b) He does not want people to understand his *modus operandi* or how he operates. [5]

c) His time is short before his impending destruction. [5]

d) His time to mislead people is running out. [5]

e) He is already defeated and sentenced to eternal damnation [5]

f) He does not have authority over believers in Christ. [5]

In Conclusion

Contrary to a relatively popular consensus of opinion that dismisses the probability of an afterlife and heaven and hell, the issues do bear heavily on the minds of countless people around the world and cannot be denied… and rightly so.

The author hopes the various presentations in this book prompt even a token obligation by the reader to ponder objectively, the ramifications pertinent to what happens after one dies. Should the possibility of heaven and hell be real, and the author believes with all his heart it is, then choosing where one will spend eternity has to be the most important decision of his or her life.

Even if someone lives for a hundred years, such a span of time is a nanosecond in comparison with eternity, which lasts forever. The cares of the temporal world pale into stark insignificance when compared to addressing the question of where one will go after he or she dies. The old and the young, the healthy and the sick, the rich and the impoverished, the educated and the unschooled – race, color or creed notwithstanding – they all stand in equal stead at the foot of the Cross of Christ. Everyone is offered the opportunity to embrace Jesus Christ or reject him.

The life of a Christian, like the life of a non-Christian, will not be without trials and tribulations. An important facet of a believer's life, however, is God's promise to stand by his children in times of temptation, hardship and suffering. The devil and his demons target Christians in the hope they might cause them to backslide and renege on their commitment to follow Jesus. They are guileful and compelling entities and will stop at nothing to prevent people from seeking the one true God of the Christian faith. They are masters of deception, consumed with a desire to take as many people as possible with them to everlasting ruin and torment in hell, especially as they know they have already been condemned to such a fate.

God is primarily a God of love. Christ offered himself as a living sacrifice on behalf of lost humankind and withstood unimaginable suffering at the hands of wicked people before they killed him on a cross at Calvary over two thousand years ago. The present world, teetering under the inspectorate of Satan, is an environment of widespread confusion and intense misery. God, however, wants his children to know he is in charge and he guarantees them victory, particularly eventual triumph that translates into an eternity in heaven. The following biblical passages attest to God's unfailing grace in guiding his children's lives and supplying their needs.

And we know that in all things God works for the good of those who love him, who have been called according to his purpose. (Romans 8:28, NIV)

But seek first his kingdom and his righteousness, and all these things will be given to you as well. (Matthew 6:33, NIV)

And my God will meet all your needs according to the riches of his glory in Christ Jesus. (Philippians 4:19, NIV)

Look at the birds of the air; they do not sow or reap or store away in barns, and yet your heavenly Father feeds them. Are you not much more valuable than they? (Matthew 6:26, NIV)

Being confident of this, that he who began a good work in you will carry it on to completion until the day of Christ Jesus. (Philippians 1:6, NIV).

Truth never changes. Religious truth withstands the test of time and attempts from all quarters to discredit and delegitimize it. The Holy Bible and its message of salvation unto eternal life through Jesus Christ is the quintessential example of enduring moral and spiritual truth.

In today's world of passionate diversity in almost every echelon human existence, it is difficult for even sincere and committed supporters of a cause to criticize alternative opinions and lifestyles without being confronted with allegations of narrow-mindedness and/or bigotry. It even becomes problematic for one to confess strict allegiance to a philosophical or more specifically, a religious belief system, unless it is palpably inclusive and not condemnatory of teachings contradictory to its own. The Christian faith is one such worldview because of its inflexible adherence to a number of deep-seated doctrines.

Proper Christian protocol revolves around the untiring dissemination of Christ's message of salvation for the sinner and the promise of eternal life in a place called heaven. Many non-Christians take offense to proactive efforts by Christian believers to convert people to Christianity even though such undertakings are hardly ever coercive or intimidatory. Christians who desperately desire to share the good news of Christ's Gospel therefore find themselves in an unenviable position. The issues at hand, i.e., the afterlife, and heaven and hell, however, are too important for political correctness and acquiescence to dubious worldly virtues to prevail.

At any given time, an individual is one heartbeat away from eternity. He or she who does not make a decision to accept Jesus as Lord and Savior essentially rejects him, and his or her soul remains imperiled every second. God does not send people to hell. They choose to go there!

A Personal Entreaty

In deciding on a name for this book and for this final chapter, I considered an alternative title, i.e., *Two Paths to Eternity*. I opted for *Two Doors to Eternity* because the term "doors," when juxtaposed against "paths," indicates a threshold or brink from which there may be no going back. A decision made when one reaches a doorway is generally final, whereas one can change his or her mind while traversing a path and decide on a new or revised strategy. Once an individual stands at either of the two "doors" to eternity, however, he or she essentially would have made a choice for Jesus Christ or against Him.

577

I pray that you, dear reader, find yourself at the *door* that leads to everlasting life in heaven!

NOTES

Chapter One

1. Dr. Andrew Corbett, Pastor of Legana Christian Church in Tasmania, Australia. National President of ICI Theological College Australia – *Five Proofs for Existence of God.* *https://www.andrewcorbett.net/articles/apologetics/5-proofs-for-the-existence-of-god/*

2. The forgoing story appears in *God In Our Midst: Making the Most Important Decision of Your Life* by Christopher Persaud in Chapter One – "A Few Recollections," under the sub heading, "A Fear of Drowning." pp.24-27. The publication was the author's first full-length book, and was published by Xlibris Corporation, USA, in 2003.

3. Oderberg, David S. (September 1, 2007). "The Cosmological Argument". In Meister, Chad; Copan, Paul (eds.). The Routledge Companion to Philosophy of Religion. Routledge. pp. 341–350. ISBN 978-0415380386.

4. PBS Thirteen, *Cracking the Code of Life.* Hosted by ABC "Nightline" correspondent Robert Krulwich. *ttps://www.pbs.org/wgbh/nova/genome/*

5. *Economic Impact of the Human Genome Project.* Simon Tripp & Martin Grueber, Battelle Memorial Institute, Technology Partnership Practice. May 2011.

https://www.battelle.org/docs/default-source/misc/battelle-2011-misc-economic-impact-human-genome-project.pdf

6. Michael Denton, *Evolution: A Theory in Crisis* (Adler & Adler, Publishers, Inc. 1986) p. 334.

7. Posted by Mario Seiglie, May 2005. DNA – *The Tiny Code That's Toppling Evolution.* Beyond Today (quoted by Lee Strobel, The Case for a Creator, Zondervan 2004, p. 224).
    https://www.ucg.org/the-good-news/dna-the-tiny-code-thats-toppling-evolution

8. Posted by Mario Seiglie, May 2005. *DNA – The Tiny Code That's Toppling Evolution.* Beyond Today (quoted by Lee Strobel, The Case for a Creator, Zondervan, 2004, p. 237).
    https://www.ucg.org/the-good-news/dna-the-tiny-code-thats-toppling-evolution

9. Bill Gates, *The Road Ahead*, Penguin Books, 1996. p.228

10. Lee Strobel, *The Case for a Creator*, Zondervan, 2004, p. 244.

11. Francis Crick, *Life Itself – Its Origin & Nature* (Simon & Schuster, 1981), p. 88.

12. Werner Gitt, *In the Beginning Was Information*, 2005) p. 95.

13. Patrick Glynn, God: *The Evidence – The Reconciliation of Faith and Reason in a Postsecular World* (Prima Publishing, a Division of Random House, 1997), pp. 53, 54-55.

14. Michael Denton, *Evolution: A Theory in Crisis* (Adler & Adler, Publishers, Inc. 1986) p. 329.

15. Quoted by Lee Strobel, The Case for a Greator Zondervan 2004.

16. Werner Gitt, *In the Beginning Was Information*, 2005) p. 124.

17. Quoted by Lee Strobel, *The Case for a Creator*, Zondervan, 2004, p. 243).

18. Quoted by Lee Strobel, *The Case for a Creator*, Zondervan, 2004, p. 77).

19. Quoted by Lee Strobel, *The Case for a Creator*, Zondervan, 2004, p. 221).

20. Quoted by Richard Ostling, *Leading Atheist Now Believes in God.* Associated Press report - December 9, 2004

21. There are three main periods in the history of ontological arguments. The first was in 11th century, when St. Anselm of Canterbury came up with the first ontological argument. Miroslaw Szatkowski (ed.), *Ontological Proofs Today*, Ontos Verlag, 2012, p. 22.

22. *Ontological Arguments*, Stanford Encyclopedia of Philosophy. *https://plato.stanford.edu/entries/ontological-arguments/* First published February 8, 1996; substantive revision February 6, 2019

23. Saint Anselm, *The Proslogion* (Latin Proslogium; English translation, *Discourse on the Existence of God* (1077-1078)

24. Dr. Peter Kreeft, Strange Notions, The Digital Aeropagus – Reason, Faith, Dialogue. *Twenty Arguments for God's Existence.* *https://strangenotions.com/god-exists/*

Chapter Two

1. COLD-CASE CHRISTIANITY with J. Warner Wallace. *Who Is Jesus, According to Other Religions?* December 4, 2017, JUDAISM https://coldcasechristianity.com/writings/who-is-jesus-according-to-other-religions/

2. COLD-CASE CHRISTIANITY with J. Warner Wallace. *Who Is Jesus, According to Other Religions?* December 4, 2017, ISLAM https://coldcasechristianity.com/writings/who-is-jesus-according-to-other-religions/

3. COLD-CASE CHRISTIANITY with J. Warner Wallace. *Who Is Jesus, According to Other Religions?* December 4, 2017, AHMADIYYA https://coldcasechristianity.com/writings/who-is-jesus-according-to-other-religions/

4. COLD-CASE CHRISTIANITY with J. Warner Wallace. *Who Is Jesus, According to Other Religions?* December 4, 2017, BAHA'I https://coldcasechristianity.com/writings/who-is-jesus-according-to-other-religions/

5. COLD-CASE CHRISTIANITY with J. Warner Wallace. *Who Is Jesus, According to Other Religions?* December 4, 2017, HINDUISM https://coldcasechristianity.com/writings/who-is-jesus-according-to-other-religions/

6. COLD-CASE CHRISTIANITY with J. Warner Wallace. Who Is Jesus, According to Other Religions? December 4, 2017, BUDDHISM https://coldcasechristianity.com/writings/who-is-jesus-according-to-other-religions/

7. COLD-CASE CHRISTIANITY with J. Warner Wallace. Who Is Jesus, According to Other Religions? December 4, 2017, THE NEW AGE MOVEMENT https://coldcasechristianity.com/writings/who-is-jesus-according-to-other-religions/

8. The Jesus Seminar – Select Your own Jesus, http://www.biblequery.org/OtherBeliefs/Skeptics/JesusSeminar.htm. Christian Debater.

9. The Jesus Seminar – Select Your own Jesus, http://www.biblequery.org/OtherBeliefs/Skeptics/JesusSeminar.htm. Christian Debater.

10. *The Five Gospels: The Search for the Authentic Words of Jesus* (1993) Polebridge Press (Macmillan), ISBN 0-02-541949-8

11. *The Five Gospels: The Search for the Authentic Words of Jesus* (1993) Polebridge Press (Macmillan), ISBN 0-02-541949-8

12. *The Gospel of Jesus: According to the Jesus Seminar* (1999), Polebridge Press (Macmillan), ISBN 0-944344-74-7

13. Michael J. Wilkins & J.P. Moreland, General Editors, Jesus Under Fire: Modern Scholarship Reinvents the Historical Jesus, Zondervan, 1995, ISBN 0-310-21139-5

14. Dale C. Allison, "Jesus of Nazareth: Millenarian Prophet," Augsburg Fortress Publishers, 1998, ISBN 0-8006-3144-7

15. *How Many Christians Are There in The World?* World Atlas. Updated by Benjamin Elisha Sawe, July 2018. https://www.worldatlas.com/articles/which-countries-have-the-most-christians-around-the world.html

16. The New Testament Documents: Are They Reliable? 5th ed., 1960, p. 119).

17. The Annals, Tacitus, XV:44

18. *Jewish Antiquities*, by Flavius Josephus. Book 18, Chapter 3, paragraphs 1-5. Paragraph 3 is the Testimonium Flavianum itself, which contains the reference to Jesus Christ.

19. *Life of Claudius,* XXV.4:

20. *Life of Nero*, XVI. 2

21. *Epistulae* (Letters), Plinius Secundus; whereby the lawyer and author asks the Emperor for instructions regarding official policy concerning Christians (Epistulae X.96).

22. *Epistulae* (Letters), Plinius Secundus; whereby the lawyer and author asks the Emperor for instructions regarding official policy concerning Christians (Epistulae X.96).

23. Clive S. Lewis, *Mere Christianity* (Harper Collins Publishers, Harper One. 1952. Revised 1980, 2001).

Chapter Three

1. Billy Graham: American Pilgrim. Oxford University Press. June 26, 2017. ISBN 9780190683528.

2. 2019 Charisma Media, Billy Graham Answers: What id the Devil's Most Successful Scheme? https://www.charismamag.com/spirit/spiritual-warfare/33294-billy-graham-answers-what-s-the-devil-s-most-successful-scheme

3. The forgoing story appears in *God In Our Midst: Making the Most Important Decision of Your Life* by Christopher H.K. Persaud in Chapter One – "A Few Recollections," under the sub heading, "The Georgetown Hospital Experience." Pps. 31-32. The publication was the author's first full-length book, and was published by Xlibris Corporation, USA, in 2003.

4. The forgoing story appears in *God In Our Midst: Making the Most Important Decision of Your Life* by Christopher H. K. Persaud in Chapter One – "A Few Recollections," under the sub heading, "The Possessed Child." Pgs. 32-34. The publication was the author's first full-length book, and was published by Xlibris Corporation, USA, in 2003.

5. The forgoing story appears in *God In Our Midst: Making the Most Important Decision of Your Life* by Christopher H. K. Persaud in Chapter One – "A Few Recollections," under the sub heading, "A Strange Happening." Pgs. 30-31. The publication

was the author's first full-length book, and was published by Xlibris Corporation, USA, in 2003.

Chapter Four

1. Book of Revelation, 21:1–4 (ESV)

2. CHRISTIAN TRUTH CENTER. Heaven – The Three Heavens. December 12, 2019. https://www.christiantruthcenter.com/the-3-heavens/

3. CHRISTIAN TRUTH CENTER. Heaven – The Three Heavens. December 12, 2019. https://www.christiantruthcenter.com/the-3-heavens/

4. CHRISTIAN TRUTH CENTER. Heaven – The Three Heavens. December 12, 2019. https://www.christiantruthcenter.com/the-3-heavens/

5. Christian Broadcasting Network (CBN) *Ian MacCormack: Sting of Death*

6. *A Glimpse of Eternity: One Man's Story of Life Beyond Death* by Jenny Sharkey, Arun Books, New Zealand (2008)

7. Don Piper on *Ninety Minutes in Heaven*. Bestselling author of "Ninety Minutes in Heaven" describes how prayer and heavenly assistance helped him survive a devastating car accident. Don Piper, Web Exclusive , February 2015 https://www.guideposts.org/inspiration/life-after-death/don-piper-on-90-minutes-in-heaven

8. *Ninety Minutes in Heaven: A True Story of Death and* Life by Don Piper & Cecil Murphey. (Revell, a division of Baker Publishing Group, Michigan, USA. 2004, 2014)

9. HeavenVisit.com - Heaven, Hell, Rapture and End Times!

10. *A Young Boy Emerges from Life-Saving Surgery with Remarkable Stories of His Visit to Heaven.* (A Christian Broadcasting Network (CBN) article)

11. http://www.heavenvisit.com/Colton_Burpo.php

12. *The Hidden Power of Healing Prayer* by Mahesh Chavda. Destiny Image Publishers Inc. 2001

13. Earthquake Kelley: Saved by a Mother's Prayers

14. *Bound to Lose, Destined to Win by Curtis* "Earthquake" Kelley and Diana Stone. Published by Copper Scroll, 2007

15. Testimonies of Heaven and Hell, End Times, Jesus Christ https://christiscoming777.com/2018/05/22/he-died-saw-the-gates-of-hell-jesus-christ-the-end-time-revival/

Chapter Five

1. A Skydiver's Near Death Experience Falling Into Heaven http://www.heavenvisit.net/mickey-robinson2.html

2. Psalm 16:11 (ESV)

3. *Falling Into Heaven: A Skydiver's Gripping Account of Heaven, Healings and Miracles* by Mickey Robinson & Don Piper (author

of Ninety Minutes in Heaven). Broadstreet Publishing Group, LLC, 2014)

4. Tamara Laroux. *Delivered From Hell - An Amazing Near Death Experience That You Will Never Forget.* December 2011 https://evidenceforchristianity.blogspot.com/2011/12/tamara-laroux-delivered-from-hell.html

5. *A Second Chance at Heaven – My Surprising Journey Through Hell, Heaven and Back to Life* (Emanate Books, 2018) Tamara Laroux (Author); Niki Taylor (Narrator).

6. Bill Wiese – *Escape From Hell.* Christian Broadcasting Network. https://www1.cbn.com/700club/bill-wiese-escape-hell

7. *23 Minutes In Hell: One Man's Story about What He Saw, Heard & Felt in that Place of Torment.* Bill Wiese. Charisma House, a Strang Company, 2006.

8. Athet Pyan Shinthaw Paul - *The Remarkable Testimony of a Buddhist monk in Myanmar (Burma) who came back to life a changed man!* http://www.heavenvisit.com/Athet_Pyan_Shinthaw_Paul.php

9. *My Descent into Death: A Second Chance at Life,* Howard Storm. Foreword by Anne Rice. (Doubleday – A Division of Random House, 2005)

10. Aline Baxley – *I Walked in Hell* http://www.heavenvisit.com/Aline_Baxley_2.php

Chapter Six

1. *Baker Dictionary of Biblical Theology* (1996) by Walter A. Elwell. Published by Baker Books, a division of Baker Book House Company, PO Box 6287, Grand Rapids, Michigan 49516-6287 (p.266)

2. *The Tragedy of Hamlet, Prince of Denmark*, often shortened to Hamlet (/ˈhæmlɪt/), is a tragedy written by William Shakespeare sometime between 1599 and 1602.

3. Sleutjes, A; Moreira-Almeida, A; Greyson, B (2014). "Almost 40 years investigating near-death experiences: an overview of mainstream scientific journals". J. Nerv. Ment. Dis. 202 (11): 833–6.

4. Griffith, LJ (2009). "Near-death experiences and psychotherapy". Psychiatry (Edgmont). 6 (10): 35–42.

5. Vanhaudenhuyse, A.; Thonnard, M.; Laureys, S. (2009). "Towards a Neuro-scientific Explanation of Near-death Experiences?" (PDF). In Vincent, Jean-Louis (ed.). *Yearbook of Intensive Care and Emergency Medicine*. Berlin, Heidelberg: Springer Berlin Heidelberg. ISBN 978-3-540-92276-6.

Chapter Seven

1. Thought Co. - Mary Fairchild, Updated September 24, 2018, https://www.learnreligions.com/christianity-statistics-700533

2. Pew Research Center Religion & Public Life. Demographic Study - December 19, 2011, Global Christianity – A Report on the Size and Distribution of the World's Christian Population

3. https://www.pewforum.org/2011/12/19/global-christianity-exec/

4. James Porter Moreland, *Scaling the Secular City*, (Baker House Books, Grand Rapids, MI, 1987, pg. 167).

5. *Evidence for the Resurrection*, Josh McDowell, Josh McDowell Ministry http://www.bible.ca/d-resurrection-evidence-Josh-McDowell.htm

6. Clark H. Pinnock - as quoted by Josh McDowell in *The Resurrection Factor*, San Bernardino, CA: Here's Life Publishers, 1981, Pg. 9).

7. Paul Maier - as quoted in *The Resurrection of Christ: Myth or Reality?* by Matthew Perman, The Skeptical Review online, 1996, July-August)

8. Paul L. Maier - as quoted by Josh McDowell in *Evidence for the Resurrection*, 1992, Josh McDowell Ministry.

9. Edwin M. Yamauchi, *Easter - Myth, Hallucination, or History?* Christianity Today, March 29, 1974.

10. Simon Greenleaf, *An Examination of the Testimony of the Four Evangelists by the Rules of Evidence Administered in the Courts of Justice*, reprint of the 1874 edition - Grand Rapids: Baker Book House, 1984 Pg. 29.

11. Thomas Arnold, *Sermons on the Christian Life - Its Hopes, Its Fears, and Its Close*, London: Fellowes, 1842 Pg. 324.

12. Ackerman, Susan (2000). "Ark of the Covenant". In Freedman, David Noel; Myers, Allen C. (eds.). Eerdmans Dictionary of the Bible. Eerdmans. p. 102.

13. The Leon Levy Dead Sea Scrolls Digital Library. *Featured Scrolls*. https://www.deadseascrolls.org.il/featured-scrolls

14. The Latin text and English translation are from B. F. Westcott, *A General Survey of the History of the Canon of the New Testament* (5th ed. Edinburgh, 1881), pp. 440, 541–2.

15. Bruce, F. F. (1988). *The Canon of Scripture*. InterVarsity Press. ISBN 978-0-8308-1258-5

16. Josh McDowell, A Skeptic's Quest, Here's Life Publishers, California, 1981.

17. Quoted in Paul D. Wegner, *Textual Criticism of the Bible,* p. 25.

18. Paul D. Wegner, Textual Criticism of the Bible, p. 25

Chapter Eight

1. Rabbi Morris N. Kertzer, revised by Lawrence A. Hoffman, *What is a Jew?* (New York: Collier Books, McMillan Publishing Co. 1993)

2. Jewish Virtual Library – A Project of the 1998-2019 American-Israeli Cooperative Enterprise. *Judaism: The Written Law –*

Torah. https://www.jewishvirtuallibrary.org/the-written-law-torah

3. *Israel 101: Stand With us.* Pgs. 2-3. https://121a6a94-37d0-4344-8957-8394c526443e.filesusr.com/ugd/46fc49_9b707b67913b45e6a4c667a5d0920871.pdf

4. academic.com *The bar Kokhba Revolt ; The Roman Point of View*, by Werner Eck (1999) The Journal of Roman Studies. Vol. 89

   http://www.academicroom.com/article/bar-kokhba-revolt-roman-point-view

5. The Jewish Agency for Israel – Jewish Population Rises to 15.7 Million Worldwide in 2023. Current Jewish Population Reports. *https://www.jewishagency.org/jewish-population-rises-to-15-7-million-worldwide-in-2023/*

6. B'rit Chadashah – The New Covenant. *B'rit Chadashah - The New Covenant of Adonai.* Hebrew for Christians https://hebrew4christians.com/Scripture/Brit_Chadashah/brit_chadashah.html

7. (Rabbi Moses Maimonides, 1134-1204) *Thirteen Principles of Jewish Faith*, Principle 12

8. Answers in Torah. Messianic Judaism (Nazarenes-Netzarim) *Messianic Jews Grow in the World in 2018.*

https://answersintorah.wordpress.com/tag/2-5-million-messianic-jews-in-2018/

9. Learn Religions – *What is the Torah?* Ariela Pelaia (April 2019). https://www.learnreligions.com/what-is-the-torah-2076770

10. Got Questions. Your Questions. Biblical Answers. *What is the Mishnah? What is a Midrash?* https://www.gotquestions.org/Mishnah-midrash.html

11. Got Questions. Your Questions. Biblical Answers. *What is the Talmud?* https://www.gotquestions.org/Talmud.html

12. Modell Klein, comp., *Passover* (New York: Leon Amyl, Publishers, 1973).

Chapter Nine

1. Luther consistently referred to himself as a former monk. For example: "Thus formerly, when I was a monk, I used to hope that I would be able to pacify my conscience with the fastings, the praying, and the vigils with which I used to afflict my body in a way to excite pity. But the more I sweat, the less quiet and peace I felt; for the true light had been removed from my eyes." Martin Luther, *Lectures on Genesis: Chapters 45–50*, ed. Jaroslav Jan Pelikan, Hilton C. Oswald, and Helmut T. Lehmann, vol. 8 *Luther's Works*. (Saint Louis: Concordia Publishing House, 1999), 5:326

2. Ewald M. Plass, *What Luther Says*, 3 vols., (St. Louis: CPH, 1959), 88, no. 269; M. Reu, *Luther and the Scriptures*, (Columbus, Ohio: Wartburg Press, 1944), 23.

3. Luther, Martin. Concerning the Ministry (1523), tr. Conrad Bergendoff, in Bergendoff, Conrad (ed.) Luther's Works. Philadelphia: Fortress Press, 1958, 40:18 ff.

4. *Tyndale's New Testament*, trans. from the Greek by William Tyndale in 1534 in a modern-spelling edition and with an introduction by David Daniell. New Haven, CT: Yale University Press, 1989, ix–x

5. Bainton, Roland. *Here I Stand: a Life of Martin Luther*. New York: Penguin, 1995, 269.

6. Bainton, Roland. *Here I Stand: a Life of Martin Luther*. New York: Penguin, 1995, p. 223.

7. Hendrix, Scott H. *The Controversial Luther, Word & World* 3/4 (1983), Luther Seminary, St. Paul, MN. Also see Hillerbrand, Hans. *The legacy of Martin Luther*, in Hillerbrand, Hans & McKim, Donald K. (eds.) The Cambridge Companion to Luther. Cambridge University Press, 2003.

8. Schaff, Philip: *History of the Christian Church*, Vol. VIII: *Modern Christianity: The Swiss Reformation*, William B. Eerdmans Pub. Co., Grand Rapids, Michigan, USA, 1910, page 706.

9. Richard P. McBrien. *The church, the Evolution of Catholicism* (New York: Harper One, 2008) 447

10. Richard P. McBrien. *The Church, the Evolution of Catholicism* (New York: Harper One, 2008) 447

11. Vatican II documents: *Pastoral Constitution On The Church in the Modern World*: Gaudium et Spes Paragraph 45.

12. Catholic Church – Wikipedia: The Free Encyclopedia

13. Joseph Francis Kelly, *The Ecumenical Councils of the Catholic Church: A History*, (Liturgical Press, 2009), 126-148.

14. Wetterau, Bruce. *World History*. New York: Henry Holt and Company, 1994.

15. The Council of Trent Documents, Fourth Session, *Decree Concerning the Canonical Scriptures*, 1546.

16. James R. White, *The Roman Catholic Controversy* (Minneapolis, MN: Bethany House Publishers, 1996) pp. 55-67

17. Austin Flannery OP, *Vatican Council II*, p.758

18. *Catechism of the Catholic Church*, paragraphs 881,882. In addition, since the decree of Vatican Council I in 1870, the pope enjoys infallibility "in virtue of his office, when as supreme pastor and teacher of all the faithful...he proclaims by a definitive act a doctrine pertaining to faith and morals," (paragraph 891).

19. James R. White, *The Roman Catholic Controversy*, (Minneapolis, MN: Bethany House Publishers, 1996) Chapter 8

20. *Catechism of the Catholic Church*, paragraph 405.

21. *Catechism of the Catholic Church*, paragraph 1519.

22. Anthony Wilheim, *Christ Among Us* (New York: Paulist Press, 1973) pp. 348,349. *Catechism of the Catholic Church*, paragraphs 1590-1600.

23. *Catechism of the Catholic Church*, paragraph 1374. Also, the Council of Trent (A.D. 1551).

24. *Catechism of the Catholic Church*, paragraph 1374. Also, the Council of Trent (A.D. 1551).

25. *Catechism of the Catholic Church*, paragraphs 1365-1367.

26. Matt Slick, President & Founder of CARM (Christian Apologetics & Research Ministry) https://carm.org/dictionary-sanctifying-grace

27. *Catechism of the Catholic Church*, paragraphs 1857-1861.

28. Anthony Wilheim, *Christ Among Us* (New York: Paulist Press, 1973) pp. 298-307.

29. *Catechism of the Catholic Church*, paragraphs 1862, 1863

30. *Catechism of the Catholic Church*, paragraph 1863.

31. *Catechism of the Catholic Church*, paragraph 1460.

32. *Catechism of the Catholic Church*, paragraph 1992

33. In direct refutation of Protestant teaching, the Council of Trent proclaimed that anyone believing the sacraments of the Roman Catholic Church were unnecessary for salvation and he or she could obtain justification through faith alone was anathema (Council of Trent, canons 9,12,14) Also *Catechism of the Catholic Church*, paragraph 1993.

34. Mario Colacci, *The Doctrinal Conflict Between Roman Catholic and Protestant Christianity* (Minneapolis, MN: T.S. Denson & Company, Inc., 1962), pp. 140-142.

35. Karl Keating, *Catholicism and Fundamentalism* (San Francisco: Ignatius Press, 1988) pp. 167,168.

36. Everett F. Harrison, Geoffrey Harrison, Geoffrey Bromiley and Carl F. H. Henry eds. *Biblical Dictionary of Theology* (Grand Rapids, MI: Baker Book House, 1960) p.282.

37. Wayne Gruden, *Systematic Theology: An Introduction to Biblical Doctrine* (Grand Rapids, MI: Zondervan Publishing House, 1994) p.748.

38. Matt Slick, 12/3/08. President & Founder of CARM (Christian Apologetics & Research Ministry) https://carm.org/catholic/purgatory

39. Anthony Wilheim, *Christ Among Us* (New York: Paulist Press, 1973) pp. 298-307. p.420

40. *Catechism of the Catholic Church*, paragraphs 1479, 1498

Chapter Ten

1. Fairchild, Mary, *Eastern Orthodox Denomination*. ThoughtCo. (2017). See also Peter, Laurence. "Orthodox Church Split: Five Reasons Why It Matters". BBC. (2018)

2. Timothy Ware, *The Orthodox Church* (London: Penguin Books, 1997) p. 7.

3. Timothy Ware, *The Orthodox Church* (London: Penguin Books, 1997) p. 246.

4. Daniel Clendenin, *Eastern Orthodox Christianity: A Western Perspective* (Grand Rapids, MI: Baker Books, 1994) p. 32.

5. Matt Slick, President & Founder, Christian Apologetics & Research Ministry (CARM). *What Is the Filioque Clause Controversy? Is it Biblical?* https://carm.org/what-is-the-filioque-clause-controversy-biblical

6. Timothy Ware, *The Orthodox Church* (London: Penguin Books, 1997) p. 27.

7. For more on how Catholics, Orthodox and Protestants see apostolic succession and the early history of the Church, see Mark A. Noll, *Turning Points* (Grand Rapids, MI: Baker Books, 1997), pp.33, 34. See also Richard E. Higginson, *Apostolic Succession*, in Harrison, Bromiley, and Henry, eds., Baker's Dictionary of Theology, p.60

8. Daniel Clendenin, *Eastern Orthodox Christianity: A Western Perspective* (Grand Rapids, MI: Baker Books, 1994) pp. 106,107.

9. Timothy Ware, *The Orthodox Church* (London: Penguin Books, 1997) p.199.

10. Timothy Ware, *The Orthodox Church* (London: Penguin Books, 1997) p.199.

11. Daniel Clendenin, *Eastern Orthodox Christianity: A Western Perspective* (Grand   Rapids, MI: Baker Books, 1994) p.105.

12. Biblica – The International Bible Society. FAQ #7: *How Were the Books of the Bible Chosen?* https://www.biblica.com/resources/bible-faqs/how-were-the-books-of-the-bible-chosen/

13. Georgi Florovsky, quoted in Daniel Clendenin, *Eastern Orthodox Christianity: A Western Perspective* (Grand Rapids, MI: Baker Books, 1994) p.105.

14. Don Fairbairn, *Partakers of the Divine Nature: An Introduction to Eastern Orthodox Thought*, an unpublished paper prepared for Christian workers doing evangelism and discipleship in the former Soviet Union. March 1993, pp. 4, 5.

15. Reverend Thomas Fitzgerald, *The Holy Eucharist*, (Brookline, MA: Greek Orthodox Archdiocese of America, department of Religious Education, (n.d., n.p.)

16. Timothy Ware, *The Orthodox Church* (London: Penguin Books, 1997) p.286.

17. Timothy Ware, *The Orthodox Church* (London: Penguin Books, 1997) pp. 285-287.

18. Timothy Ware, *The Orthodox Church* (London: Penguin Books, 1997) pp. 289, 290.

19. 19. AudioEnglish.org
https://www.audioenglish.org/dictionary/deification.htm

20. AudioEnglish.org
https://www.audioenglish.org/dictionary/deification.htm

21. Church of England (1907). *The Annotated Book of Common Prayer: An Historical, Ritual, and Theological Commentary on the Devotional System of the Church of England.* Longmans, Green and Company. p. 159.

22. When an Orthodox believer once asked his priest why the Church did not do more teaching of doctrine, he responded, "Icons teach us all that we need to know." See Daniel Clendenin, *Why I'm Not Orthodox,* Christianity Today (January 6, 1997) p. 37.

23. Daniel Clendenin, *Eastern Orthodox Christianity: A Western Perspective* (Grand   Rapids, MI: Baker Books, 1994) p.132.

24. Don Fairbairn, *Partakers of the Divine Nature: An Introduction to Eastern Orthodox Thought*, an unpublished paper prepared

for Christian workers doing evangelism and discipleship in the former Soviet Union. March 1993, p.32.

25. Timothy Ware, *The Orthodox Church* (London: Penguin Books, 1997) p. 231

26. Daniel Clendenin, *Eastern Orthodox Christianity: A Western Perspective* (Grand Rapids, MI: Baker Books, 1994) p.130.

27. Don Fairbairn, *Partakers of the Divine Nature: An Introduction to Eastern Orthodox Thought*, an unpublished paper prepared for Christian workers doing evangelism and discipleship in the former Soviet Union. March 1993 p.46.

28. Don Fairbairn, *Partakers of the Divine Nature: An Introduction to Eastern Orthodox Thought,* an unpublished paper prepared for Christian workers doing evangelism and discipleship in the former Soviet Union. March 1993. p.47

29. Daniel Clendenin, *Eastern Orthodox Christianity: A Western Perspective* (Grand Rapids, MI: Baker Books, 1994) p.18

30. Timothy Ware, *The Orthodox Church* (London: Penguin Books, 1997) p. 308

31. C.S. Lewis, Mere Christianity (New York, Macmillan, 1943), p. vii

32. Panagiotes Chrestou, *Partakers of God* (Brookline, MA: Holy Cross Orthodox, 1984)   pp. 19, 20, 28.

Chapter Eleven

1. Atheism is Shrinking – 8 Encouraging Trends in Global Christianity for 2024. Insights: Faith & Culture. *https://research.lifeway.com/2024/01/22/8-encouraging-trends-in-global-christianity-for-2024/*

2. Zuckerman, Phil (2007), *Atheism: Contemporary Rates and Patterns*, Cambridge Companion to Atheism, pp. 47–66, doi:10.1017/CCOL0521842700.004

3. 2018 Bible History Online. https://www.bible-history.com/old-testament/quicksummary.html.

4. *The New Testament Era, The World of the Bible from 500 BC to AD 100* / Author: Bo Reicke (Author) David E. Green (Translator) July 1975

5. *2018 World Atlas.com Largest Religions in the World*, https://www.worldatlas.com/articles/largest-religions-in-the-world.html, September 10, 2018, C.L. Illsley.

6. 2018 Answers in Genesis, *The Flood* https://answersingenesis.org/the-flood/

7. *Learn Religions – The 66 Books of the Bible.* Mary Fairchild, July 2018 https://www.learnreligions.com/books-of-the-bible-700274

8. Payne, J. Barton. 1973. *Encyclopedia of Biblical Prophecy*. New York, NY: Harper & Row.

9. Anon (November 2005). "Author and publisher information". *Science Speaks* by Peter W. Stoner, revised and HTML formatted by Don W. Stoner

10. Josh McDowell, *Evidence That Demands a Verdict*, Vol. 1, pp. 144, 167.

11. Richard Dawkins, *The God Delusion* (Boston: Mariner Books, 2006) p.308

12. Christopher Hitchens, *God is Not Great: How Religion Poisons Everything* (New York: Twelve/Hatchette, 2017) p.56

Chapter Twelve

1. Josh McDowell and Don Stewart, *Handbook of Today's Religions* (Nashville, TN: Thomas Nelson Publishers 1983), pp.304-306

2. The QUAD - *18 Major World Religions.* David A. Tomar, February 2019. https://thebestschools.org/magazine/world-religions-study-starters/

3. Ron Carlson & Ed Decker, *Fast Facts on False Teachings* (Harvest House Publishers, 1994, USA) pps. 23-24

4. Ron Carlson & Ed Decker, *Fast Facts on False Teachings* (Harvest House Publishers, 1994, USA) pp. 24

5. Stargardt, Janice. *Tracing Thoughts Through Things: The Oldest Pali Texts and the Early Buddhist Archaeology of India and*

Burma., Royal Netherlands Academy of Arts and Sciences, 2000, page 25.

6. ThoughtCo - *What's a Bodhisattva? Enlightenment Beings of Mahayana Buddhism* Barbara O'Brien, July 29, 2017, https://www.thoughtco.com/whats-a-bodhisattva-450136

7. Thought Co. *Bodhicitta: Practice for the Benefit of All Beings* – Barbara O'Brien. August 27, 2018, https://www.thoughtco.com/teachings-about-bodhicitta-450009

8. ThoughtCo. *An Explanation of Upaya in Buddhism* – Barbara O'Brien, March 20, 2018, https://www.thoughtco.com/upaya-skillful-or-expedient-means-450018

9. ThoughtCo - *What's a Bodhisattva? Enlightenment Beings of Mahayana Buddhism* Barbara O'Brien, July 29, 2017, https://www.thoughtco.com/whats-a-bodhisattva-450136

10. *Fast Facts & Teachings, Buddhism*, Ron Carlson & Ed Decker, Harvest House Publishers, 1994. Pg. 26

11. Encyclopedia Britannica, 11th Edition, Volume 15, New York, pp 679-680, Article on Karma; Quote - *"Karma meaning deed or action; in addition, it also has philosophical and technical meaning, denoting a person's deeds as determining his future lot."*

12. The Encyclopedia of World Religions, Robert Ellwood & Gregory Alles, ISBN 978-0-8160-6141-9, pp 253; Quote -

"Karma: Sanskrit word meaning action and the consequences of action."

13. Hans Torwesten (1994), Vedanta: Heart of Hinduism, ISBN 978-0802132628, Grove Press New York, pp 97; Quote - *"In the Vedas the word karma (work, deed or action, and its resulting effect) referred mainly to..."*

14. Karma Encyclopedia Britannica (2012).

15. Halbfass, Wilhelm (2000), Karma und Wiedergeburt im indischen Denken, Diederichs, München, Germany.

16. Lawrence C. Becker & Charlotte B. Becker, Encyclopedia of Ethics, 2nd Edition, ISBN 0-415-93672-1, Hindu Ethics, pp 678

17. "Karma" in: John Bowker (1997), The Concise Oxford Dictionary of World *Religions*, Oxford University Press.

Chapter Thirteen

1. "What are hallucinogens?" National Institute of Drug Abuse. January 2016.

2. Norman C. McClelland (2010), *Encyclopedia of Reincarnation and Karma*, McFarland, ISBN 978-0-7864-5675-8

3. World Atlas.com *Largest Religions in the World* https://www.worldatlas.com/articles/largest-religions-in-the-world.html

4. Deutsch 1988, p. 4, Quote: "Advaita Vedanta is more than a philosophical system, as we understand these terms in the West

today; it is also a practical guide to spiritual experience and is intimately bound up with spiritual experience."

5. Erwin Fahlbusch; Geoffrey William Bromiley; David B. Barrett (2005). *The Encyclopedia of Christianity*. William B. Eerdmans. p. 21. ISBN 0-8028-2416-1

6. "Pantheism and Panentheism in non-Western cultures," in: Britannica. Also,

7. Whiting, Robert. *Religions for Today*. Stanley Thomes, London 1991, p. viii. ISBN 0-7487-0586-4

8. DifferenceBetween.com *Difference between Brahma and Brahman*. 7/16/2011 https://www.differencebetween.com/difference-between-brahma-and-vs-brahman/

9. Grimes, John A. (1995). *Ganapati: Song of the Self*. SUNY Series in Religious Studies. Albany: State University of New York Press. ISBN 0-7914-2440-5.

10. Radhakrishnan, Sarvepalli (Editorial Chairman) (1956). *The Cultural Heritage of India*. Calcutta: The Ramakrishna Mission Institute of Culture.

11. For quotation defining the Trimurti see Matchett, Freda. "I realize all the three deities are avatar of Shiva. The Brahma is "Swetamber"(one who wears white clothes), Maha Vishnu is "Pitamber"(one who wears yellow/red/orange clothes) and the Shiva is "Digamber/Vaagamber"(one who doesn't wears any

cloth, only the skin of tiger)." *The Purāṇas*, in: Flood (2003), p. 139.

12. The World's Wisdom in the Palm of your Hand – *The Birth of the War-god*, http://www.sacred-texts.com/hin/sha/sha16.htm

13. Mhatre, Sandeep. *Datta Sampradaay and Their Vital Role*. Swami Samarth temple. Archived from the original.

14. Maas, Philipp A (2006). Samādhipāda: das erste Kapitel des Pātañjalayogaśāstra zum ersten Mal kritisch ediert. Aachen: Shaker. ISBN 3832249877.

15. Michele Desmarais (2008), *Changing Minds: Mind, Consciousness and Identity in Patanjali's Yoga Sutra and Cognitive Neuroscience* Motilal Banarsidass, ISBN 978-8120833364, pages 16-17 with footnotes.

16. Michele Marie Desmarais (2008). *Changing Minds : Mind, Consciousness And Identity In Patanjali's Yoga-Sutra*. Motilal Banarsidass. pp. 15–16. ISBN 978-81-208-3336-4., Quote: "The YS is widely acknowledged to be one of the most important texts in the Hindu tradition and is recognized as the essential text for understanding classical Yoga".

17. Encountering Kali

18. *In the Margins, at the Center, in the West* by Rachel Fell McDermott & Jeffrey J. Kripal (University of California Press, 2003)

19. Indiaonlinepages.com Population In India 2019

20. Busted Halo - *Do Hindus believe in Jesus?* By Neela Kale February 3, 2011, https://bustedhalo.com/questionbox/do-hindus-believe-in-jesus

21. Got Questions – *What is an Avatar in Hinduism?* https://www.gotquestions.org/avatar-hinduism.html

Chapter Fourteen

1. *Mission Islam – Basic Beliefs of a Muslim* http://www.missionislam.com/youth/belief.htm

2. The five pillars of Islam are *Pillars of Islam*. Oxford Centre for Islamic Studies. United Kingdom: Oxford University. Also, *The Five Pillars of Islam*. Canada: University of Calgary.

3. *Ibn Ishaq. Mustadrak Al-Hakim.* 3. p. 182. Muḥammad ibn Isḥāq ibn Yasār ibn Khiyār was an Arab Muslim historian and hagiographer. Ibn Ishaq collected oral traditions that formed the basis of an important biography of the Islamic prophet Muhammad

4. *Ibn Ishaq. Mustadrak Al-Hakim.* 3. p. 182. Muḥammad ibn Isḥāq ibn Yasār ibn Khiyār was an Arab Muslim historian and hagiographer. Ibn Ishaq collected oral traditions that formed the basis of an important biography of the Islamic prophet Muhammad

5. A Saginian, Armen (12 July 2011). Mission For Mohammad And Islam: Book One: *Verses of Mecca Words of Allah as Revealed to Mohammad*. Xlibris. p. 12. ISBN 978-1462873289.

6. Shaikh, Fazlur Rehman (2001). *Chronology of Prophetic Events*. London: Ta-Ha Publishers Ltd. pp. 51–52.

7. *What Makes Islam So Different?–* The Banu Qurayza The Religion of Peace.com 2002-2019 https://www.thereligionofpeace.com/pages/muhammad/qurayza.aspx

8. *What Makes Islam So Different? –* The Banu Qurayza The Religion of Peace.com 2002-2019 https://www.thereligionofpeace.com/pages/muhammad/qurayza.aspx

9. *What Makes Islam So Different? What Does Islam Teach About Violence?* 2002-2019 The Religion of Peace.Com https://www.thereligionofpeace.com/pages/quran/violence.aspx

10. Infoplease - The Top Ten: Organized Religions of the World © 2000–2018 Sandbox Networks, Inc., publishing as Infoplease https://www.infoplease.com/top-ten-organized-religions-world

11. Bart D. Ehrman (1997). *The New Testament: A Historical Introduction to the Early Christian Writings*. Oxford University Press. p. 8. ISBN 978-0-19-508481-8. The New Testament contains twenty-seven books, written in Greek, by fifteen or sixteen different authors, who were addressing other Christian individuals or communities between the years 50 and 120 C.E. It is difficult to know whether any of these books was written by Jesus' own disciples.

12. Compare: Hammer, Olav; Rothstein, Mikael, eds. (2012). "16". *The Cambridge Companion to New Religious Movements.* Cambridge University Press. p. 263. 'Jihadism' is a term that has been constructed in Western languages to describe militant Islamic movements that are perceived as existentially threatening to the West. Western media have tended to refer to Jihadism as a military movement rooted in political Islam.

13. Answering Islam – A Christian-Muslim Dialog. *The Problem of Abrogation in the Quran* by Farooq Ibrahim.

14. https://answering-islam.org/Authors/Farooq_Ibrahim/abrogation.htm

15. Neal Robinson (2013), *Islam: A Concise Introduction*, Routledge, ISBN 978-0878402243, Chapter 7, pp. 85-89

16. Mir, Mustansir. (1995). "Tafsīr". In John L. Esposito. *The Oxford Encyclopedia of the Modern Islamic World.* Oxford: Oxford University Press.

17. Compelling Truth – *What is Animism? What Do Animists believe?* Copyright 2011-2019 Got Questions Ministries - All Rights Reserved. Christian Truth

18. ThoughtCo. *A History of the Crescent Moon in Islam.* https://www.thoughtco.com/the-crescent-moon-a-symbol-of-islam-2004351

19. Women's Rights in Islam – Fighting for Equality. By Dina Elbasnaly and Lewis Sanders IV.

https://www.dw.com/en/womens-rights-in-islam-fighting-for-equality-before-the-law/a-53539222

Chapter Fifteen

1. Walter R. Martin, *Kingdom of the Cults* (Bethany House Publishers, 1992) p.87.

2. Walter R. Martin, *Kingdom of the Cults* (Bethany House Publishers, 1992) pps. 83- 87.

3. Richard Abanes, *Cults, New Religious Movements & Your Family* (Wheaton , IL: Crossway Books, 1998) pp. 235, 237.

4. Richard Abanes, *Cults, New Religious Movements & Your Family* (Wheaton , IL: Crossway Books, 1998) p. 239.

5. Richard Abanes, *Cults, New Religious Movements & Your Family* (Wheaton, IL: Crossway Books, 1998) p. 240, 241.

6. Watchtower & Bible Tract Society 2018 Grand Totals. https://www.jw.org/en/library/books/2018-service-year-report/2018-grand-totals/

7. Bible Study.org – *When was the Old Testament Written?* http://www.biblestudy.org/beginner/when-was-old-testament-written.html

8. Bible Study.org – *When was the Old Testament Written?* http://www.biblestudy.org/beginner/when-was-new-testament-written.html

9. Answers in Genesis: *How Do We Know that the Bible Is True?* Apologetics by Dr. Jason Lisle on March 22, 2011, https://answersingenesis.org/is-the-bible-true/how-do-we-know-that-the-bible-is-true/

10. Douglas Beaumont – *Theology. Philosophy. Apologetics. Jesus in the Hands of the New World Translation* https://douglasbeaumont.com/2012/03/19/jesus-in-the-hands-of-the-new-world-translation/ March 2012

11. Also, *Reasoning From the Scriptures with the Jehovah Witnesses* by Ron Rhodes. Harvest House Publishers 1993/2009

12. Ron Carlson & Ed Decker, *Fast facts on False Teachings* (Eugene, OR: Harvest House Publishers, 1994) p.126.

13. Apologetics Index, 2019 This article is related to: David Kowalski, Jehovah's Witnesses, *Trinity* http://www.apologeticsindex.org/563-trinity-doctrine-2

Chapter Sixteen

1. *Articles of Faith: A Series of Lectures on the Principal Doctrines of The Church of Jesus Christ of Latter-Day Saints,* James E. Talmage. p. 35)

2. 1 Nephi 13:28; *Pearl of Great Price*, Joseph Smith – History 1:18, 19

3. *Mormon Doctrine*, Bruce R. McConkie, 1958. p. 670; 1 Nephi 14:10

4. George A. Mather & Larry A. Nichols. *Dictionary of Cults, Sects, Religions and the Occult* (Grand Rapids, MI: Zondervan Publishing House, 1993), pp.186-188. See also Daniel H. Ludlow. Ed., *Encyclopedia of Mormonism*, vol. 2, *History of the Church* (New York: Macmillan Publishing Co., 1992) pp. 598-601.

5. Daniel H. Ludlow, *The Encyclopedia of Mormonism,* vol. 2 (New York Macmillan Publishing Co., 1992) pp. 613, 860-862.

6. See also Kurt Van Gorden, *Mormonism, Zondervan Guide to Cults and Religious Movements*, p. 11, and *Documentary History of the Church of Jesus Christ of Latter Day Saints*, 6 vols., B. H. Roberts, ed. (Salt Lake City: Desert Book Co., 1976), 7:102.

7. Roberts, David. "The Brink of War". Smithsonian Magazine. Smithsonian Institution.

8. Excerpts from three addresses by President Wilford Woodruff regarding the Manifesto," in Doctrine & Covenants , pp. 292, 293

9. Schaff-Herzog, Encyclopedia of Religious Knowledge, Vol. VIII, p. 17.

10. http://www.mazeministry.com/mormonism/mmmassacre/newmm/mm1.htm

11. The Church of Jesus Christ of Latter Day Saints. 2022 Statistical Report for the April 2023 Conference. - Salt Lake City News

Release https://newsroom.churchofjesuschrist.org/article/2022-statistical-report-april-2023-conference

12. History of the (Mormon) Church by Joseph Smith, 1991, 4:461

13. *Articles of Faith: A Series of Lectures on the Principal Doctrines of The Church of Jesus Christ of Latter-Day Saints*, James E. Talmage. p. 182–185.

14. *Teachings of the Prophet Joseph Smith*, 1977, p. 345

15. *Mormon Doctrine and Covenants* 130:22.

16. *Mormon Doctrine*, Bruce R. McConkie, 1958 p. 348

17. 2 Nephi 25:23; *Articles of Faith: A Series of Lectures on the Principal Doctrines of The Church of Jesus Christ of Latter-Day Saints*, James E. Talmage. p.79.

18. Journal of Discourses, vol. 8, p. 115; Mormon Doctrine, p. 547.

19. Doctrine and Covenants 132:20; Teachings of the Prophet Joseph Smith, p. 345–354.

20. *Latter Day Saints Bible Dictionary*, p. 697

21. *Fast Facts on False Teachings*, Ron Carlson & Ed Decker (Harvest House Publishers, 1994) pp. 167 -170

22. Joseph Smith, Times & Seasons, volume 5, page 613. Also, LDS encyclopedic work Mormon Doctrine by Bruce R. McConkie, page 321.

23. Brigham Young, *Journal of Discourses*, volume 10, page 223

24. Brigham Young, *Mormon Doctrines*, page 577

25. *Early Mormonism and the Magic World View*. Salt Lake City: Signature Books. ISBN 0-941214-46-X, 1987. Revised in 1998.

26. *The Pearl of Great Price*, Joseph Smith, chapter 2, verse 19

27. Pomeroy Tucker, *Origin, Rise and Progress of Mormonism*, p. 16, 1867, New York.

Chapter Seventeen

1. Miller, William (1845). Wm. Miller's Apology and Defense. Boston, MS: Joshua V. Himes. Pg. 5

2. W. Miller, Evidence from Scripture and History of the Second Coming of Christ, about the Year 1843. A Yesterday's World Publishing (February 7, 2020)

3. Ellen G. White Biography". Ellen G. White Estate *https://whiteestate.org/resources/pioneers/ewhite/*

4. ThoughtCo., The Arian Controversy & the Council of Nicea. By N.S. Gill, May 21, 2019, *https://www.thoughtco.com/arian-controversy-and-council-of-nicea-111752*

5. ThoughtCo., The Arian Controversy & the Council of Nicea. By N.S. Gill, May 21, 2019 *https://www.thoughtco.com/arian-controversy-and-council-of-nicea-111752*

6. The Great Controversy, Ellen White. Independently published, July 2022. Pg. 485.

7. The Gospel Coalition – The Biblical Covenants. Paul R. Williamson. *https://www.thegospelcoalition.org/essay/the-biblical-covenants/*

8. Got Questions. Your Questions. Biblical Answers. What is the Sabbath, Saturday   or Sunday? https://www.gotquestions.org/Saturday-Sunday.html

9. Counsels on Diet & Foods, Ellen G. White. Review and Herald Publishers. p. 390

10. Spirit Life Magazine – Why Seventh Day Adventism is a Cult. Jubilee Resources International Inc. April 2, 2022. https://www.spiritlifemag.com/why-seventh-day-adventists-are-a-cult/

11. Got Questions. Your Questions. Biblical Answers. What Happens After Death? https://www.gotquestions.org/what-happens-after-death.html

12. Bible & Theology - J.I. Packer on Why Annihilationism Is Wrong. Oct. 7, 2015.

13. The Adventist Ministry Magazine, October 1981, p. 8

14. *The Pillars of Adventism*, Ellen G. White. p. 28)

15. Ellen White's Role in Adventist History. Pgs. 3, 5,

16. *The White Lie* by Walter T. Rea. One Stone Press, 2021

Chapter Eighteen

1. Russell Chandler, *Understanding the New Age* (Dallas, TX. Word Publishing, 1988), p.17

2. J. Gordon Melton, *Encyclopedic Handbook of Cults in America* (New York and London: Garland Publishing, 1986) p.113

3. Russell Chandler, *Understanding the New Age* (Dallas, TX: Word Publishing, 1988), p.17

4. John Macquarie, *Existentialism*, New York (1972), pp. 14–15.2.

5. Crowell, Steven (October 2010). *Existentialism*. Stanford Encyclopedia of Philosophy. *Oxford Companion to Philosophy*, ed. Ted Honderich, New York (1995), p. 259

6. Sutcliffe, Steven J.; Gilhus, Ingvild Sælid (2013). *New Age Spirituality: Rethinking Religion*. Durham, UK: Acumen. pp. 1–16. ISBN 978-1844657148.

7. "New Age Movement" (2006). In Wouter Hanegraaff (editor) (eds.). Dictionary of Gnosis and Western Esotericism. Leiden: Brill. pp. 855–861. ISBN 978-9004152311.

8. York, Michael (1995) *The Emerging Network: A Sociology of the New Age and Neo-Pagan Movements.* London: Rowman & Littlefield. ISBN 9780847680016.

9. SensAgent: Harmonic Convergence (Wikipedia) http://dictionary.sensagent.com/harmonic%20convergence/en-en/

10. Answers in Genesis, World Religions & Cults. Volume 2. The New Age Movement (Pantheism & Monism), Dr. Don Rhodes, August 29, 2018/

11. Dr. Neil T. Anderson, *Walking Through the Darkness: Discerning God's Guidance in the New Age*, pg. 22. Here's Life Publishers, 1991

Chapter Nineteen

1. Charles Colson, Nancy Pearcey, *How Now Shall We Live?* Tyndale House Publishers, Inc. 1999, p.54

2. George M. Mardsen, index references under "Evolution" in *The Soul of the American University: From Protestant Establishment to Established Nonbelief.* (New York: Oxford University Press, 1994).

3. *NABT Unveils New Statement on Teaching Evolution,* The American Biology Teacher, 68, no. 1 (January 1996), p. 61, quoted in Colson & Pearcey, "How Now Shall We Live," p.82.

4. Douglas Futuyma, *Evolutionary Biology* (Sunderland, MA: Sinauer, 1986) p. 3.

5. William J. Provine and Philip E. Johnson, *Darwinism: Science or Naturalistic Philosophy?,* videotape of debate held at Stanford University. April 30, 1994, quoted in Colson & Pearcey, *How Now Shall We Live?* p.92.

6. Charles Darwin, *The Origin of the Species by Means of Natural Selection* (New American Library, 1958) p.450

7. David A. Nobel, *Understanding the Times* (Eugene, OR: Harvest House Publishers, 1991) p. 266

8. Lane Lester & Raymond Bohlin, *The Natural Limits to Biological Change*, 1984. Probe Books, Richardson, Texas, USA)

9. Cohen, I.L. (1984) *Darwin Was Wrong: A Study in Probabilities*, New York: New Research Publications, Inc. p.205

10. The following books and texts contain excellent discussions on how the fossil record, gene mutation and the complexity of the cell all disprove Darwinian evolution. (a) Charles Colson, Nancy Pearcey, *How Now Shall We Live?* Tyndale House Publishers, Inc. 1999, Chapter 9, "Darwin In The Dock," pp.83-90 (b) Philip Johnson, *Darwin on Trial*, (Downers Grove, IL: InterVarsity Press, 1993) Chapter 5, "Intelligent Design," pp. 75ff. (c) Philip Johnson, *Defeating Darwinism By Opening Minds* (Downers Grove, IL: InterVarsity Press, 1997) "Opening the Black Boxes of Biology." (d) Michael Denton, *Evolution In Crisis*, Adler & Adler, Publisher's Inc. 1986. (e) See Tom Woodward's article, *Meeting Darwin's Wager*, Christianity Today (April 28, 1997), pp. 15-21 for a thorough discussion of Michael Behe's work and how it destroys the theory of Darwinian macroevolution.

11. Brosius, J (2009), "The Fragmented Gene", Annals of the New York Academy of Sciences, 1178 (1): 186–93,

Bibcode:2009NYASA1178..186B, doi:10.1111/j.1749-6632.2009.05004.x

12. Ridley M (2006). *Genome: The Autobiography of a Species in 23 Chapters* (PDF). New York: Harper Perennial. ISBN 978-0-06-019497-0

13. Stephen J. Gould, *Evolution's Erratic Pace* – Natural History, May 1977, p.13.

14. Richard Dawkins, *The Blind Watchmaker*, Norton & Company, Inc. 1987, pp. 229-230.

15. Jeffrey H. Schwartz, *Sudden Origins: Fossils, Genes, and the Emergence of Species* (New York. John Wiley, 1999), p. 300.

16. Barnes, J., *Early Greek Philosophy*, Penguin Books, London, England, p. 72, 1987.

17. Cartledge, P., *Democritus*, Phoenix, London, England, pp. 20–21, 1998.

18. *The Epicurus Reader: Selected Writings and Testimonia*, translated and edited by Brad Inwood and L.P. Gerson, introduction by D.S. Hutchinson, Hackett Publishing Company, 1994.

19. Pliny the Elder, *Natural History*, translated with an introduction and notes by John F. Healy, Penguin Books, London, England, p. 13, 1991

20. From *The Mundaka Upanishad, Understanding Hinduism*, pp. 5–9, <www.hinduism.org.za/creation.htm>.

21. *The Bhagavad Gita*, translation and introduction by Eknath Easwaran, Penguin, Arkana, p. 142, 1985.

22. Pliny the Elder, *Natural History*, translated with an introduction and notes by John F. Healy, Penguin Books, London, England, p. 13, 1991.

23. Augustine of Hippo, *City of God* 18:40, about the most mendacious vanity of the Egyptians, in which they ascribe to their science an antiquity of a hundred thousand years, AD>410, <www.ccel.org/ccel/schaff/npnf102.iv.XVIII.40.html>.

24. These figures are based on the Greek Septuagint translation (ca. 250 BC), while the English Bibles are mainly translated from the standard Hebrew (Masoretic) text. Dr. Pete Williams shows why the Masoretic Text is likely to be closer to the original Hebrew in *Some Remarks Preliminary to a Biblical Chronology,* Journal *of* Creation 12(1):98–106, 1998; <creation.com/chronology>.

25. Jonathan Gray, *The Forbidden Secret*, TEACH SERVICES, Inc. www.TEACHServices.com (2011) p.43

26. Johanson, Z.; Long, J. A; Talent, J. A; Janvier, P.; Warren, J. W (2006). *"Oldest coelacanth, from the Early Devonian of Australia"*. Biology Letters. 2 (3): 443–6. doi:10.1098/rsbl.2006.0470. PMC 1686207. PMID 17148426.

27. Forey, Peter L (1998). *History of the Coelacanth Fishes*. London: Chapman & Hall. ISBN 978-0-412-78480-4.

28. Friedman, Matt; Coates, Michael I. (2006). "A newly recognized fossil coelacanth highlights the early morphological diversification of the clade". Proceedings of the Royal Society B: Biological Sciences. 273 (1583): 245–50. doi:10.1098/rspb.2005.3316. JSTOR 25223279. PMC 1560029. PMID 16555794.

29. Institute for Creation Research, *New Population Found of Damselfly 'Living Fossil'*, Brian Thomas, Ph.D., January 19, 2010. https://www.icr.org/article/5160/

30. Restak, Richard, *The Brain: The Last Frontier*, 1979, p. 390

31. The Brain, Our Universe Within, PBS Video

32. *Wonders of God's Creation*, Moody Video Series

33. Weiss, Joseph, *Unconscious Mental Functioning*, Scientific American, March 1990, p. 103

34. Webb, Jonathan (10 August 2016). "Piltdown review points decisive finger at forger Dawson". British Broadcasting Corporation.

35. Science of NBC News.com *Scientists Recover T-rex Soft Tissue – 70 million-year fossil yields preserved blood vessels*. March 2005. Associated Press /id/7285683/ns/technology_and_science-science/t/scientists-recover-t-rex-soft-tissue/#.XQpyxohKhPZ.

36. Answers In Genesis, DNA – The Language of Life, November 2010

37. *Darwin's Black Box: The Biochemical Challenge to Evolution* by Michael J. Behe Free Press, a Division of Simon & Schuster, March 2006.

38. Evolution: A Theory in Crisis – A Biochemical Challenge to Evolution. Michael Denton. Adler & Adler Publishers, Inc. (1986) p. 358.

39. *Defeating Darwinism by Opening Minds*, Phillip E. Johnson, (Intervarsity Press, 1997) p. 113.

40. Clark, Stuart (2008), *How Come Earth Got All the Good Stuff?*, New Scientist, 199[2675]: p. 29

41. Clark, Stuart (2008), *How Come Earth Got All the Good Stuff?,* New Scientist, 199[2675]: p. 29.

42. Harry Rimmer, *The Magnificence of Jesus*, Wm. B. Eerdmans (1946) p.116.

Chapter Twenty

1. Harrington, Walt. *Anton LaVey - America's Satanic Master of Devils, Magic, Music, and Madness*. The Washington Post Magazine, February 23, 1986.

2. An Interview with Church of Satan High Priest Peter Gilmore *http://en.wikinews.org/wiki/Satanism*:

3. Zachary King - 2010 U.S. census on witchcraft and Satanism (Crusade Magazine).

4. Zachary King - 2010 U.S. census on witchcraft and Satanism (Crusade Magazine).

   1980 Statistics relating to occultists, Muslims, Buddhist, Unitarians – 2% of Americans.

5. Anton La Vey (Church of Satan). Church officially established as a non-profit religious organization with the U.S. government on September 20, 1971.

6. Lists of movies retrieved from Best Simlar.com - *Occult Movies & TV Shows https://bestsimilar.com/tag/3091-occult*

7. Ron Carlson & Ed Decker, *Fast Facts on False Teachings*, Harvest House Publishers, Eugene, Oregon, USA, 1994, p.239.

   From "Reign in Blood," Rick Rubin

8. The Association for Child & Adolescent Mental Health, *Psychotic Experiences: What They Are & Why We care About Them?* JCPP Journal. Posted June 4, 2019. C. Healy, H. Coughlan, J. Williams, M. Clarke, I. Kelleher, M. Cannon (2019)

   https://www.acamh.org/research-digests/psychotic-experiences-what-they-are-and-why-we-care-about-them/

Chapter Twenty-One

Bahai Faith

1. John Boykin, *The Baha'i Faith,* chap 2 in Ronald Enroth & Others, *A Guide to Cults & New Religions*, (Downers Grove, II: InterVarsity Press, 1983), p.26; See also Walter Martin, *The Kingdom of the Cults, Updated and Expanded*, gen. ed. Hank Hanegraaff (Minneapolis: Bethany House Publishers, 1997), p. 321.

2. George A. Mather and Larry A. Nichols, *Dictionary of Cults, Sects, Religions and the Occult* (Grand Rapids, MI: Zondervan Publishing House, 1993), p.32

3. The number of 5-7 million was obtained from *Conservapedia – World Religions by Number of Followers*. Updated July 2016. *https://www.conservapedia.com/World_Religions_by_Number_ of_Followers#cite_note-1*

4. According to Baha'i teachings, there were nine manifestations in all. In addition to the even named in the text, Mirza Ali Mohammed (The Bab) was the eighth manifestation, followed 13 years after his death by Baha'u'llah, considered the last and greatest manifestation of all.

5. John Walbridge, *Sacred Acts, Sacred Place, Sacred Time*. Oxford, George Ronald, 1966

6. *http://bahai-library.com/walbridge_encyclopedia_prayer_worship*

7. Hatcher, W.S.; Martin, J.D. (1998). *The Bahá'í Faith: The Emerging Global Religion.* Wilmette, Illinois, USA: Bahá'í Publishing Trust. pp. 156–157. ISBN 0-87743-264-3.

8. Shoghi Effendi, *World Order of Baha'u'llah* (Wilmette, IL: Baha'i Publishing Trust, 1995), pp. 40,41, quoted in Enroth & Others, A Guide to Cults, pp. 30,31.

9. Ronald Enroth & Others, *A Guide to Cults & New Religions*, (Downers Grove, II: InterVarsity Press, 1983) pp. 31,32.

10. Walter Martin, *The Kingdom of the Cults, Updated, and Expanded,* gen. ed. Hank Hanegraaff (Minneapolis: Bethany House Publishers, 1997)

11. Ronald Enroth & Others, *A Guide to Cults & New Religions*, (Downers Grove, II: InterVarsity Press, 1983) pp. 31,32

12. Shoghi Effendi, *World Order of Baha'u'llah* (Wilmette, IL: Baha'i Publishing Trust, 1995), p.133, quoted in Enroth & Others, A Guide to Cults, p. 28.

Christian Science

1. Walter Martin, *The Kingdom of the Cults, Updated, and Expanded*, gen. ed. Hank Hanegraaff (Minneapolis: Bethany House Publishers, 1997) p.245.

2. Encyclopedia Britannica (2019 Encyclopedia Britannica, Inc.) *Christian Science – History, Organization & Development of Christian Science*. Written by: Stephen Gottschalk J. Gordon Melton https://www.britannica.com/topic/Christian-Science

3. Pickren, W.E. and Rutherford, A. (2010) *A History of Modern Psychology in Context*, John Wiley and Sons. p 93.

4. Walter Martin, *The Kingdom of the Cults, Updated, and Expanded*, gen. ed. Hank Hanegraaff (Minneapolis: Bethany House Publishers, 1997) pp. 249, 250.

5. Walter Martin, *The Kingdom of the Cults, Updated, and Expanded*, gen. ed. Hank Hanegraaff (Minneapolis: Bethany House Publishers, 1997) pp. 250, 253.

6. Walter Martin, *The Kingdom of the Cults, Updated, and Expanded*, gen. ed. Hank Hanegraaff (Minneapolis: Bethany House Publishers, 1997) pp. 254, 255.

7. *Science and Health with a Key to the Scriptures*, Mary Baker Eddy (1875) pp.256, 361. Quoted in Walter Martin, *The Kingdom of the Cults, Updated, and Expanded*, gen. ed. Hank Hanegraaff (Minneapolis: Bethany House Publishers, 1997) p.250

8. *Science and Health with a Key to the Scriptures*, Mary Baker Eddy (1875) p. 468. Quoted in Walter Martin, *The Kingdom of the Cults, Updated, and Expanded*, gen. ed. Hank Hanegraaff (Minneapolis: Bethany House Publishers, 1997) p.252.

9. Walter Martin, *The Kingdom of the Cults, Updated, and Expanded*, gen. ed. Hank Hanegraaff (Minneapolis: Bethany House Publishers, 1997) p.262.

10. Todd Ehrenborg - *Mind Science, Religious Science*, Unity School of Christianity, *Zondervan Guide to Cults & Religious Movements*, series ed. Alan W. Gomes (Grand Rapids , MI: Zondervan Publishing House, 1995) p.12.

11. *Science and Health with a Key to the Scriptures*, Mary Baker Eddy (1875) p. 447. Quoted in Walter Martin, *The Kingdom of the Cults, Updated, and Expanded,* gen. ed. Hank Hanegraaff (Minneapolis: Bethany House Publishers, 1997) p. 260

12. Todd Ehrenborg, *Mind Science, Religious Science*, Unity School of Christianity, *Zondervan Guide to Cults & Religious Movements*, series ed. Alan W. Gomes (Grand Rapids , MI: Zondervan Publishing House, 1995) pp. 15, 16.

13. *Science & Health, with a Key to the Scriptures*, Mary Baker Eddy (1875) pp. 256, 361, quoted in Walter Martin, *The Kingdom of the Cults, Updated, and Expanded*, gen. ed. Hank Hanegraaff (Minneapolis: Bethany House Publishers, 1997) p.259.

14. *Science & Health, with a Key to the Scriptures*, Mary Baker Eddy (1875) p. 466, quoted in Walter Martin, *The Kingdom of the Cults, Updated, and Expanded,* gen. ed. Hank Hanegraaff (Minneapolis: Bethany House Publishers, 1997) p.250

15. *Science & Health, with a Key to the Scriptures*, Mary Baker Eddy (1875) pp. 25,45, 46 quoted in Walter Martin, The Kingdom of the Cults, Updated, and *Expanded*, gen. ed. Hank

Hanegraaff (Minneapolis: Bethany House Publishers, 1997) p. 260

16. *Science & Health, with a Key to the Scriptures,* Mary Baker Eddy (1875) p. 266 quoted in Walter Martin, *The Kingdom of the Cults, Updated, and Expanded,* gen. ed. Hank Hanegraaff (Minneapolis: Bethany House Publishers, 1997) p. 261

17. *Miscellaneous Writings*, Mary Baker Eddy (Bookmark Inc., KS, 1992) p.261, quoted in Walter Martin, *The Kingdom of the Cults, Updated, and Expanded,* gen. ed. Hank Hanegraaff (Minneapolis: Bethany House Publishers, 1997) p.261

18. Todd Ehrenborg, *Mind Science, Religious Science*, Unity School of Christianity, *Zondervan Guide to Cults & Religious Movements*, series ed. Alan W. Gomes (Grand Rapids , MI: Zondervan Publishing House, 1995) p.20. Ehrenborg summarizes the teachings of *Science & Health with a Key to the Scriptures* (Mary Baker Eddy, 1875) concerning the Trinity, which appear on pp. 588:7, 8; 55:27-29.

19. *Science & Health, with a Key to the Scriptures*, Mary Baker Eddy (1875) p. 2, quoted in Walter Martin, *The Kingdom of the Cults, Updated, and Expanded,* gen. ed. Hank Hanegraaff (Minneapolis: Bethany House Publishers, 1997) p. 277

Cultural Relativism

1. Cultural Relativism. The Encyclopedia of World Problems and Human Potential. Retrieved June 1, 2024

2. What is Anthropology?. American Anthropological Association. Retrieved 1 June 2024

3. What is Anthropology?. American Anthropological Association Retrieved 1 June 2024.

4. What is Anthropology?. American Anthropological Association Retrieved 1 June 2024 Wikipedia: The Free Encyclopedia – Moral Relativism

5. *https://en.wikipedia.org/wiki/Moral_relativism*

6. Tomlinson, John (1991). Cultural Imperialism : A critical introduction. Baltimore, Md.: Johns Hopkins University Press.

The Illuminati Conspiracy

1. The Week - What is the Illuminati Conspiracy Theory? *https://theweek.com/62399/what-is-the-illuminati-and-what-does-it-control*

2. Vox – Nine Questions about the Illuminati You Were Too Afraid to Ask. By Phil Edwards. January 19, 2016.

3. Vox – Nine Questions about the Illuminati You Were Too Afraid to Ask. By Phil Edwards. January 19, 2016.

4. The Independent - What is the 'New World Order' and why has Joe Biden caused uproar by using the phrase? By Joe Sommerlad. March 24, 2022.

https://www.independent.co.uk/news/world/americas/us-politics/new-world-order-meaning-biden-b2043111.html

Transcendental Meditation

1. Beckford, James A. (1985). *Cult controversies: The Societal Response to New* Religious *Movements.* Tavistock Publications. p. 23. ISBN 978-0-422-79630-9.

2. Stark, Rodney; Bainbridge, William, Sims (1986). *The Future of Religion.* University of California Press. p. 287. ISBN 978-0520057319

3. Peterson, William (1982). *Those Curious New Cults in the 80s.* New Canaan, Connecticut: Keats Publishing. pp. 123. ISBN 9780879833176

4. Stephanie van den Berg, Sydney Morning Herald, *Beatles Guru Maharishi Mahesh Yogi Dies.* (7 February 2008) - The TM movement, which has some five million followers worldwide.

5. Maharishi Mahesh Yogi, *Transcendental Meditation*, Penguin Publishing Group, 1968 pp. 267-269

6. Maharishi Mahesh Yogi, Transcendental Meditation, Penguin Publishing Group, 1968 p. 46

7. Paul Courtright, in *Gods of Flesh/Gods of Stone* (Joanne Punzo Waghorne, Norman Cutler, and Vasudha Narayanan, eds), ISBN 978-0231107778, Columbia University Press, see Chapter 2.

8. Maharishi Mahesh Yogi, *Meditations of Maharishi Mahesh Yogi* (Bantam Books, 1973) pp.17, 18

9. Kenneth W. Morgan, *The Religion of the Hindus* (Motilal Banarsidass Publishers, 1996) p. 24.

10. Fast Facts & Teachings - Transcendental Meditation, *Ron Carlson & Ed Decker, Harvest* House Publishers, 1994. p 256

Freemasonry

1. John Ankerberg and John Weldon, *The Secret Teachings of the Masonic Lodge: A Christian Perspective* (Chicago, IL: Moody Press, 1989, 1990), p.10

2. George A. Maher and Larry A Nichols, *Masonic Lodge, Zondervan Guide to Cults and Religious Movements*, series ed. Alan W. Gomes (Grand Rapids, MI: Zondervan Publishing House, 1995), pp. 10-24

3. None of these claims is supported by historical evidence. See George Maher and Larry A Nichols, *Masonic Lodge, Zondervan Guide to Cults and Religious Movements*, series ed. Alan W. Gomes (Grand Rapids, MI: Zondervan Publishing House, 1995), pp. 7, 8.

4. Larry A Nichols, *Masonic Lodge, Zondervan Guide to Cults and Religious Movements*, series ed. Alan W. Gomes (Grand Rapids, MI: Zondervan Publishing House, 1995), pp. 7, 8.

5. Larry A Nichols, *Masonic Lodge, Zondervan Guide to Cults and Religious Movements*, series ed. Alan W. Gomes (Grand Rapids, MI: Zondervan Publishing House, 1995), pp. 7, 8.

6. Roth, Randolph A. (2002). *The Democratic Dilemma: Religion, Reform, and the Social Order in the Connecticut River Valley of Vermont.* Cambridge, UK: Cambridge University Press. p. 152. ISBN 978-0-521-30183-1.

7. Masonic Service Association of North America. Masonic member Statistics 2016-2017 http://www.msana.com/msastats.asp

8. George Maher and Larry A Nichols, *Masonic Lodge, Zondervan Guide to Cults and Religious Movements*, series ed. Alan W. Gomes (Grand Rapids, MI: Zondervan Publishing House, 1995), pp. 7, 8., p. 9.

9. Webster's New World Dictionary (New Jersey: Prentice Hall, 1970, 1988)

10. George Maher and Larry A Nichols, *Masonic Lodge, Zondervan Guide to Cults and Religious Movements,* series ed. Alan W. Gomes (Grand Rapids, MI: Zondervan Publishing House, 1995), p. 40.

11. John J. Robinson, *Born in Blood: The Lost Secrets* of Freemasonry (New York: M. Evans & Company, 1989), p. 177. Also John Ankerberg and John Weldon, *The Secret Teachings of*

the Masonic Lodge: A Christian Perspective (Chicago, IL: Moody Press, 1989, 1990), pp. 244-253.

12. George Maher and Larry A Nichols, *Masonic Lodge, Zondervan Guide to Cults and Religious Movements*, series ed. Alan W. Gomes (Grand Rapids, MI: Zondervan Publishing House, 1995), pp, 24, 25.

13. George Maher and Larry A Nichols, *Masonic Lodge, Zondervan Guide to Cults and Religious Movements,* series ed. Alan W. Gomes (Grand Rapids, MI: Zondervan Publishing House, 1995), p. 42.

14. George Maher and Larry A Nichols, Masonic Lodge, Zondervan Guide to Cults and Religious Movements, series ed. Alan W. Gomes (Grand Rapids, MI: Zondervan Publishing House, 1995), pp. 33-36

15. John Ankerberg and John Weldon, *The Secret Teachings of the Masonic Lodge: A Christian Perspective* (Chicago, IL: Moody Press, 1989, 1990), pp. 168 – 177, 215 – 243, 254 – 263. See also Ron Campbell, *Free From Freemasonry* (Ventura, CA: Regal Books, 1999).

16. John Ankerberg and John Weldon, *The Secret Teachings of the Masonic Lodge: A Christian Perspective* (Chicago, IL: Moody Press, 1989, 1990) p. 97, quoting Albert Mackey's Revised Encyclopedia of Freemasonry, revised and enlarged by Robert I. Clegg, 3 vols. (Richmond VA: Macoy, 1966) vol. 1 p. 133.

17. *Coil's Masonic Encyclopedia*, quoted in Mackey's Revised Encyclopedia of Freemasonry, vol. 2, pp. 735,746, referenced in John Ankerberg and John Weldon, *The Secret Teachings of the Masonic Lodge: A Christian Perspective* (Chicago, IL: Moody Press, 1989, 1990) pp. 119,120.

18. Thirty-third Degree Masonic leader Jim Shaw, Past Worshipful Master of the Blue Lodge, Past Master of all Scottish Rite Bodies and Knight Commander of the Court of Honor, quoted in John Ankerberg and John Weldon, *The Secret Teachings of the Masonic Lodge: A Christian Perspective* (Chicago, IL: Moody Press, 1989, 1990) p.131. See also Jim Shaw and Tom McKenney, *The Deadly Deception: Freemasonry Exposed By One of Its Top Leaders* (Lafayette, LA: Huntington House, 1988) pp.126,127.

19. John Ankerberg and John Weldon, *The Secret Teachings of the Masonic Lodge: A Christian Perspective* (Chicago, IL: Moody Press, 1989, 1990) pp. 126-129.

20. Albert Pike, *Morals and Dogma of the Ancient and Accepted Scottish Rite of Freemasonry* (Charleston, SC: The Supreme Council of the 33rd Degree for the Southern Jurisdiction of the United States, 1906) pp. 219, 161, quoted in John Ankerberg and John Weldon, *The Secret Teachings of the Masonic Lodge: A Christian Perspective* (Chicago, IL: Moody Press, 1989, 1990) p.200.

21. Carl H. Claudy, *Little Masonic Library*, 4 (Richmond, VA: Macoy Publishers and Supply Company, 1946) p. 51.

Hare Krishna

1. J. Isamu Yamamoto, *Hare Krishna (ISKCON)*, chapter 6 in Ronald Enroth & Others, *A Guide to Cults & New Religions*, (Downers Grove, II: InterVarsity Press, 1983) p.94

2. George A. Mather and Larry A. Nichols, *Dictionary of Cults, Sects, Religions and the Occult* (Grand Rapids, MI: Zondervan Publishing House, 1993), pp. 117, 137. See also J. Isamu Yamamoto, *Hare Krishna (ISKCON)*, chapter 6 in Ronald Enroth & Others, *A Guide to Cults & New Religions*, (Downers Grove, II: InterVarsity Press, 1983) pp. 92-93

3. George A. Mather and Larry A. Nichols, *Dictionary of Cults, Sects, Religions and the Occult* (Grand Rapids, MI: Zondervan Publishing House, 1993), p.139.

4. George A. Mather and Larry A. Nichols, *Dictionary of Cults, Sects, Religions and the Occult* (Grand Rapids, MI: Zondervan Publishing House, 1993), p.138.

5. Ron Rhodes, *The Challenge of the Cults and New Religions: The Essential Guide to Their History, Their Doctrine, and Our Response* (Zondervan, Grand rapids, Michigan, USA, 2001) p. 176.

6. A.C. Bhaktivedanta Swami Prabhupada, *Bhagavad Gita As It Is* (Los Angeles, CA:ISKCON, 1975), p.168.

7. Siddha Swarup Ananda Goswarm, *Jesus Loves Krsna* (Los Angeles CA: Vedic Christian Community and Life Force, Krsna Yoga Viewpoint, 1975) p.14, quoted in Walter Martin, *The Kingdom of the Cults, Updated and Expanded,* gen. ed. Hank Hanegraaff (Minneapolis: Bethany House Publishers, 1997), p. 400.

Secular Humanism

1. Modinos, Antonis (2013). *From Aristotle to Schrödinger: The Curiosity of Physics, Undergraduate Lecture Notes in Physics* (illustrated ed.). Springer Science & Business Media. p. 43. ISBN 978-3-319-00750-2. Extract of page 43

2. Charles E. Hummel, Christianity Today - *Christian History, The Faith Behind the Famous: Isaac Newton.* *https://www.christianitytoday.com/history/issues/issue-30/faith-behind-famous-isaac-newton.html*

3. Matt Slick, *What Is Higher Criticism & the Historical Critical method of Examining the Bible?* 5/22/2016. Christian Apologetics & Research Ministry.

   https://carm.org/what-is-higher-criticism-and-the-historical-critical-method-of-examining-the-bible

4. Fr. John A. Hardon S.J. Archives - Real Presence Eucharistic Education and Adoration Association, "Communism." *Atheistic Communism: The Destruction of Human Person, Family, Civilized Society* Copyright © 2003 Inter Mirifica

*http://www.therealpresence.org/archives/Communism/Communi
sm_001.htm*

5. Djupe, Paul A. and Olsen, Laura R., "American Humanist
    Association", Encyclopedia of American Religion and Politics",
    Infobase Publishing, 2014

6. Paul Kurtz and Edwin Wilson, *Humanist Manifesto I & II*
    (Buffalo, NY: Prometheus Books, 1973). Also, see James
    Hitchcock, What Is Secular *Humanism?* (Ann Arbor, MI:
    Servant Books, 1982), pp. 11, 13.

7. Paul Kurtz and Edwin Wilson, *Humanist Manifesto I & II*
    (Buffalo, NY: Prometheus Books, 1973). Also, see James
    Hitchcock, *What Is Secular Humanism?* (Ann Arbor, MI:
    Servant Books, 1982), pp. 17, 18.

8. Paul Kurtz and Edwin Wilson, *Humanist Manifesto II*, (Buffalo,
    NY: Prometheus Books, 1973) statement 6, p.22..

The International Churches of Christ

1. ICOC Hot News. The Editors of ICOC, About the ICOC. March
    2019.

2. Charles Caldwell Ryrie, *Ryrie Study Bible* (Chicago: Moody
    Press, 1978) p. 1869.

3. Randy Frame, *The Cost of Discipleship? Despite Allegations of
    Abuse of Authority, the International Churches of Christ
    Expands Rapidly*. Christianity Today (September 1, 1997), p.
    66. Also see Julianna Gittler, *Church or Cult? A Look at the*

Controversial Los Angeles Church of Christ, The Long Beach Union, California State University, Long Beach, student newspaper, Nov. 29, 1993

Postmodernism

1. Jim Leffel, *Post Modernism and The Myth of Progress – Two Visions*, in Dennis McCallum, ed., *The Death of Truth* (Minneapolis: Bethan House Publishers, 1996), p.50

2. Jim Leffel, *Post Modernism and The Myth of Progress – Two Visions*, in Dennis McCallum, ed., *The Death of Truth* (Minneapolis: Bethan House Publishers, 1996), p.50

3. Jim Leffel, *Our New Challenge: Post-Modernism.* Also, *The Death of Truth*, Dennis McCallum, ed. (Minneapolis. MN: Bethany House Publishers, 1996), p.31

4. Jim Leffel, *Our New Challenge: Post-Modernism.* Also, *The Death of Truth,* Dennis McCallum, ed. (Minneapolis. MN: Bethany House Publishers, 1996), p.32

5. Bob Hostetler & Josh McDowell, *The New Tolerance: How A Cultural Movement Threatens to Destroy You, Your Faith, and Your Children* (Tyndale House Publishers, Inc.1998) p.19.

6. Bob Hostetler & Josh McDowell, *The New Tolerance: How A Cultural Movement Threatens to Destroy You, Your Faith, and Your Children* (Tyndale House Publishers, Inc.1998) p. 20

7. Bob Hostetler & Josh McDowell, *The New Tolerance: How A Cultural Movement Threatens to Destroy You, Your Faith, and Your Children* (Tyndale House Publishers, Inc.1998) pp. 26, 27.

8. *The Death of Truth*, Dennis McCallum, ed. (Minneapolis. MN: Bethany House Publishers, 1996), pp. 199-212

9. *The Death of Truth*, Dennis McCallum, ed. (Minneapolis. MN: Bethany House Publishers, 1996), p.31

10. *The Death of Truth*, Dennis McCallum, ed. (Minneapolis. MN: Bethany House Publishers, 1996), p.35

11. *The Death of Truth*, Dennis McCallum, ed. (Minneapolis. MN: Bethany House Publishers, 1996), 34, 35, 99.

12. Charles Colson, The Searing of the Conscience, Jubilee (Summer 2000) p. 23.

13. Potter, Garry and Lopez, Jose (eds.): After Postmodernism: An Introduction to Critical Realism. London: The Athlone Press 2001, p. 4.

14. Kirby, Alan. *The Death of Postmodernism and Beyond.* Philosophy Now 58 (2006): 34-37.

Unification Church (the Moonies)

1. *Prophets and Protons: New Religious Movements and Science in Late   Twentieth- Century America,* Benjamin E. Zeller, NYU Press, Mar 1, 2010, page 13.

2. Sontag, Fredrick (1977) *Sun Myung Moon and the Unification Church.* Abingdon. pp. 102–105

3. Daske, D. and Ashcraft, W. 2005, *New Religious Movements*, New York: New York University Press.

4. *The Advent of Sun Myung Moon: The Origins, Beliefs and Practices of the Unification Church*, George Chryssides, Springer, Apr 5, 1991, 247 pages, pages 155-157

5. Bednarowski, Mary Farrell (1995). *New Religions and the Theological Imagination in America.* Indiana University Press. p. 103.

6. Title*; "Moonies" in America: Cult, Church, and Crusade*: SAGE Library of Social Research; Authors: David G. Bromley, Anson D. Shupe, Jr.; Editor: David G. Bromley; Publisher: SAGE Publications, p. 197.

7. Daske, D. and Ashcraft, W. 2005, *New Religious Movements*, New York: New York University Press.

8. *From Slogans to Mantras: Social Protest and Religious Conversion in the Late Vietnam War Era*, Stephen A. Kent, Syracuse University Press, 2001, page 168.

9. "Executive Summary". U.S. Department of State. *https://2009-2017.state.gov/j/drl/rls/irf/2003/27185.htm*

10. Respectively Articles 2, 6 and 7 of the Schengen Agreement, eur-lex.europa.eu;.

11. Steven Hassan, Founding Director of Freedom of Mind Resource Center. *The Truth About Sun Myung Moon, May 2017.* https://freedomofmind.com/the-truth-about-sun-myung-moon/

Unitarian Universalism

1. Unitarian Universalist Association – *7th Principle: Respect for the Interdependent Web of All Existence of Which We Are a Part.* https://www.uua.org/beliefs/what-we-believe/principles/7th.

2. Zavada, Jack. *What Do Unitarian Universalists Believe?* Learn Religions, Apr. 17, 2019, learnreligions.com/unitarian-universalist-beliefs-and-practices-701571

Chapter Twenty-Two

1. Gary Kitmacher (2006). *Reference Guide to the International Space Station.* Canada: Apogee Books. pp. 71–80. ISBN 978-1-894959-34-6. ISSN 1496-6921.

2. *Key Findings about Americans' Belief in God* by Dalia Fahmy, April 2018

3. John Walvoord, *The Literal View* in William Crockett (ed.), *Four Views on Hell* (Grand Rapids: Zondervan, 1992), pp.19-20.

4. Reuters, "Organic Food Is No Healthier, Study Finds," July 2009. Quoted in *Losing Our Religion – The Liberal Media's Attack on Christianity,* by S.E. Cupp. Threshold Editions, A Division of Simon & Schuster, Inc., 2010. Pgs. 64-65.

5. Six Things Satan Doesn't Want You To Know About Himself

   https://agapegeek.com/2009/11/01/six-things-satan-doesnt-want-you-to-know-   about-himself/

www.ingramcontent.com/pod-product-compliance
Lightning Source LLC
Chambersburg PA
CBHW070855120626
46546CB00001B/11